Revitalizing Our Social Group Work Heritage:
A Bridge to the Future

Proceedings of the XXXV International Symposium
of the International Association for Social Work with Groups,
Boston, Massachusetts, USA, June 6th-9th, 2013

Revitalizing Our Social Group Work Heritage:
A Bridge to the Future

Edited by

Mark Gianino
and
Donna McLaughlin

**Followed by selected papers
from the XXVI International Symposium,
Detroit, October 21st-24th, 2004
'Group Work Reaching across Boundaries:
Disciplines, Seasons of Life, Practice Settings,
Cultures and Nations'
edited by Alice Lamont and Dale Swaisgood**

w&b

MMXVI

Published by Whiting & Birch Ltd,
Forest Hill, London SE23 3HZ

ISBN 9781861771391

Printed in England and the United States by Lightning Source

CONTENTS

The XXXV International Symposium
Boston, Massachusetts, USA, June 6th-9th, 2013
'Revitalizing Our Social Group Work Heritage: A Bridge to the Future'

Selected Papers from the XXVI International Symposium, Detroit, October 21st-24th, 2004 'Group Work Reaching across Boundaries: Disciplines, Seasons of Life, Practice Settings, Cultures and Nations'

Acknowledgements

International Association for Social Work with Groups (IASWG)
XXXV Annual International Symposium
Boston, Massachusetts, USA June 6-9, 2013

Symposium International Honorees
Hubie Jones
Jürgen Kalcher

Symposium Local Honorees:
Boys and Girls Clubs of Boston
Boston Children's Hospital
Lois Levinsky
Riverside Community Care

Symposium Co-Chairs
Mark Gianino
Dana Grossman Leeman
Donna McLaughlin

We are indebted to the phenomenal support we received for Symposium from our co-sponsors: Boston University School of Social Work, Simmons College School of Social Work and Springfield College School of Social Work. Much appreciation goes to our benefactor, the IASWG Massachusetts Chapter and our planning partner, the NASW Massachusetts Chapter, who helped foster a productive collaboration between our organizations. We extend our gratitude to sustainers: Florida International University and Wheelock College School of Social Work and supporter, Salem State University School of Social Work.

We are grateful beyond words for the efforts of our planning committee. They contributed their considerable talents and ideas to the creation of a memorable symposium, and in a pinch could be found shuttling attendees from the dorms to the event venue! We could not be prouder of our planning committee which consisted of Melissa Brown, Jim Canning, Crystal Carrington, Marcia Cohen, Mary DeChillo, Nicole Dubus, Adam Glick, Sera Godfrey Grantz, Anthony Hill, Liz Hudson, Nate Bae Kupel, Lucy Mograss, Leah Hart Tennen, Patty Underwood and Erika Vargas. We want to offer a special shout out to our event planner, Kristina Whiton-O'Brien for her wisdom, organizational talents and immense calm throughout Symposium. We also wish to thank our many student volunteers and our regional MA IASWG board members for their support.

We wish to thank our many contributing authors for their vital scholarly contributions to this volume. It is heartening to have received such a diversity of substantive writing on social group work. Lastly, we are grateful for the guidance and patience of our publisher, David Whiting.

Tribute
Jim Garland

We dedicate this volume to Jim Garland. We offer the following tributes written by colleagues, former students, and mentees of Jim upon the occasion of his passing on March 27, 2012. Throughout his esteemed and distinguished career, Jim Garland was devoted to exploring the origins of the social groupwork method and movement. Jim was committed to social work with children and youth and the agencies doing this work. His love of the social work profession and the richness of the groupwork process was contagious at the Boston University School of Social Work and far beyond.

Personal Reflections

"Jim Garland was on my mind this week as I agreed to speak at the Social Work with Groups' meeting next June 2013. I began my social work career sharing an office with Jim at the Boston Children's Services. I served as his program director at its camp. We collaborated on writing the "Stages of Development in Social Work Groups." He was one of the finest group practitioners that I ever saw in action. He had a great conceptual and theoretical mind. I fondly remember lots of discussions with him about his ideas about loneliness in groups. I had the good fortunate to join him again when I became Dean at the School of Social Work. He was an excellent and beloved teacher. I will always treasure his work, his life and his enduring support of my life's work. I will dedicate my speech next June to the memory of James Allen Garland. What a great loss!!"
Hubie Jones, BUSSW Dean Emeritus

"I like to picture Jim with his wife and children all snuggling him as he passed away—a perfect "group ending." Jim was such a warm

and hugely well informed colleague...so many talks at conferences, so many classes that piqued attendees' interests, lots of articles with Hubie and others, a hardy insistence not to let group work fade from the knowledge base when many were trying to diss it. My office was near his for some time, and both of us came early in the mornings to prepare before early classes, and enjoyed many a laugh together. He'd worked well at McLean Hospital, with Golda Edinburg, I think. I'm glad to think of her welcoming Jim back to a fold....I feel sad today to get this news. Yet, I want to recall with a big smile that when Trudy Duffy and I were about to retire in the spring of 2005, Jim and 3 or 4 others of his eating group —called "Really Old Men Eating Out," or "ROMEO"–asked Trudy and me over to eat with them, which I considered a great honor that was bound to be full of a lot of laughter and musing on the past. He told us that we had to start this get together with an Organ Recital....... Huh??   Well, he and Archie explained that ROMEO meetings always began with an "organ recital"...each member was allowed 5 minutes and no more, to complain about health problems or specific troubles with this or that organ–and then they would compare bodily complaints and laugh a lot about aging. So, I'm going to take a few minutes here at home now, to light a candle and think of Jim's welcomes and supports and helps to so many of us... and all that he left within us about the importance and dynamics of groups in our lives. Jim is now free forever from organ recitals and from feeling like a ROMEO.   I know that Jim will have already organized a few angels at the gates in order to have dinner together quite often so as to develop fun and strong relationships. God bless you, Jim and family, and give you peace."
Carolyn Dillon, BUSSW Professor Emerita

"I have been connecting all day with people who have been touched by the warmth and compassion that Jim Garland exuded. I first met Jim when I was a social work student here at BUSSW and Jim was my faculty advisor. I was placed at the Dorchester House Multi-Service Center and Jim was amazing and inspiring as we talked about group work in the community, on the streets, and in the office. We stayed in touch and he modeled the critical importance of social group workers finding each other. Now, long after my years as a student with Jim, and others (Trudy Duffy and Lois Levinsky) as mentors, I find myself living that role – trying to do my best work in teaching about group work, supporting group workers in the field and connecting with new students who venture a curiosity about the practice of group work. I

owe so much gratitude to Jim for his support and encouragement. I am glad for the opportunity to remember him today as I ready myself to go and teach the BUSSW Group Work Specialists seminar in just a few moments."
Donna McLaughlin, BUSSW Clinical Associate Professor

"Jim Garland made major contributions to group work theory, yet always kept his feet firmly planted in practice. He was an outstanding group worker, an iconic classroom instructor, a terrific colleague, and most important, a wonderful human being. His passion for group work was legendary. Jim was dearly loved by all who knew him (well maybe not some in the upper echelons of the BU Administration during faculty union days) and I can't count the times I've spoken with colleagues and alumni who spoke glowingly about him."
Lee Staples, BUSSW Professor Emeritus

"If ever there was someone who had a real twinkle in his eye, it was Jim Garland. I had heard that phrase but never knew what it meant until I met Jim. I saw it so often when we talked or when I observed him with others. His joy and his appreciation for relationships was infectious. He served as my mentor when I had to get up to speed in teaching the group work content in the Introduction to Clinical Practice course. He was patient and reassuring with me. He encouraged me to take risks and coached me when I reported or he observed my missteps. He was all-knowing in the field of group work but shared his knowledge in a gentle way. I will miss him."
Cassandra Clay, BUSSW Professor Emerita

"Jim was my first real hero and a most generous and passionate group work teacher, supporter and mentor throughout my career. His spirit, energy and humor reside in my mind and heart.....My pleasure, privilege and good fortune to have known Jim for 40 years, and experienced him as professor, mentor, supervisor, consultant, coach, cheerleader, and colleague.

Jim's big presence -a big man with a big voice, big laugh, quick to joke, to be playful, to see the good, the funny and the inspirational in people and situations~

An inspiring group worker with talent, passion, intuition and skills to promote positive and effective group experiences for many people, in the classroom, in the field, in agency settings, faculty meetings and professional events.

A brilliant and prolific writer of group theory and practice, whose seminal works in group development, group types and models, group dynamics and processes educated, engaged, challenged and inspired generations of group workers.

An enthusiastic, thoughtful and attuned group worker who enjoyed teaching and learning with students, clients, colleagues.

A consummate professional with a sensitive soul, a big heart, contagious humor and boundless joy for all things groupwork."
Lois Levinsky, BUSSW Professor Emerita

Many thanks for these contributions in Jim's memory. Jim reached many with his love of group work and his passion lives on through those of us he impacted so deeply.

Adapted from: http://www.bu.edu/ssw/2012/03/28/bussw-remembers-professor-emeritus-jim-garland/

About the Editors

Mark Gianino, MSW, PhD joined the full time faculty at Boston University School of Social Work in September of 2005 where he now is a clinical associate professor. In this capacity he teaches a range of courses within the MSW program. His research interests include gay and lesbian parenthood, transracial adoption, continuing professional education in Social Work, education and training in suicide prevention and intervention, and group work. He has enjoyed a 30-year social work career as a clinician, supervisor, and administrator in outpatient and inpatient mental health settings as well as group and independent private practices. Areas of clinical expertise include the following: treatment of trauma and mood disorders; emphasis on practice with gay, lesbian, bisexual, and transgender populations and group psychotherapy; treatment approaches include CBT, solution-focused, narrative, and emotionally focused therapy (EFT) in clinical practice with individuals, couples, families, and groups.

Donna McLaughlin, MSW, LICSW, is Clinical Associate Professor at the Boston University School of Social Work where she directs the Groupwork Specialization Program. She teaches a range of foundation and advanced level courses at BUSSW; and designed and teaches the Clinical Practice with Groups course for the BUSSW On-Line program. Donna's scholarly and practice interests include the supervision and mentoring of students and new workers; community training in group work; trauma and homelessness; and issues facing the LGBTQ community. She practices as a clinician/consultant in private practice and presents and trains on social group work practice, supervision and mentoring locally and internationally. Donna is a past board member-at-large with the International Association for Social Work with Groups (IASWG). She is the recipient of the 2015 Group Worker of the Year Award presented by the Massachusetts Chapter, International Association for Social Work with Groups (IASWG) and a 2014 Platinum Award for Best Practices in Distance Learning Programming from the United States Distance Learning Association (USDLA).

The Contributors

Charlla Allen, PhD, is a Professor and the Director of the Social Work Program at Central State University in Wilberforce, Ohio. As a social work educator, practitioner, and group worker, Dr. Allen has contributed to the education and professional development of social work students throughout Ohio, Michigan and internationally in Ethiopia. Sharing her experience as a practitioner and group work leader in the classroom environment has been her area of expertise and passion. Email: charllaka777@yahoo.com; callen@centralstate.edu

Dale Asis, MA, is a lecturer at Loyola University Chicago School of Social Work. He earned his Masters of Arts Program in Social Sciences (MAPSS) at the University of Chicago. He is the President of the Bayanihan Foundation Worldwide, a public charity promoting Filipino diaspora philanthropy. He is the founder of the Coalition of African, Arab, Asian, European and Latino Immigrants of Illinois and United Congress of Community and Religious Organizations. In 2009, he established a network of over 150 diaspora donors that donate to 50 countries. Email: dasis@luc.edu

Frank Bartolomeo, MSW, PhD, is Director of Behavioral Health Services at The Southfield Center for Development in Darien, Connecticut. From 1998 to 2003, Frank taught at the Boston University School of Social Work and in 2003 was awarded the *Saul Bernstein Memorial Group Worker of the Year* by the Massachusetts Chapter of IASWG. He was honored to give the The *Robert Salmon Invitational* address at the 2013 IASWG Symposium. Email: fbartphd@gmail.com

Stephanie Bell, MSc, is a graduate of the London School of Hygiene and Tropical Medicine and has been working in the field of HIV prevention in Toronto, Canada since 2012. Email: steph.l.bell@gmail.com

Jessy Benjamin, MSW, RSW, secured her Masters degree in Social Work (M.A. in, Social Work) from Stella Maris College, Chennai, India, and also has a Certificate in Canadian Social Work Practice -

Internationally Educated Social Work Professional Bridging program (IESW) from Ryerson University, Canada. She is also a Registered Social Worker (RSW) with Ontario College of Social Workers and Social Service Workers (OCSWSSW) currently practicing as a clinical Social Worker with The Hospital for Sick Children, Toronto, Canada. Email: jessy.benjamin@sickkids.ca; jessy.benjamin@gmail.com

Erin Bishop Daigle, LCSW, is a 2013 graduate of the University of New England. She works for The Opportunity Alliance and Alternative Wellness Services, Portland, Maine, USA. Email: erin.daigle@opportunityalliance.org

Ariane Bowie, LCSW is a 2013 graduate of the University of New England. She works for KidsPeace New England, South Portland, Maine, USA. Email: ariane.bowie@kidspeace.org

Kristen Cianelli, MSW, CADC is a 2014 graduate of the University of New England. She works for Day One, Buxton, Maine, USA. Email: kcianelli@une.edu

Marcia B. Cohen, MSW, PhD, is Professor at the University of New England in Portland, Maine, where she has been a faculty member since 1988. She has been a group worker for more than 25 years and has published books and articles on a variety of group work themes. Email: mcohen@une.edu

Santiago Delboy, MBA, MSW, LSW, S-PSB, is a psychotherapist at Wellington Counseling Group in Chicago, Illinois, US. Email: sdelboy@wellingtoncounselinggroup.com

Kerry Dunn, JD, PhD, is an Associate Dean of Curriculum and Innovation at the College of New Rochelle in New Rochelle, NY, USA. Email: kedunn@cnr.edu

William Dunn, PhD, is an Associate Professor in the Faculty of Education at the University of Alberta. Email: wdunn@ualberta.ca

Kyle Taylor Ganson, LICSW, is a clinical social worker at Monte Nido & Affiliates, an adjunct professor at Simmons College School of Social Work, has a private practice in Concord, MA, and is an artist. Email: kyletaylorganson@gmail.com Web: www.kyletaylorganson.com

Erika Gilbert, LMSW-cc, is a 2013 graduate of the University of New England. She works for Maine Medical Partners Family Practice, Portland, Maine, USA. Email: gilbee@mmc.org

Rebecca Halperin, LCSW, is a clinical social worker at the Multiple Sclerosis Comprehensive Care Center at New York University Langone Medical Center located in New York City. Email: rebeccajhalperin@gmail.com

Anthony C. Hill, MSW, EdD, is an Assistant Professor at Springfield College School of Social Work, Springfield, MA. USA. Email: ahill@springfieldcollege.edu

Stephanie Holt is an Assistant Professor of Social Work in the School of Social Work & Social Policy, Trinity College Dublin. Prior to her current academic post she worked as a child and family social worker and coordinated a Family Support Service in Dublin. Her academic and research interests include domestic violence, intimate partner homicide, post-separation child contact, child care and family support. Email: sholt@tcd.ie

Hubie Jones is Dean Emeritus of the Boston University School of Social Work. He has served as Special Assistant to the Chancellor for Urban Affairs at the University of Massachusetts Boston, as Acting President of Roxbury Community College, and as Associate Professor at the Massachusetts Institute of Technology. Mr. Jones has played a key role in the formation, rebuilding and leadership of at least thirty community organizations within the black community and across the city. Mr. Jones founded the Boston Children's Chorus in 2002. Email: hjones@cityyear.org

Dara Kammerman, LMSW, is a graduate of Hunter College School of Social Work. She currently works at Origins High School, a public high school in Sheepshead Bay, Brooklyn. Email:dkammerman@originshighschool.org

Gloria Kirwan, BSS, CQSW, MA, MSc Appl Soc Res, MLitt, is Assistant Professor of Social Work in the School of Social Work and Social Policy at Trinity College Dublin, Ireland, where she is currently Director of Undergraduate Teaching and Learning. Email: kirwangm@tcd.ie

Linda McArdle, MSW, LISW-S, is a Senior Instructor at the University of Akron School of Social Work in Akron, Ohio, USA. Email: linda15@uakron.edu.

Donna McLaughlin, MSW, LICSW, is Clincal Associate Professor at Boston University School of Social Work, Boston, MA, USA. Email: dmmclaug@bu.edu

Barbara Muskat, PhD, RSW, is the Director of Social Work at the Hospital for Sick Children in Toronto, as well as an Assistant Professor (status-only) at the Factor Inwentash Faculty of Social Work, the University of Toronto. Email: barbara.muskat@sickkids.ca

Jane Ngo, MSW, is a recent graduate of Trinity College Dublin. She is the founder of Aer Remedy, Sligo, Ireland. Email: janeyngo@gmail.com

Claude Olivier, PhD, is an Associate Professor in the School of Social Work at King's University College. As a social worker, he has over 10 years of experience with community-based AIDS organizations. His teaching and research interests include anti-oppressive social work practice, social group work, and community organization. His most recent research involves exploring the use of forum theatre in assisting people in telling their stories to foster empowerment and to bring about social change. Email: colivier@uwo.ca

Elisa Orme, LMSW-cc, is a 2013 graduate of the University of New England. She works for Pathways, in Scarborough, Maine, USA. Email: elisa.orme@pathways.com

Biswas Pradhan earned his Master of Social Work degree with a specialization in Leadership and Development in Social Services from Loyola University Chicago. Currently, he is working at the Asian Health Coalition as a program coordinator for Affordable Care Act (Obamacare) and substance abuse treatment programs. Email: bpradha@luc.edu

Mamadou M. Seck, LSW, MSSA, PhD. A nine year elementary school teaching experience in a village working with parents and children inspired me to become social worker with at risk youth. My experiences in Social Work as student, field supervisor, instructor, and school administrator inspired me to write on issues related to juvenile justice, social work education and student success, group work, developmental disability, and economic and social development. Email: m.seck@csuohio.edu

Simone Shindler, MA, MSW, RSW, is a graduate of the University or Toronto, and works as a clinical social worker in the field of child and adolescent mental health. Email:simoneshindler@gmail.com

Thelma Silver, MSW, PhD, is Professor of Social Work at Youngstown State University where she teaches Groupwork in both the BSW and MSW Programs. She has also been a member of the executive committee of the Northeast Ohio Chapter IASWG. Email: tsilver@YSU.edu

Shirley R. Simon, ACSW, LCSW, is Associate Professor, School of Social Work, Loyola University Chicago. A social work educator for over thirty-five years, she has published on group work education, practice and history, is Book Review Editor for Groupwork, and has facilitated over 150 student presentations at IASWG. Email: ssimon@luc.edu

Mary Tangelder, MA, is a graduate from OISE, University of Toronto. She has over 15 years experience researching and designing education programmes, and currently lives and works in Kenya, as an Education Advisor. Email: marylouiset@gmail.com

Mary B. White, MSW, LCSW, is a graduate from the University of Maine and has had an extensive career working in mental health. Currently, she is a Clinical Professor in the School of Social Work at The University of New England located in Portland, Maine. Email: mwhite5@une.edu

Introduction

It is with great pleasure that we present the Conference Proceedings of the XXXV Annual Symposium of the International Association for Social Work with Groups (IASWG). This Symposium, titled "Revitalizing Our Heritage: A Bridge to the Future," was co-sponsored by the Boston University, Simmons College and Springfield College Schools of Social Work and was held at the beautiful Simmons College campus. The title of this year's Symposium reflected our vision to honor the traditions of our cherished group work heritage including that of the beloved founders of the Boston Model. At the same time we affirmed cutting edge practices that advance excellence in group work practice, theory, research and advocacy.

The Symposium year of 2013 was one of challenge, tribulation and loss for our members and client populations. The devastating flooding in New York and New Jersey, the shootings in Newtown, Connecticut and the shocking Marathon bombings that took place in Boston just two months prior to Symposium tested our resilience and resolve. The power of group work is vital to provide healing, to mobilize action and reawaken our passion for the enduring power of social justice that lives at the heart of social group work. The Boston Planning Committee aspired for Symposium to be a means of revitalizing attendees through the myriad events that advanced skills, promoted social engagement, and inspired through plenaries, diverse workshops, theater and musical events and fondly regarded traditions such as dine- a-round. The spirit of Symposium was beautifully reflected in the image that graced the program book cover which was of the iconic Leonard P. Zakim Bunker Hill Memorial Bridge (or Zakim Bridge). The bridge serves as a beacon for the city of Boston and stands as a tribute to Boston civic leader and civil rights activist Leonard P. Zakim, former executive director of the New England region of the Anti-Defamation League. Lenny Zakim was a leader in tolerance education, ethnic reconciliation and inner-city youth programs. He died tragically in 1999 at the age of 46 from myeloma. According to the New York Times, Mr. Zakim used his political connections and friendships with African-American ministers, Roman Catholic leaders and sports celebrities to establish community organizations and public-service events, including the

12,000-member Team Harmony antiracism rally for youth. We believe that the image of the Zakim Bridge was a fitting tribute to a man championed for "building bridges between peoples."

This year, Symposium XXXV happened to coincide with Boston Pride – a weeklong celebration and affirmation of the LGBTQ community and its allies. In recognition of the political and cultural significance of Pride, we were pleased to offer several special events that interlaced Symposium activities with those of Pride including a special plenary on group work across the lifecycle for LGBTQ populations, and a break in scheduled programming offering members an opportunity to march with our Massachusetts National Association of Social Workers (NASW) LGBT Shared Interest Group. Thirty plus attendees hopped on the MBTA to the launch site of the Pride march, and representing a high- spirited national and international crew, we marched at Pride under our very own IASWG banner. For the first time since the start of Boston Symposium the clouds parted, and the sun and cheering crowds greeted our attendees all of whom made it back in time for Saturday afternoon Invitationals!

Symposium showcased many talents of all types commencing with a lively and engaging opening reception featuring Urban Improv, an interactive program for young people that uses improvisational theater workshops to teach violence prevention, conflict resolution, and decision-making. Attendees were invited to display their acting chops by stepping into role plays dealing with serious issues such as bullying among others in a manner that proved to be moving, vibrant and fun! This event was preceded by Massachusetts regional IASWG Board members who, recognizing the importance of warm ups, led the audience in creative, nonverbal activities that served to connect all assembled attendees in the room across the span of culture and language. Saturday morning kicked off an impressive array of over 160 papers, workshops and invitationals. Among these eclectic array of offerings, and serving as a testament to the engagement of students in the life of social group work, we had 30 student posters on display at Boston University prior to the Beulah Rothman Plenary. Here the symbol of the bridge was much in evidence as students beamed while their work was viewed and discussed by mentors and authors whom they have both read and revered in their course work!

Symposium offered impressive plenaries commencing with the Sumner Gill Memorial Plenary entitled, "Weaving a rainbow from our past to our future: Using group work to support LGBTQ people across the lifespan." Presenters gave vivid testimony to the power of group work in working across diversity on multiple dimensions through their use of personal narrative, practice examples and film. Friday was topped off at the Beulah Rothman Plenary with an unforgettable keynote offered by Hubie Jones - "Group Work in an Era of Rage and Disunity" who amplified how the power of groups can be used to achieve social healing and greater solidarity. His talk was preceded by a moving and stirring performance of the Boston Children's Chorus, which Dean Emeritus Jones founded. Hubie served double duty as both a speaker and an international nominee. Jürgen Kalcher was also honored at the Gala. The Joan K. Parry Memorial Plenary featured Lorrie Greenhous Gardella who mesmerized attendees as she drew from her recent book, *The Life and Thought of Louis Lowy: Social Work through the Holocaust*, which explored Louis Lowy's enduring legacy as a social group worker and implications for social workers today. Finally, a unique and unprecedented offering was presented at the MA Chapter Plenary. Produced in collaboration with Wheelock College and Boston University, MSW students and recent graduates, David Carpenter, Kyle Ganson, Mya Ribot and Kelly Mogren premiered "Better together: IASWG MA Chapter highlights innovative group work in the Commonwealth." The culmination of a yearlong project, this film takes an intimate look at the inspired and leading edge group work taking place in Massachusetts.

*

We are delighted to offer you the 16 chapters that represent a sample of the many ways as to how, in keeping with our Symposium theme, social group work is both revitalized and vital as we integrate the value of justice that lay at the heart center of social group work alongside cutting edge practices and pedagogies.

In *Chapter One,* we are honored to present the keynote address by Hubie Jones entitled, "The Power of Groups for Healing at a Time of Great Anxiety and Fear." In this memorable chapter which is dedicated to his friend and colleague, the late James Garland, Hubie Jones enlightens readers to the power of groups as an antidote to social isolation and as forces of social hearing. This chapter chronicles three very different types of groups that realize these goals – community choruses (specifically the Boston Children's Chorus which the author founded), Black women's book groups and groups for mothers of murdered children. Be prepared to be stimulated and moved!

Jessy Benjamin explores in *Chapter Two* how social determinants of health impact the families of patients receiving care at the Hospital for Sick Children in Toronto. Through the Parent Coffee Hour, a caregiver support group, families meet together to share their experiences of caring for an ill member. The author describes, with the use of case examples, how family member's health is impacted by determinants such as poverty, inadequate housing, unemployment and cultural factors.

In *Chapter Three,* authors Marcia Cohen, Shirley Simon, Donna McLaughlin, Barbara Muskat, and Mary White examine the obstacles and opportunities for using group work principles to advance learning in online education. Three examples of online social group work courses that are fully online, mixed synchronous and asynchronous and online field seminars are discussed in order to highlight these issues. The potential role of group work educators as leaders in facilitating effective online learning is explored.

Santiago Delboy offers readers in *Chapter Four* a cogent conceptual paper that integrates constructs of group psychotherapy and 12-step recovery programs that are the most common interventions used for addiction treatment. Conceptualizing addictions as an attachment disorder, this chapter explores how opportunities for participants to develop interpersonal relationships and repair attachment injuries are central processes in group therapy, and also play a critical role in 12-step recovery groups.

In *Chapter Five,* faculty mentor Kerry Dunn collaborates with students Erin Bishop, Ariane Bowie, Kristen Cianelli, Erika Gilbert and Elisa Orme to pen an engaging chapter about how in the Spring 2013, 10 second-year MSW students facilitated support groups in five housing units at a county jail. The idea for these groups arose from discussions with inmates about needs at the jail. In this chapter, students and their faculty mentor discuss the challenges and rewards of doing group work in this under-resourced setting. This UNE-CCJ support group project provides readers an excellent example of community-based social work education.

In *Chapter Six,* contributor Anthony Hill provides the reader a vivid testament to the power of social group work in faith-based organizations to promote academic, social, and cultural success for urban at-risk youth. This chapter describes The Black Leadership and Enrichment Society of Springfield (B.L.E.S.S.) that is a group mentoring project serving elementary and middle school-aged participants. Implications for the use of group mentoring sessions to provide long-term benefits for at-risk young males are discussed.

Claude Olivier and William Dunn offer readers in *Chapter Seven* a fascinating report on the use of theatre workshops as a group format to give voice to international university students' experiences of inclusion and exclusion. The workshops they present are comprised of five skits presenting themes such as: awareness, responsibility and action; loneliness and exclusion; developing empathy and transcending cultural differences; benefits of social interaction; and accessing informal interaction through formal structures. Group work is in abundant evidence with the creative use of theatre as the vehicle for empowerment and connection.

Online pedagogy is explored in *Chapter Eight* where author Mamadou Seck describes the stages of group development of an online task group in a social work course on diversity, racism, and discrimination. The author describes numerous dimensions of the online task group such as group processes, leadership, roles and management of intra-group. This descriptive theoretical paper raises awareness about the fundamental group factors that may emerge of at each specific stage of a task group.

Thelma Silver, Charlla Allen and Linda McArdle in *Chapter Nine* offer an engaging conceptual paper that integrates the three theoretical models representing the backbone of social work with groups; the Strengths Perspective, empowerment, and mutual aid. Multiculturalism and diversity factors in group work are also explored. Finally, a case vignette is presented that effectively displays how these theories live in group work assessment and practice.

In *Chapter Ten*, contributor Kyle Tyler Ganson describes the creative work he engaged in with adolescents through a therapeutic photography group entitled Finding Focus. Here the reader is introduced to a mode of expressive therapy that highlights the use of cameras and self-expression. Adolescents present their reality through photographic representations of the symptoms they experience as they struggle with issues of trauma and, at times, persistent mental illness. The chapter demonstrates how the mutual aid process helps the members understand themselves as well as describe to another their inner most emotions.

In *Chapter Eleven*, authors Biswas Pradhan and Dale Asis describe a series of group workshops called the GROW project designed to help community-based organizations (CBOs) in the Chicago area strengthen strategic organizational capacity building for small ethnic community-based organizations. The authors emphasize the importance of group work in organizational capacity building, especially for organizations that serve small and vulnerable ethnic populations.

The reader travels to Ireland with author Stephanie Holt in *Chapter Twelve* where she examines the impact of a group work program for mothers and children who have experienced domestic abuse. The author offers an extensive review of the literature describing the barriers mothers and children face when living with abuse and describes the research and evaluative outcome learned from a joint collaboration of services offered by Ireland's Statutory Child and Welfare Services and a local voluntary agency. The findings confirm the importance of supportive and therapeutic interventions with this population and the positive impact this has on the mother-child relationship, while describing key components of the group program.

Using a narrative approach to her presentation, Rebecca Halperin in *Chapter Thirteen* tells a story of resilience and mutuality in working with Mothers living with Multiple Sclerosis. The author describes her varying experiences with the individual therapy and the group work with this population. Using psychodynamic theory, she reflects on the critical authentic self that surfaces in therapeutic work while describing 'a second true self' that emerges through the support of group membership. In all, the reader experiences a feeling of uplift for the story told here.

In *Chapter Fourteen*, Simone Shindler, Stephanie Bell and Mary Tangelder, present an evaluation of The Teresa Group's Prenatal Program for women living with HIV in Toronto, Canada. The authors describe the barriers to participation in the program and the significant benefits women experience when they have the opportunity to interact genuinely with other women living with HIV. The model presented highlights a positive impact for group members stemming from key group work factors including increases in confidence, feelings of hope and the capacity to cope with stigma attached to living with HIV.

Readers are taken on a journey in *Chapter Fifteen* with author Dara Kammerman who invites the reader along with her as she describes the challenges and successes in using group work to reduce conflict and stigma among a group of school-aged boys in an after-school youth program. From group formation, to developing group purpose and structure, to the purposeful use of activities in the group, the author demonstrates how mutual aid and positive regard transform and deepen the interactions between the boys.

In *Chapter Sixteen,* readers are treated to advice in the form of a "survival guide" for working with involuntary groups. Frank Bartolomeo integrates 25 years of group work practice with involuntary groups with diverse populations in an array of settings combined with the findings of his doctoral research. Eight essential guidelines for social group work with involuntary groups are illustrated by personal experiences, anecdotes from practice and research findings.

We wish you a renewed experience of groupwork, creativity, and innovation as you read these proceedings.

Mark Gianino and Donna McLaughlin

The Power of Groups for Healing at a Time of Great Anxiety and Fear: Keynote Address for the 2013 IASWG Symposium Gala

Hubie Jones

Introduction

Good evening. It is a great pleasure and honor to speak at this gala this evening. I do so in memory of my colleague and friend James Allen Garland, an extraordinary practitioner and teacher of group work at Boston University School of Social Work. I had the good fortune of beginning my social work career as his colleague at the Boston Children's Service Association's Department of Neighborhood Clubs. In fact, we shared an office together. Jim was the lead author with Ralph Kolodny and me in writing the seminal paper: Stages of Development in Social Work Groups, which found its way around the world. It became known is some circles as the "Boston Model." Jim had a fine conceptual, theoretical mind, often hard to keep up with. I served as program director of the summer camp that he directed in Cohasset, MA, for Boston Children's Services. It was there that I saw him work directly with young people in groups – a tour de force. He was a great clinician and practitioner – and always a teacher. Jim Garland, struggling with Alzheimer's disease, passed away on March 27, 2012. He is greatly missed. So here's to the memory of Jim Garland.

Current Societal Context

I begin with some societal context: Our society is being rocked by major transitional challenges: Acceptance for same-sex marriage is growing as expressed by the passage of new legislation in 12 states in the nation – and that number will grow. A major adjustment and acceptance of this reality is now required by our citizens. Women's sexual freedom is under assault as politicians and some religious leaders attempt to impose constraints on their freedom, including repeal of Roe vs. Wade by the U.S. Supreme Court.

We are experiencing a demographic revolution in America seen in the enormous growth of immigrants, Latino citizens and other people of color. They are having a substantial political impact, which was experienced in the last presidential election. They made the difference in winning in some key states. Politicians and other citizens are having difficulty accepting this trend and, therefore, have devised schemes to limit access to the voting booth.

The continuing debate about immigration reform focused on providing routes to citizenship for 11 million immigrants has stirred up xenophobic behavior that is toxic. The election of a Black president of the United States has not been accepted by many of our political leaders and prominent citizens, so his leadership is thwarted at every turn, hoping to render him ineffective and result in a failed presidency, no matter the consequences for our country.

Too many citizens are expressing fear and dislike of government, reflected in far right politics and the surge in the sale of guns in response to legislative efforts to curb access to guns and their use by mentally incompetent people. The revelations that the IRS unfairly targeted conservative groups and that the US Justice Department violated the privacy of journalists in the name of national security surveillance has exacerbated these anti-government sentiments that are abroad in the land.

Due the tragedy on 9/11/2001 at the World Trade Center in New York City, the killings in Aurora, Colorado, the massacre of 20 children in Newtown, CT and the bombings at the Marathon in Boston, the American people are on edge, gripped by anxiety, fear, anger and grief. Our people are traumatized as they cope with the realities of a new world. At times it feels like the country is coming apart at the seams. Disunity abounds and we are in a world of hurt.

However, there is good news: When Alexis de Tocqueville came to America in 1831 to study our society, he was most impressed with our citizens' freedom to associate in groups of their own choosing. He said. "In America there is a group for every imaginable purpose and cause." This is still the great strength of the American society. It plays a big role in holding us together. In a real sense, it is our irreplaceable glue. When a society is in turmoil like America is now, group life at least allows for a constructive way to blow off steam. We may not like what many groups say or do, but within the constraints of the legal system they have a right to do it, as long as it doesn't do harm to others. These actions may annoy us and frustrate us, but we better appreciate the gift of democracy that is sometimes messy. Of course, we are troubled by individuals and groups, which use enormous amounts of undisclosed money to unfairly discredit other groups. Nevertheless, our commitment to unfettered group life is a great societal asset.

The Power of Groups as an Antidote to Social Isolation

This is where we come in. We know the power and dynamics of groups, so we are positioned to apply our knowledge and experiences to groups of all sorts, just not traditional small treatment groups. The benefits of groups bear repeating here: groups can serve as an effective antidote to social isolation and loneliness. Groups provide a place to be cared about and to care about other people. Groups provide a valuable sense of belonging and being a part of community. Groups can provide a place to commune and do necessary grief work. Groups offer the opportunity to acquire social skills and access valuable social resources. Groups can contribute to healthy identity formation and provide a sense of protection from external harm. Groups can embolden individuals to become empowered to assert their rights as citizens, advocating for social justice.

Treasuring these valuable properties of groups, we ply our knowledge and our craft as practitioners. This is what set us apart from other clinicians: We know that there are stages of group development, which require specific work to successfully move groups from formation through dissolution. We understand that change, even positive change, brings feelings of loss and with loss comes grieving. We know that giving up the victim role also leads to grieving. Consequently, we know how to deal with sadness in groups. We know that many people do not feel that they are worthy of pleasure and joy. Group life can help them to embrace pleasure. We know that groups, like any social system, have boundaries, which define its membership and its purposes. Boundary maintenance functions to keep other external people and influences from penetrating group boundaries in order protect its work and integrity. Therefore, transactions with other groups and social systems are not easily achieved. We know that power and control struggles within groups are necessary to assure group members that the power of the group leader will not be exercised in malevolent ways. We know that such assurance is necessary for group members to experience intimacy. We know that physical mastery is a prerequisite to mastery of the social world. So we skillfully introduce and offer activities to help group members gain physical mastery. We know that group members calculate whether the benefits of group membership are worth the risks involved. Until this calculus is completed, the decision to own affiliation cannot really be made. Most important, for the potential group member is the matter of trust: can group members and its leaders be counted upon to be fair, honorable and behave in the best interest of everyone?

So this is the frame of reference and social context for the work we currently do. I will focus on three group trends that I believe are providing social healing and constructive ways to deal with the grief and anxiety that is prevalent today. First, I will focus on the value of community choruses and their role in social healing. Second, I will look at women's book clubs as a route to gender and racial solidarity. Third, I will look at groups being formed by victims of violence, which are acting to reduce homicides in urban communities and cope with unspeakable grief and chronic sadness.

Community Choruses as Forces in Social Healing

The National Endowment for the Arts (NEA) has documented through recent surveys that choral singing is the number one way in which people participate in the performing arts. There has been a slight increase in the number of community choruses since 9/11. It is understood that music for many people is a way for people to find inner peace. It also provides a way to be a vibrant part of community, particularly at a time when there is a great need for social healing. For the last decade, I have used my knowledge of groups to build the Boston Children's Chorus. Its mission is to use the power of singing for social healing, youth development and community building. I was motivated to found the Chorus in 2002 as a way to achieve authentic social integration of young people across the divides of race, ethnicity and social class. Over my 50 years as a social group worker, I had tried other means to achieve this result, but with limited success. After the Federal Court ordered the desegregation of the Boston Public Schools in 1974, Boston witnessed violent resistance to the Court order in Charlestown and South Boston. In those communities, White mobs attacked Black students as their buses approached their new schools. It was downright ugly. Those events branded Boston as a racist place in the eyes of the nation. The branding still lingers. So the Boston Children's Chorus was founded to contribute to social healing and rebranding. When its diverse singers come on to a stage to perform, as they did tonight, Boston sees what it can become: A community that celebrates diversity and supports its talented youth.

In 2003 we began the work with 30 singers. Today we have 500 singers in 12 choirs, including neighborhood choirs in South Boston, Dorchester, Allston-Brighton and the South End. 35% of our singers come from the suburbs and the rest from inner city neighborhoods in Boston and nearby cities – in all, from over 70 neighborhoods. 47% of our singers are white. 58% are non-white – 22.4% Black, 17.5% Hispanic, 7.5% Asian, 2.4% multi-racial. Singers range in age from 7 to 18 years old. 98% of our graduates have gone on to college. Some of our singers are disabled, including a young man on a walker and a young girl who is blind. All choirs perform at public and private events in the Boston region and beyond, as ambassadors for the city of Boston. Every other year, the top choirs go on an international tour. They have been to Japan, Mexico, Jordan, Scotland and England. On June 22nd, they will head to Vietnam and Cambodia. The Boston Globe calls them: "The Ambassadors of Harmony". In a world plagued with disunity, it is critical that our singers interact with young people through workshops in other countries and sing to global audiences. For our young people, these experiences have been life-altering. They come to understand that they are global citizens.

In a focus group conducted by an external evaluator, our Premier Choir singers said this concerning matters of race: "We do not evaluate each other based on race. We evaluate each other based on maturity.

Are you reliable; do you show up on time; do you know your music; do you reach out and help another singer in need." This is the evaluation that matters to them. It is evidence that authentic social integration is happening at the BCC.

While learning to sing at a level of excellence, our singers are introduced to lyrics and music that speak to social issues that are troubling – historic racism, religious intolerance and xenophobia. They also sing songs about hope and change. Consequently, their singing is infused with powerful emotion. This is clearly apparent at our annual concert celebrating the life and legacy of Dr. Martin Luther King, Jr. on the national holiday celebrating his birthday. An audience of 1,000 people at Jordan Hall is transformed into a "beloved community" by the inspirational singing. One of our singers wrote the following in her college application:

> I gained a greater appreciation for the dreamer. It is because of MLK that my chorus strives to breakdown barriers in Greater Boston and around the globe and unite people of all different backgrounds. After my first MLK concert in 2011, I gained a greater appreciation for the dreamer – I formed a connection with him, and finally could see the impact his vision has made on my life. This day was life-changing.

A few years ago, the friend of one our high school singers committed suicide. Four of her choir colleagues supported her by attending the funeral and singing at the service. About two months later, on their own, they went to see the Samaritans organization and requested that it hold a workshop on depression and suicide at our central rehearsal site. It happened with the support of the BCC staff. The 20 plus singers who attended the workshop came out of the session crying, in touch with the grief that was pent-up and in need of expression. A couple of the singers became trained to be hotline counselors for the Samaritans, handling calls from very depressed callers, some contemplating suicide.

The family of one of our singers was burned out of their apartment by a fire. Within a week through contributions from the BCC community, the family received everything that they needed to start over. The healing power of community was clearly on display. The BCC has a mentor system, which allows the older singers to mentor a younger singer. Giving back to others is strongly encouraged. Our singers created a blog which is on the BCC website. It is used to communicate to the public the pleasure they receive from their major performances. I call it: "spreading joy."

Last year, 19 singers graduated and their loss of the BCC was palpable – they wept as they sang the last song in their last concert. So the support from other singers and staff members is critical to help them deal with the pain of termination. All I know about termination in groups gets applied by our staff.

You have just heard our Premier Choir and Young Men's Ensemble sing Up to the Mountain, written by Patti Griffin in tribute to Dr. King. They sang this song at the interfaith service, which sought to heal the city after the Marathon bombings. President Obama and Governor Patrick spoke at the service. This was the BCC's contribution to social healing. One of our singers was singing through tears, which had a great impact on a global television audience. It made the rounds of You Tube. The Boston Children's Chorus is just one example of how community choruses are contributing to social healing and building community and social bonds

Women's Book Groups Provide Social Bonding

I am fascinated by the emergence and growth of women's book clubs. These are groups that feed the intellect and souls of it members. They provide opportunities for social bonding and gender and cultural solidarity. Men appear not to be able to pause like this and engage in introspection and bonding. I have looked closely at one Black woman's book club that has been going for 15 years. It selects books to read principally written by Black authors, seeking to deepen their knowledge of black culture, history and life perspectives. The membership composition is inter-generational, with some members in their 70s and 60s and the rest in their 30s and 40s. The older members share their wisdom, gained from a lifetime of struggles with young professionals who are still making their way in their careers and raising children. The transfer of intergenerational learning is powerful. The social interactions at and between meetings meet important social needs. This book club had some difficulty concerning boundary matters: how should new members be considered and invited into the club? Fortunately, they worked out rules for admitting new members before differences turned into harsh conflict. There was also disagreement about whether to accept the offer of another book club to have a joint meeting. After some contentious debate, the invitation from the other book club was accepted. However, some members, who thought that the joint meeting would be a diversion from the purposes of their book club, refused to attend. Fortunately, the book club was able to get beyond boundary issues and to move ahead to have a fulfilling experience. During this time of pain and disunity, the book club is a place for learning, laughter and social bonding. Going 15 years with no end in sight. I know of another Black women's book club that has been meeting for 25 years. It would be a good thing if qualitative research would be done to understand the factors and group dynamics that sustain book clubs for such a long time, beyond usual group life.

Groups for Mothers of Murdered Children

Finally, I lift up another group phenomenon in response to homicides that are rampant in urban neighborhoods in Chicago, Philadelphia and Boston. Mothers of murdered children have formed groups to console each other, to grieve and take actions that would prevent further violence in the community. One such group in Boston is Mothers for Justice and Equality. Its members have a program of mobilizing others to prevent violence in Roxbury, Dorchester and Mattapan. They met with Governor Patrick, Mayor Menino and Police Commissioner Davis to demand greater governmental efforts to end the scourge of violence. They are enraged by the inability of the police to find most of the perpetrators of murders. The group's work is a combination of advocacy, community mobilization and social healing. It has received enormous support from other nonprofit organizations in the community. I mentor one of the leaders of the group, who lost her nephew to violence. She retired after 38 years of work at Citizens Bank where she had risen to senior management status. She is now responsible for the group's major fundraising and strategic planning.

Conclusion

Here is my main point this evening: In a world tormented by wars, terrorism, violence, civic discord, partisan gridlock and all manner of divisiveness, the watchword is HEALING – SOCIAL HEALING.

Retreat into social isolation will not work; it just won't cut it. What we most need is the embrace of others in order to heal. That embrace may come at the workplace, in a church, in a synagogue, in a mosque, in a community chorus, in a book club, in an anti-violence group or any other group association. We bring to these settings our eternal knowledge of the power of group life and practice wisdom to advance healing. Our gifts are needed more than ever.

I was dean of the School of Social Work here at Boston University for 16 years. Before arriving here, I had acquired managerial and organizational development skills that would stand me in good stead. But I am a social group worker to my core who basically saw the School of Social Work as a big group. I gave it a group work hug – a big embrace. That means I used my group leadership skills to get everyone – faculty, students and staff members to profoundly embrace each other and our institutional mission and to create a healing culture. And the legacy of those embraces lives on. During those 16 years, we had some difficult times, particularly when faculty union members were challenging the BU administration with threats of strikes and execution of strikes. To say that things got tense is a gross understatement. It was my job to make sure that we continued to embrace each other while respecting each other's roles and rights. Jim Garland was one of the union leaders – and believe me, he put his group work skills to work. But we got through it all intact as a WHOLE community. The operational word here is WHOLE.

As social group workers, we operate in every conceivable arena in this country. Through direct practice, consultation, training, mentoring and organizational leadership, we have the opportunity to contribute to healing. This may require that you practice mega-group work, using your knowledge and skills to have healing impact on large numbers of people. HEALING is the watchword and the mission that must drive you. Just go out and give group work hugs – with love, with humility, with wisdom and with skill. This is the work that you are called upon to do. Embrace it!

Thank you for having me speak tonight.

Hubie Jones
June 6, 2013

Social Determinants of Health and Parent Coffee Hour

Jessy Benjamin

Introduction

This chapter describes and examines social determinants of health and its impact on the families of patients receiving care at the Hospital for Sick Children in Toronto. As a result of these socially determined circumstances, families are faced with difficulties and disadvantages, in addition to providing support to pediatric patients. In keeping with the mission of the hospital to provide family-centered care, the social work department developed a caregiver support group in the form of Parent Coffee Hour to enable families to meet each other and share their experiences. It also allowed families to learn about the various resources available within and outside the hospital that helps in mitigating the emotional and financial strain experienced by families functioning as caregivers to a child patient.

Background

According to the Public Health Agency of Canada: "It is evident that research is telling us to look at the big picture of health to examine factors both inside and outside the health care system that affect our health. At every stage of life, health is determined by complex interactions between social and economic factors, the physical environment and individual behavior. They do not exist in isolation to each other. These factors can be referred to as determinants of health" (Public Health Agency of Canada, 2011).

This premise is further supported by publications such as Social Determinants of Health: Canadian Facts (Mikkoken & Raphael, 2010) that identified and evaluated the role of various social and economic factors contributing to health inequities in Canada, namely, income and income distribution, education, unemployment and job security, employment and working conditions, early childhood development, food insecurity, housing, social exclusion, social safety network, health services, aboriginal status, gender, race and disability.

Social determinants of health

Social determinants of health are "conditions in which people are born, grow, live, work and age including the health system. These circumstances are shaped by the distribution of money, power, and resources at global, national and local levels" (World Health Organization, 2013). Families of patients receiving care at hospitals experience stressful situations as a result of their family dynamics and troubles associated with social determinants of health such as poverty, inadequate housing, unemployment and social exclusion. Cultural background also plays an important role in determining how soon a family can adapt to functioning effectively as caregivers, especially in an unfamiliar city or new surroundings.

Diversity

Toronto is one of the most multicultural cities in the world. The population of Toronto in 2011 was "2,615,060, or 7.8% of Canada's total population of 33,476,688" (Toronto Backgrounder, 2012). Toronto's population is composed of 49.1% visible minorities; which makes up 20.2% of Canada's visible minority population (Statistics Canada, 2011b). According to the 2011 census, only 50.9% of Torontonians have English as a mother tongue (Statistics Canada, 2011a).

Immigration and New Comer Health in Toronto

The National Household Survey by Statistics Canada showed that in 2011 Canada had a foreign-born population of about 6,775,800 people (Statistics Canada, 2011b). They represented 20.6% of the total population, the highest proportion among the G8 countries (Statistics Canada, 2011b). National and provincial research shows that newcomers are healthier than Canadian-born residents when they first arrive to Canada. They have lower rates of heart disease, cancer and mental health problems. The first comprehensive report on newcomer health in Toronto was released in 2011 (Khandor & Koch, 2011). The report identified health as a settlement issue and highlighted that most newcomers arrive in Toronto in good health but lose that health advantage over time. Newcomers experience a decline in their health due to the stress associated with migration, settlement and adaptation. High rates of unemployment, discrimination, social isolation, housing insecurity and barriers to health and other services also contribute to declining health over time.

Education, Income distribution, Poverty and Housing: A Health Issue

Poverty affects some newcomers more than others. Ethnic newcomers earn less. The following data show that newcomers are disproportionately poorer than the population at large. In 1980, newcomers earned 85 cents for every dollar earned by Canadian-born residents. By 2005, it was reduced to 63 cents. This demonstrates the growing income gap between resident and immigration population (Khandor & Koch, 2011).

In 2009, the unemployment rate among newcomers was 17% compared to 10% of all residents. In 2006, 46% of male newcomers and 40% of female newcomers had a university education compared to corresponding figures of 26% and 21% of longer-term immigrants (10 years or more). Nationally, the proportion of newcomers with university degree working at jobs with low educational requirements grew from 22% in 1991 to 28% in 2006 for men and 44% for women (Khandor & Koch, 2011).

Persons who rent their housing, 1.6 million households, have an annual income of less than $14,000. This means that 1 in 3 tenant households in Canada cannot afford to pay more than $360.00 per month in rent. Canadian Public Health Association recognises that "adequate shelter" is a prerequisite for health and that homelessness is a health issue. Many newcomers do not have social support networks or an extended family support in Toronto to help them cope with the stress of migration and resettlement. They end up settling in neighbourhoods that lack affordable and quality housing and have poor access to transportation and other services. Almost half the population of newcomers live in low-income households (Kandor & Koch, 2011). As of 2005, 46% of newcomers lived in low-income housing compared to 23% of longer-term immigrants and 20% of Canadian-born residents. In 2006, 58% of newcomers spent more than 30% of their income on housing compared to 30% of long-term immigrants and 22% of Canadian born residents (Khandor & Koch, 2011).

Inadequate housing has been a concern for many of these families. Many large families live in small apartment buildings and are unable to maintain a healthy life, particularly if the building is not maintained with proper heating and pest control by the property management.

The Parent Coffee Hour (PCH) Group

Parent Coffee Hour (PCH) is a caregiver support group offered for the families of General surgery, Orthopedic, Urology and Gynaecology divisions at the Hospital for Sick Children (SickKids) – a North American Pediatric Hospital. The vision of the hospital is "Healthier Children. A Better World." The purpose of the Parent Coffee Hour group is for parents to meet other families; experience a relaxing time outside of their child's hospital ward; and to have an opportunity to express their needs and difficulties to staff and to learn of the various resources within and outside the hospital. In essence, this is a single-session, mutual aid, support group facilitated by different social workers in their respective divisions. This group meets once a week.

Composition of Parent Coffee Hour group

Parent Coffee Hour is a group of families with varying national, cultural and language backgrounds gathered together for a short break to meet with the other families, share their experiences and learn from each other. PCH members belong to different socio-economic backgrounds. Almost 50% of the group members are landed immigrants who are struggling to settle down in a new country and have the additional stress of experiencing the hospitalization and nursing of a family member. It is understood from the group meetings that these families have either not found a job or were laid off from employment. In several cases, insufficient hours of work and single parenthood are contributing factors to the stress experienced by families, particularly with a child hospitalized for a chronic disease. Most parents are unemployed and survive on income received from employment insurance funds or social assistance. Some of the families have no insurance coverage while others may be on refugee status.

The duration of a family's stay at the hospital depends on the severity of the patient's illness. General Surgery department mostly treats patients with chronic and complex disorders, and these patients tend to have a longer duration of stay at the hospital. These families require additional financial support for travel, parking or hotel expenses, especially if their primary residence is out of town.

SickKids Patient Amenities Fund and Other Resources

The Patient Amenities Fund is a composite fund, which is administered through the Hospital and encompasses financial support for newcomers who are unemployed and dealing with unforeseen circumstances. It covers parking and transportation, prescription drugs, dental coverage, meals and hotel accommodation. Interpreter services are available if the families are unable to understand medical terms and conditions. Mental health services are available off-site for parents older than 18 years, particularly for assessment and treatment. If patients are observed as neglected by their caregivers, Child Protection Services are notified to investigate and this child welfare agency follows up for support and safety of the children at home, once discharged.

Case Example

Background

The following case example highlights the various social determinants that play an important role in the physical, emotion and mental well being of the patient and the caregivers. It also brings to light the role of social workers and a group, such as the one that meets through Parent Coffee Hour, in alleviating the challenges caused by social circumstances, which inadvertently affect health. Parents voice their issues, which are focused on coping with prolonged hospitalization, various psychosocial issues, and the impact of hospitalization. The group members share information and receive parent-to-parent support. This group process is an opportunity to not only have a break from the four walls of their room but also to meet with other parents with a range of problems/issues. Parents also get an opportunity to verbalize their questions and seek information about how to fund expensive medical supplies and also other children's charity resources. Low-income status and financial stress is huge for parents when their children are hospitalized. The group also helps in building networks outside of the group, thereby maintaining a continuum of social support.

The group is open ended and may have different members each week as well as parents returning from previous weeks due to re-hospitalization. The opportunity to share experiences as parents of surgical patients, to problem solve, clarify information and develop supportive networks through participation in the group will ideally reduce parental stress and will positively impact on their experience of surgical unit and hospital system at large. Involvement in the group will enhance parental coping with issues related to the hospitalized child, family, school and community. "The constant variety of people who attend the group increased the range of problem solving ideas, of talents and information shared, and of relationship opportunities available to group members. Families increased their coping skills through their encounters with a range of people and problems" (Lassner, 2013, p. 89).

Sarah* (name changed for protection of identity) was brought to the Hospital for Sick Children (SickKids) for surgery soon after birth. She suffered from a congenital disorder, the severity of which was difficult for her family to comprehend. Sarah's mother and her parents were permanent residents of Canada and had been living in the country for 5 years. Sarah's father remained in their native country and could not be present for Sarah's birth or for after-care. Sarah's father is from a South Asian country, unknown to the hospital. The extended family is the basis of social structure and loyalty and respect to "seniors" in the family is very important. Elders in the family are viewed wise and they make decisions for the family. A referral letter to the immigration department from a social worker at the hospital explaining the need for the father's presence as a caregiver expedited his application to visit Canada.

Sarah's mother had difficulty grasping the meaning of the complex medical terms associated with Sarah's condition due to English being her second language. Despite her best intentions, language barriers often resulted in Sarah's mother falling short of fulfilling her responsibilities as primary caregiver where she had to be prompted by the social work team to attend to her daughter's medical needs. At this point, Sarah's father's arrival was timely. He was able to grasp the severity of Sarah's illness through frequent updates by the medical and social workers' team in a very short period of time. Sarah's father's physical presence in the hospital provided additional support to the mother. Additionally, he took upon himself the role of the primary caregiver.

Upon his arrival, Sarah's father became responsible for a portion of the medical expenses, but as a newcomer and as a primary caregiver, he could not find a job to support the family's needs. He finally had to seek social assistance for basic needs such as food, housing and medication. The family came from a conservative cultural background and relied solely on income earned by male members. Women were forbidden from working. Thus, the family's cultural practice and belief system prevented Sarah's mother from seeking employment. The family also struggled with domestic issues involving Sarah's parents' lack of freedom as a result of a joint family system.

Social Worker Assessment and Role of PCH

Sarah suffered from a congenital disorder known as persistent cloaca, which results in confluence of the rectum, vagina, and urethra into a single common channel. The pediatric surgery involves anatomical reconstruction (Levitt & Penna, 2013). Consequently, the duration of the stay required at the hospital was relatively long, leading to increased cost of care. Also, the cost of urinary catheterization, gastrostomy tube for feeding issues and ostomy supplies could not be met by the income from social assistance alone. Through social workers' guidance the family was able to learn about and seek additional government funding such as Assistance for Children with Severe Disabilities and Ostomy grants to mitigate these needs. The family also had to consider subsidized housing to live closer to the hospital. Through Parent Coffee Hour interactions, Sarah's mother learned about and was referred to community counseling for assessment of learning ability, and also received emotional support.

Information regarding subsidized housing, tax returns for medical expenses, etc. was provided to the families during Parent Coffee Hour sessions.

PCH is a weekly group mainly for parents of children admitted as in-patients. The group is open-ended and may have new members who join more ongoing members each week. Sarah's mother continuously attended the group, as her baby was a long-term patient. She enjoyed the opportunity to meet other members from her community, speak in her first language and build a social network and friendships. This mom would say, "When I come to this group, I get a special energy. My eyes open up more. I learn and get more wisdom listening to others." Caring for a sick baby is a big responsibility. Sarah mother's friends from the group often offer parenting tips, how to wake up the baby to feed on time, how to watch for the infant's cues, etc. The group is also a forum to normalize feelings. One member stated, "Yeah, all of us went through this, losing sleep is the main thing, but it is for our child."

Pearlin, Menaghan, Lieberman, & Mullen (1981) state, "Research of stress elucidates how people come to experience challenging circumstances, potentially caused by socio-economic deficits, exclusion, illness and disability and how they are mediated by coping, social supports, and a sense of control and mastery (as cited in Mechanic & Tanner, 2007, p. 1222). Sarah's father's physical and mental health was deteriorating as he relentlessly worked on stabilizing Sarah's clinical condition by providing financial and emotional support. He had no extended family support in Canada. His lack of employment and financial independence along with his unfamiliarity to the new culture and country took a toll on his health and his ability to play the strong role of a primary caregiver. The social work team's continued efforts and correspondence enabled his mother (Sarah's grandmother) to visit Canada and provide secondary support to the family.

Group members express feelings of frustration/anxiety around chronic illness or medical conditions, loneliness, extra expenses, loss of job, housing and accessing appropriate resources. For instance, members support each other by having their lunch together, listening to each other, exchanging contact information or caring for a sibling for a short time, or providing a cultural meal.

PCH helps parents to meet, share, understand difficulties and support and receive attention for concerns and feelings. For Sarah's mother it has been a consistent growth from not knowing anything to gaining confidence and knowledge of how to manage better with a chronically ill child. Sarah's father occupied a difficult position in the family, as he had to negotiate supporting his wife and child alongside navigating cultural expectations about his role within the family. Beliefs around who controls finance and how money is distributed for daily needs were another social and economic dynamic and struggle for this family. This single session group helped in receiving information, provided an opportunity for expression of feelings, and helped to generate new ideas. Sarah has been continually in association with the hospital whenever she had emergence of medical issues alongside her diagnosis. She always has medical appointments as follow-up and comprehensive pharmaceutical care. Whenever possible the group work meetings are open for dad, mom and grandmother.

There are seven possible benefits for single session groups. These are:

1. Receive information
2. Provide an opportunity for expression of feelings
3. Generate new ideas
4. Become inspired
5. Receive attention for concerns and feelings
6. Can provide consensual validation
7. Practice a skill

(Brown, 2014, p. 110.)

Conclusion

The impact of the Parent Coffee Hour group at the Hospital for Sick Children in Toronto highlights the importance of a social support group as a complementary aid in the provision of health care services to patients.

An ethnically diverse city like Toronto is made up of a large proportion of newcomers from different socio-economic and cultural backgrounds. Each of these newcomers go through the experience of adapting to a new country, living a life that is different from one that they are used to, struggle through unemployment, underemployment, new languages and a new legal system, especially concerning the role of women and children in society. In such a scenario, the health of an individual or family member is likely to be affected by a number of social determinants such as income levels, housing conditions, unemployment and social standing. When children of such families are hospitalized, these families experience added pain and social and financial struggles, which may lead to anxiety, depression and other mental health issues.

By providing a safe and supportive social aid group through the Parent Coffee Hour, parents of these patients have an opportunity to alleviate some of their stress. Also, they gain access to knowledge of various resources available to them including the SickKids patient amenities fund and other government aid. In many instances, this has led to better quality health care for the patient through the development of a more stable social support system.

Author's Note

The author wishes to thank Barbara Muskat, Director of Social Work at the Hospital for Sick Children for her continuous encouragement and support and Elsa Jacob, Research Technologist, Department of Physiology and Experimental Medicine at the Hospital for Sick Children for assistance with Research expertise and fine tuning this paper.

References

Brown, N. W. (2014). *Facilitating Challenging Groups: Leaderless, Open, and Single-Session Groups*. Routledge.

Khandor, E., & Koch, A. (2011). The Global City: Newcomer Health in Toronto. Toronto Public Health and Access Alliance Multicultural Health and Community Services.

Lassner, J. (2013). *Social Group Work: Competence and Values in Practice*. Routledge.

Levitt, M., & Pena, A. (2013). Cloacal Malformations: Background. Retrieved from http://emedicine.medscape.com/article/933717-overview

Mechanic, D. & Tanner, J. (2007). Vulnerable people, groups, and populations: Societal view.*Health Affairs*, Sep/Oct 2007, 1222.

Mikkonen, J., & Raphael, D. (2010). *Social determinants of health: The Canadian facts*. York University, School of Health Policy and Management.

Pearlin, L. I., Menaghan, E. G., Lieberman, M. A., & Mullan, J. T. (1981). The stress process. *Journal of Health and Social Behavior, 22*(4), 337-356.

Public Health Agency of Canada (2011). Population Health: What Determines Health? Retrieved from http://www.phac-aspc.gc.ca/ph-sp/determinants/index-eng.php

Statistics Canada (2011a). Focus on Geography Series, 2011 Census: Census subdivision of Toronto, C – Ontario. Retrieved from https://www12.statcan.gc.ca/census-recensement/2011/as-sa/fogs-spg/Facts-csd-eng.cfm?LANG=Eng&GK=CSD&GC=3520005

Statistics Canada (2011b). Immigration and Ethnocultural Diversity in Canada: National Household Survey, 2011. Retrieved from http://www12.statcan.gc.ca/nhs-enm/2011/as-sa/99-010-x/99-010-x2011001-eng.pdf

Statistics Canada (2011c). Population and dwelling counts for Canada and census subdivisions. Retrieved from http://www12.statcan.gc.ca/census-recensement/2011/dp-pd/hlt-fst/pd-pl/Table-Tableau.cfm?T=301&S=3&O=D

Toronto Backgrounder (2012). 2011 Census: Population and Dwelling Counts. Retrieved from https://www1.toronto.ca/city_of_toronto/social_development_finance—administration/files/pdf/2011-census-backgrounder.pdf

World Health Organization (2013) Health Topics: Social determinants of health. Retrieved from http://www.who.int/topics/social_determinants/en/

Challenges & Opportunities for Applying Group Work Principles to Enhance Online Learning in Social Work[1]

Marcia B. Cohen, Shirley R. Simon, Donna McLaughlin, Barbara Muskat, Mary White

Introduction

The recent increase in social work courses being offered on line as well as fully online social work programs raises challenges for social work educators. The literature suggests that group work principles can serve as a foundation for effective online education. This chapter will examine the obstacles and opportunities for using group work principles to advance learning in online education. Three examples of fully online social work courses will be discussed in order to highlight these issues. The potential role of group work educators as leaders in facilitating effective online learning will be explored.

Background

In recent years, there has been a large increase in the number of social work programs offering online and hybrid/blended (partially online) courses along with the traditional classroom based courses. Furthermore, there has also been an increase in the number of fully online MSW programs. Despite initial unease on the part of many social work educators, online education has increasingly been embraced as a valid teaching method in social work. There is a growing literature which suggests that group work principles can serve as a foundation for effective online education. The development of group cohesion, in particular, a cornerstone of group work education and practice, has been found to improve online learning outcomes. (Parr & Ward, 2006; Stauber & Simon, 2009; Wilke, Randolph & Vinton, 2009). As Stauber and Simon (2009, 2011) have noted, group work educators are in an ideal position to assume a leadership role in facilitating the development of online communities. We have the group work knowledge and skills necessary to facilitate group development and build online environments conducive to mutuality, group cohesion and learning. This chapter discusses the challenges and opportunities inherent in online teaching in social work, with an emphasis on the use of group work principles to advance student learning. It describes and assesses three examples of fully online education in social work - an online BSW group work course, an online MSW group course and an online MSW field work seminar - to demonstrate the role of group work principles in the effective delivery of online education.

Deterrents to Faculty Engagement in Online Education

Teaching via an online format brings its own set of unique challenges. Being an online educator requires understanding and adapting to a new form of instructional delivery. While one must still be a content expert, it is additionally necessary to understand the delivery system itself and to design and conduct one's course to be effective without the physical presence of a teacher in the classroom.

To be effective, instructors must become familiar with best practices in online education and apply those practices to their courses. This could involve "re-packaging" existing course content and transcribing lecture notes from yellow legal pads to audio, video, or formal written outlines. It would likely require revising assignments and composing additional written descriptors in order to adapt to an online environment. This would necessitate a higher level of organization since the opportunity for informal, face-to-face (F2F) interactions is generally diminished, and thus, the questions and explanations typically handled via in-class exchanges require written communications. Clarity and detail are essential in online education in order to provide the framework for more independent student learning. Overall, instruction via the online platform necessitates additional effort (Allen & Seaman, 2013), and faculty may not be interested in learning about this type of instruction. They may even consider "virtual instruction" less rewarding.

The additional time and effort is not limited to learning new pedagogy, but also to gaining familiarity with the online and technological systems (Simon & Stauber, 2011). Instructors need to learn about delivery platforms such as Blackboard and Sakai. They need to develop a reasonable degree of comfort and skill with the technology in order to create, post, conduct, manage and evaluate course material. And this is not simply an initial investment of effort. Upgrades, advances in software, and administrative changes in university platforms can necessitate additional demands for time and effort. Technical "glitches" can cause further frustrations. The system "going down" or data seemingly lost by a crashing computer can be monumental stressors. In the academic world where "publish or perish" still exists, it may be hard to commit the additional time and effort.

Fear can also play an inhibiting role in the desire to embrace online education. Needing to learn something new can be intimidating. Faculty who lack technological expertise may be particularly fearful of making mistakes with irreversible consequences, causing data loss and/or system malfunction. Moreover, faculty are not used to operating in a "virtual" environment. The classroom, from both sides of the desk, is familiar and comfortable. Conducting a course online is new and potentially scary. It exposes instructors to a different set of expectations and responsibilities where they may feel vulnerable. In addition, students typically know more about the virtual environment than faculty members, since they have grown up with computers, Wi-Fi, Facebook, Google, etc. This disparity can readily add to the instructor's discomfort.

Other challenges for educators include the sense of distance implicit in the lack of face-to-face contact. Questions naturally arise about whether online education will diminish the sense of satisfaction derived from engaging students in a typical classroom setting. Instructors may also be concerned about the 24/7 accessibility inherent in online interactions. Given the instant access and flexibility that accompanies online communication, instructors may justifiably feel pressure to respond outside of the typical workday hours. The traditional boundaries of nine to five, Monday through Friday, no longer provide the structure and accepted limits that once were commonplace. Working with the newer technological modalities can also be deterred by a lack of interest and patience. Both pedagogical and technological learning demand attention and diligence. Finally, since communication in online education frequently occurs via written formats, instructors may feel a need to be more deliberate and careful in their interactions with students. We live in a litigious society, and online communication provides a formal record of those interactions.

While many educators find teaching in an online format challenging, it is particularly daunting for social group work educators. Group workers' stock in trade has been the communications and dynamics of the face-to-face interaction. The very definition of social group work had been predicated on required face-to-face interaction (Schwartz, 1971). Group workers, and by extension, group work educators, typically enjoy and are adept at the give and take of the group work process. Transferring these skills and interests to the online environment requires a critical conceptual and practical shift in perspective. It is understandable that many of today's group work educators, most of whom were trained in the years before the explosion of online technology, are reticent to embrace this new medium (Simon & Stauber, 2011). Thus, it is clear that online education provides myriad challenges. So why do it?

Opportunities

Despite the many obstacles associated with online instruction, there are compelling reasons to embrace it. First, online education efficiently reaches new and underserved populations. These individuals include those who cannot abandon roles as primary wage earners or family care takers, those with accessibility issues, and those who live at a distance from campuses and cannot relocate (Tandy & Meacham, 2009; Wolfson, Marsom & Magnuson, 2005; Frey, Yankelov & Faul, 2003; Conklin & Osterndorf, 1997). The students in rural communities, the caretakers unable to leave home, the working mothers who want to be home with their families, and the military men and women whose locations may change at any time, can now be served via online education. For most of these populations, F2F instruction is not a viable option. Post secondary academic institutions have been increasingly attentive to the needs of individuals who are not able to access traditional F2F education. This has led to the development and delivery of increasing numbers and types of innovative teaching methods, including a variety of web-based courses (York, 2005). Both for practical and social justice considerations, online education fills a critical societal need.

Online education offers convenience and scheduling flexibility - two characteristics that are highly valued in our fast-paced, overcommitted society. Students have greater control over the day and time they do most of their work. They are not bound by the parameters of one or two weekly F2F class meetings. Instead, they can learn while a dependent is napping or while traveling away from home. Students can work late at night or early in the morning, depending upon their own lifestyle choices. In our consumer-driven environment, offering convenience and flexibility in educational delivery creates a strong marketing advantage.

Online technology allows for greater speed and efficiency in instructor-student communication. Instantaneous, around the globe communication, unimaginable in prior decades, is now a reality. Students no longer need to wait until the next class session to connect with an instructor or their classmates. Email communication has become an expected component of most contemporary educational experiences. Online courses build in additional communication channels - blogs, forums, discussion boards - that enhance and expedite interaction and connection.

Instruction via online platforms also prompts better organization and clarity in course delivery. It is much more difficult to go to class and "wing it". With little or no opportunity for informal F2F interactions, and with a need to post course material before class begins, advanced planning and organization are critical. Whether courses are delivered in hybrid/blended or entirely online formats, online teaching requires a higher degree of structure and specificity.

Instruction in the virtual arena is typically cost effective, a benefit recognized by the leaders of educational institutions. Once "packaged", courses can be opened to large numbers of students without much of the overhead costs implicit in "brick and mortar" settings; this can be an advantage but also has the potential to dilute online course effectiveness if class sizes grow disproportionately. Students can also save money - on travel expenses, childcare, and even residential housing.

Perhaps most importantly, online education is here to stay. Distance education is one of the fastest growing educational options and social work education is quickly adapting to this new reality (Allen & Seaman, 2013; CSWE, 2012). In 2012, the CSWE annual report, *2012*

Statistics on Social Work Education in the United States, began to include formal data on course offerings in online or distance education formats. Twenty-three programs, or 11% of those reporting, offer entire master's programs in online or distance formats. Moreover, another 106 programs, or 50.5% of those reporting, offer part of the master's program online, and seven additional programs anticipate that online/distance education courses will be in operation during the next academic year. It is clear that online education within social work is widespread and growing.

As social work education has joined in the development and expansion of online education (Coe Regan & Youn, 2008; MacFadden, Moore, Herie & Schoech, 2005; Petracchi, 2000), web-based approaches have been employed for a variety of social work courses, including research (Faul, Frey & Barber, 2004), policy (Moore, 2005), and more recently to direct practice courses (Coe Regan & Youn, 2008; Ouelette & Chang, 2004). Despite this growth in online education in social work, there is very little written about the use of online methodology in teaching group work and even less about fully online instruction in group work education (Levine, 2013; Muskat & Mesbur, 2011; Simon & Stauber, 2011).

For group work educators, the widespread increase in online education provides a timely opportunity to assume a leadership role in the development of effective online teaching strategies. Group cohesion is a critical component for improving learning in online education (Fisher, Phelps, & Ellis, 2000; Parr & Ward, 2006; Randolph & Krause, 2002). Who knows more about building cohesion than group workers? Strategies for enhancing participation, engagement, and cohesion fall within group workers' expertise, and community building is at the core of social group work. So while the technical aspects of online teaching may be new to many group work educators, these critical elements of effective online pedagogy are fundamental to the discipline. Although teaching in an online environment may not provide the face-to-face interactions familiar to group workers, the core need for community is the same. Thus, online education provides a perfect opportunity for social group work educators to demonstrate the value of group work principles and practices to the broader academic community. Working collaboratively with colleagues in other departments as well as with technical experts to establish best practices in online education can assure group work educators a leadership role in this burgeoning form of instruction.

Considerable scholarly research focuses on best practices in online education (Coe Regan & Youn, 2008; Madoc-Jones & Parrott, 2005; Maidment, 2005; Palloff & Pratt, 2007; Parr & Ward, 2006; Siebert, Siebert, & Spaulding-Givens, 2006; Simon & Stauber, 2011; Wilke & Vinton, 2009) and group work educators need to be a part of this emerging literature. There are currently vibrant efforts to teach and assess the effectiveness of group work courses in online formats - a task that was thought impossible not so very long ago. The results of these efforts and those of others throughout the group work community should be widely disseminated to claim our expertise and promote the value of social group work methodology. As a beginning effort, we will present three examples of online courses that provided both opportunities and challenges to using group work principles to enhance teaching and learning.

Example #1: A Fully Online, Asynchronous Course on Social Work with Groups

Course Development and Overview

The course, "Social Work with Groups", was developed as a pre-requisite for entry into a BSW program. The program was situated in a college that is part of a large Canadian university. The university has a well-regarded distance education program that includes fully online undergraduate degrees. The course was designed to increase access to professional education for non-traditional learners.

This course evolved from an earlier type of distance education format, which included the use of audiotaped lectures, readings and simulated exercises, completed independently by each student. The course was managed by an instructor who evaluated and graded assignments and answered questions posed by students. The instructor had no face-to-face contact with students, and students did not have any contact with one another.

The course was re-designed as part of an upgrading strategy by the university's distance education service. The upgrade process included the integration of input from university administrators, program consultants and staff from the distance education service. The design team included an instructor with experience teaching this course F2F and members of the university distance education services, notably one expert in web-design and a second expert in on-line instructional design. The intent was to mirror the F2F version of the course, taught regularly on-campus. The web design team utilized the in-class course syllabus and teaching notes. This was supplemented by audio material that was created by audio taping the F2F class.

The purpose of the course was to provide an overview of group work: the basics of group theories, group leadership, group stages, and the application of group work within a variety of social work settings. Group process and dynamics were explored through the use of group activities in which students participated online. The course included twelve units, presented over twelve weeks. Each unit consisted of 20-30 minutes of lecture supplemented by colorful graphics, diagrams and photos that illustrated the material. Readings were assigned for each unit. Students were randomly assigned to online 'pods' - groups of 5-6 students who participated together in small group exercises and discussions. The activities provided students with the experience of participation in a group, mirroring group stages and offering experiential examples of the course material. A different student facilitated each activity within the pods. This also provided students with an opportunity to function as group facilitators.

Communication among students and between students and the instructor were in writing only and asynchronous, with individuals participating at times of their choice. The course requirements included a quiz, a final examination and two written submissions. The quiz was carried out on-line, the final examination was administered at a university exam setting and the written assignments were submitted online. The first submission was an analysis of a group experience, focusing on one or two topics covered in the course material and linking to readings and lecture material. The second assignment was a reflection paper, related to students' experiences in their pods and to their group activities. It was expected that students would participate in the group activities. These activities were not graded, but participation was essential in order to complete the second assignment.

Experiences with the course: Challenges and benefits

Students participated from locations across Canada as well as from a variety of international locations. Students also varied by age, life experience and cultural background. The course allowed many non-traditional students, such as those returning to school while raising children or those working full-time, to participate in group work training.

The asynchronous online format allowed for participation at any time of day or night. This was a great advantage for students who participated from other time zones and for those who worked or cared for children during the day. However, this also presented challenges for the activity portion of the course. Some students preferred to complete activities immediately, while others would rather wait until the last minute. Some students took vacations, had illnesses or experienced life crises. These sorts of situations impacted the timing and completion of exercises. While these experiences can happen in F2F classes as well, in this course it seemed like the very limited amount of interaction/relationship/connection between student and the instructor made it more likely that the issues would not be reported to the instructor and hence not addressed. This led to frustration and resentment, as expressed by some students in their course evaluations. Conflicts also arose in some of the pods. Again, conflicts tended not to be communicated to the instructor, and were not easily 'visible' to the instructor in the traditional F2F manner. Although dealing with conflict in groups was a topic in the course, the students themselves did not address the conflicts. There are several potential reasons for this. Conflict is difficult to acknowledge and deal with in many groups, particularly for students who are new to group theory and practice. Moreover, the potential impact of having pod members who have not met face-to-face is unclear. As well, the course grading was not contingent upon addressing group processes. Thus, when conflicts arose in relation to pod activities, students tended to complete the assignments and to leave the processing of affect to their reflective journals. And as the journals were the final assignment, handed in at the end of the course, conflicts were never discussed or resolved, but merely reflected upon by the students. Although the instructor provided written feedback based upon review of the journals, there was no further dialog, thus missing an important teaching opportunity, especially for group work education.

Another challenge related to students' ability to navigate the technological aspects of the course. Although this is decreasing as an issue for online education as a whole, students in this course often ran into technological glitches. However, this challenge also presented an opportunity. Students who successfully navigated the course site began to offer online advice to other students, thus beginning the development of positive communication and mutual support among some students, an element of mutual aid (Steinberg, 2014). The course instructor also included a message in an early post to the class describing her own inexperience with online education, thus placing her 'in the same boat' as the students, reinforcing another element of mutual aid.

The reflective journals completed by the students indicated that their feelings and experiences throughout the course were quite similar to those typically described by group members at various stages of a group. These included uncertainty about other members, caution in disclosing too much information too soon, excitement to get started, doing the work in the middle phase and reflecting on unresolved issues and gains made at the end. Students offered positive comments about the course in both the reflective journals and in course evaluations. A number of students stated that they clearly advanced their knowledge about groups and group work. Several noted that they would have liked to experience the course in a F2F context; however they did gain a unique experience in an online group.

From the instructor's point of view, the relationship with online students was different than that with F2F students. The online instructor only 'met' the students by reading posts, monitoring activities, responding to questions and grading assignments. This relationship was adequate when the group processes in the pods were proceeding well. However, it was more challenging when students required assistance. It was difficult for the instructor to recall details about each student, as the more nuanced information that can be generated in F2F meetings was not available. Students' relationships with one another were also more limited. They had little exposure to the class as a whole and mainly interacted with their pod-mates. This is in contrast to a F2F class where students can see one another participating in activities, working through conflicts, and engaging in discussions.

Communication in this course was carried out strictly through the written word. Non-verbal communication could not be observed. This was a challenge, especially when dealing with a social work approach that emphasizes the importance of visually scanning group members and observing non-verbal cues (Kurland & Salmon, 1998). While there has been an increase in the use of computer graphics and 'emoticons', they are not a full substitute for the breadth and depth of nonverbal communication. The sole use of written language can also be problematic for students who have specific challenges with writing or reading.

Finally, there is evidence that online learning has cost-saving benefits (Regehr, 2013). This is true with regard to the sponsoring institution, since classroom rental and maintenance are not needed in the virtual classroom. However, course instructors in online teaching formats must spend considerable time moderating, monitoring and maintaining the course (Fisher et al, 2000). In this experience, it was crucial for the instructor to log on frequently, monitor work within the pods and answer the many questions posted by students in relation to assignments and course material. This is especially critical in a group work course, where group process is just as important as content. Monitoring was particularly crucial due to the presence of what is known as "Online Disinhibition Effect" (Suler, 2004). The absence of non-verbal cues and the presence of written material that cannot be stopped ahead of its appearance online resulted in some students sharing personal thoughts, feelings and histories that went beyond the boundaries of the usual instructor-student communication. It is challenging to prevent this from happening and to help these individuals to learn 'netiquette', the rules of what is appropriate and not appropriate to share with virtual classmates. In a F2F classroom, the instructor is present to guide discussions to include information suitable for an educational setting and re-focus students if needed. While the topic of boundaries was conveyed in the online course material, disclosures only surfaced after they had already occurred in a pod or through student-instructor communication.

Lessons learned

The fully online group work course successfully provided students with the basics of social group work theory and a specific type of online educational group experience. An online group work course has the additional potential to prepare students to work with online groups. The role of the instructor is one of observation and monitoring, with potentially less opportunity for modeling and group facilitation.

Based upon the above experience, the following recommendations are offered to enhance the online delivery of education and to better meet the requirements of a group work course:

1. Although it might negatively impact accessibility, synchronous on-line communication, with all students and the instructor online

at the same time, would allow for better monitoring and modeling of communication. With this in mind, course designers in group work must pay close attention to web-based discussions, in order to deal with the "interactivity and responsivity integral to e-learning" (Madoc-Jones & Parrot, 2005, p. 766).

2.   Inclusion of a mandatory face-to-face meeting at the start of the course, with all students attending, would allow students to meet, begin to form relationships, have online technology and norms explained, and begin to build a sense of belonging to the class group. If this is not possible, newer forms of online conferencing software, such as SKYPE, can create an opportunity for students to see and hear one another. This requires that students have a computer with a camera, microphone and the drive space needed to host the program.

3.   Online group work courses should be created with specific attention to issues common to the group work process: (a) explicit and clear expectations about the purpose of the course, (b) the development of group norms, including agreements on content and timings of posting and the development of norms around personal safety, (c) attention to confidentiality, (d) attention to group stages: proper introductions, monitoring of group process and conflict, and preparation for endings and (e) enhancement of the development of mutual aid.

4.   Instructors should anticipate that issues that commonly arise in groups, such as conflict among members, may also arise in the course. Preparation for these issues is important, and mechanisms must be put into place to help resolve conflicts that may arise.

Example #2: A Combined Synchronous and Asynchronous Online Group Work Course Development and Overview

In approaching the design of an online, master's level course in group work, a robust and active connection with and among the students was emphasized as a priority. An online "Clinical Practice with Groups" course was designed, developed and implemented. The goal of the course was for students to learn conceptual group theory and practice skills in facilitating groups with clients. There was a keen awareness that experiential learning and teaching in social work relies heavily on adult learning theory. This theory maintains that adult learners are most effectively educated in a style that is interactive, includes feedback and role playing, and incorporates specific elements that foster changes in attitude, cognition, and behavior (Knowles, 1980; Garavaglia, 1993; Kirkpatrick, 1998; Mott, 2000; Daley, 2001). The "Clinical Practice with Groups" course provides a meaningful learning experience for the students that is skills-based, culturally-based, incorporates current theory and research, and is accessible to students with varying learning styles.

Experiences with the course: Challenges and benefits

The main design challenge for this online group course was how to give the students an opportunity to *practice and engage* in group work. In teaching group work online, the Live Classroom (LC) experience is a key component. LC for this course is defined as one that uses the technology of Adobe Connect where participants appear in 'real time' by both video and audio so that all participants can talk with one other in the virtual classroom. While the concepts, course literature, lectures and exercises can occur via asynchronous learning on an individual basis, active and dynamic interaction must occur as a weekly component of the course. As previously noted, synchronous learning can be challenging. However, "a real-time, instructor-led online learning event in which all participants are logged on at the same time and communicate directly with each other" is quite beneficial to all participants (Daydov, Emery, Lahanas, & Potemski, 2010). During LC, students often comment positively about the effectiveness of this technology. It is helpful that role play exercises, for example, can be seen, heard, felt and critiqued right in the moment of action. Over the duration of this five weeks' long course, students will meet in LC five times. Participation is a required component of the online Group Work course. For multiple reasons, attention to the scheduling of the LC's is important. Students have very full daily schedules that often include familial obligations, work and field placements. In order to minimize conflicts with these additional student priorities, as well as allow for time zone differences where the students reside, LC's are arranged for Sunday or Monday evenings.

Segments of recorded LC sessions demonstrate how students and instructors can negotiate the enacting of role plays, and offer support and encouragement to one another as the students practice their newly acquired skills. The EPAS (Educational Policy Accreditation Standards) put forth by CSWE (Council on Social Work Education) call upon educators to teach students to *demonstrate* their learning in diverse practice areas (Council on Social Work Education, 2008). Utilizing the LC for activities such as role plays offers students the opportunity to experience being a group member or a group facilitator and to discuss core group work concepts by debriefing after a demonstration. Real-time practice increases students' comfort level with group facilitation and with the dynamics that occur in groups. For those students not directly taking part in the exercise, there is an opportunity to observe and share viewpoints as part of the critique, since students often pick up on actions and words that the participants do not necessarily notice. Critical to the online experience is the fact that students are engaging from locations all over the country, yet can engage in practicing skills together. The technology enables students to connect in ways that would be impossible otherwise, facilitating a robust and effective learning experience.

The next critical piece of the Group Work course is the institution of a Peer Support Group component. In learning group work skills, it is essential that students have a lived experience of group membership and the opportunity to 'try on' group facilitation. In this course the overarching purpose of the peer support group is to socialize students to group norms as group members, facilitators and consultants. It also aims to increase knowledge, skills and comfort in conducting groups as well as to learn about the stages of group work in real-time as members and as group facilitators. The goals for the group are to (a) provide students the opportunity to discuss school and field related issues and learn about the experiences of other students; (b) offer students additional peer support related to balancing work and the demands of graduate school, and (c) facilitate hands-on experiential learning about group leadership and group membership. During these groups students meet without a course facilitator, in a live virtual "room" arranged through Distance Education, and the session is recorded. The course instructor reviews the session so as to garner important themes to bring back to the LC to discuss. Again, the instructor and students have the opportunity to view the peer support groups after the fact, and then utilize these clips for learning and integration of key group work concepts.

Lessons learned

The Peer Support Group component of the course was very successful in helping the students to feel part of a learning community. Important to the course learning objectives is that after each peer support group session, the group will have a debrief conversation. It is here that students critique and identify the group concepts, skills practiced, techniques learned, and potential improvements. As well, there is a course assignment connected to the student's experience of facilitating the peer support group. It is here that the students will integrate the group work literature, support their statements with examples from the support group, and critique their skills. The assignment provides further opportunity for the students to internalize their learning experience.

In summary, the key synchronous components of the Clinical Practice with Groups course are critical to a successful experience for the students and for the instructor. The students' experience of group cohesion, while participating as a member in both the course and in the peer support group, contributes to their professional growth as group workers. Relationships and connections are made, and students experience support and build confidence in the core practice skills needed to be effective practitioners in social work with groups.

Example #3: Online Learning in a Field Work Seminar

Social work is a collaborative and relationship based profession. Collaboration goes beyond two or more people working together towards a common goal; it is about open learning, relationships, and sharing. Collaborative skills developed through group work in a F2F or online environment are essential transferrable skills for social workers. As noted previously in this chapter, students learn best when they are engaged with their classmates and when they connect, share, communicate and collaborate with one another (Randolph & Krause, 2002). The power of learning from and through peers simply cannot be overstated.

Course Development and Overview

Field education in social work must be a robust experience. In fact, it is the signature pedagogy of a student's academic experience (CSWE, 2008). In one fully online MSW program based in the Northeastern U.S., each student is enrolled in an asynchronous integrated field seminar course while completing 32 weeks of field placement. Integrated seminars in the online environment are structured in the same manner as in the traditional classroom setting. The seminar provides students with an opportunity to discuss and reflect on professional social work issues from their practicum experience regarding assessment, specific interventions with client systems and the application of practice theories. Students use the seminar to monitor their own learning experiences and their progress towards attaining their professional goals with respect to membership in groups and communities distinguished by class, ethnicity, gender, sexual orientation, age, ability and culture while honoring each person's individuality.

The traditional F2F seminar classes are comprised of 10-12 students sitting in a circle, led by an instructor. The instructor opens the class by asking students to do a check-in and then proceeds to invite students to share and discuss their prior week's field experiences with one another. In the online integrated field seminars, the course is also comprised of 10-12 students. Each student must upload a video describing her/his experiences from the previous week. Videos are five minutes in length and focus on receiving feedback or suggestions with how to proceed regarding a particular situation. Students are instructed to post a question to their classmates about either an ethical dilemma or a specific scenario from their placement. In turn, each student must respond to each video/question, thus ensuring that all students both share and respond.

Experiences with the course: Challenges and benefits

One challenge in the traditional field seminar classroom is inadequate class time; there never seems to be enough time for all students to share their experiences. Class time is quickly absorbed by the more vocal, assertive students, leaving the quieter students to go unheard for the week. One benefit of an online integrated seminar is that this cannot happen. Students cannot hide in the online classroom environment. All students are expected to post and respond to weekly videos. This lends itself to much more robust conversations. Also, online students have the benefit of interacting with others from outside their geographic areas, including students from all over the U.S. and around the world. Our students represent 47 states, 5 countries (non-military), 3 US territories, and 3 Military 'states'. We have 17 students in the Armed Forces, in Africa, Canada, Europe, Middle East, the Americas, and the Pacific. Students in online integrated seminars therefore learn about social work in their own back yards while simultaneously learning how it is practiced worldwide. This creates a very rich experience in terms of culture, norms, social mores and ethical dilemmas. Obviously, the cross-cultural exchange is of great benefit to students as it demonstrates the necessary flexibility and open mindedness students must have in order to meet the needs of clients.

Another benefit of the online group experience, particularly in field work, is that students must develop essential communication skills such as clarity, assertion and brevity — all of which are transferrable to social work practice. These skills are honed in the online seminar course by limiting the amount of video time students have to present their cases. Students are given five minutes to update their classmates about their practicum including presenting clinical questions. This is not unlike an outpatient setting whereby clinicians have only a brief amount of time to present salient clinical points so to develop appropriate treatment recommendations.

The profession of social work is built upon the premise that the worker is able to develop positive rapport with clients. The skills acquired by participating in a group-based field seminar are essential to this work. The instructor and student have many ways to ensure that the group work is effective. The use of social media and other technological modalities (Facebook, Twitter, and Skype, for example) allows for instant communication. Skype and other video formats enable students to virtually be in the same room. Skype is the video format utilized most often in order to achieve this goal. Instant chat and other real-time communications can simulate a function of group work in the online classroom. Students are incredibly creative when it comes to connecting with one another in online formats. Many online learners embrace technology because they want to be connected to their classmates and ultimately to their social work program.

There are of course some challenges in conducting field work seminars in an online environment, just as there are in F2F seminars. For example, in both formats, some students may be anxious about the equity and fairness of workload in online group situations. However, in online courses, many platforms that are used (Blackboard, Moodle, etc.) have tools built within their frameworks to provide the instructor with an objective way to measure individual participation and overall group involvement. Thus, the use of online methodology actually offers an advantage over F2F education.

Lessons learned

There are significant benefits in online field seminars. Students must stretch beyond their comfort zones, increase their assertiveness, become clear and concise in their conversations, rely upon others, and constantly be involved in the group process. These are critical components of social work education and of field education in particular.

Conclusion

As discussed, online social work education has grown exponentially in the past decade, posing both challenges and opportunities for instructors. The relationship between the use of such group work principles as mutuality, cohesion, and effective learning has now been well documented. The three case studies presented here - the asynchronous online BSW group work course, the combined synchronous/asynchronous online MSW course, and the online field seminar - suggest a number of important recommendations. Group work principles such as clarity of group purpose, attention to group norms and stages of development, and emphasis on the development of mutual aid are all important to the success of online learning. Where possible, opportunities for direct, synchronistic contact (either actual or virtual) should be made available for students in fully online courses. The various communication mechanisms discussed in this article require labor intensive involvement on the part of students and instructors, but potentially yield worthwhile results. For example, creative ways of sharing field experiences, such as videotaping and responding to classmates' videotapes, require considerably more participation from students than in F2F instructional formats, thus providing more reticent students with opportunities to increase their assertiveness and involvement in group process. Creative uses of technology can overcome the challenges of asynchronistic communication by providing opportunities for interaction in 'real time' so that students can communicate with each other, face to face. However, the potential for positive group dynamics yielding a high level of learning in the online environment cannot be realized without skilled facilitation on the part of instructors. Course instructors with group work knowledge and skills are particularly well suited to harness group dynamics and apply group work principles to their online teaching. We can utilize our group work expertise and creativity to enhance online course design, development and delivery, providing a leadership role in online social work education.

References

Allen, I. E. and Seaman, J. (2013), *Changing Course: Ten Years of Tracking Online Education in the United States,* Babson Survey Research Group, and Quahog Research Group. Retrieved October 20, 2013, from http://www.onlinelearningsurvey.com/reports/changingcourse.pdf

Coe Regan, J.R. & Youn, E. (2008). Past, present and future trends in teaching clinical skills through web-based learning environments. *Journal of Social Work Education, 44*(2), 95-115.

Conklin, J.J. & Osterndorf, W. (1997). Distance education and social group work: The promise of the year 2000, in A. Alissi, & C.G. Corto Mergins (Eds.), *Voices from the field. Group work responds.* New York: Haworth Press.

Council on Social Work Education (2008). Educational policy and accreditation standards. Retrieved July 11, 2011, from http://www.cswe.org/File.aspx?id=41861

Council on Social Work Education (CSWE), *Guidelines for using distance education in social work programs,* downloaded October 6, 2006 from the website of the Council on Social Work Education, www.cswe.org.

Daley, B. J. (2001). Learning and professional practice: A study of four professions. *Adult Education Quarterly, 52(1),* 39-54.

Daydov, T., Emery, D., Lahanas, S., & Potemski, B. (2010). E-Learning Glossary. Retrieved from http://www.astd.org/LC/glossary.htm

Faul, A., Frey, A. & Barber, R. (2004). The effects of web-assisted instruction in a social work research methods course. *Social Work Education, 23(1),* 105-118.

Fisher, K., Phelps, R. & Ellis, A. (2000). Group processes online: Teaching collaboration through collaborative processes. *Educational Technology & Society 3*(3), 484-495.

Frey, A., Yankelov, P. & Faul, A. (2003). Student perceptions of web-assisted teaching strategies. *Journal of Social Work Education, 39*(3), 443-457.

Garavaglia, P. (1993). How to ensure transfer of training. *Training and Development, 47,* 63-68.

Kirkpatrick, D. L. (1998). *Evaluating training programs: The four levels.* San Francisco, CA: Berrett-Koehler Publications.

Knowles. S. (1984). The Adult Learner: A Neglected Species (3rd ed).

Houston, TX .Gulf.Kurland, R. & Salmon, R. (1998). *Teaching a methods course in social work with groups.* Alexandria, VA: Council on Social Work Education.

Levine, J. (2013). Teaching groupwork at a distance using an asynchronous on-line role-play. *Groupwork, 23*(1), 56-72. DOI: 10.1921/1601230104.

Madoc-Jones, I. & Parrott, L. (2005). Virtual social work education: Theory and experience. *Social work education, 24*(7), 755-768.

Madoc-Jones, I. & Parrott, L. (2005). Virtual social work education: Theory and experience. *Social Work Education, 24*(7), 755-768.

Maidment, J. (2005). Teaching social work online: Dilemmas and debates, *Social Work Education: The International Journal,* 24(2), 185-195.

Moore, B. (2005). Faculty perceptions of web-based instruction in social work education. In MacFadden, R.J., Moore, B. Herie, M. & Schoech, D., *Web-based education in human services: Models, methods and best practices.* New York: Haworth Press.

Mott, V. (2000). The development of professional expertise in the workplace. *New Directions for Adult and Continuing Education, 86,* 23-31.

Muskat, B. & Mesbur: E.S. (2011). Variations in teaching social work with groups in the age of technology. *Groupwork, 21*(1), 6-27.

Oulette, P.M. & Chang, V. (2004). The acquisition of social work interviewing skills in a web-based classroom instructional environment: Preliminary findings. *Advances in social work, 5*(1), 91-104.

Palloff, R. M., & Pratt, K. (2007). *Building online learning communities: Effective strategies for the virtual classroom.* San Francisco: Jossey-Bass

Parr, J. & Ward, L. (2006). Building on foundations: creating an online community. *Journal of Technology and Teacher Education*, 14, (4), 775-794.

Petracchi, H.E. (2000). Distance education: What do our students tell us? *Research on Social Work Practice, 10*(3), 362-376.

Randolph, K. A., & Krause, D. J. (2002). Mutual aid in the classroom: An instructional technology application. Journal of Social Work Education, 38, 259–271.

Regehr, C. (2013). Trends in higher education in Canada and implications for social work education. *Social Work Education*, 32(6), 700-714.

Schwartz, W. (1971). On the uses of groups in social work practice. In W. Schwartz, & S. Zalba (Eds.), *The practice of group work* (pp. 3 -24). New York: Columbia University Press.

Simon, S.R., & Stauber, K. W. (2009). Group Work Education—Use of Technology in Teaching. In A. Gitterman, and R. Salmon (Eds), *Encyclopedia of social work with groups* (pp.128 -130). New York: Routledge.

Simon, S. R., & Stauber, K. W. (2011). Technology and group work: A mandate and an opportunity. *Groupwork: An Interdisciplinary Journal for Working with Groups.21*(3), 71-85.

Siebert, D.C., Siebert, C. F. & Spaulding-Givens, J. (2006). Teaching Clinical Social Work Skills Primarily Online: An Evaluation. *Journal of Social Work Education*, 42 (2), 325-36.

Suler, J. (2004).The On-line Disinhibition Effect. *The Psychology of Cyberspace*. Downloaded December 24, 2009 from http://www-usr.rider.edu/~suler/psycyber/disinhibit.html

Steinberg, D.M. (2014). The Mutual-Aid Approach to Working with Groups: Helping People Help One Another, Third Edition, Binghamton, NY: Haworth Press.

Tandy, C. & Meacham, M. (2009). Removing the barriers for students with disabilities: Accessible on-line and web-enhanced courses. *Journal of Teaching in Social Work, 29,*313-328. DOI: 10.1080/088412309022118

Wilke, D.J. Randolph, K. A. & Vinton, L (2009): Enhancing Web-based Courses through a Mutual Aid Framework, *Journal of Teaching in Social Work*, 29(1), 18-31.

Attachment and Recovery: Combining 12-Step Programs and Group Psychotherapy to Treat Addiction

Santiago Delboy

Introduction

Group psychotherapy and 12-step recovery programs are the most common interventions used for addiction treatment. While their structure and process are different, both of them provide opportunities for participants to develop interpersonal relationships, which play a critical role in recovery. Attachment theory provides a useful framework to understand the relational challenges present as either a cause or a consequence of addiction, and how group interventions can help address them. This chapter conceptualizes addiction as an attachment disorder. With this framework in mind, 12-step programs and group psychotherapy are described in terms of their ability to repair attachment injuries and modify intrapsychic processes and mental representations underlying interpersonal patterns. Finally, the similarities and differences of both group modalities are discussed, highlighting the ways in which, when used concurrently, they serve complementary functions that enhance the client's capacity to develop healthy attachments.

Background

Group therapy and 12-step programs (programs of recovery based on the principles of Alcoholics Anonymous) are the most common approaches for substance abuse treatment (Panas, Caspi, Fournier & McCarty, 2003). While these interventions have different structures and processes, both emphasize the importance of developing interpersonal relationships as a cornerstone the recovery process. Attachment theory provides a useful framework for conceptualizing the interpersonal challenges underlying addiction and the reparative processes that take place during recovery. Understanding addiction as an attachment disorder (Flores, 2001, 2004) helps articulate the similarities, differences and complementarity of both treatment approaches.

The disease model of addiction (Jellinek, 1960; McLellan, Lewis, O'Brien & Kleber, 2000) suggests addiction is not a symptom but a primary condition that can be treated. Not without criticism, this view has been widely accepted in the social work community, the medical community, and among policy makers and the general public (Frans, 1994; Flores, 2004). The recognition of addiction as a disease encouraged the understanding of its potential causes, development and treatment.

Substance or process dependence alone is not a sufficient condition for addiction development (Köpetz, Lejuez, Wiers & Kruglanski, 2013), which makes addiction a biopsychosocial condition. In addition, while the biological and social processes involved can be different depending on the specific "drug of choice" (e.g., alcohol, drugs, gambling, sex), there is a "psychological sameness" (Johnson, 1993, p.26) across addictions. At a fundamental level, this commonality rests on understanding addiction as a "solution" to underlying psychological issues and a way to avoid being overwhelmed by anxiety, a view that has been recognized for over 80 years (Johnson, 1993). The inability of addicted individuals to cope with anxiety and stress underlies their dependence process. Moreover, individuals who rely on their "drug of choice" to accomplish affect-regulation goals (e.g., anxiety reduction, mood elevation), "are more prone to become addicts than are individuals who have at their disposal alternative ways of pursuing these goals" (Köpetz, Lejuez, Wiers & Kruglanski, 2013, p.10).

Addiction as an Attachment Disorder

Addiction can be defined as a disorder of self-regulation (Köpetz, Lejuez, Wiers & Kruglanski, 2013; Sayette & Griffin, 2007) and specifically affect-regulation (Kohut, 1977, cited by Flores, 2001). Recent neurobiology research provides evidence that neurophysiological development and functioning are influenced by the availability and experience of secure attachments (Flores, 2010). Thus, interpersonal relationships define our capacity for neurophysiological regulation. Attachment theory provides a privileged perspective to understand this process. For instance, Thorberg and Lyvers (2010) offer evidence that insecure attachment predicts poor affect regulation among people with substance abuse disorders, affecting interpersonal relationships. On the other hand, lack of available and supportive attachment figures undermines the development of a sense of security, which impairs affect regulation by relying on avoidance and anxiety strategies (Mikulincer & Shaver, 2007). Addicted individuals use their "drug of choice" as a compensatory mechanism for self-regulation; however, as the addiction progresses, "the results serve to deepen the dysregulation within the attachment system" (Padykula & Colkin, 2010, p. 352).

The connections between self-regulation and attachment support the definition of addiction as an attachment disorder (Flores, 2001, 2004), both in terms of its etiology and its consequences. The addicts' "drug of choice" becomes at the same time a substitute for and an obstacle to developing interpersonal relationships (Flores, 2006a). Addictions have been understood as a way to solve attachment issues from diverse theoretical standpoints. For example, a traditional psychoanalytic approach (Johnson, 1993) might view addiction as the "union with an ideal object/ideal mother" (p.30) based on an impaired "superego's ability to regulate the aggression which is needed to separate from the mother" (p.32).

While not all clinicians agree that addiction is always rooted in severe attachment issues, it is recognized that impaired attachment "paves the way" for addiction development. Lack of early secure attachment, physical proximity and containment impacts the individual's brain development by limiting the capacity to release oxytocin (Strauss, 2013, personal communication). Later in life these people cannot develop secure interpersonal experiences, which makes them more likely to become attached to addictive substances or processes, over which they believe they have more control. At the same time, they avoid attaching to people, since "human relationships are messier, there are disagreements and ups and downs" (Strauss, 2013, personal communication). Again, addiction operates as a "solution" to the insecurely attached individual's inability to cope with the exigencies of interpersonal relationships.

The capacity to form secure attachments starts to develop in early childhood, based on the child's relationship with a primary caregiver, which shapes internal working models (IWM). IWMs comprise mental representations of self, others and the nature of our relationships (Berzoff, Melano Flanagan & Hertz, 2011). Attachment needs have a biological origin, which shifts toward a psychosocial need during adolescence for individuals who experienced "sound attachment relationships, internal working models, and a helpful system for meaning and values" (Höfler & Kooyman, 1996, p. 513). Individuals who do not experience secure attachment in their early years become more vulnerable to developing addictive behaviors as they transition into adulthood, as the drug of choice "seems to offer a solution to those adolescents who feel unlovable, who might have felt like this for a long time, who have sometimes suffered a history of early trauma and neglect and, consequently developed a negative self-concept" (Höfler & Kooyman, 1996, p. 516).

Early trauma, rejection or neglect is often found in the histories of addicted people (Höfler & Kooyman, 1996), lacking physical and emotional closeness during childhood. Sachs (2009) notes that many individuals struggling with alcoholism have had a hard time making a healthy separation from parental figures, leaving individuals overly attached to their parents or emotionally distant from them. Many addicts' upbringing fluctuates between emotionally unavailable or enmeshed parenting, resulting in individuals who become detached, isolated or overly self-sufficient. Addicts fluctuate between emotional restraint, driven by feelings of shame and isolation, and indulgence when acting out on their addictive behavior, highlighting the challenge of affect-regulation. This insecure attachment includes holding negative self-perceptions that prevent people from developing intimate relationships, making them more vulnerable to use addictive behaviors to meet their attachment needs. In fact, Bowlby and Ainsworth - founders of attachment theory - describe insecure attachment as a set of "defensive strategies designed to maintain contact with abusive, rejecting, unavailable, or inconsistent caregivers" (Flores, 2010, p.549).

Adult relationships incorporate elements of early attachment, such as secure base-effect, separation protest and inaccessibility of conscious control (Höfler & Kooyman, 1996). As an addicted person continues to rely on addictive substances or behaviors to compensate for interpersonal relationships, his or her ability to develop healthy relationships is further undermined. Relational issues (e.g., coping with interpersonal conflict, developing intimate relationships) are present in the majority of individuals with addiction issues (Strauss, 2013, personal communication).Whether relational issues are the cause or consequence of addiction, "addicts and alcoholics are best treated by helping them develop a capacity for healthy interpersonal relationships" (Flores, 2006a, p.6). Laudet, Morgen & White (2006) highlight multiple purposes of developing relationships in recovery: addicts can acquire additional coping strategies from peers, and supportive networks will compensate the letting go of friends that were associated to the addiction (e.g., drinking buddies). The authors found positive impact of developing a recovery support network on recovery outcomes.

In addition to the value of attachment processes to understand interpersonal issues in addiction, similar processes take place between addicted individuals and their drug of choice. For example, alcohol or drugs may provide, at least initially, a "secure base" that compensates for feelings of insecurity and negative self-concept (Höfler & Kooyman, 1996). Thus, addicted individuals must first detach from addictive substances, processes and relationships (Flores, 2006a; Laudet, Morgen & White, 2006) in order to develop the capacity to build healthy attachments (e.g., therapeutic alliance, recovery support network) and maintain those attachments in the long run, despite conflict or tension (Flores, 2006a).

Addictive behaviors can be considered misguided attempts at self-repair to compensate for missing or damaging relationships. In order to give up dependence on these behaviors, people need to substitute them with healthy and responsive relationships (Flores, 2007). From an attachment perspective, development is not a transition from dependence to independence, but rather from "immature dependence to mature interdependence" (Flores, 2006a, p.15). In the context of addiction, development toward recovery involves experiencing a sense of community and belonging, and the capacity to develop healthy attachments, instead of relying solely on individual self-regulation. While personal responsibility is required, addiction is a disease of isolation (Roth, 2004) and "mature interdependence" can address relational issues and soften emotional insularity (Sachs, 2009).

Twelve Step Programs and Attachment Repair

Founded in 1935, Alcoholic Anonymous (AA) became the largest self-help group aimed at helping alcoholics achieve sobriety and addiction recovery. Currently, AA includes approximately two million members, who gather in 114,000 groups in 170 countries (Alcoholic Anonymous General Service Office, N.D.). In addition, a wide range of support groups were developed based on the principles set forth by AA, including programs for substance addictions (e.g., Narcotics Anonymous, Nicotine Anonymous), process addictions (e.g., Overeaters Anonymous, Sex Addicts Anonymous, Gamblers Anonymous), and relationship with addicted individuals (e.g., Al-Anon/Alateen for friends and relatives of alcoholics, S-Anon/COSA for people affected by someone else's sexual behavior). While there are some differences between programs (e.g., sobriety is defined differently for substance and process addictions), all of them are based on AA's 12-steps of recovery (AA, 2001) and will be collectively referred to in this paper as twelve-step programs (12SP).

12SP involve multiple components directly addressing relational elements, consistent with the view of addiction as an attachment disorder. Specifically, interpersonal relationships are addressed by three key "tools" of the recovery program: attending meetings, reaching out to other members to receive or provide support, and working the steps with a recovery sponsor. All these relationships are developed in a context of communion and acceptance. Meetings allow members to hear others' stories and experience, helping members break the feeling of isolation and shame (Flores, 2007). According to the 12SP "traditions", the only requirement to become a member is a desire to stop the addictive behavior (AA, 2001). Continuous attendance of meetings is one of the basic components of the program (most programs recommend newcomers attend at least six meetings). The emphasis on story-telling and sharing personal experiences provides a sense of communion and service (Lederman & Menegatos, 2011), which serves as a meaningful way to connect with others and develop attachments. At the same time, sharing personal experiences with a group deepens their personal meaning and implications for the individual (Sachs, 2009), as it becomes a bridge to connect with others.

This sustained interaction with others helps addicted individuals modify their dysfunctional interpersonal patterns, thanks to the relationships established with specific members and with a recovery sponsor (Flores, 2007). Sponsorship gives members the opportunity to receive personal ongoing support from a more experienced member. This relationship can be a reparative emotional experience as the new member is encouraged to develop a trusting, vulnerable and honest relationship in a non-judgmental setting. Much of the step work itself in 12SP has a reparation quality (Sachs, 2009). The steps allow addicted individuals to change beliefs about self-worth, about their ability to develop intimate interpersonal relationships, and about the role of the addictive processes (Carnes, 2001).

A study conducted by Majer, Droege and Jason (2012) provides evidence suggesting that deeper involvement in 12SP increases the addict's utilization of social support as a coping mechanism, while reducing the reliance on emotion-focused coping strategies (e.g., managing one's emotional distress). This supports the notion that 12SP helps repair its members' ability to develop healthier relationships, within and outside the program (Ronel & Libman, 2003). In a survey conducted by Narcotics Anonymous (NA) among its members, 90% declared that "family relationships" and "social connection" were the two areas most favorably impacted by the program (NA, 2012). In addition to addressing interpersonal relationships, 12SP offer other reparative dimensions. For instance, 12SP increase self-intimacy, by setting forth "rigorous honesty" and integrity as core values of recovery, which can lead to developing a renewed sense of purpose. 12SP also involve developing a relationship with a "higher power" as a critical component of the recovery program, attempting to establish an attachment addicts can rely on for recovery, which can lead to spiritual healing.

Le, Ingvarson and Page (1995) criticize 12SP suggesting that its principles of powerlessness and surrender (AA, 2001) are inconsistent with basic tenets of the counseling profession, which emphasize personal empowerment and accountability. This criticism does not seem to take into account the role of 12SP role in self- regulation and attachment repair. By asking its members to accept their powerlessness and surrender any attempts of control their addiction, 12SP attempts to change their "self-centered" mindset and develop relationships and attachments in their path to recovery. For 12SP, recovering addicts are powerless over the disease but they are not helpless in using the "tools of recovery" and developing relationships is a way to strengthen their recovery.

In contrast to the criticism offered by Le, Ingvarson and Page (1995), research by Laudet (2003) suggests that clients' and clinicians' attitudes toward 12SP are positive. Obstacles to participation and effectiveness relate to "motivation and readiness for change and on perceived need for help, rather than on aspects of 12SP often cited as points of resistance (e.g., religious aspect and emphasis on powerlessness)" (p. 2018).

Group Therapy and Attachment Repair

Group therapy is recognized as a critical component of treating substance addictions such as alcoholism (Flores, 2007) and process addictions such as sex addiction (Hook, Hook & Hines, 2008). Experimental studies suggest the positive impact of group therapy on recovery outcomes and relapse prevention (Ahmed, Abolmagd, Rakhawy, Erfan & Mamdouh, 2010). In addition, Panas, Caspi, Fournier and McCarty (2003) provide evidence suggesting that clients "engaged during their treatment mostly in group rather than individual counseling achieved better rates" (p. 276) on measures of treatment completion and goal achievement upon discharge from substance abuse outpatient programs.

Connors, Donovan & DiClemente (2001) describe the benefits of group therapy in addiction treatment, which include: (a) provision of a safe environment to repair interpersonal deficits, (b) peer feedback and modeling that can be more powerful than counselor input, (c) experiences with group members which serve as "practice" for "real life" interactions (outside of the therapeutic setting), (d) promotion of a sense of belonging that helps reduce feelings of isolation and low self-worth, (e) a meaningful support system (as cited in Velasquez, Stephens & Ingersoll, 2006). Another important outcome of group psychotherapy is the ability to develop intimate relationships with others (Hook, Hook & Hines, 2008). A distinct group culture emerges, usually different from the culture of other groups such as family and colleagues, in which group members develop new ways of relating to others and new coping skills (Line & Cooper, 2002).

Yalom's therapeutic factors (Yalom & Leszcz, 2005) provide a more structured starting point to understand how group therapy helps in addiction recovery (Nerenberg, 2000). Some of these factors constitute reparative attachment processes, allowing clients to develop basic relationship and intimacy skills (e.g., trust through "universality" factor, vulnerability through "catharsis" factor), connect with others ("altruism" factor), and experiment with new relational patterns ("corrective recapitulation", "socializing skills" and "interpersonal learning" factors). For example, people in recovery starting group therapy would develop trust in other members by learning that they share common experiences. This might enhance their feelings of connection with the rest of the group, which would in turn allow them to modify the way they relate to other group members, take in feedback from them, and use this learning to modify relational patterns outside of the group.

Group cohesiveness allows clients to experience the group as an object of attachment that can substitute the existing attachment to their "drug of choice". Thus, group therapy helps people in recovery replace unhealthy attachments and relationships for healthier ones. The importance of cohesiveness as a source of belonging and driver of relational shift has been observed across cultures and addictions (Nerenberg, 2000; Ahmed, Abolmagd, Rakhawy, Erfan & Mamdouh, 2010). While the impact of specific aspects of the disease (e.g., neurochemical impact, level of social stigma) might be different depending on the specific type of addiction, the underlying issues related to attachment and the opportunities the group provides operate in similar ways.

As Yalom points out in an interview with Flores (2006b), the power of group therapy comes from "the actual interaction with members and interpersonal changes that occur" (p.8). He adds that the object of group therapy with addicted populations is to teach clients how to establish enduring, nurturing and loving relationships, by understanding the obstructions to form these kinds of relationships (Flores, 2006b). The group can be defined as a "lab for creating change" (Korshak, 2013, personal communication). It is the group leader's task to enable and encourage interactions among clients, fostering the development of attachment with each other (Flores, 2007).

Additionally, there is evidence that short-term group psychotherapy can increase secure attachment and decrease certain types of insecure attachment, as well as improve interpersonal relationships (Kinley & Reyno, 2013). Washton (1992) summarizes some of the reasons why group therapy works: it provides a setting to find identification and acceptance, positive role modeling, confrontation and positive peer pressure, affiliation and support to communicate feelings, structure and boundary setting, and installation of hope in own recovery (as cited in Flores, 2007). Group therapy can "meet the struggling individual where it suffers the most: in the nonverbal need of a reliable holding relationship" (Höfler & Kooyman, 1996, p.517).

12-steps and Group Psychotherapy: Similarities and Complementarity

12SP and group therapy have different processes and rules. The former is highly structured, following the same script each week, and interpersonal interaction during meetings is mostly discouraged. The goal is to create a predictable, comfortable and safe environment for participants. Some members have an assigned role (e.g., chairperson) but these roles rotate periodically to avoid conflicts of interest or power struggles. Participants in 12SP meetings are not required to speak. Those who do are encouraged to talk about their experience, strength and hope in recovery, focusing on how they are working the steps, using the tools of the program, developing a spiritual practice, or dealing with challenges to their sobriety. In contrast, group therapy is less structured and encourages interaction during the sessions. The potential conflict or discomfort that follows these interactions is seen as part of the therapeutic work: the feelings that are evoked and the group processes that trigger them are as important as the content discussed by group members. Therapy groups are less likely to have a defined agenda or protocol, and they usually do not have formally assigned roles. Even if they are focused on recovery from addiction, they tend to be more open to discuss elements seemingly unrelated to their members' recovery program, including group dynamics in the here-and-now. While both approaches are complementary and synergistic, the nature of their relationship is complex (Brown & Yalom, 1977; Yalom & Leszcz, 2005).

From an attachment theory perspective, detaching from addictive behaviors requires the development of alternative coping strategies, particularly early in the recovery process. The strategies provided by both 12SP and group psychotherapy stem from the "regulating power of a strong attachment relationship" (Flores, 2006a, p.10). Early attachment failures can be processed and revisited in a group setting, as groups can "provide the context for supporting authentic connection with one's own affect and encourage resonance with the affect of others" (McCluskey, 2002 as cited in Mikulincer & Shaver, 2007, p.238). Establishing a renewed capacity to develop and nurture relationships and interpersonal attachments are fundamental goals of both 12SP and group therapy. The group can then become a source of safety and a secure base for exploration of the unknown territory of recovery. Developing a support network comprised of recovery-oriented members improves the likelihood of long term recovery and self-efficacy (Majer, Jason, Ferrari, Venable & Olson, 2002).

In group therapy, "success" depends on how new attachments created in group challenge IWMs developed during early traumatic attachment experiences (Flores, 2010), which can also be accomplished in 12SP. This change in IWMs entails a shift in the individual's mental representation of self, of others, and of interpersonal relationships. Furthermore, 12SP address directly the IWM related to the addictive attachment (i.e., attachment to the drug of choice or to an addictive behavior). The first step of 12SP ("We admitted were powerless, that our lives had become unmanageable", AA, 2001) calls for a redefinition of the relationship between the individual and the addiction.

Yalom's curative factors (Yalom & Leszcz, 2005) apply to both group therapy and 12SP, even though they emphasize different elements given their different principles and process. For example, the factor of universality plays a critical role in 12SP as newcomers meet, probably for the first time, others who share their own struggle. This is not necessarily the case in group psychotherapy. In contrast, factors such as corrective recapitulation are less present in 12SP given the lack of interaction during the meetings, but are an intrinsic part of psychotherapy groups. Flores (2007) summarizes the differences between the two interventions: "AA groups place more emphasis on guidance, identification, and instillation of hope, while professional group therapy relies more on interpersonal learning, catharsis, insight, and existential awareness" (p.688).

Used in combination, the two interventions emphasize different but complementary aspects critical for addiction recovery. The synergy created when these modalities are used concurrently deepens the client's experience, as he receives support in settings with different structure and processes, but connected to the same goal of recovery.

It is important to note, however, that while 12SP are useful throughout the life-long recovery process, the most appropriate type of therapy group will depend on the stage of treatment. For example, the emphasis at the beginning of treatment ought to be on "abstinence, relapse prevention, and managing the cravings" (Flores, 2001, p.70), which would warrant groups with a heavier psychoeducational or CBT orientation. As clients become more stable and ready to explore underlying relational issues, they might be ready to transition to groups with a focus in interpersonal process. Interpersonal process groups, similarly to Yalom's interactional groups (Yalom & Leszcz, 2005), are defined by their emphasis on here-and-now feelings and thoughts expressed, or not, in the group. These elements "take precedence over the events in the past or current life of each member outside of the group" (Flores, 2007, p. 305).

12SP will be most helpful to keep sobriety, while group psychotherapy deepens the client's understanding of emotional and interpersonal issues (Flores, 2007). However, 12SP also address individual personality or relational issues. There is an important emphasis on identifying and dealing with "defects of character" through the program steps (AA, 2001), which include mindsets or behaviors that impact the addict's relationships with others. Both treatment approaches will meet with resistance when trying to remove these "defects of character". From a 12SP perspective, working on these issues defines the transition from sobriety to recovery. In a therapy setting, the group's task is to shift these traits from ego-syntonic to ego-dystonic (Sachs, 2009). 12SP provide a structure to work through these individual traits, whereas group therapy provides the opportunity for a more in-depth exploration.

Korshak (2013, personal communication) suggests that 12SP are superior to group therapy to attain sobriety, developing a sense of spirituality and meaning, and enhancing recovery by being of service to others. These constitute reparative experiences for people with attachment problems. In contrast, group therapy would be superior to address issues underlying addiction, regulating emotions, owning projections and letting go of defenses. 12SP have a well-defined structure and an underlying belief system, which facilitates cohesion and commitment, but members can self-select by choosing which meetings to attend. Self-selection allows individuals to avoid meetings where they feel challenged or uncomfortable, which might keep them from working through interpersonal difficulties. Clients in group therapy learn how to relate to the group, expressing and regulating emotions without the benefit of self-selection.

Developing a new sense of self-worth, accountability and healing relationships with others are critical components of recovery (Flores, 2007), but they are achieved in different ways. Group therapy should provide an environment where the tension and conflict that inevitably arise in interpersonal relationships can be safely explored, experienced and processed, without fear of abandonment or rejection (Flores, 2010). Clients can work through their barriers to establish intimate relationships in the "here-and-now" of the group, providing a safe environment to acknowledge their defense systems and try alternative reaction to anxiety, stress and interpersonal conflict. Some therapists might request members not to have contact outside of group, although they do not really have a way to keep this from happening. In contrast, 12SP emphasize unconditional mutual support rather than processing of interpersonal conflict. The barriers to establish intimate relationships are addressed as part of the program steps, by identifying situations that trigger these barriers, acknowledging associated thoughts, feelings and behaviors, and developing alternative ways to react. Individuals may find it easier to develop attachment in 12SP, since they can work the program at their own pace and avoid confrontation. Interactions outside of the meetings are sometimes encouraged, and 12SP might choose to participate in them or not. Korshak (2013, personal communication) calls 12SP a "basic course" and group psychotherapy, particularly interpersonal process groups, an "advanced course" in affect regulation and attachment repair.

Conclusion

Despite their procedural and structural differences, group therapy and 12SP serve a similar and complementary reparative function for attachment issues, whether they are the cause or consequence of addiction. When both group modalities operate differently, they are still complementary in two ways. First, both approaches may address similar attachment challenges in different ways. For example, interpersonal issues are processed through acceptance and self-reflection in 12SP, and through conflict and in-depth processing in group psychotherapy. Second, each approach addresses specific aspects of attachment that the other typically doesn't, hence providing a more rounded reparative experience when used together. For example, 12SP's focus on a "higher power" helps its members add a spiritual focus to their attachment repair experience not usually emphasized in group psychotherapy. In contrast, the role of the therapist in group psychotherapy provides an opportunity to work through relationship issues with authority and, through transference processes, attachment issues with paternal figures. While transference may occur in 12SP as well (e.g., in the relationship with the sponsor), the relationships in that program are not aimed at an in-depth reflection of the underlying emotional and relational processes. The complementarity between these two modalities creates a synergetic process that deepens the experience of recovery for clients.

Understanding addiction as an attachment disorder is not an attempt to reduce the complex drivers of addiction to interpersonal issues, but instead provides a useful framework to understand the impact of group psychotherapy and 12SP on recovery from addiction. The former can support the objectives of the latter by identifying defenses preventing compliance with abstinence, and adhering to the principles and structure of the steps (Flores, 2007). It is also important for therapists to be familiar with 12SP principles, dynamics and history, as that will allow them to speak the same language of their clients, increase empathy with clients' recovery experience and increase the therapist's credibility (Flores, 2007).

While not all people with addictions have significant attachment issues or will want or need to address them in depth, 12SP and group therapy provide significant benefits during treatment. The more impaired the attachment ability is, the more important it is to combine both treatments. For clients who are ready and willing to address relational challenges, using both interventions concurrently would provide a more holistic path to recovery.

Acknowledgements

The author wishes to thank Shelley Korshak, M.D., C.G.P. and Barney Strauss, L.C.S.W., C.G.P. for their contribution in the early stages of this paper

References

Ahmed, S. Abolmagd, S., Rakhawy, M., Erfan S. & Mamdouh, R. (2010). Therapeutic factors in group psychotherapy: a study of Egyptian drug addicts. *Journal of Groups in Addiction & Recovery*, 5(3-4), 194-213. doi: 10.1080/1556035X.2010.523345

Alcoholic Anonymous (4th ed.). (2001). New York, NY: Alcoholics Anonymous World Services.

Alcoholic Anonymous General Service Office (N.D.). A.A. at a glance. Retrieved from http://www.aa.org/pdf/products/f-1_AAataGlance.pdf

Berzoff, J., Melano Flanagan, L. & Hertz, P. (2011). *Inside out and outside in: Psychodynamic clinical theory and psychopathology in contemporary multicultural contexts* (3rd Ed). Lanham, MD: Rowman & Littlefield Publishers, Inc.

Brown, S. & Yalom, I.D. (1977). Interactional group therapy with alcoholics. *Journal of Studies on Alcohol*, 38(3), 425-456

Carnes, P.J. (2001). *Out of the shadows: Understanding sexual addiction* (3rd Ed). Center City, MN: Hazelden.

Flores, P.J. (2001). Addiction as an attachment disorder: implications for group therapy. *International Journal of Group Psychotherapy*, 51(1), 63-81. doi: 10.1521/ijgp.51.1.63.49730

Flores, P.J. (2004). *Addiction as an attachment disorder.* Lanham, MD: Jason Aronson.

Flores, P.J. (2006a). Conflict and repair in addiction treatment: an attachment disorder perspective. *Journal of Groups in Addiction & Recovery*, 1(1), 5-26. doi: 10.1300/J384v01n01_02

Flores, P.J. (2006b). Interview of Dr. Irvin D. Yalom, MD. *Journal of Groups in Addiction & Recovery*, 1(3-4), 5-16. doi: 10.1300/J384v01n03_02

Flores, P.J. (2007). *Group psychotherapy with addicted populations: An integration of twelve- step and psychodynamic theory* (3rd Ed). New York, NY: Routledge.

Flores, P.J. (2010). Group psychotherapy and neuro-plasticity: an attachment theory perspective. *International Journal of Group Psychotherapy, 60*(4), 547-570. doi:10.1521/ijgp.2010.60.4.546

Frans, D. (1994). Social work, social science and the disease concept: new directions for addiction treatment. *Journal of Sociology and Social Welfare, 21*(2), 71-89

Höfler, D.Z. & Kooyman, M. (1996). Attachment transition, addiction and therapeutic bonding –an integrative approach. *Journal of Substance Abuse Treatment, 13*(6), 511-519. doi:10.1016/S0740-5472(96)00156-0

Hook, J.N., Hook, J.P. & Hines, S. (2008). Reach out or act out: long-term group therapy for sexual addiction. *Sexual Addiction & Compulsivity, 15*(3), 217-232. doi: 10.1080/10720160802288829

Jellinek, E.M. (1960). *The disease concept of alcoholism.* New Haven, CT: Hillhouse Press.

Johnson, B. (1993). A developmental model of addictions, and its relationship to the twelve stepprogram of Alcoholic Anonymous. *Journal of Substance Abuse Treatment, 10*(1), 23-34. doi: 10.1016/0740-5472(93)90095-J

Kinley, J.L., & Reyno, S.M. (2013). Attachment style changes following intensive short-term group psychotherapy. *International Journal of Group Psychotherapy, 63*(1), 53-75. doi:10.1521/ijgp.2013.63.1.53

Köpetz, C.E., Lejuez, C.W., Wiers R.W. & Kruglanski, A.W. (2013). Motivation and self- regulation in addiction: a call for convergence. *Perspectives on Psychological Science, 8*(1), 3-24. doi: 10.1177/1745691612457575

Laudet, A.B. (2003). Attitudes and beliefs about 12-step groups among addiction treatment clients and clinicians: toward identifying obstacles to participation. *Substance Use & Misuse, 38*(14), 2017-2047. Retrieved from http://www.ncbi.nlm.nih.gov/pmc/articles/PMC1855195/

Laudet, A.B., Morgen, K. & White, W.L. (2006). The role of social supports, spirituality, religiousness, life meaning and affiliation with 12-step fellowships in quality of life satisfaction among individuals in recovery from Alcohol and Drug Problems. *Alcoholism Treatment Quarterly, 24*(1-2), 33-74. doi: 10.1300/J020v24n01_04

Le, C., Ingvarson, E.P. & Page, R.C. (1995). Alcoholics Anonymous and the counseling profession: philosophies in conflict. *Journal of Counseling & Development, 73*(6), 603-609. doi: 10.1002/j.1556-6676.1995.tb01803.x

Lederman, L.C. & Menegatos, L.M. (2011). Sustainable recovery: the self-transformative power of storytelling in Alcoholics Anonymous. *Journal of Groups in Addiction & Recovery, 6*(3), 206-277. doi: 10.1080/1556035X.2011.597195

Line, B.Y. & Cooper, A. (2002). Group psychotherapy: essential component for success with sexually acting out problems among men. *Sexual Addiction & Compulsivity, 9*(1), 15-32. doi: 10.1080/107201602317346610

McLellan, A.T., Lewis, D.C., O'Brien C.P. & Kleber, H.D. (2000). Drug dependence, a chronic medical illness: implications for treatment, insurance, and outcomes evaluation. *The Journal of the American Medical Association, 284*(13), 1689-1695. doi:10.1001/jama.284.13.1689

Mikulincer, M. & Shaver, P.R. (2007). Attachment, group-related processes, and psychotherapy.*International Journal of Group Psychotherapy, 57*(2), 233-245. doi: 10.1521/ijgp.2007.57.2.233

Majer, J.M., Droege, J.R. & Jason, L.A. (2012). Coping strategies in 12-step recovery: more evidence for categorical involvement. *Journal of Groups in Addiction & Recovery, 7*(1), 3-14. doi: 10.1080/1556035X.2012.632317

Majer, J.M., Jason, L.A., Ferrari, J.R., Venable L.B. & Olson, B.D. (2002). Social support and self-efficacy for abstinence: is peer identification an issue? *Journal of Substance* Abuse *Treatment, 23*(3), 109-215. doi: 10.1016/S0740-5472(02)00261-1

Narcotics Anonymous Worldwide Services (2012). Information about NA. Retrieved from http://www.na.org/admin/include/spaw2/uploads/pdf/PR/Information_about_NA.pdf

Nerenberg, A. (2000). The value of group psychotherapy for sexual addicts in a residential setting. *Sexual Addiction & Compulsivity, 7*(3), 197-209. doi: 10.1080/10720160008400218

Padykula, N.L. & Colkin, P. (2010). The self regulation model of attachment trauma and addiction. *Clinical Social Work Journal, 38*(4), 351-360. doi: 10.1007/s10615-009-0204-6

Panas, L., Caspi, Y., Fournier, E. & McCarty, D. (2003). Performance measures for outpatient substance abuse services: group versus individual counseling. *Journal of Substance Abuse Treatment, 25*(4), 271-278. doi: 10.1016/S0740-5472(03)00142-9

Ronel, N. & Libman, G. (2003). Eating disorders and recovery: lessons from overeaters anonymous. *Clinical Social Work Journal, 31*(2), 155-171. doi: 10.1023/A:1022962311073

Roth, J. (2004). *Group psychotherapy and recovery from addiction: Carrying the message.* Binghamton, NY: The Haworth Press.

Sachs, K.S. (2009). A psychological analysis of the 12-steps of Alcoholics Anonymous. *Alcoholism Treatment Quarterly, 27*(2), 199-212. doi: 10.1080/07347320902784825

Sayette, M.A. & Griffin, K.M. (2011). Self-regulatory failure and addiction. In K.D. Vohs & R.F. Baumeister (Eds.), *Handbook of self-regulation:*

Research, theory, and applications (2nd ed.) (pp. 505-521). New York, NY: The Guilford Press.

Thorberg, F.A. & Lyvers, M. (2010). Attachment in relation to affect regulation and interpersonal functioning among substance use disorder in patients. *Addiction Research and Theory, 18*(4), 464-478. doi: 10.3109/16066350903254783

Velasquez, M.M., Stephens, N.S. & Ingersoll, K. (2006). Motivational interviewing in groups.*Journal of Groups in Addiction & Recovery, 1*(1), 27-50. doi: 10.1300/J384v01n01_03

Yalom, I.D. & Leszcz, M. (2005). *The theory and practice of group psychotherapy* (5th ed.).New York, NY: Basic Books.

Challenges and Rewards of Facilitating Support Groups in an Under-Resourced County Jail

Kerry Dunn, Erin Daigle, Ariane Bowie, Kristen Cianelli, Erika Gilbert, Elisa Orme

Introduction

In Spring 2013, 10 second-year MSW students facilitated support groups on five housing units at a county jail. The idea for these groups came out of discussions about needs at the jail that students had with inmates in an elective class. In this chapter, students and their faculty mentor discuss the challenges and rewards of doing group work in this under-resourced setting.

Background

People living in US jails and prisons have higher rates than the average population of a variety of economic, social, health, and mental health challenges (Visher & Travis, 2012). The experience of being incarcerated itself can create or exacerbate psychological issues, strain family relationships, and reduce social capital (Mazza, 2008). The challenges inmates face are especially stark in county jails where needs are immediate, resources are scarce, and services are limited and short-term (Freudenberg, 2001). As a result, people are often released from jails with many unaddressed needs.

To begin identifying ways to address this resource disparity, social work students at the University of New England partnered with students from other health professions as well as inmates and staff at the nearby county jail. The goal of the University of New England-Cumberland County Jail (UNE-CCJ) Collaboration is to create an enduring and mutually beneficial relationship between the two institutions in order to mobilize university resources to improve the well being of incarcerated people. UNE has varied health profession programs and vast resources while CCJ has many health-related needs. The purpose of the CCJ-UNE Collaboration is to harness UNE and other community resources to benefit CCJ, in ways deemed helpful by CCJ inmates and staff.

The Collaboration grew out of an "Inside-Out" model class taught at CCJ in the summer of 2012. In the Inside-Out model, college students and inmates study issues of crime and justice together as peers, and several elements of the model are designed to create space for multiple experiences, viewpoints, and agendas (Pompa, 2005). The Collaboration is guided by a similar spirit of inclusion with and evolving mix of inmates, staff, faculty, and students working together in the Planning Group to design projects to benefit students and inmates. The support groups are one such project.

Group work has the power to improve the lives of incarcerated people by providing a forum for asking questions, sharing concerns, and identifying new paths of action (Dixon, 2000). However, the challenges of doing social justice group work in a correctional setting are numerous (Sarri & Shook, 2005). The jail setting is a dehumanizing environment, where people have little control over their lives. The daily routine is both highly rigid and punctuated by constant change; people are sent to court, randomly drug tested, transferred to other housing units, and sent to segregation. Many inmates stay at the jail for a very short period; the average length of stay is seven days. For those who are incarcerated longer, many are awaiting trial or sentencing, facing unknown futures. In the midst of these barriers to authentic relationships, social work students and inmates created productive forums for learning and growth. This paper describes the challenges and rewards, from the facilitators' perspective, of running support groups at the jail.

Goals

The mutual and collaborative foundation of the Collaboration Planning Group led to a shared and democratic process of creating goals for the support group project. It was important to develop and articulate a clear sense of purpose for the support groups (Kurland & Salmon, 2006), particularly since this was a new project within the jail. The Planning Group worked to set clear and mutually agreed upon goals (Gitterman, 2005) in order to provide coherent direction, answer any questions from jail staff, and establish a basis for evaluating the project.

There were three types of goals identified by the Planning Group: those of the facilitators, those of the support group members, and those shared by facilitators and members. The Planning Group recognized the development of group facilitation skills as an important goal for facilitators. The most important skill for the facilitators was to maintain flexibility within each group meeting. An ability to 'go with the group' was identified as vital by the inmates in the Planning Group.

For the group members, the central identified goal was to improve an individual's wellbeing at CCJ by making it easier to cope with being there. The remaining goals for the group members laid the groundwork for that to happen. These included learning to trust group members, experiencing a sense of community, and having a safe place to vent without fear of backlash from CCJ staff (a teacher from the jail was present for some of the groups but no correctional officers (COs)). Shared goals included recognizing the humanity of people, seeing each person as a unique individual, and providing and receiving psycho-education as requested/needed. These goals provided guidance for the development of the support group format (Gitterman, 2005).

Group Structure

The planning group decided on the following parameters for the groups: groups should run once a week for 90 minutes in 6-week sessions; each group will have 8-10 participants and be facilitated by 2 social work students; groups will be closed, meaning that new people cannot join after the first meeting; and groups will reopen after the first six weeks. Group members would be recruited by the jail's education staff, who would post sign up sheets on the housing units. In order to join the group, inmates would need to be on good disciplinary status and be expecting to be at the jail for 6 weeks. During the first meeting of the group, each facilitator would share an introduction that described their background and motivation for facilitating the group at the jail. Also, during the initial meeting, group rules would be discussed and established and later reviewed at subsequent meetings. One key task of the facilitators was to make sure everyone was aware of the group process.

The planning group decided that facilitators would start each group with an icebreaker activity. There were a variety of reasons for engaging the group in icebreakers, such as developing trust, lightening the mood, and introducing participants and facilitators in non-threatening ways (Doel, 2006). Icebreakers are especially important for facilitators coming into the jail from the outside as a means to break down the barriers of "us and them" and begin the process of developing relationships with the participants. Beyond these parameters, facilitators were allowed to tailor the structure of each group meeting to the needs and interests of the participants.

In terms of content, the Planning Group decided it would be best to approach these groups with an open structure where the group members would decide what would be covered in each group meeting. The Planning Group discussed many topics that people incarcerated at CCJ may find useful--such as transitions, parenting and family connections, substance abuse, and ways to avoid coming back to jail-- and we debated the merits of creating groups based on these identified topics. Most members of the Planning Group had participated in the Inside-Out model class, which had a set curriculum with pre-selected readings and assignments tailored to facilitate learning by all participants on the criminal justice system. The Planning Group members consciously decided that the support groups should be different from the class, with a specific focus on the needs and interests of the incarcerated participants as determined by the participants themselves. The Planning Group did not want facilitators to come into the support groups with their own assumptions about what the specific members in their group wanted or needed. They wanted to focus on what the group participants needed and what topics they wanted to explore.

Another reason why the Planning Group chose to keep a flexible format for the support groups was their awareness that each group would have different needs. For example, when creating the ground rules for the support group, one group might believe swearing is acceptable while another group may find it offensive. Planning Group members wanted the group to be a break from routine, an opportunity for a more "normal," less predictable social experience. "For the great bulk of prisoners, this [every day life] consists of a relentlessly unchanging, grimly gray routine" (Morris, 1998, p. 202). The Planning Group did not want to give group members more guidelines and directions to follow; they follow rules and are told what to do all day, every day. By following an open format, the facilitators would be provided an opportunity for participants to collectively create group norms and guidelines and choose the content/topic for each meeting. Additionally, through maintaining this structure, the support group members could change the meeting topic, if desired. For example, group members may want to process an incident that occurred earlier that day on the housing unit, which is unrelated to list of topics previously identified by the group.

To communicate the goals of the groups to potential participants, incarcerated members of the Planning Group worked with the education director at the jail to create recruitment flyers. They called the groups "Jail Sucks," inviting people to come and talk about whatever is on their mind. It was then a challenge for the facilitators on the first day to find a balance between following the parameters developed by the Planning Group while establishing an open, flexible forum.

The Group Process

In Spring 2013, 5 pairs of students ran groups on 5 different housing units, including a unit for women and for special needs men. Some of the groups worked with sentenced and some with un-sentenced inmates. CCJ is the federal detention center for Maine, and 2 of the 5 groups had a mix of state and federal inmates. All groups happened on the housing unit in a visible classroom. Groups range from 5-9 participants, which decreased over time for most groups due to people getting released, sentenced, or transferred. All groups were racially diverse, though not hugely so given Maine's primarily White demographic.

Facilitators were excited but nervous. They were not sure how the open structure would go and how inmates would receive them coming in to provide these groups. During the first support group meeting, the facilitators asked the inmates what topics they would like to cover during the life of the group and worked with the groups to identify a six-week schedule. The most common topics chosen across the 5 groups were parenting, reentry, available resources, and stress management. Many of the inmates expressed their fear of what would happen to them when they were released from jail. They were concerned about obtaining housing, finding a job, and caring for their families. Facilitators tailored group meetings to these concerns as they arose and created resource packets and educational tools as needed. Each of the five groups took on their own flavor based on the characteristics of facilitators and participants. For the last meeting, each set of facilitators chose closing exercises and rituals suited to their group's process.

Throughout the first six-week session, facilitators debriefed not only with their facilitation partner but also with a buddy from another facilitation team. Teams reached out to their faculty mentor as needed to process logistical challenges, negative interactions with jail staff, and challenging group dynamics but also powerful group-process moments and facilitation epiphanies. It became clear through the level of reflection in these debriefs that the goal of facilitation skill building was being met.

At the end of the first six-week session, the planning group developed a brief survey to assess whether the Planning Group's other goals were indeed met and to elicit more general feedback about the group experience. The surveys were administered by the director of the jail's education program, and the results were discussed in the Planning Group in order to help facilitators think about whether any changes should be made to the structure of the groups before starting the next six-week session. The feedback was generally positive, and the Planning Group decided to maintain the original structure for the second session. The most important lesson from the evaluation was the need for better communication among the facilitators, the jail's education staff responsible for keeping accurate lists of group members, the COs, and jail administrators. The Planning Group must continue to work on increasing support among COs and administrators for the support groups so the groups can more fully reach their goals of providing a humanizing, safe space.

Challenges of Conducting Groups within Jail Setting

Support groups at the Cumberland County Jail provided many challenges for student facilitators, including how to work within the correctional system (i.e., encountering unsupportive COs and strict rules and procedures while inside), how to respond to inmates who may talk about their crimes, and how to establish a sense of safety in an unsafe environment. Overall, the challenges reflected an attempt to create a sense of cohesion and organization in an unpredictable environment. It required facilitators to be flexible, to think on their feet, and not to take personally any of the negative feedback they might encounter from unsupportive jail staff.

Students faced a few barriers, within and without our small classroom inside the housing unit. Entering the housing unit felt very uncomfortable, but that was not due to the presence of the inmates. Rather, it was due to the uncertainty of how student facilitators would be treated by the COs who oversee the housing unit. While the education staff at the jail was completely supportive, the security staff was fairly skeptical of the facilitators and groups. A few COs were openly hostile. In one example a CO ignored the facilitators for 20 minutes, delayed calling the group members to the group, and ended the group early. As a result, this group lost 45 minutes of what should have been a 90-minute meeting. The actions of the CO created a very uncomfortable environment for the facilitators and the group members.

Incarceration carries a stigma in our society, which is evident as the formerly incarcerated begin to look for work, return to reintegrate within their families and within their neighborhoods (Council on Crime and Justice, 2006; Mauer, 2006). The stigma exists inside the jail as well; students witnessed the staff expressing disdain for the support group projects—through words and actions--and other inmates judging one another based on the crimes they have committed (i.e. one group consisted of sex offenders who expressed that their housing unit was better than the other units where there were murderers). Many (not all) COs made it clear that incarcerated people do not deserve services, and that the students were wasting their time trying to help.

Student facilitators quickly discovered that inconsistencies within jail are not uncommon. Facilitators were briefed on procedures within the jail and were told that COs change housing units at the beginning of each month, but one group had four different COs during a six week group. This made it difficult to establish and maintain a relationship with the COs.

The jail environment made it difficult to create a sense of "safe space." In jail, people under stress with uncertain futures are kept in close quarters with one another and are stripped of privacy, dignity, and means of self-expression. As a result, hierarchies develop and are enforced as people search for a sense of respect and security. The hierarchy is often maintained through verbal and physical aggression, which added a challenge for many groups. For instance, one group member told another member who was due for transfer to prison that he was so small that he was "definitely going to be someone's bitch." On another occasion a member who had shared with the group his struggle with dark, violent thoughts essentially threatened another group member. On both occasions the target of these statements ceased participating for the remainder of the meeting. The facilitators were taken aback by these comments and addressed it in the following group by identifying how comments like this could target and isolate a group member and create a negative space/violate the safety of the group. Group members acknowledged how this could be true and no further comments were made.

The negative comments and violent statements brought forward a new challenge for the student facilitators: holding all group members accountable to the group rules. This proved to be difficult on a few occasions, specifically after one group member confessed to killing two people. He was not bragging or apologizing, but talking matter-of-factly about his criminal history. After his confession, the inmate began talking over other group members and became quite disruptive. Other members appeared to be evaluating the truth of his statements. The motives of the speaker were unclear, and the facilitators honored his sharing and recognized the difficulty he had faced being in and out of the system. The facilitators processed the meeting together. It was challenging for these facilitators because their purpose was to create a safe space where inclusion and respect were paramount. As facilitators, they wondered if they treated this man differently after learning of his crime, specifically whether they would be less likely to reinforce group rules with him because they were scared or would they respond the same way to him as they would respond to a man who confessed to credit card theft? While the group was able to move forward in both instances without any further threats, it brought to light the intense dynamics in the jail setting, and how difficult it is to neutralize them in a way that keeps everyone feel safe and respected.

Facilitators had to learn how to navigate challenging topics that spontaneously arose. The support groups were not necessarily the best place to have super charged conversations about some of the topics like race, privilege, class that were brought up. The unpredictable nature of the groups – will we have all group members next week, will the COs allow us all of our allotted time – made it hard to try to discuss highly charged, sensitive or political issues because facilitators could not assume they could fully address the topic. And, ultimately, the overarching purpose of the group was supportive rather than educational, and the facilitators needed to keep the group focused on engaging in mutual support.

Rewards of Facilitation

It may seem antithetical to begin speaking about the rewards experienced by facilitators by first mentioning a challenge, but this challenge is worth noting as it laid, at least in part, a positive cornerstone for many support groups. As facilitators entered housing units at the beginning of each meeting, they were often met with predominately pejorative attitudes directed at them by COs. The short time working with a few unsupportive COs gave facilitators an opportunity to consider how it must feel for inmates who experience this lack of support, and worse, on a daily basis. Mauer (2006) writes that the effects of incarceration "are persistent and pervasive and can include personal, social, financial, emotional, psychological, and physical concerns" (p. 4). For the facilitators who experienced hostile COs, it became clearer how the experience of incarceration could negatively impact a person's emotional wellbeing, even after being released. It was, however, an opportunity for the facilitators to connect on a more direct level with the incarcerated members by inviting them to discuss any similar experiences of being ignored or judged by COs and how those experiences impacted their daily lives.

The facilitators, as social workers, worked hard to examine the issues of race, discrimination and privilege and to keep those issues in the forefront of practice, but we seldom hear social workers talking about the rights of the oppressed behind bars. The people on the inside expressed such a deep genuine gratitude that the facilitators not only would have an interest, but that they actually cared. This type of gratitude is not always given so freely by many who have freedom and privilege on the outside, and the sincerity was itself a reward.

An additional benefit of participating in the CCJ support groups was that even though the inmates knew that the facilitators were all students running the programs, none of the group members were condescending towards them. At times, during internships, a student can be made to feel like they have to "pay their dues" or "earn their way" before they are afforded respect. CCJ participants however gave that respect without question and often looked to the students as role models.

Another big reward included building enough trust and relationship within the group to be able to witness participants become a cohesive group and support one another. This may seem obvious since this is a stated purpose of group work, but in an institutionalized setting such as a jail where the very nature of letting one's guard down and relying on another is not only taboo but perhaps even dangerous, it can be very gratifying to witness such trust and development of mutual aid. The many rewards for UNE students participating with the CCJ support groups are as unique and individual as each group. One major reward for all of the group members was that, at least for a short time, inmates did not feel solely like criminals, and facilitators did not feel solely like students. CCJ participants were people who were valued and heard, facilitators were gaining valuable experience doing truly people-centered social work, and together we were all human beings remembering a bit of our humanity.

Conclusion

The UNE-CCJ support group project is an example of community-based social work education. Working at the jail required students to build on learning gained in field placements and classrooms and draw on multiple skills and forms of knowledge. All facilitators completed a required course on group work before embarking on the support group project, and designing and facilitating groups at the jail gave students the opportunity to put their newly acquired knowledge of group process into practice. Working together with incarcerated people as colleagues to design the support group project taught the facilitators an unforgettable lesson: service design itself can be an empowering process for all. Students should be encouraged to work with community partners to design and initiate new groups as part of their social work education.

References

Council on Crime and Justice (2006). The collateral effects of incarceration on fathers, families, and communities. Retrieved from http://crimeandjustice.org/researchReports/Collateral%20Effects%20of%20Incarceration%20on%20Fathers,%20Families,%20and%20Communities.pdf

Dixon, L. (2000). Punishment and the question of ownership: Groupwork in the criminal justice system. *Groupwork*, 12 (1), 6-25.

Doel, M. (2006). *Using Groupwork*, London: Routledge.

Freudenberg, N. (2001). Jails, prisons, and the health of urban populations: A review of the impact of the correctional system on community health. *Journal of Urban Health*, 78(2), 214-235.

Gitterman, A. (2005). Building mutual support in groups. *Social Work with Groups*, 28 (3/4), 91-106.

Hallinan, J. T. (2003). *Going up the river: Travels in a prison nation*. New York: Random House.

Kurland, R. (2005). Planning: The neglected component of group development. *Social Work with Groups*, 28 (3/4), 9-126.

Kurland, R. and Salmon, R. (2006). Purpose: A misunderstood and misused keystone of group work practice. *Social Work with Groups*, 29(2/3), 105-120.

Mauer, M. (2006). *Race to incarcerate*. New York: The New Press.

Mazza, C. (2008). A pound of flesh: The Psychological, familial and social consequences of mandatory long-term sentencing laws for drug offenses. *Journal of Social Work Practice in the Addictions*, 4(3), 65-81.

Morris, N. (1995). "The contemporary prison: 1965-Present." In N. Morris & D. Rothman (Eds.) *The Oxford history of the prison: The practice of punishment in Western society*. New York: Oxford University Press.

Pompa, L. (2005). Service-learning as crucible: Reflections on immersion, context, power, and transformation. In D.W. Butin (Ed.), *Service learning in higher education*. New York: Palgrave/Macmillan.

Sarri, R.C., Shook, J.J. (2005). The future for social work in juvenile and adult corrections. *Advances in Social Work*, 6(1), 210-20.

Visher, C., Travis, J. (2012). The characteristics of prisoners returning home and effective reentry programs and policies. In J. Petersilia & K. Reitz (Eds). *The Oxford handbook on sentencing and corrections*.

Social Workers Collaborating with Faith Based Organizations to Create a Group Mentoring Program for African American Youth

Anthony C. Hill

Introduction

This chapter describes a group mentoring project that collaborates with a faith-based organization serving elementary and middle school-aged participants. The Black Leadership and Enrichment Society of Springfield (B.L.E.S.S.) program is a low cost group intervention that mentors, supports, and raises the academic achievement of urban youth. This paper examines how social workers promote academic success for urban at-risk youth by describing the B.L.E.S.S. program. The primary goals of B.L.E.S.S are to address issues of poor academic performance, negative peer pressure, and the lack of positive male role models for African American youth. B.L.E.S.S serves as an example of how social workers can use groups to partner with faith-based institutions to promote academic, social, and cultural success for urban at-risk youth.

> The pain is in their eyes. Young black men in their late twenties and early thirties living in urban America, lost and abandoned, aimlessly walking and hawking the streets with nothing behind their eyes but anger, confusion, disappointment and pain... (Madhubuti, 1991)

Background

The quote above shows why it is important to focus our attention on providing support to African American boys. Social workers can be proactive and work to mentor, provide guidance and uplift young African American boys today, or have to deal with dire consequences facing African American men later. Too many African American males are the subject of negative media, gangs, drugs, poor education, unemployment, crime, violence, and death. African American students in our nation's urban centers fare poorly in education, employment, health, housing, high school graduation, and college attendance rates (Children's Defense Fund (CDF), 2013; CDF, 2010; Noguera, 2008). African American men are also disproportionately represented in our nation's criminal justice and penitentiary system (Alexander, 2010; Noguera, 2008). The Schott Foundation (2010) examines the drop-out rate for African American males and finds that Black boys' graduation rates are less than 50% and they are less likely to enroll in or graduate from college. School failure during one's childhood and adolescence inevitably leads to negative adult life experiences. There is limited discussion or connection by mainstream media as to how these negative school indicators contribute to a negative self-identity for young African American boys. It appears that too many young Black males internalize negative messages that they receive from our educational system and do not value education or see it as an important element toward their development and future success.

There is a disproportionate number of African American youth that are retained, do not graduate, and drop out of school (Noguera, 2008; CDF, 2010). This negatively impacts African American youth's life choices and opportunities to be productive citizens in American society. The role of the social worker is integral to the academic achievement of African American students. It is essential that social workers provide guidance and work directly with students to help them process the stigma of being an African American male in American society and motivate them about the importance of obtaining a quality education. The inability of African American youth to acquire advanced skills in reading, writing, mathematics, and science will hinder their overall development in life. It is important that social workers come up with proactive interventions to address the crisis among African American youth. Social workers can be at the forefront of promoting and sustaining academic success for urban youth of color by confronting issues such as poor academic performance, high truancy and drop-out rates, and punitive disciplinary practices within mainstream educational systems.

The B.L.E.S.S. Program

One concrete way that social workers can impact student achievement is to offer a community mentoring group in places of worship that provides them with a group experience where students discuss specific issues such as promoting academic achievement, the developmental challenges of growing up as a male and the specific obstacles one faces as a young African American male in American society. Corey, Corey and Corey (2014) point out that individual therapy may not be the best way to engage male clients. The authors discuss that groups for males can be helpful in helping males to clarify gender roles and cope with life's struggles. The group provides a context where the males can be transparent and bring their feelings and fears into the open and gain support from other members. Themes such as "trust, vulnerability, fear, shame, strength, weakness, male-male relationships, competition, family of origin issues, sexuality, friendship, dominance, submissiveness, love, hatred, dreams, grief, obsessions, work, and death" are all topics that can help males explore their feelings and get the support from the group facilitator and other members (Corey et al., 2014, p. 376).

The B.L.E.S.S. program was established for young boys in the third to eighth grades to receive support, gain insights, find solutions, and improve self-image. Students have discussed with the group ways to intervene when they feel that a teacher does not like them, how to handle situations where they feel that they are being unfairly punished in school, how to save face when confronted with a peer that wants to fight, and how to interact appropriately with females. This group format is an important area where the social worker can play an instrumental role in encouraging students to reach their academic potential and identifying, preventing, and helping children eliminate, overcome, or reduce the problems that are obstacles to successful academic, social, and cultural learning. As a result of an assessment of need in the community, the seriousness of the issues facing African American young males, I founded the B.L.E.S.S. program.

As an MSW social worker and a member of an urban church with about 300 members, I had a discussion with the Pastor of my house of worship that I wanted to establish a mentoring program for African American boys. The Pastor was supportive of the idea and provided space in the church, allowed us to advertise in the church bulletin to recruit members, and allowed use of the Church van to take the boys on recreational and cultural events. The Pastor noticed the high number of single parent homes led by mothers, grandmothers, and extended family members and was agreeable to the program as a way of providing positive role models for the African American males in the church and in the community. This was a win-win intervention for the church members and for families in the community. The church wanted to reach out to the community as well as be a support to single parent families in the congregation. As a leader in the church with a MSW degree, I volunteered my time so there were few costs in establishing the program other than those associated with utilities, use of an adequate meeting room, and the use of the church van for occasional field trips. Advertising of the program took place in the weekly church bulletin and through making a connection with a local public school in close proximity to the church. Due to being a member of the church and a strong working relationship with both the Pastor and the church congregants, there were no issues of distrust or fears of my social work background. Usually there is confusion about the role and responsibilities of social workers in the community and there is a misconception and a strong stigma that social workers "remove children from families". As this was a mentoring program and not a clinically based group, there were no issues of confidentiality and it was understood that information would be shared and parents were invited to sit in on groups at any time.

The mission of the B.L.E.S.S. program is to provide mutual aid and to help each individual meet their goals (Association for the Advancement of Social Work with Groups [AASWG], 2006). Additionally, this program serves as an antidote to an increase of drugs, poverty, violence, loss of positive male models, and a soaring school dropout and incarceration rate in an urban community. I established this group in a faith-based setting (urban Baptist church) that wanted to help African American male youth, in grades three through eight from the church and the outlying community improve their school performance and cultivate successful habits early in their lives. This program served as both a prevention and an enrichment program that strived to (a) provide youth with male adults who can serve as competent, capable, caring male role models; (b) provide opportunities for youth to practice leadership; (c) teach African American history and culture; (d) enhance Christian values and moral development; (e) promote life skills such as overcoming peer pressure, addressing healthy ways to deal with anger, and stressing the importance of education; and finally (f) provide opportunities for participants to engage in field trips, recreation, and public speaking.

Our decision to form a group for boys in grades three through eight was based on research which demonstrates that African American boys start to disconnect from their schooling experience around the third grade (Price, 2002). Therefore, in an effort to address youth disengagement, our program was developed to provide young students with the additional academic, emotional and spiritual support that this group could provide. The program is held on Saturdays from 9:00 AM to 12:00 PM with the last half hour dedicated to recreational activities such as football, basketball, and tag. There are usually 8-12 boys who attend regularly and we meet for 15 consecutive sessions in the fall and spring. There is a small nominal fee to participate.

The group starts off with prayer and then each member recites the B.L.E.S.S. pledge, which the students have memorized. The B.L.E.S.S. pledge, developed by B.L.E.S.S. founder Dr. Anthony C. Hill, is meant to inspire and help participants create a positive Black male identity. Below is the pledge:

God help us,
To be strong black men.
Role models with our actions as well as our words.
Help us to protect and respect our women, family, elders, community and each other.
God, give us a vision.
If we cannot do any good,
Let us do no harm.
Let Your will be done in us.
Help us to submit to your will.
We know that You have a special plan for our lives.
Help us to realize that it is better to build up than to tear down.
Help us to refrain from criticizing, putting down, or destroying the character or reputation of others.

And to always remember to encourage, uplift, and support each other
in all positive endeavors.
Help us to make this world a better place than we found it.
Bless us Lord!!!
AMEN

This pledge is powerful in that it incorporates spirituality, how
to relate to peers, family members, women, elders, and how to be
responsible members of the community. It also speaks to each person's
uniqueness, potential, and encourages the students to take advantage
of educational opportunities and to make use of their talents, skills,
and positive attributes for themselves as well as take responsibility for
making their community safer and better for everyone.

The activities for each week allow students the opportunity to
enhance their writing skills as the students have to complete a weekly
writing prompt during the session. An example of a writing prompt
is: "What positive changes would you make in your neighborhood if
you had one million dollars?" Other activities during each session
include the following: a read-a-loud session discussing African
American history and culture, a Bible study twenty minutes in duration
discussing key male figures in the Bible such as Joseph, David, and
Jonathan, Scripture from the book of Proverbs and Psalms, guest
speakers from the community, and field trips (1-2 a semester). Activities
also include recreational events such as playing football in the church
parking lot thirty minutes before the end of the session.

One central theme for the group is emphasis on the importance of
education and attending college so that these boys would persevere in
school, attain academic success, and eventually graduate with their
high school diploma. In order to highlight the importance of college,
we tour the campus of a local college that is in the community to open
up their minds about the value and accessibility of a college education.
In this group setting it is stressed that the youth must not succumb
to poor academic effort, low teacher expectations, or to negative peer
pressure, which can sabotage their academic potential and success.
Ford, Grantham, and Whiting (2008) examine negative peer pressures
on gifted African American students and their perceptions of "acting
White" and "acting Black" as it relates to their identity and academic
achievement. According to the authors, "acting White" refers to
behaviors of students of color being studious, raising one's hand in class
to answer teacher questions, obtaining a good report card, and speaking
"standard" English (Ford et al., 2008). Some examples of "acting Black"

cited by the authors are students of color devaluing education, not studying or reading, getting poor grades, being aggressive to adults and peers, and using slang (Ford et al., 2008). This topic of what it means to "act White or Black" is incorporated in several of our group sessions and students are able to discuss the pressures that they face from their peer groups in not putting forth maximum effort academically. We explore with the students the meaning of an anonymous quote about the importance of "postponing immediate gratification in favor of long term success!" The adult facilitators also highlight several successful and influential African Americans locally and nationally as a way to counteract negative peer pressures and to promote academic success. We also identify both national and successful African American men in the local community who have overcome poverty, trauma, and societal ills. We also teach and role-play with the boys about how to interact with authority figures such as teachers, police officers, bus monitors, and principals. The boys liked having a safe space to discuss issues that they faced with peers, girls, parents, and teachers. The boys commented that this group gave them an opportunity to learn essential life lessons while having fun by engaging in sports, field trips and learning from successful men in the community. Here is an example of some of what the B.L.E.S.S. activities covered and what each letter of the B.L.E.S.S. acronym represents:

- **Black:** African America leaders represent the first letter of B.L.E.S.S.; we read, study and discuss significant historical figures such as: Malcolm X, Rev. Dr. Martin Luther King, Marian Wright Edelman, Jesse Owens, George Washington Carver, Rosa Parks, Rev. Jesse Jackson, Sojourner Truth, Michael Jordan, Harriet Tubman, Booker T. Washington, Maya Angelou, Frederick Douglass, Nelson Mandela, and local community leaders as guest speakers.
- **Leadership:** The second letter of B.L.E.S.S. stands for leadership. We discuss with the young men the importance being a role model, a leader, taking charge and the importance of doing the right thing, fairness, caring for others, thinking for themselves, following directions and being responsible, honest, doing their best and respecting themselves and others.
- **Enrichment:** The third letter of B.L.E.S.S. stands for enrichment. The young men are given the opportunity to practice reading, writing, public speaking, and learn about African American culture and history, Christian values, and key Scriptures from the Holy Bible.

- **Society:** The fourth letter of B.L.E.S.S. stands for society. We establish a supportive, community like environment in the group where the youth support each other and we have as a motto: "We are our brother's keeper."
- **Springfield:** The final letter of B.L.E.S.S. stands for Springfield. The young men are given the opportunity examine the positive characteristics of their community and to make a difference here by pursuing educational excellence.

Some of the group topics and activities center on helping students learn and practice effective conflict resolution, decision-making, problem solving, and coping skills. We want to make sure that we address areas and equip students with strategies to help them overcome incidents that interfere or distract them from doing their best academic work in school. It should come to no surprise that young Black males desire to emulate athletes, hip-hop stars, entertainers, Hollywood celebrities and even criminals. We challenge the boys to have a back up plan and also aspire to have a career in law, education, medicine, politics, and business in addition to pursuing their dreams of being an athlete or a hip-hop recording artist. Through the content of the group sessions and our guest speakers we wanted to expand the images of Black men as actors, athletes, celebrities and criminals that are routinely depicted in the media as seemingly the only avenues for Black boys to attain success in life. Below are examples of journal entries from the students. The students were asked to define what a "good Black man" is and what they themselves will do to become a "good Black man". Below are some powerful examples of participant responses to these questions

Participant 1:
A good Black man is strong and determined.
A good Black man is willing.
A good Black man is educated.
A good Black man has a job.
I will become a good Black man by educating myself.
Striving to reach my goals.
And I will have a good job.

Participant 2:
A good Black man treats a woman with respect.
A good Black man does his best at all times.

A good Black man does not take drugs.

A good Black man does not use guns.

A good Black man uses words instead of violence.

I will become a good Black man by listening to my elders.

Focusing on my goals.

And I will make good choices in my life.

Participant 3:

A good Black man does not hit a woman.

A good Black man will get a job.

I will become a good Black man by going to college and getting a college degree.

Participant 4:

A good Black man is someone who is trustworthy.

A good Black man is responsible.

A good Black man is kind.

A good Black man is hard-working.

I will become a good Black man by being loyal, responsible, trustworthy, and hardworking.

The group also serves as a supportive environment for students who exhibit inadequate academic, behavioral, and social performance in school. The group focuses on life skills, character building, and career exploration. This group also offers academic tutoring in math and provides social support for at-risk students so that they could attain academic success. As indicated earlier in this chapter, the group presents successful male guest speakers that include teachers, police officers, businessmen, firemen, financial advisors, ministers, high school and college graduates, and civic and governmental leaders such as the National Association for the Advancement of Colored People's (NAACP) local president. These guest speakers expose group participants to different career options as well as share their family background and struggles that they successfully overcame when they were young people. They also motivate students by sharing with them their lived experiences and how their hard work in studying in school shaped them individually and allowed them to lead a very successful life.

We say to the students that the next five to ten years of your life will dictate the quality of the rest of their life for the next 40-50 years. We share with them the meaning of the United Negro College Fund's slogan: "A mind is a terrible thing to waste!" and that it carries a significant long lasting message. It is important for students to take advantage of the educational opportunities and realize that their hard work and studying now will lead to greater opportunities in the future. Additionally the students are taken on field trips 1-2 times per semester. The field trips include visits to local colleges, museums, sporting events, and the aquarium. In addition, the students receive Bibles that they are allowed to keep and use as a reference when we have weekly Bible lessons.

The use of group mentoring sessions provides many long-term benefits. This group could be classified as a psychoeducational group that helps the young males to "develop the knowledge and skills necessary to cope with specific issues in their lives" (Furman, Rowan, & Bender, 2009, p. 79). The students in the group provide mutual aid to each other and have an opportunity to learn and grow from each other, share insight and solutions to common problems such as how to get along with teachers and to deal with peers who were picking on them. Through the group, members are able to learn and practice new behaviors and skills through observation and role-plays where they gain confidence while working collaboratively with others. The group members also learn from the knowledge, experiences, and positive modeling of the group facilitators as they seek to emulate key concepts and apply this information to their individual situations (Furman et al., 2009). As a result of their participation in the group, the young males were able to identify behaviors that were maladaptive in the classroom that impeded student achievement. Most importantly, as a result of group participation, students verbalized that they are motivated to overcome life's challenges, excel academically, and improve the quality of their lives in the future while having fun on a Saturday morning.

Conclusion

In the words of Pedro Noguera (as cited in Casserly, M., Lewis, S., Simon, C., Uzzell, R., & Palacios, M., 2012), it is essential that we are proactive in addressing the plight of young African American males:

The continued failure of so many young men is costly to the entire society. Every dollar spent to incarcerate a Black or Latino man or boy, to support them during periods of unemployment, to house them when they are homeless and destitute, to police them when there is a lack of safety in the neighborhoods where they reside, to pay for the cost of medical care when they show up with chronic health conditions at hospital emergency rooms, or to support their children because they are unable to provide as fathers, could easily be redirected to address other needs. We need a proactive, preventative strategy, and education must be at the center of it. (p. 185)

This group was a way as a social worker I could play a crucial role in helping young male African American students have access to competent male role models, learn important social and life skills, and attain academic success. This program allowed me to address the vulnerability, negative perceptions, self-degradation, and common obstacles that face African American males in American society. This is a creative way to provide services to the community and it is my hope that this initiative would spur other social workers to partner with faith based organizations to meet the social, emotional, and educational needs of children through a group format. Through the use of this group, I was able to partner with the Black church and give back to the community and utilize my expertise as a professional social worker to provide support and help students overcome obstacles that interfered with academic proficiency.

References

Association for the Advancement of Social Work with Groups. (2006). Standards for social group work practice. Retrieved from http://iaswg. org/Practice_Standards

Alexander, M. (2010). The new Jim Crow: Mass incarceration in the age of colorblindness. New York: The New Press.

Boykin, A.W. & Noguera, P. (2011) Creating the opportunity to learn: Moving from research to practice to close the achievement gap. Alexandria, VA: ASCD.

Casserly, M., Lewis, S., Simon, C., Uzzell, R., & Palacios, M. (2012). A Call for Change: Providing Solutions for Black Male Achievement. Council of the Great City Schools.

Children's Defense Fund. 2013. Each Day in America for Black Children. Retrieved from http://www.childrensdefense.org/child-research-data publications/eachday-in-americablack-children.html#sthash. Fq95maum.dpuf

Children's Defense Fund (2010). Annual Report. Washington, DC: Children's Defense Fund.

Corey, M.S., Corey, G. & Corey, C. (2014). Groups, Process and Practice. 9th edition. Belmont, CA: Brooks/Cole Cengage Learning.

Ford, D.Y., Grantham, T.C., & Whiting, G. W. (2008). Another look at the achievement gap: Learning from the experiences of gifted black students. *Urban Education*, 43(2), 216-239.

Furman, R., Rowan, D., & Bender, K. (2009). An Experiential Approach to Group Work. Chicago: Lyceum.

Madhubti, H. (1991). Black men: Obsolete, single, dangerous?: The Afrikan American Family in Transition. Chicago: Third World Press.

Noguera, P. (2012). Saving Black and Latino boys: What schools can do to make a difference. *Phi Delta Kappan*, 93(5), 8-12.

Noguera, P., Hurtado, A., & Fergus, E. (2012). Invisible no more: Understanding the disenfranchisement of Latino men and boys. New York: Rutledge

Noguera, P. (2008). The trouble with black boys and other reflections on race, equity, and the future of public education. San Francisco, CA: Wiley & Sons.

Price, H.B (2002). Achievement matters: Getting your child the best education possible. New York: Dafina Books.

Schott Foundation. (2010). Yes, we can: The 2010 Schott 50-state report on public education of black males. Retrieved from www.blackboysreport. org.

Theatre Workshops as a Group Format for Promoting Intercultural Understanding

Claude Olivier and William Dunn

Introduction

This chapter reports on the use of theatre workshops as a group format to give voice to international university students' experiences of inclusion and exclusion. The workshops were associated with a research project that investigated the social interactions between international university students whose first language is not English and domestic university students whose native language is English. Fourteen students took part in an initial workshop that focused on writing scripts, and twelve students took part in a second workshop to perform and record them. The students completed written evaluations that assessed the impact of participating. The workshops resulted in five skits presenting themes such as: awareness, responsibility and action; loneliness and exclusion; developing empathy and transcending cultural differences; benefits of social interaction; and accessing informal interaction through formal structures. In general, participants expressed satisfaction with the workshops. They also reported changes in their thinking about domestic and international student experiences and interaction. In addition to workshop outcomes, key issues examined in this chapter include: benefits of using theatre in social work with groups; developing research-based performances; challenges related to authenticity versus adaptation; and the impact on audiences.

Background

Our interest in using theatre workshops arose from a research project investigating informal social interaction between international and domestic university students. We wanted to find creative and meaningful ways of giving voice to students' experiences of inclusion and exclusion. In addition, we were looking for interesting ways to present the research findings to various university stakeholder groups including students, administrators, instructors and service providers. We anticipated that theatre held potential to involve socially excluded or marginalized groups in research and to communicate research findings beyond the more usual routes of journal articles and paper presentations, thus allowing us to engage a broader audience. What follows is what we learned about the benefits of using theatre in research, including possible ways to dramatize findings, as well as challenges related to authenticity versus adaptation, the impact on audiences, and the practical aspects of developing and performing skits. All of these issues are illustrated through our experience of using theatre within the university student interaction study. Moreover, readers will have the opportunity to view one of the resulting skits from this research through a provided YouTube link.

A review of the literature revealed that many disciplines have incorporated theatre into research, including education, sociology, anthropology, business and commerce, and health and medicine (Ackroyd & O'Toole, 2010; Butler-Kisber, 2010). However, social work is a relative newcomer to publishing reports on the use of theatre in research. This is surprising given the potential benefits of this approach, discussed below. Of particular relevance to social work is the opportunity theatre provides oppressed groups to tell their stories and the resulting increase in audience awareness that can lead to both personal and structural change. Many terms are used to indicate the use of theatre in research, including: ethnodrama, ethnographic performance, readers theatre, verbatim theatre, community theatre, documentary theatre, docu-drama, reality theatre, performance inquiry, performance research, performance ethnography, research-based theatre, theatre of reenactment, and applied theatre (Ackroyd & O'Toole, 2010; Beck, Belliveau, Lea, & Wager, 2011; Butler-Kisber, 2010; Dennis 2009). One of the most commonly used terms and approaches is ethnodrama, which we focus on in this chapter. Saldaña (2005) states that ethnodrama "consists of dramatized, significant selections of narrative collected through interviews, participant observation, field notes, journal entries and/or print and media artifacts" (p. 2). Although there are differences between the various approaches, Butler-Kisber (2010) acknowledges that all "are informed by a performative epistemology" (p. 137) that can provide an embodied and empathic means of understanding research findings. In addition, Leavy (2009) notes that "although often considered a representational form, performance can be used as an entire research method, serving as a means of data collection and analysis as well as a (re)presentation form" (pp. 135-136).

Benefits of Using Theatre in Research

Leavy (2009) points out that "the move by some qualitative researchers toward ethnodrama results from the ability of dramatic performance to get at and present rich, textured, descriptive, situated, contextual experiences and multiple meanings from the perspectives of those studied in the field" (p. 145). The literature details numerous benefits of using theatre in research, including its potential to: 1) provide vivid and embodied narratives; 2) reach and involve broader audiences; 3) foster empathy; 4) contribute to social change; and 5) enable participation of research participants—including those who are oppressed.

Research findings can be communicated through an actor to convey the associated spoken words, feelings and gestures, all presented within a real-life context. As underscored by Leavy (2009), "performance-based methods can bring research findings to life, adding dimensionality, and exposing that which is otherwise impossible to authentically (re)present" (p. 135). Theatre also enables the dissemination of research findings in a clear and accessible manner, and to a wider range of audiences, than is typical of academic reports (Mienczakowski, 2006; Rossiter et al., 2008). Furthermore, some theatrical methods involve the audience by temporarily stopping the performance to invite comments or suggestions for an actor on how he or she should proceed in the story being conveyed. Another method of audience participation is to have an open discussion following the play. Theatre enables connections with an audience both on an emotional and intellectual level (Mienczakowski, 2006). Such connection can foster empathy. Ackroyd and O'Toole (2010) point out that "one of the characteristics of drama is that participants—actors and audience—put themselves into others' shoes, empathising with the subjects of the drama while simultaneously maintaining distance and detachment... This may make the research site and the subjects' lives accessible subjectively, emotionally and existentially...." (pp. 4-5). Similarly, Saldaña (2010) states that ethnodrama holds potential to increase awareness, understanding and empathy. This resulting deeper level of understanding may then move people to individual change and social action (Butler-Kisber, 2010; Dennis, 2009; Saldaña, 2010), following the tradition of Augusto Boal's 'theatre of the oppressed' (Boal, 1985). Through involving the audience in analysis and consciousness raising, Boal used theatre as a means of promoting social and political change. As Saldaña (2010) states "Ethnodrama provides opportunities for participants with marginalized 'offstage' status in everyday life to stand centre stage and tell their stories" (p. 67). A good example of this is Conrad and Campbell's (2008) use of theatre to explore the stories of adolescent boys in a young offender facility. Using theatre with this aim was one of our main reasons for incorporating ethnodrama into the dissemination of our research on social interaction between international and domestic university students.

Developing Research-based Performances

Saldaña (2010) writes, "if a shared goal of theatre and qualitative inquiry is to explore and learn more about the human condition, then the outcomes are doubly if not exponentially increased when the two disciplines merge, bringing with them their best representational and presentational modes of expression through dramatic text" (p. 61). This merging is facilitated by similarities between conventional approaches to qualitative research and the processes for transforming data into script. Data can be collected through such means as interviews and focus groups, themes then emerge through data analysis, and the resulting themes are used to inform the script which can stay close to the actual research transcripts or be adapted into more elaborate skits or plays (Butler-Kisber, 2010). Rossiter et al. (2008) examined published health studies that have used theatre for data analysis or to communicate findings, and based on their review, they divided and categorized the literature into four theatre genres representing a continuum "moving from a very close alignment with data to purely fictional accounts of health-related topics" (p. 131). Their four categories are non-theatrical performances, ethnodramas, theatrical research-based performances, and fictional theatrical performances. This categorization provides a useful way of thinking about the various approaches to using theatre in research.

In non-theatrical performances, such as readers theatre, research transcripts and field notes are used verbatim or nearly verbatim to produce a script, resulting in "performances that employ a minimum of traditional theatrical convention, such as a story line or dialogue, and may even eschew theatrical 'staples' such as sets and costumes" (Rossiter et al., 2008, p. 132). Ethnodramas entail "the creation of 'real-life' vignettes that emerge directly from data such as interviews, focus groups or ethnographic notes" (Rossiter et al., 2008, p. 134). They use theatrical techniques while also remaining true to research participants' narratives, and can be interactive with the audience or not. Theatrical research-based performances use similar techniques as ethnodramas and "are informed by the research process, but do not strictly adhere to the data as script" (Rossiter et al., 2008, p. 136). Finally, fictional theatrical performances (e.g., plays, poetry) are not based on research.

Some genres or methods are easier to carry out than others. Non-theatrical performances, for example, "may simply consist of a dramatized reading of interview transcripts that, through their performance, have been transformed into monologues" (Rossiter et al., 2008, p. 132). Ethnodramas and theatrical research-based performances, in comparison, generally require greater theatrical expertise in developing characters, and writing dialogue and story lines. Saldaña (2010) notes that "play scripts written by those with theatrical experience tend to include lengthier storylines with more impactful, emotion-evoking monologue and dialogue in a variety of styles and genres" (p. 62).

Beck et al. (2011) provide a useful framework to assist in selecting the most suitable genre of theatre for use in a research project. The authors "delineate a spectrum of research-based theatre...based on two defining continua: the research continuum, which distinguishes among many types of research used to inform research-based theatre, and the performance continuum, which distinguishes among different kinds of performances, audiences, and purposes of a given research-based theatre piece" (p. 687). At one end of the research continuum is systematic research that is carried out with intentionality and follows a formal research process while at the other end of the continuum is "inquiry into historical facts" where the "story aspect is fictionalized"

(Beck et al., 2011, p. 691). At one end of the performance continuum are "closed/conferences performances" (Beck, et al., 2011, p. 692) for specific audiences such as research participants and other key stakeholders. These performances "explore source data closely, often with a minimum of theatrical conventions" (Beck et al., 2011, p. 692). At the other end of the performance continuum are "performances created for aesthetic engagement" (Beck et al., 2011, p. 693) that may not closely adhere to specific research data. Such performances may appeal to a broader, general audience. The two continua are combined to assist in determining the type of theatre that is best suited to the type of research and intended purpose and audience.

Illustrative Example:
Our Use of Theatre-based Research

We drew upon the 'theatrical research-based performance' genre (Rossiter et al., 2008) in our research on university student interaction. As a key part of the research dissemination, we engaged students in writing and performing skits based on findings and themes that had been previously identified during the analysis of the research findings. An important aspect of our use of theatre was that the skits were created by students who had much in common with the students who had participated in the actual research project. Before proceeding to discuss our use of theatre, we will provide an overview of the research in order to place the use of theatre in context.

The study was carried out to investigate the social interactions between international university students whose first language is not English and domestic university students whose native language is English (see Dunn & Olivier, 2011). The research goal was to explore the social dynamics of inclusion, focusing in particular on: 1) strategies used by international students to gain access to informal social interaction with domestic students, and the barriers and supports encountered; and 2) overtures and responses of domestic students to social interaction with international students. The primary source of data was individual interviews with 60 international and domestic undergraduate students at two Canadian universities. Key factors that hindered interaction included cultural differences, language, and a lack of cultural knowledge and understanding. Both international and domestic students shared personal strategies for addressing these barriers and working toward social inclusiveness. International students, for example, spoke of building their courage to initiate conversation and not personalizing rejection. Domestic students recognized their "gate-keeping" role in facilitating the entry of international students into the broader campus community. Strategies in common for both groups included learning about the other's culture and developing social empathy. Participants also identified structural factors that can either advance or deter cross-cultural social interaction such as having formal means to gain access to informal interaction. Examples of formal means included organized clubs and social events, student residences/housing, volunteering, orientation week, international student support programs, and classroom activities and course assignments. The findings also pointed to processes of oppression that encompassed personal, cultural and structural locations (Thompson, 2011).

As previously noted, we became interested in theatre as a means to involve participants and creatively communicate our research findings in a way that would engage a broad audience. To this end, two full-day theatre-based workshops were held at one of the universities where the original research project had taken place. The objective of the first workshop was to produce written skits of key themes that had been previously identified in the data analysis phase of the project. The themes were organized into the following four categories: (1) Awareness, responsibility and action as a process towards initiating and sustaining interaction between international and domestic university students; (2) Developing empathy for the loneliness and exclusion experienced by international students and issues of cultural differences; and then transcending cultural differences through such means as friendly gestures and initiatives, patience, and suspending judgment about difference; (3) The benefits of social interaction in fostering a sense of belonging and promoting cross-cultural knowledge and awareness, and (4) Accessing informal interaction with domestic or international students through formal or organized events and activities.

The purpose of the second workshop was to have students act out the skits for which scripts had been written in the previous workshop. The skits were video-recorded for future use in presentations to various stakeholders. Both workshops included an evaluation component to assess the logistics and organization of the workshops as well as the perceived impact, if any, of participating. The workshop participants were international and domestic university students who were recruited through flyers posted and distributed around the university campus. Students were given an honorarium to acknowledge their time commitment and creative contribution.

Fourteen students took part in the first workshop, which focused on writing scripts. The workshop began with a general welcome, explanation of the workshop goals, and presentation of the research findings. Next, a large group discussion took place, which included student introductions, icebreakers, general reactions to the research findings, a presentation of theatrical methods, and preliminary brainstorming. Afterwards, the workshop participants were divided into smaller working groups, each of which was given an assigned theme from the research findings and asked to begin writing a script to illustrate the theme. These smaller working groups later re-convened as a large group for a progress check before returning to continue development of scripts. Participants then re-convened as a large group to present the final drafts of their scripts. Finally, the workshop concluded with completion of the written evaluations.

The outcome of the workshop was five scripts that cover each of the four thematic categories presented to the students at the beginning of the workshop. Some of the skits illustrate more than one theme, and all of them involve imagined yet plausible stories based on the research findings. In some instances, the students generated their ideas for the skits through a creative blending of the experiences of the research participants with their own experiences as domestic or international students.

Twelve students took part in the second workshop, which focused on performing and recording the skits that had been written in the first workshop. This workshop began with a general welcome and explanation of the workshop goals, followed by a large group discussion that included student introductions and ice breakers. Next, the workshop participants were divided into smaller groups, and each group was assigned one of the skits. In their groups, participants were asked to distribute the roles, prepare props, do a preliminary read through, and rehearse their skit. Following rehearsal, the five skits were video-recorded and information was prepared for the closing credits of the video. The workshop ended with the completion of the written evaluations.

All five skits developed at the first workshop were performed and recorded thus attaining the objective of producing recorded dramatizations of key research findings. As an example, one skit entitled 'Free Hugs' illustrated cultural differences through the reaction of some international students to a student offering hugs during orientation week. The skit depicts how some international students experienced surprise, confusion, uncertainty, and fear in response to this event that was seen by some as transgressing their own cultural boundaries between personal and public activity. The intent of the skit was not to judge the 'free hugs' event but to utilize the skit as a stimulus for discussion of cultural differences. Readers can view this skit at the following unlisted video link on YouTube: http://www.youtube.com/watch?v=QGoZZh9gXVM.

Project Evaluation

The workshops were evaluated using quantitative and qualitative measures. As detailed in Tables 1 and 2, workshop participants were satisfied with the organization and delivery of the workshops. Participants' mean satisfaction with aspects of the workshops ranged from 3.1 to 3.9 on a 4-point scale where 4 was defined as "very satisfied" and 1 was defined as "very dissatisfied."

In addition to questions about satisfaction, the workshop evaluation questionnaire asked: "Did participation in this workshop result in any changes in your thinking about domestic and international student interaction? If yes, please describe". Students did report changes in their thinking about domestic and international student experience and interaction. For example, one workshop participant wrote: "I did come to realize a lot more the alienation that many International students feel toward what Canadian students do at university. I have found now a lot more interest in the topic and will personally take more steps to welcome International students to our school." Another stated: "Yes, although I've interacted with International students, I've underestimated how isolating it can be for International students. I think I've learned to make a greater effort to meet more of these students." A third wrote: "I realize that I should be more understanding of international students and their predicaments and I should treat them like how I would like to be treated." These responses are consistent with benefits of theatre reported elsewhere. They illustrate that theatre can foster awareness and empathy leading to a commitment to action.

From the organizers' perspectives, factors that contributed to the success of the workshops included: having the workshops facilitated

Table 1: Writing Workshop Evaluation (14 participants)

4 point scale ranging from 1 (very dissatisfied) to 4 (very satisfied):	Average of Ratings
Overall organization	3.9
Overall scheduling and timing of workshop components	3.8
Explanation and instruction regarding goals for day and writing tasks	3.1
Presentation and discussion of findings	3.5
Presentation and discussion of theatrical methods	3.4
Small group writing time	3.6
Large group presentation and discussion of writing	3.4

Table 2: Acting Workshop Evaluation (12 participants)

4 point scale ranging from 1 (very dissatisfied) to 4 (very satisfied):	Average of Ratings
Overall organization	3.5
Overall scheduling and timing of workshop components	3.6
Explanation and instruction regarding goals for day and acting tasks	3.8
Presentation of scripts and discussion	3.7
Rehearsal time	3.8
Video recording of sketches	3.8

by a student with skill in both group facilitation and theatre, having the researchers available to present the research findings and be resource persons for the participants, and having international and domestic students participate together in writing and performing the skits. Workshop activities were structured and sequenced with an aim of fostering participant comfort and group cohesion before participants moved into smaller-sized groups for task completion. For example, beginning workshop activities included a general welcome, an explanation of the workshop goals and the provision of background information. This allowed participants time to observe and listen while the facilitator and researchers did most of the talking. These beginning activities were followed by large group discussion, introductions and icebreaker activities, which required greater group participation. Participants were then able to proceed to their smaller groups with knowledge of workshop expectations and some comfort in interacting with the other participants. Involving both international and domestic students in the workshops fostered dynamics and processes associated with social group work. For example, discussion and task completion benefited from a diversity of perspectives and mutual aid. In addition, students demonstrated cross-cultural empathy in their discussion of their experiences in relation to the skit storylines. They also experienced vicarious learning as they reflected upon how they might react in some of the situations depicted in the skits.

Discussion

In this final section, we discuss the project by focusing on some of the challenges we faced related to the tensions between authenticity and dramatization, maximizing trustworthiness, and impact on the audience. The literature on the use of theatre in research provides a number of suggestions for maintaining authenticity with the findings and maximizing the 'validity' or trustworthiness of the performances. These include: the script reflecting the research participants' multiple perspectives including similar and disconfirming positions (Saldaña, 1999); evidential support that links the performance's dialogue and actions back to the research findings in the same way written reports often include verbatim text (Sallis, 2010); the research participants' validation of research findings as well as of the scripts and performances (Butler-Kisber, 2010; Mienczakowski, 2006); a preview performance with an audience familiar with the research topic (Mienczakowski, Smith & Morgan, 2002); and avoiding sensationalizing (Butler-Kisber, 2010).

We chose the 'theatrical research-based performance' genre (Rossiter et al., 2008), which allowed the script writers considerable latitude in communicating the research findings without closely adhering to the research participants' transcript data. However, we did present four key themes from the research findings that we wanted communicated through theatre. The 'trustworthiness' of these themes had already been established in earlier phases of the research through such means as involving several members of the research team in analyzing the transcripts and conducting a focus group with university students to 'member check' the findings (Lincoln & Guba, 1985). So while the students had creative room to develop the scripts, they carried out this task within the parameters of key research findings. This is also similar to Saldaña's (2010) position that research performances are an "imaginative yet reality-based reconstruction of participants' concerns" (p. 65). Having international and domestic students write the skits also served as another means of member checking (Lincoln & Guba, 1985) as they developed scripts consistent with both the data and their own experiences as students. This also served to foster their control and empowerment with respect to the research process. Our approach was consistent with that of Ackroyd and O'Toole (2010) who state that "fictionalisation is not the same as a retreat from authenticity. It can enhance the truthfulness of the research as well as the experience of the audience" (p. 64). Fictionalization can also help preserve the confidentiality of the original research participants. This safeguard was important in this project, given that the theatrical skits were designed for use within the original research sites, in addition to being used elsewhere.

The literature also alerted us to the need to be concerned about the impact of our performances on prospective audiences. Mienczakowski (2006), for example, noted that "for some people and under some circumstances, exposure to theatre that seeks to redefine a person's relationship to a particular personal, health, or social topic may be loosely understood as entering the therapeutic realm" (p. 249). As such, the researcher using theatre to communicate findings needs to anticipate any potential harm to the audience (Mienczakowski et al., 2002). With our study, this concern was greatly alleviated through the development of skits that reflected scenarios commonly reported by international students, and that were presented with sensitivity and often humor (as illustrated by the YouTube "Free Hugs" skit). As another safeguard, the researchers primarily used the recorded skits as part of larger presentations of research findings and where there was opportunity to discuss the findings and context illustrated in the performances. The literature provides other suggestions for anticipating and responding to audience reaction including: preview performance with a knowledgeable audience in order to identify any difficult or distressing reactions, the use of program booklets with performances in order to provide members of the audience with additional information, and having experts on hand following performances for audience debriefing and discussion (Mienczakowski & Morgan, 2001).

Conclusion

Findings support the potential use of theatre workshops as an effective means of involving community members, including those vulnerable to social exclusion, in the research process, and as an impactful means of communicating research findings. Furthermore, participating in producing the skits can be personally transformative with potential to enhance empathy and cross-cultural understanding. Since these workshops, the recorded skits have been used in presenting the research findings to university stakeholders as well as in classroom instruction. Our hope is that any increase in audience empathy and awareness about the struggles international students face in attaining social inclusion will lead to personal and structural change. We hope that this account of our experience will encourage others to explore the use of theatre in enabling various groups to tell their stories with the goal of bringing about social change.

References

Ackroyd, J., & O'Toole, J. (2010). Performing research: Tensions, triumphs and trade-offs of ethnodrama. Staffordshire: Trentham Books.

Beck, J. L., Belliveau, G., Lea, G. W., & Wager, A. (2011). Delineating a spectrum of research-based theatre. *Qualitative Inquiry, 17,* 687-700.

Boal, A. (1985). *Theatre of the oppressed.* New York: Theatre Communications Group.

Butler-Kisber, L. (2010). Qualitative Inquiry: Thematic, narrative and arts-informed perspectives. Thousand Oaks: Sage.

Conrad, D., & Campbell, G. (2008). Participatory research—An empowering methodology with marginalized populations. In P. Liamputtong & J. Rumbold (Eds.), *Knowing differently: Arts-based and collaborative research methods* (pp. 247-263). New York: Nova Science Publishers.

Dennis, B. (2009). Acting up: Theater of the oppressed as critical ethnography. *International Journal of Qualitative Methods, 8,* 65-96.

Dunn, W., & Olivier, C. (2011). Creating welcoming and inclusive university communities. *Canadian Diversity, 8*(5), 35-38.

Leavy, P. (2009). *Method meets art: Arts-based research practice.* New York: The Guilford Press.

Lincoln, Y.S., & Guba, E.G. (1985). Naturalistic inquiry. Newbury Park, CA: Sage.

Mienczakowski, J. (2006). Ethnodrama: performed research—limitations and potential. In S. N. Hesse-Biber & P. Leavy (Eds.), *Emergent methods in social research* (pp. 235-252). Thousand Oaks, CA: Sage.

Mienczakowski, J., & Morgan, S. (2001). Ethnodrama: Constructing participatory, experiential, and compelling action research through performance. In P. Reason & H. Bradbury (Eds.), *Handbook of action research* (pp. 219-227). London: Sage.

Mienczakowski, J., Smith, L., & Morgan, S. (2002). Seeing words—hearing feelings: Ethnodrama and the performance of data. In C. Bagley & M. B. Cancienne (Eds.), *Dancing the data* (pp. 34-52). New York: Peter Lang.

Rossiter, K., Kontos, P., Colantonio, A., Gilbert, J., Gray, J., & Keightley, M. (2008). Staging data: Theatre as a tool for analysis and knowledge transfer in health research. *Social Science and Medicine, 66,* 130-146.

Saldaña, J. (2005). An introduction to ethnodrama. In J. Saldaña (Ed.), *Ethnodrama: An anthology of reality theatre* (p. 1-36). Walnut Creek, CA: AltaMiras.

Saldaña, J. (1999). Playwriting with data: Ethnographic performance texts. *Youth Theatre Journal, 13,* 60-71.

Saldaña, J. (2010). Writing ethnodrama: A sampler from educational research. In M. Savin-Baden & C. H. Major (Eds.), *New approaches to qualitative research: Wisdom and uncertainty* (pp. 61-69). New York: Routledge.

Sallis, R. (2010). Investigating masculinities in school. In J. Ackroyd & J. O'Toole (Eds.), *Performing research: Tensions, triumphs and trade-offs of ethnodrama* (pp. 187-202). Staffordshire: Trentham Books.

Thompson, N. (2011). *Promoting equality: Working with diversity and difference* (3rd ed.). New York: Palgrave Macmillan.

Participant Observation of an Online Task Group Process: A Narrative

Mamadou Seck

Introduction

This chapter describes the stages of development of a model of an online task group based on the Tuckman's (1965; Tuckman & Jensen, 1977) theory of group development. I identify each stage which task-groups undergo based on Tuckman's framework. Phenomena that occur at the forming, storming, norming, and performing stages are described as well as those taking place during the adjourning phase. The purpose of this descriptive theoretical paper is to raise group workers' awareness that fundamental group factors may emerge of at each specific stage, thereby enabling these practitioners to predict group members' behaviors, group phenomena, and outcomes. The model task group described in this chapter was developed in the context of an online Social Work course on diversity, racism, and discrimination, entitled "The Black Experience and Contemporary Society", listed as a general education course in the curriculum of a School of Social Work in a large research university located in the Northeast. Fourteen groups have been organized to complete the final assignment of the course. Each group was composed of six students who signed up to work on one specific topic among fourteen listed in the course syllabus. As a participant observer, I analyze students' interactions and communication processes, and their engagement in completing their tasks. Group processes such as formalization of an agreement as a group contract, leadership, roles completion, intra-group conflicts, and decision-making strategies are described.

Background

There is an extensive literature focusing on online courses and task groups (Gray & Smyth, 2012; Hodge, 2004; Hsu, Y., Ching, Y., Mathews, J.P., & Carr-Chellman, A., 2009; Jacinto & Hong, 2011). Meanwhile, none of the authors reported a study on task groups developed in an online course. The new trends in the implementation of online programs illustrate the popularity of online courses. This popularity is enhanced by their use in distance learning programs as a content delivery format. In effect, previous studies (Brown, 2012; Mason, Helton, & Dziegielewski, 2010) explored the reasons students choose web based courses, their performance levels in online courses, and their perceptions of online courses. Brown (2012) found that students choose web-based courses for various reasons. Among these reasons, the researcher pointed out (a) that students thought that distance learning course would be less difficult; (b) they lacked time to attend regular classes; (c) online courses could be combined with family responsibilities; and (d) they reduced travel time. In addition, students wanted to try a new method of learning which could be more advantageous to them. These findings were aligned with those reported by Hsu et al. (2009). These researchers noted that the online delivery format of distance learning provided advantages such as "breaking geographic barriers, saving time and transportation expense, and flexible scheduling" (p. 110). Aspirations to receive higher grades were cited as another reason that students pursued online courses. However, research comparing the performance of students attending web based and land based courses found that there was not much difference between the average grades of these two groups of students, and that the only difference found was related to the lower rate of retention in web based courses (Brown, 2012).

Despite the popularity of online courses, researchers (Mason et al., 2010) reported that students noted that there were disadvantages in taking online courses. These authors noted that research participants felt removed from instructors due to limited student-faculty interactions, rare opportunities to discuss personal issues with instructors, and low degree of personal relationship among students. In order to overcome these challenges as well as the occurrence of technical problems that occur during online courses, instructors should be ready to use alternative teaching methods, and students should prepare themselves to face those challenges by developing successful self-regulated learning styles (Hsu, et al. 2009; Rakap, 2010; Rogers & McNeil, 2009). Hsu et al. (2009) introduced the concept of self-regulated learning (SRL) in a thematic analysis examining students' learning styles. They found that students exerted a variety of SRL strategies with the facilitation of instructors, in order to plan activities, monitor progress, and sustain motivation. Other authors reported correlation between students' learning styles and performance. Rogers and McNeil (2009) found that there was a significant difference in student performance across the four learning styles they determined based on four combinations of the eight traits from Myers Brigg Types Indicators (MBTI). Further, Rakap (2010) found that students' learning styles/preferences had significant effects on the performance of adult students whose success in online courses was correlated with computer skills and the management of online tools, which Singh, Mangalaraj and Taneja (2012) studied. These researchers reported that instructors' mastery of online tools and technologies greatly enhanced student learning experience. Specifically, they found that resources like course collaboration tools, interactive communication tools, and assessment and learning tools were the most effective functionalities in the dissemination of course content in various forms, and improving collaboration between students, groups, and instructors. In the present course, these tools contributed to the completion of specific tasks required to complete a collective paper that each group should submit as the outcome of their group process.

Previous literature reported the use of task groups in community change (Chupp, 2009) and in social work education (Cohen, 2011; Seck, 2010). In fact, Chupp (2009) noted that "today, neighborhoods and communities continue to organize themselves through task groups" (p. 270). He further reported the prevalence of the task group approach to community change and emphasized that the social action mode relied extensively on task groups to affect change. In another study on the use of task groups to teach group process and development, Cohen (2011) noted that a task group assignment was used in conjunction with didactic and other experiential teaching methods, primarily role-plays and vignettes, to provide students with learning about group work across the practice continuum, from therapy groups to task groups. Cohen reported that after completing the assignment, students increased their knowledge of diverse group approaches, experienced, identified, and applied group work concepts to their small-group experiences. Cohen's conclusions were aligned with those reported by Seck (2010) who noted the extent to which students, who completed a generic group work course focusing on task completion, enhanced their practical knowledge of group concepts and group processes as they implemented community development activities. Using experiential learning methods, participants applied group concepts and processes to showcase their level of understanding of the course content. One of the findings Seck (2010) reported was the interest most students expressed regarding Tuckman's fourth stage of group development during which their brainstorming sessions took place. They noted that these sessions allowed them to enhance their understanding of group concepts. This finding revealed that students had a good knowledge of proponents of theories that focused specifically on stages of group development. Tuckman's theory was used to identify the different stages through which this online task group evolved.

The Context in Which this Online Task Group Evolved

The purpose of designing this model task group was to organize students so they would complete a collective paper as a final assignment of a 100 level Social Work course that aimed at introducing undergraduate students to the concepts of diversity, cultural competency, and sensitivity through the understanding of race relations. This assignment was to provide them with the opportunity to engage and collaborate with other classmates using Blackboard tools such as "course collaboration", "assessment tools", and "group tools" that included group emails, discussion board, file exchange, and group tasks. Each of these tools contributed to the development of this model of online task group. As the course instructor, I gained the status of participant observer by registering in each group as a member. This membership enabled me to participate in most verbal and written communication within the groups, and to play an active role that contributed to my understanding of the members' behaviors from my group work practitioner's frame of reference. As a participant observer, I deemed that using a phenomenological approach would more likely reflect my intent to narrate the different ways I experienced these students' interactions as they happened, and only then, express my personal feelings about them. In effect, Stenfors-Hayes, Hult, and

Dahlgren (2013) suggested that "the result of a phenomenological analysis is the description of the essence of the lived experience of a given phenomenon" (p. 262). I need to stress that, at times, I chose to withdraw from the picture and distance myself from the discussions. My objectives were to allow students to fully express themselves but also to enable myself to assess the group process and predict events that could occur later.

Distance learning and web-based courses have become buzzwords in the academic environment. Colleges and universities have been investing more and more efforts in the area of information services and technology (IST) as their retention and graduation rates constantly drop. In addition, they spend more financial and human resources in order to meet faculty and students' needs, and to diversify their IST equipment. The complexity of the various techniques colleges and universities develop reflects the high number of strategies used to meet the expectations of all stakeholders involved in the educational system. Distance learning programs are comprised of course management systems such as Springboard and Blackboard which support traditional "brick and mortar" classes, hybrid classes that combine in-person and web courses, and distance learning web-based classes (Mason et al., 2010). In this third model limited to online courses only, students and instructors are not required to meet face to face but may do so when students seek a more direct personal contact with the instructor. Activities described in this chapter took place during an online class. Students were organized in task groups in order to complete collective papers at the end of the semester. This model of task group is a close-ended group with a limited lifetime, which coincides with a college semester. Task groups have been discussed in the literature but specific references to task groups developed in online courses are limited. Therefore, describing the context of the activities may provide a better picture of this group.

The Stages of Development of this Model of Online Task Group: What I Learned

In this section, I identify the stages which this course-based task-group underwent. In addition, I will describe the phenomena that occurred at each phase, and highlight the determining factors that led to a positive outcome for the groups. A number of theories of group development have been discussed extensively in the literature (Bales & Strodtbeck, 1950; Balgopal & Vassil, 1983; Garland, Jones, & Kolodny, 1965; Hartford, 1972; Northen, 1969; Sarri & Galinsky, 1967). Previous literature documented Tuckman's (1965; Tuckman & Jensen, 1977) contribution to the debate on group process and content as he provided the framework for this description. In effect, Tuckman (1965) first identified four stages of group development: the forming, storming, norming, and performing stages based on the models of groups he studied. Additional research on stages of group development led Tuckman and Jensen (1977) to include a fifth phase they titled "adjourning." As group workers, we are aware of Garland et al.'s (1965) reflection that earlier stages may appear at later points in time. Some of us may also remember Northen's (1969) observation that progress is made unevenly with steps forward and backward and then ahead to a new level of consolidation and gains. However, despite the wisdom expressed by these group work scholars, I present the stages of development of this online course-based task group in a linear manner to better clearly describe and illuminate the phenomena and activities occurring during each stage.

Forming: Setting Up a Group Contract

The group started when students signed up to be member of a group after selecting the topic on which they wanted to work. As indicated above, fourteen topics were listed on the syllabus, and each topic number corresponded to that of a group. As soon as a group size of six was reached no new members were admitted. Blackboard enabled students to send emails to each other and post their ideas on their group discussion board. The group could decide to include as many sections they thought the paper should include and make their own choice regarding responsibilities and task assignment. This written agreement or group contract was then sent to me as the course instructor for feedback. I would then look at each member's responsibility on completing the paper. I also check the subtitle of each section of the paper to make suggestions aimed at deterring overlapping responsibilities and repetitions.

At this stage, I mainly learned that leadership had started to emerge and members initiated self-orientation as they identified and tested their boundaries. Interactions were initiated, and bonding relationships started as students exchanged personal phone numbers and email addresses. The principle of democratic group functioning facilitated the decision making process as members selected their own tasks and roles were determined. I learned also that conflict started to occur, leading some members to express their intent to leave the group. The main reasons invoked were the lack of communication as some members did not respond in a timely manner to emails and did not post their contribution on the discussion board. The lack of communication raised the anxiety level in the group as the deadline for submission of the contract approached. Some other students delayed registering in a group prompting me to send them a reminder.

Storming: Boundary Setting and Conflicts

Student group members became more aware of the important dates set as deadlines for completing their drafts. Members started to know each other better, and see patterns of missing appointments or delayed actions that exacerbated intra group conflicts. For example, as some members began missing deadlines set by the group or by the instructor, other members started to send out emails to me or the group to report their frustration or emotional responses about the process as a reaction to these behaviors. Deadlines for turning in sections of the paper or for completing important tasks were missed. This behavior raised some members' level of frustration, and the group atmosphere became tense. This negative feeling was exacerbated when concerned members noticed that a few group mates were not responding to their emails that were sent to address these specific group problems. Therefore, due to frustration, intragroup conflicts were exacerbated and could be noted in the communication process. For example, members clashed with one another regarding late responses to emails, or not attending group meetings. Reactions of defensiveness, resistance and hostility could be observed.

During this "storming" stage, the instructor's perspicacity in predicting events was tested as the level of tension rose requiring an immediate intervention to prevent any incident and to address major differences. Awareness of members' motivation to attend this course was important since many students were required to take this course although they were not majoring in social work. Therefore, many students resented being part of the group. Consequently, they asked the instructor if they could move to another group, or write the paper as a single author. Meanwhile, once the contract was done, many of them began immediately to address issues involved with writing the paper. This was the period where the instructor had to make some adjustments in order to facilitate the communication process. Phenomena occurring in this stage illustrated Tuckman's suggestion that group processes were cyclical, not linear although some critics noted that the model he developed had overlapping stages.

Norming: Rule Setting and Reinforcement

Members' feelings toward the group functioning and other members' procrastination developed positively in some groups but negatively in other ones. In effect, many students voiced their frustration due to their colleagues' lack of communication and late responses to emails regarding scheduling meetings or sending input for the paper content. In other groups satisfactory communication processes contributed to complete tasks related to contract completion and timely submission. A group became more cohesive as members' roles and tasks became more precise and clearly defined, thereby avoiding any confusion. Members became more sensitive to each other's concerns as they would reach out to another one who expressed his or her struggles in completing specific tasks. Group cohesion was reinforced with clearly defined rules. My role was to remind students that existing as well as new rules were agreed upon to address unsettled questions and avoid task conflicts that still could occur. At this point, group cohesion could build up as groups tended to become an entity that members wanted to maintain. Students looked for consensus in their decision-making. Their awareness of the rules enabled them to overcome some of their differences. They were able to devise a number of methods for ensuring effective face-to-face interactions and collaboration. In fact, some group members found out that they all were coming to school to attend other courses on the same days and at the same time period. Therefore, they agreed to meet on campus to discuss the content of their paper, tasks and responsibilities, and set deadlines for completing their sections. Leadership of the groups was discussed and one member was assigned the responsibility to coordinate members' contributions.

These defined roles, interpersonal relationships, interactions, as well as group rules contributed to the development of the group structure.

Performing: Group Functioning and Task Completion

Most groups became functional as members got to know each other and succeeded in forging strong relationships around their responsibilities. Although the course was exclusively online, some groups deemed that their decision making process would be more effective if they met face to face on campus or at a more convenient place. Consequently, meetings were scheduled on campus, either in the university library or in some restaurants around campus. More verbal and written communication took place between meetings enhancing collaboration. Sections of the paper were completed and submitted to the group leaders so they could put together a draft of the document. Members shared responsibility for the final product by reviewing group mates' sections but also the final draft of the paper, its reference list, and formatting requirements. My main learning was that in most groups, members reached a high level of intimacy and maturity as demonstrated in the emails but more specifically on the peer rating forms. For example, a student responding to a groupmate wrote, "I agree with what you are saying. I think a group effort intro/concl [*sic*] paragraphs would be best because it will keep one person from making false conclusion regarding another's topic and saying partially false conclusions." Another student noted, "Does anyone want to volunteer to complete the introduction and/or conclusion of the research paper…I feel it is appropriate for us to work as a group." In fact, students knew that after completing their tasks, they would evaluate each one of their group members on a number of areas including their willingness to work in a group environment, consideration for other group members, and ability to consider minority viewpoints. So in order to be able to complete the form, they needed to enhance their level of intimacy and maturity. Most groups that completed a well-structured contract and maintained effective communication strategies were able to submit their work ahead of the deadline. The other groups, which struggled in setting up a contract and communicating, experienced more tension and conflicts but were able to meet the submission deadline.

Adjourning: Group Outcome and Termination

The adjourning phase (Tuckman & Jensen, 1977) was the last stage, when all groups were expected to have completed their collective paper and submitted it as an email attachment to me for grading. At this point, students also had to submit their peer review form to me after assessing their group mates in a number of areas. For example, they assessed each member on the leadership they provided to the group, reliability in completing the assigned tasks, and the amount of efforts put forth. In addition, each evaluator was asked if they would want to work with the evaluated classmate again in the future. The students' peer evaluation forms were kept confidential. No student was to communicate group mates' scores. All these assessment activities took place before a final grade was assigned to each student and sent to the registrar. At this stage, I was convinced that students were reluctant to evaluate themselves. In effect, despite specific instructions regarding evaluating their individual and personal contribution, and although there was a column explicitly prepared for them to meet that requirement, many students "forgot" (or refrained) to assign a grade to themselves. Although I was convinced that some of those students effectively forgot to grade themselves, I also was convinced that many of them were aware that I knew how they performed in the group and consequently did not want to write on the form a grade that would not reflect their performance in the group. In fact, some of them were prompt in correcting their error by sending a complete form before the deadline when the other ones did not do anything to meet that expectation despite being notified that they had to entirely fill the peer rating form.

Remarks on Next Step

My goals moving forward are to conduct an empirical study on this specific model of an online task group, employing the Tuckman (1965; Tuckman & Jensen, 1977) model's conceptual framework and assumptions to guide the inquiry. Constructs which will be central to future investigation entail the model's predictive power with regard to membership, emerging leadership, solidarity, relationships, making suggestions, giving and asking for opinions, and also showing antagonism. The aim of this proposed study will be to provide a strong empirical foundation on teaching and training strategies through online courses to educators in general and more specifically to social work instructors, field practice supervisors, and students.

References

Bales, R.F., & Strodtbeck, F. L. (1951). Phases in group problem-solving. *Journal of Abnormal and Social Psychology*, 46(4), 485-495.

Balgopal, P. R., & Vassil, T. V. (1983). *Groups in Social Work: An Ecological Perspective*. New York, Macmillan Publishing Co., Inc

Brown, J.L.M. (2012). Online Learning: A Comparison of Web-Based and Land-Based Courses. *The Quarterly Review of Distance Education*, 13(1), 39-42.

Chupp, M. (2009). Community Change. In A. Gitterman & R. Salmon (Eds.), *Encyclopedia of social work with groups* (p. 269-272). New York, NY: Routledge.

Cohen, M. B. (2011). Using Student Task Group to Teach Group Process and Development. *Social Work With Groups*, 34(1), 51-60.

Garland, J. E.,, Jones, H. E., & Kolodny, R. L. (1965). A model for stages of development in social work with groups. In S. B. Berstein, ed., Explorations *in Group Work*. Boston: Charles River.

Gray, C. & Smyth, K. (2012). Collaboration Creation: Lessons Learned From Establishing an Online Professional Learning Community. *The Electronic Journal of e-Learning*, 10 (1), 60-75

Hartford, M.E. (1972). *Groups in social work: Application of small group theory and research to social work practice*. New York: Columbia University Press.

Hodge, D. M. (2004). Creating a Virtual Community of Learners Using WebCT: Lessons Learned. *Journal of Technology in Human Services*, 22(3), 69-78

Hsu, Y., Ching, Y., Mathews, J.P., & Carr-Chellman, A. (2009). Undergraduate Students' Self-Regulated Learning Experience in Web-Based Learning Environment. The Quarterly Review of Distance Education, 10(2), 109-121.

Jacinto, G. A. & Hong, Y. J. (2011). Online Task Groups and Social Work Education: Lessons Learned. *Contemporary Rural Social Work*, 3, 17-28

Mason, J. A., Helton, L. R., & Dziegielewski, S. (2010). Psychosocial Environmental Relationships Among MSW Students in Distance Learning and Traditional Classrooms. *Journal of Social Service Research*, 36, pp. 230-247.

Northen, H. (1969). *Social work with groups.* New York: Columbia University Press.

Rakap, S. (2010). Impacts of Learning Styles and Computer Skills on Adult Students' Learning Online. *The Turkish Online Journal of Educational Technology*, 9(2), 108-115.

Rogers, P. R., & McNeil, K. (2009). Student Learning Styles and Online Course Performance: An Empirical Examination of Student Success in Web-Based Management Courses. *Business Education Digest* XVIII, p.1-15.

Sarri, R. C., & Galinsky, M. J. (1967). A conceptual framework for group development. In R. D. Viner, ed., *Readings in group work practice. Ann Arbor, MI: Campus.*

Seck, M. M. (2010). Evaluating Experiential Learning of Group Practice: Engaging Social Work Students in Community Development Activities in Senegal. *Intervention*, 133 (2), 21-30.

Singh, A., Mangalaraj, G., & Taneja, A. (2012). Bolstering Teaching through Online Tools. Journal of Information Systems Education, 21(3).

Stenfors-Hays, T., Hult, H. & Dahlgren, M. A. (2013). A phenomenographic approach to research in medical education. *Medical Education*, 47, 261-270

Tuckman, B. W. (1965). Developmental sequences in small groups. *Psychological Bulletin.* 63 (6) 384-399.

Tuckman, B. W., & Jensen, M. A. C. (1977). Stages of Small-Group Development Revisited. *Group & Organizational Studies*, 2(4), 419-427.

Integration of Strengths and Empowerment into Group Work Practice

Thelma Silver, Charlla Allen, Linda McArdle

Introduction

This chapter defines and integrates the concepts of strengths (Saleebey, 1997) and empowerment (Anderson, 1997) with mutual aid groups (Shulman, 1999). Moreover, concepts of diversity and multiculturalism (Anderson) are also added to this model. A case example is given of the application of this model in an assessment of a youth for groupwork intervention, and then suggestions are given for implementation of this model into groupwork practice, in general.

Since the early days of our heritage in groupwork, social workers have emphasized the empowerment and the strengths of the client systems with whom we work. Today, in much of social work practice there is emphasis on the Strengths Perspective (Saleebey, 1997; 2009). Some authors in their work about groupwork have focused on concepts that can be integrated with the Strengths Perspective (Saleebey), particularly Anderson (1997), with his attention to empowerment in groups, and Shulman (1999) with his attention to strengths in mutual aid groups.

We also need to recognize the increasing diverse nature of our client systems demands that we work within a multicultural perspective. A Strengths Perspective can support a multicultural diversity framework (Appleby, Colon, & Hamilton, 2010). Effective practitioners can act on the social work commitment to respect human diversity by placing all clients in groups in their own cultural context and then drawing on a Strengths Perspective (Saleebey, 2009). Thus, we need to be sensitive and mindful of people's differences regarding culture, meaning race, ethnicity, age, gender, social class, etc., and accept their unique strengths. This assumes that all clients possess untapped reservoirs of mental, physical and emotional resources that help them develop, grow and overcome their problems (Appleby et al., 2010), while contributing as well to the group process.

This discussion will focus on the integration of concepts in the three models of the Strengths Perspective (Saleebey, 1997; 2009), empowerment (Anderson, 1997), and mutual aid (Shulman, 1999). Attention will also be given to the factors of multiculturalism and diversity in regard to empowerment and groupwork (Anderson). Following this, this chapter will then center on the utilization of concepts of strengths (Saleebey), empowerment, and diversity (Anderson, 1997) into an assessment of a youth for group intervention. The final section of this paper will focus on the implementation of these concepts into groupwork practice. By connecting concepts of mutual aid (Shulman), the Strengths Perspective (Saleebey), and diversity and empowerment (Anderson), we are making vertical connections linking different theories of social work that are closely connected (Steinberg, 2002). These theories were developed separately, but the concepts are related and build on one another.

Background

Concepts of the Strengths Perspective and Mutual Aid

One of the principles of the Strengths Perspective is that every individual and group has strengths; each person possesses knowledge, wisdom and assets that can be used as a resource to assist them in reaching their goals (Saleebey, 1997). In groupwork, there is also the belief that everyone has strengths that can be accessed to help reach these goals (Steinberg, 2002).

Saleebey (1997) discusses the concept of resilience, which is the state of people rebounding from adversity. Thus, resilience is connected to potential for change. There is the belief that people can grow when they meet the challenges of their lives in positive ways. In groupwork, the camaraderie of the group can lead to resilience. When people in the group care about what happens to each other, or when people are able to share experiences with each other, this can lead to growth in the group members (Goldstein, 1997).

Group members are familiar with the ways in which groups can help members cope with loss as illustrated in a support group of parents who had lost children. For example, when one parent shared the beginning steps of socializing again with friends, or when every member laughed at a funny memory that was shared by the parents, this led to a strong sense of being understood and connected to the other group members. In turn, this helped those experiencing deep loss in their process of rebounding from adversity. The sharing of experiences demonstrated resilience of those who had the socialization or the memory, but also contributed to the resilience of the other group members in moving forward in their recovery process. When one parent shares the beginning steps of socializing again with friends, or when every member laughs at a funny memory of a deceased child that was shared by his parents, this can lead to resilience.

Another concept outlined by Saleebey (1997) is dialogue. According to Saleebey:

> Humans can only come into being through a creative and emergent relationship with others. Without such transactions, there can be no discovery and testing of one's powers, no knowledge, no heightening of one's awareness and internal strengths. In dialogue, we confirm the importance of others and begin to heal the rifts between self, others, and institution (p. 10).

Thus, dialogue requires that one empathizes with, identifies with, and includes others (Saleebey, 1997). This concept of dialogue is central to groupwork and mutual aid as the very nature of groupwork requires that each person be present, make his/her individual contribution and demonstrate appreciation of others. This is an interpersonal and active process of helping others, and being helped (Steinberg, 2002; Shulman, 1999). Thus, the Strengths Perspective (Saleebey) assumes that a relationship with others affects change, and mutual aid also requires a relationship with others (Steinberg).

In a support group for widows, dialogue (Saleebey, 1997) and mutual aid (Steinberg, 2002) are present as one member shares the discomfort she feels in informal social settings and another group member empathizes with her, but also states ways that she has begun to socialize again.

In the Strengths Perspective, Saleebey (1997) discusses the concept of collaboration or partnership where the relationship of the social worker to the client is one of working together. The social worker needs to be open to the views and dreams of clients by respecting, caring about, listening to, and believing in clients. In the mutual aid process in groups, working relationships are created by the worker and group members, and among group members (Steinberg, 2002). In groupwork, the social worker respects the members and believes in the client's ability for growth-oriented change, and also believes in the client's power to help him or herself (Weick & Chamberlain, 2002), with the worker as facilitator of this process. For example, in a group of family members of persons with mental illness, when one member asked about the court probate process, the other family members shared their experiences while the groupworker encouraged this exchange. Thus, we see members helping each other and sharing data, and the worker facilitating this exchange; we see the partnership in action.

Saleebey (1997) also introduces the concept of suspension of disbelief, where as workers we honor clients' perceptions and perspectives even if these differ from ours. In social groupwork, there is the belief that the only limits to possibilities of change are lack of imagination or understanding (Steinberg, 2002). Thus, in a support group of persons with serious mental illness, when one group member said that he aspired to work in a mental health agency, the group members and groupworker helped him look at ways to accomplish this dream. The concept of membership is also introduced by Saleebey (1997). This relates to a sense of belonging or people's need to feel they are members of the community. In groups, the process of engaging in mutual aid also lends to the sense of belonging. There is the "all in the same boat" experience (Shulman, 1999). Empowerment is another key element of the Strengths Perspective, which involves the process of helping people to gain control over their lives (Saleebey, 1997). Empowerment entails both the social worker encouraging the clients to engage in social action and helping those who have been oppressed to access their strengths and resources. In a support group for families of persons with mental illness, when family members were concerned about the lack of coordination of mental health services, the social worker helped them engage in social action. The group members were encouraged to bring their concerns to the local mental health board for improved case management services. This support helped empower the group to undertake this action. This concept of empowerment will be further addressed below.

Saleebey (1997) notes that in the Strengths Perspective, problems become the focus of the work with clients when problems become obstacles to reaching clients' goals. In groupwork, one type of obstacle to reaching clients' goals has been identified as taboo subjects that are often avoided in groups (Shulman, 2002). These taboo subjects include race, sex, sexual orientation, disability or angry feelings, to name a few. To accomplish the goals of the group, these taboo subjects need to be addressed. For example, in a support group for young widows, the subjects of grief and death were readily discussed. However, the group members avoided the issue of their own mortality evoked by a group member who had been seriously injured in the car crash that killed her husband. Because this group became comfortable discussing the taboo subject of death, as the members proceeded with the group they were able to derive strength from each other and address issues of their own mortality.

If we believe in the strengths of the group and its members, then we realize that we can confront problems or taboo subjects together. Shulman suggests that as the worker and group members confront these obstacles, they continue to grow and gain in strength. Therefore, the pillars of the Strengths Perspective such as resilience, dialogue, collaboration, suspension of disbelief, membership, and empowerment (Saleebey, 1997) are integral to and intensify the mutual aid process in groups (Shulman, 1999).

Implementing strengths and empowerment in groups

In mutual aid groups, the Strengths Perspective (Saleebey, 1997) is related to the belief in the fundamental possibility of change through the use of the resources within the group. In groupwork, members report that they are able to express a variety of feelings that they have not been able to with family and friends. Being able to "talk about it" and apply the resources from the group experience is linked to a sense of trust and cohesion with group members. This reflects the development of skills related to the individual's ability to cope in new ways rather than trying to control the situation (Anderson, 1997). This becomes a dramatic representation of the group's ability to identify and further develop self-determination and resiliency inherent within each individual.

As the social groupworker implements the mutual aid approach (Shulman, 1999), this should include the promotion of individual self-determination. When members take control of their lives, they become able to develop new affirmations about their "problematic life situations" leading to a new sense of empowerment. The role of the group leader should be to develop members' new perceptions regarding their experiences. The facilitator should provide member activities that will enhance strength identification within the group setting. The focus of these strength-based activities should be to promote a strong sense of self based on the group's input. This ultimately allows members to embrace a self-image that reflects the newly internalized strong and competent self. Empowerment, as a tool during the group process, can be viewed as an individual's ability to increase power over their personal and interpersonal situations. Throughout the group process, members are encouraged to "take action" and "control" over their lives and problem situations. Members recognize that they share power through engagement in the mutual aid process. Empowerment assumes that individual self-determination is an inherent component of the human condition (Gutierrez, 1990). The development of personal empowerment as a result of the group process should focus on the "psychological outcome of increasing self-efficacy and competence" (Anderson, 1997) that becomes translatable to everyday life. In the case example below, the youth can utilize the resources of the group to gain a sense of identity and personal empowerment.

The goal of the group process should be to reduce personal alienation and associated powerlessness. Strength-based techniques typically instill a sense of power and control in members who have been unable to achieve desired goals through their own efforts. Self-determination encourages "client centered" decision-making and identifies that the solution to the client's problem situation lies within the individual group members and not the group leader (Corey, 2008). Utilizing this approach allows members to "tap into" and identify the fact that they possess their own resiliency. Drawing on their personal resources during the group process allows them to recognize and build coping skills based on their identified strengths. As discussed in the case example above, the youth has a lot of strengths, and the group can help her acknowledge the strengths.

Leadership skills in the development of resiliency in the group setting requires that social workers locate the strengths and resources of clients to remind them of the personal assets and social capabilities that they possess. Leadership skills also involve assisting clients in recognizing these assets as a powerful means to achieve goals they have developed throughout the group process. The process of empowerment assists clients in recognizing their personal power in applying the new skills they have developed as a result of the mutual aid process (Borst, 2010).

During the intervention phase of the group process, strength-based leadership techniques involve engaging the group members to employ efforts leading to individual change. This can be achieved through member-to-member interactions structured to facilitate communication to enhance self-esteem building. This allows the group to develop positive perceptions of personal worth. In addition, the development of member support and concern lead to helping relationships within the group that lead to constructive lives outside of the group.

The group leader has to focus on moving between both the individual needs and the group needs through the group process. This is especially noted in the differentiation and interdependence stage of the group process (Anderson, 1997). Members often have both independent and interdependent needs, and to encourage cohesion in the group, the leader has to keep the group in the here and now process. During this stage of the group, the mutual aid process develops a conscious recognition of the resources needed to achieve individual and group goals. This is achieved through open communication and sharing as a result of leader facilitation of open feedback. Member differences become accepted and used as a resource in achieving individual empowerment and improved self-esteem for the members. Interdependence on the group members continues until individual and group goals are achieved and the group terminates.

The next phase of the intervention process should include techniques that develop goal development and planned change. The identification of "action strategies" should involve utilizing the members' existing strengths and resources to facilitate change. Leadership skills revolve around facilitation of group goals that achieve an individual's improved sense of self-worth (Anderson, 1997). Self-determination can become a function of activities designed to facilitate group goals that achieve an individual's sense of self-worth. Incorporating activities that focus on goals that improve member self-determination may be achieved through understanding and altering long existing self-concepts, attitudes and behaviors (Anderson, 1997).

Strengths, Diversity and Groupwork

Applying the strengths perspective to multicultural diversity when working with groups is a process of acknowledging that each individual is (1) like no other in uniqueness; (2) like some others in cultural and other contexts; and (3) like all others in human spirit and potential (Anderson & Carter, 2003). Acknowledging diverse strengths in group practice requires an ability to discover the unique resources of each individual, opportunities in the cultural context, and motivations and capacities for growth and change in human nature (Anderson & Carter, 2003). The focus is on how the practitioner can use this perspective in preparation for group practice, especially in assessing prospective members' needs and expectations, in preparing members for the therapeutic culture that evolves in social work practice through the group process, and when composing groups with sensitivity to significant issues of diversity (Chau, 1992).

Members of social and cultural groups who have survived a history of marginalization and oppression often demonstrate evidence of special adaptive strengths (Anderson & Carter, 2003). These strengths generally evolve from three sources: (1) personal transformation qualities as a result of overcoming self-depreciating forces (Chestang, 1982); (2) family and community structures that develop self-esteem and provide a network of psychosocial and economic resources (Billingsley, 1992); and (3) survival determination and skills (Hopps, Pinderhughes, & Shankar, 1995).

Marginalization results from a cultural perspective that views the center of power, strengths and superiority as belonging to those who are of European descent, middle-class, heterosexual, able-bodied, mentally healthy, church-going Christians and describes any differences as "less-than" deviance (Van Voorhis, 1998). This view is historically embedded in our North American structural arrangements that benefit those privileged by birth through ascribed social status and systematically excludes those who differ from this central norm through discrimination and oppression (Anderson & Carter, 2003). This elite privileged group need not represent a numerical majority; however, it maintains control through institutional and economic power (Pharr, 1988). When viewed from this dominant center of political, economic, and social power that controls resources, and influences cultural linguistic dominance in a social structure, those not in this group are identified on the margin, lacking in power and resources (hooks, 1984; May & Sletter, 2010; Pedwell, 2012).

Forming an identity as a member of a marginalized group in such oppressive conditions can deter members from claiming and being proud of their differences (Collins, 1991; Gould, 1987; hooks, 1983). Such negative identity and self-image can lead to the denial of one's own perceptions, experiences, strengths, power, and opportunities in relationships with those at the center (Van Voorhis, 1998). Thus, social work practice requires (1) critical consciousness raising regarding oppression (Freire, 1970); (2) the affirmation of strengths; and (3) empowerment approaches (Anderson & Carter, 2003). These components are most central to multicultural competency to develop and deliver services to individuals and groups who have been marginalized because of the difference from the "center" in regard to color, ethnicity, gender, class, sexual orientation, disability, age, religious affiliation or some combination thereof (Anderson & Carter, 2003).

Traditionally, multicultural competence and diversity have been defined primarily from a racial and ethnic perspective (Mackelprang, 2011). However, this conceptualization is being challenged as myopic and incomplete (Colligan, 2004; Mackelprang & Salsgiver, 2009; McRuer, 2006). Cultural competence and diversity concerns must address more than race; it must address multiple social identities and their unique intersection for each individual, organization, and society (Ridley, Baker, & Hill, 2001). Hence, the inclusion of disability has been a major recent leap in conceptualizing diversity (Mackelprang, 2011)

Disability culture has arisen from identity-based communities (Longres, 2000). Surviving and resisting oppression and marginalization have created a foundation for a culture for persons with disabilities (Mackelprang, 2011). As Fine and Asch (1993) contend, minority group status resulting from shared experiences within the larger society provide persons with disabilities common identity and shared interest. Consequently, people who identify as persons with disabilities and embrace disability have recognized the importance of moving the agenda of independence and equality forward through the political process (Mackelprang & Salsgiver, 2008). Persons with disabilities and their allies have become active in developing political agendas and establishing policies that recognize disability culture, and educating both persons with and without disabilities about disability culture, resulting in advocacy and resistance to mainstream disability views (Riddell & Watson, 2003). The resilience of persons with disabilities is manifest in the art, music, literature, and other expressions of their lives and culture, drawn from their personal experiences (Brown, 1996).

Cultural competent practice entails multiple identities and intersection of these identities within society (Ridley et al., 2001). People's attitudes about life and person identity for a multicultural diversified society are strong determinates of individual and group values (Lum, 2011). These values provide commonality of understanding and perceiving the world (Anderson & Carter, 2003).

In our practice with groups, initial and ongoing assessments of prospective members' needs and goals benefit from our understanding of the nature of particular members' group identities. We need to develop ways to "tune in" to what others tell us indirectly and directly about their identifications with cultural influences and to reach for more communication of cues, letting prospective members define their group-based identities for us (Anderson, 1997).

The following case example provides an illustration of the integration of the concepts of strengths, empowerment, mutual aid and multicultural practice. The case study is an assessment of a youth who is struggling with her identity. In assessing this prospective member's needs and goals, we also have to attend to factors of culture and diversity.

Case study: Marion

Marion is an African-American female who is a sophomore in a college preparatory program at an urban parochial high school. She entered this school from one of the poorest performing parochial grammar schools in the city, where she had been a star student. Adjusting to the college preparatory curriculum at the new school has been difficult for Marion and she is no longer considered to be scholarly advanced. She has been referred to the social worker due to behaviors her teachers reported as disrespectful. The social worker has been told that Marion is in danger of expulsion, although she had not exhibited problematic behavior in her grammar school, or during her freshmen academic year. Marion's mother has been incarcerated for drug-related charges for almost a year, and Marion lives with her maternal grandmother and five- year-old sister. Her father is no longer in the picture, although Marion remembers him fondly. He left the family after the birth of her little sister who has profound developmental disabilities. Marion was 12 years old when her father left the home.

Marion's grandmother is a widow from Jamaica who works as a nurse at a local hospital. Her apartment is well kept and furnished. The grandmother is overwhelmed by the demands of taking care of her two grandchildren, particularly attending to the needs of her special needs granddaughter, and working full-time. Up to now she has not worried about Marion who seemed to be a "model child" in grammar school. From the age of 13, Marion often became easily annoyed with others, while displaying an unwillingness to accept responsibility for her behavior. Marion, while resentful of the attention her little sister requires, has been helpful with her sister's care. The grandmother is now angry with Marion for causing trouble at school and fearful that she will follow in the steps of neighborhood youth whom she describes as unmotivated, and who exhibit bullying behaviors, which are reportedly violent. The grandmother is extremely worried about these influences. She is overburdened and believes the only way to protect Marion is to contact child welfare officials to place Marion in a foster home in order to escape the dangers of the neighborhood.

Recommended initial intervention

Based on the assessment of Marion and her family, it was recommended that Marion attend an intensive after-school group. Marion will work with the social worker who conducted the assessment and is the facilitator of the group. Marion will work with the school social worker and attend an intensive after school group. The purpose of the group is to help adolescents develop social skills, increase academic study skills and habits, and identify feelings/emotions, discussing how this has previously contributed to their choices and behaviors, and how to improve upon these skills (Adapted from Appleby et al., 2010). Facilitation of the group will utilize a multicultural practice approach, with a focus on each individual's diversity, identifying each group member's strengths, by exploring what has been their experience of positive ways of coping, and the strategies taken to achieve previous goals. Group members will explore and identify feelings of empowerment and self-actualization. The group process of sharing experiences on similar and common problems will develop an alliance between the group members, enhancing mutual aid and support from one another. This process demonstrates how group members are unique yet have commonalities in human needs and in possessing a human spirit. Thus, in the case study we can see the importance of assessing strengths (Saleebey, 1997), while acknowledging empowerment and diversity (Anderson, 1997). These factors then become integrated with the groupwork intervention of mutual aid (Shulman, 1999).

Conclusion

This chapter presents the three models, including the Strengths Perspective (Saleebey, 1997), empowerment (Anderson, 1997), and mutual aid (Shulman, 1999), which have been defined and integrated into groupwork. Concepts of diversity-based groupwork were also added to this model, and a case example was presented of an assessment of a youth for groupwork intervention. Then, practice technologies were presented of ways that this model can be implemented. With the Strengths Perspective (Saleebey, 1997) being a prominent model in social work practice, and the concepts being so closely aligned with mutual aid (Shulman, 1997), this integration seems a natural fit for social groupwork practice today.

References

Anderson, J. & Carter, R. (2003). *Diversity perspectives for social work.* Boston: Allyn & Bacon.

Anderson, J. (1997). *Social work with groups: A process model.* Boston: Pearson.

Borst, J. (2009). *Social work and health care: Policy, practice, and professionalism* (1st ed.). Boston: Pearson.

Appleby, G., Colon, E., & Hamilton, J. (2010). *Diversity, oppression, and social functioning: Person in environment assessment and intervention.* Boston: Allyn & Bacon.

Billingsley, A. (1992). *Climbing Jacob's ladder: The enduring legacy of African American families.* New York: Simon & Schuster.

Brown, S. (1996). Deviants, invalids, and anthropologists: Cross-cultural perspectives on conditions of disability in one academic discipline. *Disability and Rehabilitation,* 18 (5), 273-275.

Chau, K. (1992). Needs assessment for group work with people of color: A conceptual formulation. *Social Work with Groups,* 15, 53-66.

Chestang, L. (1982). Racial and personal identity in the black experience. In B. White (ed.) *Color in a white society,* Silver Spring: NASW Press.

Collingan, S. (2004). Why the intersexed shouldn't be fixed: Insights from queer theory and disability study. In B. Smith & B. Hutchinson (Eds.), Gendering disability. (pp. 45-60). Piscataway: Rutgers University Press.

Collins, P. (1991). *Black feminist thought.* New York: Routledge and Kegan Paul.

Corey, G. (2008). *Theory and practice of group counseling,* (7th ed.) Belmont, CA: Brooks/Cole.

Fine, M. & Asch, A. (1993). Disability beyond stigma: Social interaction, discrimination, and activism. In M. Nagler (Ed.), *Perspectives on disability: Text and readings on disability* (pp 61-74). Palo Alto: Health Markets Research.

Freire, P. (1970). *The pedagogy of the oppressed.* New York: Seabury.

Goldstein, H. (1997), Victor or victim. In D. Saleebey (Ed.), *The strengths perspective in social work practice* (2nd ed.). (pp. 21-36). New York: Longman.

Gould, K. (1987). Feminist principles and minority concerns: Contributions, problems, and solution. *Affilia,* 2, 6-19.

Gutierrez, L.M. (1990). Working with women of color: An empowerment approach. *Social Work,* 35.

hooks, b. (1984). *Feminist theory: From margin to center.* Boston: South End Press.

hooks, b. (1983). Ain't I a woman: Black women and feminism. *The Black Scholar,* 14, 38-45.

Hopps, J., Pinderhughes, E., & Shankar, R., (1995). *The power to care.* New York: The Free Press.

Longres, J. (2000). *Human behavior in the social environment.* Itasca, Il: F.E. Peacock.

Lum, D. (2011). *Culturally competent practice: A framework for understanding diverse groups and justice issues.* Belmont: Brooks Cole.

Mackelprang, R. (2011), Cultural competence with persons with disabilities. In D. Lum (Ed.), *Culturally competent practice: A framework for understanding diverse groups and justice issues,* (4th ed.). (437-463). Belmont: Brooks Cole.

Mackelprang, R., & Salsgiver, R, (2009). *Disability: A diversity model in human service practice.* Chicago: Lyceum Books.

May, S., & Sletter, C. (2010). (Eds.). Critical multiculturalism: Theory and praxis. New York: Routledge Press.

McRuer, R. (2006). *Crip theory: Cultural signs of queerness and disability.* New York: New York University Press.

Pedwell, C. (2012). Affective (self)-transformation, empathy, neoliberalism and international development. Feminist Theory (13), 163-179.

Pharr, S. (1988). *Homophobia: A weapon of sexism.* Berkley: Chardon Press.

Riddell, S., & Watson, N. (Eds.). (2003). *Disability, culture and identity,* London: Pearson.

Ridley, C., Baker, D., & Hill, C. (2001). Critical issues concerning cultural competence. *The Counseling Psychologist,* 29 (6), 822-232.

Saleebey, D. (2009). *The strengths perspective in social work practice* (5th ed.). Boston: Pearson.

Saleebey, D. (1997). *The strengths perspective in social work practice* (2nd ed.). New York: Longman.

Shulman, L. (1999). *The skills of helping individuals, families, groups and communities* (4th ed.) Itasca, IL: F.E. Peacock.

Shulman, L. (2002). Learning to talk about taboo subjects: A lifelong professional challenge. In R. Kurland & A. Malekoff (Eds.), *Stories celebrating group work: It's not always easy to sit on your mouth* (pp. 139-150). New York: The Haworth Press.

Steinberg, D. (2002). The magic of mutual aid In R. Kurland & A. Malekoff (Eds.), *Stories celebrating group work: It's not always easy to sit on your mouth* (pp. 31-38). New York: The Haworth Press.

Taylor, S. & Kennedy, R. (2003). Feminist framework. In Anderson, J. & Carter, R. (Eds). *Diversity perspectives for social work practice.* Boston: Pearson.

Van Voorhis, R. (1998). Culturally relevant practice: A framework for teaching the psychosocial dynamics of oppression. *Journal of Social Work Education,* 34, 121-134.

Weick, A., & Chamberlain, R. (1997). Putting problems in their place: Further explorations in the Strengths Perspective. In D. Saleebey (Ed.), *The strengths perspective in social work practice* (2nd ed.). (pp. 39-48). New York: Longman.

Finding Focus: Adolescents Experiencing Major Mental Illness Explore Their Photographic Realities

Kyle Taylor Ganson

Introduction

Adolescents today are increasingly experiencing and viewing their lives, and the lives of others, through photographic images. The current adolescent reality is one where photographs are viewed through social media, advertisements, news outlets, and magazines, and are taken with the simplicity of a camera phone. As a creative medium, photography enables self-expression, self-awareness, and is a direct and unique means of communication, which can assist adolescents who are searching for identity and a sense of self. This chapter presents the therapeutic photography group, *Finding Focus*, which was designed and implemented at an outpatient day treatment program for adolescents experiencing symptoms of major mental illness in the Greater Boston area. The group purpose, process, and case presentations are outlined to highlight the effectiveness of using photography with adolescents in a group setting.

Adolescents today are surrounded by photographic images through a variety of social media (Facebook, Instagram, Twitter, Snapchat), advertising, news outlets, and magazines, and they are making photographs in seconds, often with the technology of cellphone cameras. *Finding Focus* is a therapeutic photography group for adolescents experiencing symptoms of major mental illness. It was designed for group members to utilize creative expression in order to develop and enhance self-esteem. The group facilitator encourages members to make their own photographs by offering weekly prompts to inspire creativity. The prompts elicit self-discovery, the development of self-esteem, and provide the opportunity for creative expression. Through the presentation of each group participant's photograph during the weekly group session, group members witness a peer's perspective on their own reality. Open-ended questions about the group participants' photographs excite emotions, thoughts, beliefs, and interpretations from the group; and the group interaction generates relatedness, mutual aid, and the development of interpersonal relationships between group participants. However, it is important to note that the benefits of the *Finding Focus* group are not limited to those listed above.

This chapter provides specific case studies that demonstrate how group participants create visual representations of their thoughts, feelings, interpretations, and beliefs as well as further develop a sense of self, discover a new means of creative expression, and increase their self-esteem. The case studies display how the group format provides support for group participants, and how adolescents experiencing symptoms of major mental illness can utilize photography to better understand, and literally show, their own reality. Finally, this chapter discusses implications for future research regarding the benefits of using photography in therapeutic groups with all populations.

Background

Photography is a powerful tool that can be used for many different purposes. Whether a photograph is made for advertising purposes, a family portrait, fine art, or simply a snapshot, there is an inherent meaning and feeling that is associated with the photograph by the photographer, the subjects, and the viewers. With the increase in visual social media (Instagram, Twitter, Facebook, Snapchat) over time, individuals are increasingly making meaning and living their lives through the photographic image. Visual social media is even more prevalent for the younger generation, who have been raised with significant technological advances during the past 25 years.

Photography fundamentally allows for self- and creative expression, enhances self-awareness by the acts of looking and photographing, and crosses cultural and linguistic barriers (PhotoVoice, 2013).

Additionally, photography is a direct medium of communication (Bell, 2002). The *Finding Focus* group's basic premise aligns with the statement, "every image embodies a way of seeing" (Berger, 1972, p. 9), in that each photograph made by the group member shows how they perceive the world, themselves, and others. Photography can record facts and realities and can be enjoyable for participants. These qualities deem photography as a positive medium in many fields. It is currently used in the fields of sociology through Photo-Elicitation (Harper, 2002), research practice with Auto-Photography (Noland, 2006), social action though Participatory Action Research (Wang & Burris, 1994), and therapeutic treatment with Photo Therapy (Stevens & Spears, 2009).

Auto-Photography asks participants to make photographs that best represent themselves by asking the question, "Who are you and how do you see yourself?" (Noland, 2006, p. 3). Auto-Photography allows participants to use and photograph their surroundings, people, objects, and issues that are most important to them and their "construction of self" (Noland, 2006, p. 3). Researchers will ask questions to participants about the photographs to gather information relevant to the research questions. Similar to Auto-Photography, Photo-Elicitation uses photographs to prompt research interview responses from participants (Harper, 2002). The interviews allow the participant to define how they interpret the photograph based on the participants' individual experiences with the subjects within the photographs. The interviews and photographs connect "core definitions of the self to society, culture and history" (Harper, 2002, p. 13). Auto-Photography and Photo-Elicitation use photography to allow the participant to be the experts and lead the interviewer through the photographs (Harper, 2002). Just as with social group work, utilizing a mutual aid model, it is fundamental when using these photography methods that a need is identified by "hanging out" and developing relationships with potential members, that a purpose is determined collaboratively with members, and to allow the group purpose to adapt and change as it develops and the needs of the group change (Malekoff, 2014).

PhotoVoice is a Participatory Action Research (PAR) method that was created for the purpose of allowing outsiders in. Wang and Burris (1994) stated that PhotoVoice permits us "the world from the viewpoint of people who are leading lives that are different from those traditionally in control of the means of imagining the world" (p. 172). PhotoVoice has three main objectives: 1) to enable people to record their community's strengths and difficulties; 2) to promote a dialogue about important issues through the use of photographs; and 3) to engage policy-makers in creating change (Thompson et al., 2008). Objectives one and two directly relate to Steinberg's three "primary functions of mutual-aid practice": harnessing strengths, group building, and purposeful use of self (Steinberg, 2014, pg. 14). By harnessing the strengths, group members feel supported in the group process and are more open to sharing. Once the group members feel supported, group building occurs and the group begins to see their "we-ness" (Steinberg, 2014, pg. 16). Finally, the self-reflection and self-reference process of mutual aid occurs for the group members through the process of making the images (Steinberg, 2014). Additionally, one of the core values of social work is the advocacy for social justice and social change (Poulin, 2010). PhotoVoice participants are often a group of community participants who are given a single prompt to guide their photographs. After the allotted time period in which participants make their photographs, participants display their photographs, often accompanied by written text, to the public (PhotoVoice). This enables the community to engage in a larger dialogue regarding the central issues of the images and text.

Finally, PhotoTherapy is a therapeutic practice that uses clients' personal snapshots, family albums, and photographs taken by others as catalysts to develop insight and increase communication during individual therapy sessions (Stevens & Spears, 2009). PhotoTherapy focuses on the feelings, thoughts, and memories that the photographs elicit in the client. The objective is for the client to use the items as tools to express their thoughts and emotions that are triggered by the images, and to discover a new skill in communicating (Stevens & Spears, 2009). PhotoTherapy is most effective when the facilitator generates discussion with open-ended questions regarding the clients' thoughts, feelings, and interpretations of the photographs. Importantly, the photographic aesthetic itself is not of significance, but the meaning and interpretation the client assigns to the photograph (Stevens & Spears, 2009).

Theoretical Framework

Finding Focus was developed from the practices previously mentioned. As well, narrative techniques were used to assist the *Finding Focus* group members in creating order, links, and consistency for their life events (Bell, 2002). Unique to photographic narratives, is the subjectivity of interpretation by viewers (Bell, 2002). Different photographic interpretations by group participants were crucial for the group's success and inevitable due to the differences in upbringing, developmental stage, socioeconomic status, culture, religion, and diagnosis.

The creator and lead facilitator of *Finding Focus* holds a Bachelors in Fine Arts with a concentration in photography, in addition to an MSW degree. The facilitator's background in photography was a benefit in the design and implementation of the group, while the social work experience and education lends critical clinical insight and opportunities for intervention with the group members, individually and as a whole. The protocol for photography critiques and techniques for the conceptualization of photography projects had a significant influence on the group format, as well as selecting the prompts used each week.

Group Purpose

Finding Focus is a therapeutic photography group that allows for group participants to create visual representations of their thoughts, feelings, interpretations, and beliefs of their own reality. This group promotes self-discovery, creative expression, self-esteem development, and uses the group format to foster mutual aid, relatedness, and to strengthen interpersonal relationships.

Group Composition, Structure and Content

The *Finding Focus* group described here was a 15-week, 30 minute, open group, in an outpatient day treatment program in the Greater Boston area. Adolescents aged 13-18 years old, with a variety of mental health diagnoses, experiencing a range of social and cultural stressors, self-harming behaviors, and suicidality, composed the group. The group utilized a co-facilitation model, however, occasionally the group was facilitated with only one leader. Group members were asked to make photographs with their own cameras. Group participants primarily used their cell phone cameras or personal point and shoot cameras, and were asked to send one image via text message or email to the lead facilitator the day before the group was scheduled to meet. The lead facilitator of the group would create a PowerPoint presentation of all the images to display during the group session.

During the first session, the lead facilitator explained the group purpose and the logistics of making and sending photographs. Confidentiality was also explained thoroughly, as well as personal boundaries regarding communicating with the lead facilitator via text message and email. The facilitator stated, "Texting was to be used solely for the purposes of sending images. Casual, conversational text messages would not be replied to or allowed." The facilitator asked that the members respect his privacy as he would theirs. All group members agreed to this norm. It should be noted that the facilitator and group members had an already existing relationship prior to the start of the group as they were familiar with each other from the milieu setting. The decision to have the members text the facilitator on a personal cell phone was discussed and approved by both the facilitator's supervisor and the program director. To offer inspiration to the group, a slideshow of images made by professional photographers, as well as the lead facilitator, was presented. To end the first session, the facilitator provided the first prompt that would be due the following week: *Photograph something you see or do everyday.*

In the following group sessions, a standard, outlined agenda with the goal of stimulating group collaboration was followed. At the beginning of each session, the facilitator asked a group participant to restate the prompt that was assigned for the week. Next, a PowerPoint presentation was shown to the group for discussion and questioning. The PowerPoint was constructed so that each group member's photographs were shown on separate slides. The name of the group participant did not display initially with their photograph. Instead, there is an "on-click" transition for each name. This anonymity allowed for objective feedback about the photograph from the group members. Once the first stage of discussion was complete, the facilitator would "on-click" to show the name of the group participant who made the photograph. The photographer would then have an opportunity to explain their photograph to the group and to describe how they believed it related to the prompt. At this time, the photographer would also answer any questions from the group. The group facilitators guide the time spent on each photograph in order to allow for the completion of both stages of discussion for all photographs.

Finally, at the end of each session, the prompt for the following week was assigned. Prompts were created before each group session and were assigned based on multiple factors, including the group stage, the addition of new participants, what happened for each group participant, and the group as a whole, during the day or week (i.e. Was there a difficult family session for a client? Is the group presenting more depressed, anxious, suicidal, etc. than usual? Was the previous group emotionally tiring?), and the level of challenge involved in the prompt. Sample prompts included: *Photograph something you see & do everyday, Photograph something that represents a past self,* and *Photograph something or someone that is good in your life.* While the facilitators would allow for some clarifying questions from group participants regarding the prompts, it was essential that the group participants were encouraged to interpret the prompt in their own way, and make a photograph that visually represents that interpretation. The facilitator would often explain that there is no wrong way to interpret the prompt. To encourage group participation, facilitators had the option to participate in the group by making their own images related to the prompt. Facilitators' involvement in the group process seemed to enhance group development and intimacy, as well as support the concepts of authenticity, use of self and genuineness (Murphy & Dillon, 2015). In a milieu-based setting, like the outpatient day treatment program that operates on a relational model (Schiller, 2007), it was important to build strong a rapport with each group participant. Strong client-social worker relationships build trust and inspire growth and progress on therapeutic goals (Poulin, 2010).

A main task for the group facilitators was to reach for feedback and discussion among the members regarding the photographs. As outlined in the group session agenda, the facilitators would ask open-ended questions to the group first and the photographer second. Sample questions included: "What do you think the photographer is trying to say?" (to the group) and "What does this photograph mean?" (to the photographer). It was also important for the facilitators to ask questions that link the photographs to the group participants' and photographer's feelings, thoughts, and interpretations. Two examples are: "Describe this photograph to the group." (to the photographer) and "How do you think this photograph represents the prompt?" (to the group). At times, it was helpful for the facilitator to inform group participants of photographic techniques and provide constructive criticism. However, the technical aspects and aesthetic qualities of the photographs were not as important as the content, conceptualization, and meaning the group participant assigned to the photograph, as well as the relationship to the group's purpose.

Case Vignettes

The following case vignettes are examples that emphasize the purpose of the *Finding Focus* group. How the photographer conceptualized and created images to visualize their own interpretation of the prompts is described. Additionally, the group discussion related to each of these examples emphasized the tenets of group therapy practice, including mutual aid, relatedness, interpersonal learning, and catharsis (Yalom, 2005).

Case Vignette #1

During week six of the group, a 17-year-old female experiencing symptoms of major depression, with a suicidal baseline, presented a photograph of her psychiatric medication bottles (Figure 1) for the prompt: *Photograph an emotion you currently feel.* During the first stage of discussion, a 14-year-old female group participant reported that she interpreted the feeling of being "labeled". After her statement, other group participants agreed with the interpretation of the photograph and related to the feeling of being "labeled" with a mental illness.

The photographer reported to the group that she made this photograph to show her feelings of being "controlled," specifically by her medications. While the group facilitators remained quiet, the group members discussed what it is like to be on medications and how their moods, feelings, and actions change when they are on and off of them. Since all of the group participants were prescribed at least one psychiatric mediation, the entire group was able to relate to this feeling and the uncertainty of taking medications for the rest of their lives. The facilitator then made some inquiries, asking the group

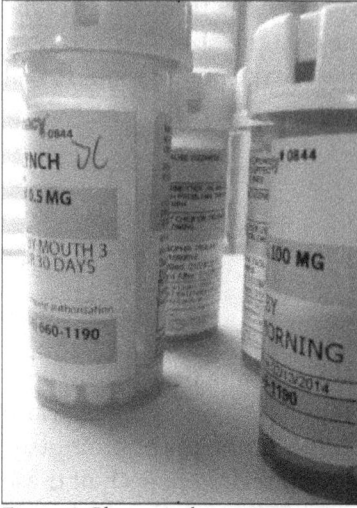

Figure 1. Photograph an emotion you currently feel - Week 6

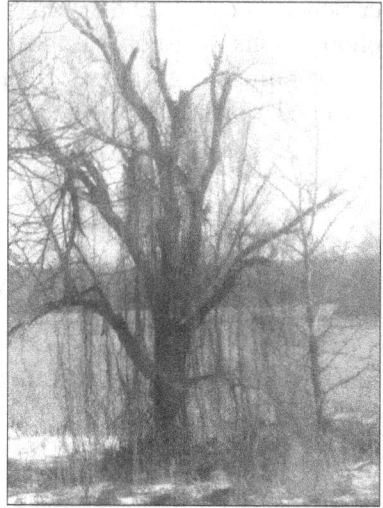

Figure 2. Photograph an emotion you currently feel - Week 6

members if they ever felt like they wanted to stop their medication intake one day, as well as how they viewed the positives and negatives of taking medications. Most group members reported wanting to stop taking medications at some point in their life. However, they each described the current positive effects their medications have on them and on their progress towards improving their daily functioning.

The image of the bottles (Figure 1) shows how the photographer was able to conceptualize and visually represent her feelings and reality to the other group participants. She was able to receive positive feedback from the other members, which afforded mutual aid and acceptance, as well as an understanding that only the group participants could experience this "all in the same boat" phenomenon (Steinberg, 2014).

Case Vignette #2

During the same week as the previous vignette, a 16-year-old female experiencing symptoms of major depression and post-traumatic stress disorder, who has attempted suicide multiple times, made this photograph of a dead tree (Figure 2) for the prompt: *Photograph an emotion you currently feel.* The other group participants immediately praised this image for it beauty and authenticity. During the first stage of questioning, the group was able to accurately guess which group participant made this photograph based on their knowledge of her experiences and daily presentation. The group knew about this photographer's suicidal thoughts and previous attempts, as well as her poor self-esteem and significant bullying history. Because of this, the group was able to remind her of her positive qualities, skills, why they care about her, and why she is a great friend.

The photographer reported she made this photograph because she wanted to be dead and that she felt numb. Some group participants stated that they have similar feelings, but reassured her that things will get better, as well as reminded her of the positives in her life. The photographer used photography to express her feelings about herself to the group and receive positive feedback that helped increase her self-esteem if only for a short time. Because of the intense level of intimacy in the group, the facilitators allowed for the group to support and help the photographer process her current feelings, though after the group she was checked-in with individually to assess for safety. Overall, it was evident that the photographer felt supported by the group, as she smiled and was engaged throughout the remainder of, and after, the group.

Case Vignette # 3

During week nine, a 15-year-old female experiencing symptoms of obsessive-compulsive disorder (OCD) made a photograph of a pencil, pen, and sheet of paper (Figure 3) for the prompt: *Photograph why you are here [the outpatient program]*. Because she was the only group participant diagnosed with OCD, the group immediately recognized this as her photograph. The photographer reported to the group that it took over an hour to make her photograph, stating that she wanted the pencil, pen, and sheet of paper to be perfectly lined up. She reported that she was never satisfied, so she continued to rearrange the items in hopes that it would be perfect. She reported she eventually became frustrated that she couldn't line everything up as she wanted, so she decided to make the photograph as it is and move forward with her day.

This photograph visually introduced the group to some of this photographer's OCD behaviors and allowed her to use the image as a visual guide while explaining her compulsions to the group. The

Figure 3. Photograph why you are here [the outpatient program] - Week 9

Figure 4. Photograph why you are here [the outpatient program] - Week 9

facilitator was able to help the group member connect the photograph to the compulsions she was exhibiting in school prior to her admission to the program. Many of her compulsions occurred during that time and were exacerbated due to feelings of inadequacy and imperfection. The act of making this photograph was also an experiment of exposure for her. While making the photograph, she reported feeling frustrated and anxious, and when she was able to move forward, she was able to see that the world did not end and she did not die, which she often reported would happen if things were not perfect.

Case Vignette # 4

During week nine, an 18-year-old male experiencing symptoms of depression with psychotic features, and possible schizophrenia, made a drawing of a robot and photographed it (Figure 4) for the prompt: *Photograph why you are here [the outpatient program]*. Because the group was familiar with the photographer's symptoms, they were able to identify this image as his. The photographer presented daily with extremely flat affect and rarely spoke unless spoken to. He reported to the group that he felt "mechanical" and did not have the ability to feel emotions, like robots, and that's why he was at the outpatient program. He reported in *Finding Focus,* and other groups, that he often felt like he was not in his body, but hovering over himself, controlling his actions as if playing a video game. He repeatedly reported the desire to get better, but due to his intense symptoms, struggled to fully engage in treatment. While the group did not directly address his feeling "mechanical" during the discussion, they were able to give him feedback about his daily presentation, mood, and affect, which led to the start of a peer-led daily check-in scale with him. The group encouraged the photographer to keep working hard on his goals and things would get better. Problem-solving, a key element of mutual aid, described as the process in which the group helps explore and find solutions for one member's needs by utilizing their own experiences (Steinberg, 2014), often occurred during the sessions.

During the discussion, a 14-year-old female group participant reported that the photograph might show someone letting life pass by, because robots do not have any control of themselves. All of the group participants, including the photographer, were able to relate to feeling like their life was passing by and that they did not have control of themselves or what is happening in the world around them. The group was able to use this discussion to further understand their reality and where they are in their life, as well as what they can and cannot control. This session was a point in which the group moved further into the intimacy stage of group development (Garland, Jones, & Kolodny, 1965), and began doing deeper therapeutic work.

Case Vignette #5

During week 15, the same 18-year-old male made this photograph of a transformer (Figure 5) for the prompt: *Photograph who you are now [at the end of the 15 week group].* After 15 weeks of the group, the photographer reported that he was feeling less "stiff" and it was "easier to move." He referenced his photograph of the robot to show how much he feels he has improved. The group told him that they had also seen significant changes in his mood and presentation, saying that he talks, laughs, and smiles more, and was now social in the milieu.

This prompt was specifically designed to assist in the

Figure 5. Photograph who you are now [at the end of the 15 week group] - Week 15

termination process. It allowed for time traveling and reflection on areas of growth, with this example showing the process. As a transitional object, a small booklet was made with one image from each group member and facilitator, along with the prompt associated with the photograph. The booklet was meant as a reminder for the group members of their "groupness" (Malekoff, 2014, p. 230) and of a space where they felt supported, accepted, and connected to others (Malekoff, 2014).

Vignette Summary

These case vignettes show how the use of prompts in eliciting conceptualization and creation of photographs by group members can aid the member to visually represent their thoughts, feelings and perception of their reality to the group. The 18-year-old male's growth in the group is profound because of his diagnosis, initial presentation, and difficulty verbally engaging in treatment due to his symptoms. The camera gave him a voice to show the group, the facilitators, and most importantly, himself, how he was feeling, what he was thinking, and where he was in his life. In each case vignette, group members were able to provide positive feedback, support and validation to the photographer and to relate to the each other's feelings and experience. Members' verbal and nonverbal cues during discussion made it evident to the facilitator that they often felt "all in the same boat" (Steinberg, 2014), and the members felt understood by each other. The prompts were assigned to quickly develop intimacy, which assisted the group participants in processing openly about themselves and discussing their lives in the group.

Limitations of the *Finding Focus* Group

Like in most therapeutic groups, there were group participants who were more challenging to engage than others. In activity-based groups like *Finding Focus*, it is important to allow group participants the option of not directly engaging in an activity. For this group, this meant to pass on making photos. However, these participants were encouraged to engage during the group discussion portion of the session. Members who do not participate are akin to the "silent member"; their presence in the group is important to the dynamics of the "group as a whole" and facilitators need to tune-in to these members just as they do with other more outwardly active members of the group. Most importantly, these group participants were asked about why they were having difficulty engaging and in what ways could it be made easier. This ensured that they knew they still had the option to engage. Additionally, the discussion portion of the session was ultimately therapeutic for the group participant due to the nature of processing, both listening and engaging. This was demonstrated when a 16-year-old male member of the group, who experienced OCD, made photographs for prompts only five of the 15 weeks. In discussing with the group why he struggled to make his photograph, he reported feeling unsure of what to photograph and self-conscious that is would not align with the prompt. The group was able to assure him that the prompts were just starting points and that there were no wrong answers. Additionally, the group accepted where he was at and helped him see that they enjoyed his participation in the group during discussion and that he did not have to make photographs if he did not want to. He felt supported and validated by the other group members.

It is important to note that the group participants of *Finding Focus* had cameras accessible to them through their cell phones or family point-and-shoot cameras. A quite obvious and highly significant limitation is the accessibility of cameras. Therefore, in specific settings where cameras are unavailable, the *Finding Focus* group may be challenging to implement. Adapting the model to two or three group members working together in order to share the equipment, or asking the group to creatively strategize about how to manage the use of one camera, for example, are possible solutions to this limitation. Fundraising for donations of equipment or targeted funds to purchase equipment to loan to group members could enhance and sustain the group over time.

Implications for Future Research

Photography has many benefits in helping client's voice feelings and thoughts about their lives through visual images. Implementing the *Finding Focus* group with a variety of client populations in various settings may provide a better understanding of how photography in a group setting can foster mutual aid, strengthen interpersonal relationships, further develop self-esteem, and inspire self-discovery. Additionally, conducting the *Finding Focus* group in new settings with new populations could aid in the creation of thorough and standardized quantitative and qualitative tools to measure all aspects of the group purpose and outcomes. Stronger data outlining the benefits of photography as a therapeutic modality will enable its use as an evidenced-based practice and will open more possibilities for social workers, and other helping professionals, to utilize it when assisting clients of different ages, cultures, and backgrounds, in a variety of settings.

Conclusion

The *Finding Focus* group demonstrates that photography has many therapeutic benefits when used in a group setting. The case vignettes detail how the adolescents who participated in *Finding Focus* experienced mutual aid, connection to other members, and received positive feedback that fostered self-esteem and personal growth. The group participants were able to realize through making their photographs that they have a story that is important and it is within their power to tell it through photographs. In support of this, one group participant wrote in an anonymous open-ended question evaluation, "I've learned that every part of my story exists and that I can see it in more ways than one."

Another group participant wrote, "[photography] really is an effective way to convey something that you might not be able to express in words." This quote demonstrates how the group participants were able to use their photographs to speak for them and show others what they are feeling, thinking, and how they see their own reality. This is especially important for group participants who have difficulty expressing themselves verbally. Similarly, another group participant wrote, "I liked sharing my photos [to family & friends]; it was less stressful than explaining through words how I am."

To show the value of subjectivity in photographic interpretation, one group participant wrote, "it is a great feeling when two people interpret a picture differently." The different interpretations were catalysts for group discussion, individual processing, and the giving and receiving of positive feedback. Finally, one group participant wrote, "*[Finding Focus]* helped others figure out my life..." They continued, "[photography] made me more comfortable explaining my life through pictures." The vignettes presented and the members' stories and comments describe how the unique process of photography (seeing, photographing, and reflecting) used in a group modality can be beneficial to adolescents experiencing symptoms of major mental illness. The *Finding Focus* group prompts inspired group participants to make photographs to further understand who they are, where they are, what they think, and how they feel. The entirety of the *Finding Focus* group process allowed members to identify and focus on the realities of their past, present, and look to a new life in the future.

References

Bell, S. E. (2002). Photo images: Jo Spence's narratives of living with illness. *Health: An Interdisciplinary Journal for the Social Study of Health, Illness and Medicine, 6*(1), 5-30.

Berger, J. (1972). *Ways of seeing*. London: Penguin Books.

Combs, J. M., & Ziller, R. C. (1977). Photographic self-concept of counselees. *Journal of Counseling Psychology, 24*(5), 452-455.

Dollinger, S. J., & Clancy, S. M. (1993). Identity, self, and personality: II. Glimpses through the autophotographic eye. *Journal of Personality and Social Psychology, 64*(6), 1064-1071.

Erdner, A., & Magnusson, A. (2011). Photography as a method of data collection: Helping people with long-term mental illness to convey their life world. *Perspectives in Psychiatric Care, 47*, 145-150.

Garland, J., Jones, H., & Kolodny, R. (1965). A model for stages of development in social work groups. *Explorations in Group Work*, 17-71.

Harper, D. (2002). Talking about pictures: A case for photo elicitation. *Visual Studies, 17*(1), 14-26.

Krauss, D. A. (1983). Reality, photography, and psychology. In D. Krauss & J. Fryrear (Eds.), *Phototherapy in Mental Health*. Springfield: Charles C Thomas Publisher, Ltd.

Malekoff, A. (2014). *Group work with adolescents: Principles and practice* (3rd ed.). New York, NY: The Guilford Press.

Murphy, B.C., & Dillon, C. (2015). *Interviewing in action in a multicultural world* (5th ed.). Stamford, CT: Cengage Learning.

Noland, C. M. (2006). Auto-photography as a research practice: Identity and self-esteem research. *Journal of Research Practice, 2*(1), 1-19.

PhotoVoice, (2013). PhotoVoice methods and process. Retrieved from http://www.photovoice.org/whatwedo/info/photovoice-methods-and-process

Poulin, J. (2010). *Strengths-based generalist practice: A collaborative approach* (3rd ed.). Belmont, CA: Wadsworth, Cengage Learning.

Schiller, L.Y. (2007). Not for women only: Applying the relational model of group development with vulnerable populations. *Social work with groups, 30*(2), 11-26.

Steinberg, D. M. (2014). *The mutual-aid model for social work with groups* (3rd ed.). New York, NY: Routledge.

Stevens, R., & Spears, E. H. (2009). Incorporating photography as a therapeutic tool in counseling. *Journal of Creativity in Mental Health, 4*, 3-16.

Thompson, N. C., Hunter, E. E., Murray, L., Ninci, L., Rolfs, E. M., & Pallikkathayil, L. (2008). The experience of living with a chronic mental illness: A PhotoVoice study. *Perspectives in Psychiatric Care, 44*(1), 14-24.

Wang, C., & Burris, M. A. (1994). Empowerment through photo-novella: Portraits of participation. *Health Education Quarterly, 21*(2), 171-186.

Woychik, J. P., & Brickell, C. (1983). The instant camera as a therapy tool. *Social Work, 28* (4), 316-318 .

Yalom, I. (2005). *The theory and practice of group psychotherapy* (5th ed.). New York, NY: Basic Books.

Ethnic Nonprofit Organizations During the Economic Recession: An Examination of the Role of Organizational Capacity and Leadership Building for Long-Term Sustainability

Biswas Pradhan and Dale Asis

Introduction

This chapter examines a series of group workshops designed to help community-based organizations (CBOs) strengthen strategic organizational capacity building by incorporating group methods as effective strategies for long-term sustainability as social service agencies. These capacity and leadership group workshops are especially effective for small ethnic community-based organizations struggling in the current economic recession. In 2012, the authors conducted a series of strategic organizational capacity building workshops called the GROW Project, for seven small, ethnic community-based organizations in the Chicago area. As a group work series, it focuses on the important impact of groups on individual and organizational levels and thus utilize group processes to accomplish individual, group, and organizational goals as a whole. This chapter portrays the importance of group work that encompasses the need for organizational capacity building for long-term sustainability, especially for organizations that serve small and vulnerable ethnic populations.

Background

Introduction to the Agency

The Coalition of African, Arab, Asian, European, and Latino Immigrants of Illinois (CAAAELII) is a registered, nonprofit 501(c)(3) organization in Chicago. Established in 1996, CAAAELII is a coalition of 34 ethnic community-based organizations (CBOs) serving 16 different ethic communities in 13 different neighborhoods throughout the Chicago area (CAAAELII, 2013). CAAAELII's mission is to strengthen the diverse voices of intergenerational immigrant and refugee communities by building alliances through a transformative process that develops grassroots power to impact public policy (CAAAELII, 2013).

The GROW Project Leadership Institute

The GROW Project Leadership Institute was a workshop series designed for the immigrant community-based organizations to build their capacity, develop leadership, and increase collaboration among other groups in order to better serve their immigrant communities and promote integration and self-reliance (CAAAELII, 2013). This project was a collaborative effort between CAAAELII and the Loyola University Nonprofit Management and Philanthropy Program. The GROW project conducted nine workshops comprising of one introductory workshop and eight core course workshops and were held at CAAAELII office located at 4300 N. Hermitage Ave., Chicago, IL 60613. The seven participating organizations in these group workshops were CAAAELII's member organizations; they have been participating in its 501(c)(3) working group since 2008. In addition, other interested community-based organizations and graduate students from the Loyola University School of Social Work Leadership Development Series were also welcomed to attend the workshop series.

The GROW Project as a Group Work

There are numerous definitions and explanations of group work practice that can be interchangeably referred to as group treatment, group counseling, or group therapy (Alle-Corliss & Alle-Corliss, 2009). Common to all, group work is a collaborative approach where the facilitator and the group members interact and engage with each other to exhibit mutual learning, understanding, support, and cooperation. Likewise, the GROW project was designed explicitly for the mutual benefit of both - the group members in the individual level and their organizations in the macro level in terms of organizational capacity building and enhancing leadership skills. According to Olmstead (as cited in Alle-Corliss & Alle-Corliss, 2009), the small group is defined as:

> Plurality of individuals who are in contact with one another, who take one another into account, and who are aware of some significant commonality. As essential feature of a group is that its members have something in common and that they believe what they have in common makes a difference. (p. 4)

As a group type, the GROW project corresponded to a task group where the project was solely focused on achieving its goals and objectives primarily organizational capacity building and leadership development. For example, each group session outlined specific goals, identified specific points to learn, and provided appropriate handouts. The GROW project was implemented to enhance capacity building and leadership development of the participating community agencies by promoting steps to integration, leveraging resources, and long-term sustainability of the organizations. The project was designed to vitalize the leadership abilities of the participating ethnic community leaders and increase resources for the organizations in order to meet the organizational and community needs. As stated by Alle-Corliss and Alle-Corliss (2009), an effective task group is comprised of these nine components: (a) clear group purpose; (b) balance between process (dynamics) and content (information); (c) encouragement of culture building and appreciation of diversity; (d) mutual collaboration, cooperation, and respect; (e) addressing of conflicts; (f) immediate exchange of feedback; (g) group issues are addressed; (h) encouragement of active participation among group members; and (i) allocation of time between facilitator and members to reflect upon their work.

The GROW project incorporated all the above nine major components of group work to effectively run the group sessions. The participating members comprised of diverse backgrounds, cultures, and countries of origin and they all expressed eagerness to learn from each other. The GROW project emphasized the significance of working in the community as a joined venture in dealing with an issue or set of issues that affect all of them. At the same time, the ethnic community leaders participating in the GROW project acquired new life skills and self-awareness to acculturate with the social, political, and economical fabric of the United States. Participating members also noted that the small group sessions have resulted in creating opportunities of employment, self-sustainability, interdependence, training, and education for their community members. The group sessions have provided the participating members with a wealth of resources to build their organizational capacity by increasing partnership with other organizations and by reaching out to their community members for their support and contribution.

Need for the GROW Project

During the recent economic recession, resources for human service agencies especially for ethnic community organizations have decreased dramatically affected by huge cuts in funding for social services. Social service programs are often among the first places governments look to cut when tax revenues decrease. Private philanthropy dedicated to social services - another critical source of funding - also declined during economic downturns (Harms, 2008). In 2011, funding provided by foundations has decreased by 1.3 percent, followed by a decline of two percent in the previous year (Giving USA, 2012). Ironically, funding to service programs is cut when the need for help rises (Harms, 2008).

Despite current economic crisis, the Chicago metropolitan area continues to see an influx of immigrants and refugees. In recent years, the region has seen rising numbers of Iraqi refugees as well as Nepali immigrants and Bhutanese refugees, among other populations (Schmadeke, 2011). Through difficult economic times, immigrants and refugee communities of all ethnicities are establishing community-based organizations to help address their most pressing problems. Unfortunately, these newly founded organizations face myriad challenges as they need to learn how to operate nonprofit organizations, and how to secure funding in very difficult times. Moreover, small community organizations that serve ethnic communities with a low literacy rate and low-income populations are even more vulnerable.

Many micro-ethnic organizations have already shut down leaving those that are left standing to fend for themselves to navigate the labyrinth of the US bureaucracies. Without these ethnic community agencies as lifeboats and as places of vital information and services, many ethnic community residents are swimming upstream to navigate the US mainstream society on their own (Newland, Tanaka, & Barker, 2007).

Initiation of the GROW Project

In 2011, CAAAELI established a 501(c) (3) working group project to provide technical assistance to newly founded immigrant and refugee-based nonprofit organizations and community groups to help them achieve their tax exempt status and incorporate in order to positively impact their local communities. A year after the project's inception, CAAAELII realized that completing their nonprofit tax incorporation is only one step among numerous capacity building steps to help immigrant and refugee organizations survive the financial crisis, build their organizational strength and eventually thrive as a nonprofit organization to serve their specific ethnic community. In 2012, CAAAELII initiated the GROW project and invited all emerging micro-community organizations to join the workshop. Altogether, seven organizations signed up to join this workshop and they became the first cohort of the CAAAELII GROW project. Each participating organization sent at least one ethnic community leader and one board member to all the GROW project workshops.

Formation of the Group

Group formation is one of the critical components of any group session. It is imperative to understand that there are many factors that need to be addressed in group formation. These elements consist of but are not restricted to: the group composition, group size, frequency and duration of sessions, length of group, and group type i.e. either open ended or close ended (Alle-Corliss & Alle-Corliss, 2009). Below, the chapter describes the group structure of the GROW project.

Group Composition

As indicated earlier, there were seven ethnic community-based organizations that participated for the entire workshop series and learned together as a cohort. All participating group members also shared similar organizational goals, mission, and values, even though they came from diverse ethnic backgrounds and represented different ethnic communities. The CAAAELII group workshop provided nine comprehensive organizational training topics including: 1) organizational management and structure; 2) governance; 3) transparency; 4) accountability; 5) program planning; 6) community fundraising; 7) effective organizational communications; 8) community organizing; and 9) advocacy.

In any group work, group membership is determined according to the fulfillment of established criteria that is decided beforehand to the establishment of the group (Alle-Corliss & Alle-Corliss, 2009). All participating organizations and their representatives came from emerging ethnic nonprofit organizations striving to accomplish their mission and community services by enhancing organizational capacity and leadership building for long-term sustainability. The diversity represented by the seven participating community organizations can be seen in their names and the constituencies they represented. The participating organizations were: 1) Alliance of Filipinos for Immigrant Rights and Empowerment (AFIRE); 2) Centro Informativo Quetzalcoatl; 3) Community Defense Foundation (CDF); 4) Guatemalan-Cultural Community Organization (GCCO); 5) Lao American Community Services; 6) Midwest Asian American Center; and 7) Nepalese American Society (NAS).

Group Size

About a range of 10-15 participants attended each GROW project session, with at least one ethnic community leader and one board member consistently attending the eight workshops series. The representatives of these participating organizations included executive directors, program directors, student interns, and general staff members. Throughout the group session, the diverse participants engaged in group discussions, shared their stories, knowledge, and resources, developed camaraderie among each other, and provided constructive feedback to help reach their organizational goals. Thus, the GROW project became an iconic group work to create networks and friendship among one another.

Frequency and Duration of Sessions

For any group, the frequency of group sessions and time estimated for each group session play an instrumental role in the optimal functioning of the group (Alle-Corliss & Alle-Corliss, 2009). For instance, if the group session is too short, the group members may not have equal chance of participation. On the contrary, if the group session is very lengthy, the group work may be less effective and the participants may feel bored and tired. Considering the time schedules of all the participants, the GROW project was conducted on Thursday evenings, once a month from 6 pm until 9 pm (including dinner and a short break in the middle of the session). The project commenced on April 5, 2012 and concluded on December 12, 2012, comprising of nine group sessions. The final session was also celebrated as a graduation day where each participating member was conferred a non-degree graduate certificate recognized by the Loyola University Nonprofit Management and Philanthropy program.

Close-ended group

This GROW project was a close-ended group where there were a fixed number of participants from each organization. However, there were occasions where participants invited their guests and friends to share their experiences/perspectives pertaining to the group topic. Although the group was close-ended, besides the mandatory participation of the executive heads of the respective organizations, there were a few new members who joined the group in the mid sessions. In other words, the group was close-ended featuring the participating organizations and its executive heads but the group allowed members from their organizations to participate during particular sessions. As a close-ended group, this project was highly effective in promoting cohesiveness among group members and was very productive in achieving its stated goals.

Design of the Agenda

Each of the nine sessions was entitled with a specific topic that corresponded with organizational settings and goals. The workshop series were designed based on the needs of the emerging participating organizations and the discussion topics were conferred with them ahead of time. The agenda for the group session was subdivided into six parts. For instance, the first fifteen minutes were allocated for registration and dinner. The next part of the group work was for the introduction of the group session, its goals, and objectives followed by the main group facilitation that was allocated for an hour. Subsequently, the agenda was paused for a fifteen-minute break period and for questions and answers session. During the second part of the group session, the guest speakers, as deemed appropriate by the facilitators, occasionally led the sessions. The last ten minutes were allocated for evaluation and quick review of the session and for take-home assignments that needed to be implemented at their respective organization during that particular month.

Understanding Diverse Ethnic Organizations and Client Populations

Each participating agency's organizational setting was comprised of unique features, and each agency served but did not restrict themselves to their own ethnic community members and immigrants to acclimate with the American mainstream society. Many ethnic community leaders participating shared specific issues and challenges pertinent to their specific community while other community leaders and participants chimed in and shared their personal experiences with the group. In the end, the participants coordinated a seamless fashion of working and discussing issues together that were supportive to all (Alle-Corliss & Alle-Corliss, 2006).

The GROW project also manifested a unique avenue for participating ethnic organizations to create an interconnected platform where all the participating members in the group focused on a common purpose. In this project, each of the participating organizations can be compared to a system and the participating members as smaller sub-systems. A system is not only made up of interrelated parts, but is itself an interrelated part of a larger system (Brill & Levine, 2002). Each ethnic community leader takes the learning and changes back to their ethnic community and the changes and actions take place in different ethnic communities. The effective system becomes complex and effective as a whole as both synergy and information happen within the complex environment of ethnic community organizations working together as a cohort.

Socializing among Group Members

Many traditional forms of group therapy discourage members from mingling with one another outside of group (Wenger, McDermott, & Snyder, 2002), however in the GROW project the group members were able to create and sustain a mutually supportive environment. Although conflict may arise where there is a formation of cliques, common interest sub-groups, or in situation encountering hidden agendas (Corey, 2004), this was not the experience with the GROW project. The participating members rather eagerly embraced the GROW project and no such conflict appeared during the entire eight group sessions. In addition, in cases where participating members struggled to understand English where, for instance, Spanish was the native language, an interpreter was hired to translate the group discussion to the member's native language. The GROW project initiative was instrumental to creating supportive networks among the group members and their organizations.

Evaluation of the GROW Project

The evaluation of the GROW project was based on both quantitative and qualitative methods. For each participating organization, the success of the project was measured by: (a) completion of their nonprofit registration and status; (b) establishment of an active board of directors helping the community organization; (c) detailed program plans and objectives; and (d) detailed plans of grassroots community fundraising and budget. Most significantly, all CAAAELII GROW project participants raised $80,000 in community grassroots fundraising for 2013. The responses in the video interview also validated the positive qualitative outcome of the project. The participants were interviewed for what they have learned from the workshop and how they have implemented those lessons in their organizations (Pradhan, 2013).

In addition to the above evaluation strategies, the effectiveness of the GROW project was also evaluated based on the following four criteria:

1. The number of consistent attendees at each workshop counted based on their completion of the attendance sheets.
2. The positive response of the attendees at the end of the workshop as an indicator of the members experience based on their comments and feedback provided in the evaluation forms. It was found that 80% of the respondents have rated each workshop as above average to excellent.
3. The participating organizations achieved the four concrete benchmarks for group work success.
4. The final measure was the long-term achievement of the GROW project and the continued sustainability and continued growth of these organizations beyond the first two years as many nonprofit organizations fail after a two-year period.

Conclusion

When immigrants step onto a foreign land, ethnic nonprofit organizations play a crucial role in providing critical social services and information in helping them to acculturate into a new culture and integrate into the US way of living. These emerging ethnic community organizations helped their ethnic communities navigate the US bureaucracy and eventually integrate their ethnic community members to contribute to the larger society as well (Weerawardena, McDonald, & Mort, 2010). While larger umbrella organizations and national nonprofits fulfill a vital need, it is also important that smaller, micro-ethnic community organizations serve the niche and specific needs of individual immigrant and refugee communities. Integration and adapting to life in America takes a long time. With the help of ethnic nonprofit organizations, immigrants get more personalized and effective support. Not only this, but by empowering the immigrants themselves to work for their own needs, more empowering opportunities open up for them. Emerging ethnic organizations gain tremendous resources and innovative ideas in networking and collaboratively working. The diverse ethnic organizations that participated with the GROW project were committed in their organizations' missions but they also provided valuable, mutual exchange and integration of information and knowledge to their community members as part of successful group work practice. The GROW project's group workshops became the building blocks to the emerging ethnic nonprofit organizations in creating self-sustainability and organizational capacity building. The GROW Project not only supported the ethnic community organizations but in the process also empowered the grassroots immigrant communities themselves.

References

Alle-Corliss, L., & Alle-Corliss, R. (2006). *Human service agencies: An orientation to fieldwork.* Belmont, CA: Thomson Brooks/Cole.

Alle-Corliss, L., & Alle-Corliss, R. (2009). Group work: a practical guide to developing groups in agency settings. Hoboken, N.J.: Wiley.

Brill, N., & Levine, J. (2002). *Working with people: the helping process* (7th ed.). Boston: Allyn & Bacon.

CAAAELII. (2013, June 4). *About The Grow Project.* Retrieved from '

CAAAELII. (2013, June 4). *Mission.* Retrieved from https://sites.google.com/a/caaaelii.org/caaaelii2009nov/about-caaaelii

CAAAELII. (2013, June 4). *Welcome to CAAAELII.* Retrieved from http://www.caaaelii.org/

Corey, G. (2004). *Theory and practice of group counseling.* Belmont, CA: Thomson/Brooks/Cole.

Delander, L., Hammarstedt, M., Mansson, J., & Nyberg, E. (2005). Integration of Immigrants. *Evaluation Review, 29,* 1, 24-41.

Giving USA. (2012). *The Annual Report on Philanthropy for the year 2011. Annual Report.* Indianapolis, IN: Retrieved from http://www.alysterling.com/documents/GUSA2012ExecutiveSummary.pdf

Harms, W. (2008). An economic downturn impacts social services' ability to aid poor. *The University of Chicago Chronicle, 28*(6). Retrieved from http://chronicle.uchicago.edu/081211/poor.shtml

Newland, K., Tanaka, H., & Barker, L. (2007) Bridging divides: The role of ethnic community-based organizations in refugee integration. *Migration Policy Institute.* Retrieved from http://www.migrationpolicy.org/research/bridging-divides-role-ethnic-community-based-organizations-refugee-integration

Pradhan, B. (2013, May 30). *CAAAELII GROW project-I* [Video file]. Retrieved from https://www.youtube.com/watch?v=ORqc20M_UNQ

Schmadeke, S. (2011, December 22). Regugee agency aids newcomers. *The Chicago Tribune.* Retrieved from http://articles.chicagotribune.com/2011-12-22/news/ct-met-holiday-giving-refugee-one-1221-20111222_1_refugee-status-kenyan-refugee-camps-bhutanese

Weerawardena, J., McDonald, R. E., & Mort, G. S. (2010). Sustainability of nonprofit organizations: An empirical investigation. *Journal of World Business, 45,* 4, 346-356.

Wenger, E., McDermott, R., & Snyder, W. M. (2002, March 25). Cultivating communities of practice: A guide to managing knowledge – seven principles for cultivating communities of practice. *Harvard Business School Working Knowledge.* Retrieved from http://hbswk.hbs.edu/archive/2855.html

Yalom, I. D. (1995). *The theory and practice of group psychotherapy* (4th ed.). New York: Basic Books.

Appendix

Coalition of African, Arab, Asian, European and Latino Immigrants of Illinois (CAAAELII) & Loyola University Nonprofit Management & Philanthropy Program GROW Project: Workshop Series & Certificate Program

Session	Eight Series Workshop Series & Certificate Program	Who	Materials
Thurs April 5, 2012, 6 pm – 9 pm	**Introduction GROW Project:** Pre-Assessment, Asset Mapping, Potential Sharing of Resources	D a l e A s i s , CAAAELII	Community Asset Mapping Exercise, Pre-Assessment Survey
Thurs April 26, 2012, 6 pm – 9 pm	**1. Community and Identity:** Who we are and why do we care? 21st century immigrant narrative and steps to Integration	Dale Asis, CAAAELII	Critical reading list: 1) US immigration history; 2) globalization; 3) human rights; and 4) rights based and asset based approach
Thurs May 31, 2012, 6 pm – 9 pm	**2. Organizational Structure & Management:** From Sparks to Sustainability Fiscal Sponsorship, 501c3 structure & application	I v a n M e d i n a , Loyola University & A l e x a n d e r D o m a n s k i s of Boodell & Domanskis	Handouts: 1) fiscal sponsorship; 2) Bylaws of the Organization (sample); 3) Duties of Directors (memorandum); 4) Internal Revenue Service Section 501(c)(3) Application (sample); 5) Ongoing filing requirements

Date	Topic	Speaker	Handouts
Thurs, June 28, 2012, 6 pm – 9 pm	**3. Proper Governance:** Board Development, Transparency & Accountability	Ivan Medina, Loyola University & Dale Asis, CAAAELII	Board development handouts: 1. What is the role of board governance? How can board members help raise money?/ 2. Board Member Fundraising Checklist/ 3. Whatever Board Member Needs to Know about Fundraising/ 4. Facing the Financial Crisis: 10 Smart Things Your Board Can Do Now
Thurs July 26, 2012, 6 pm – 9 pm	**4. Program planning:** From vision to reality, clear steps to get there	Dale Asis, CAAAELII	Guest speakers and handouts (to be determined)
Wed August 29, 2012, 6 pm – 9 pm	**5. Community Fundraising I:** Methods & Tools of Tapping into Local Community Resources	Dale Asis, CAAAELII & other Executive Directors of CAAAELII member agencies	Fundraising handouts: a. Fundraising Basics/ Nuts & Bolts b. Choosing a Fundraising Program c. Different Avenues for Nonprofit Fundraising
Wed Sept 26, 2012, 6 pm – 9 pm	**6. Community Fundraising II & Finding Volunteers:** Joint Fundraising, more community resources and finding volunteers	Dale Asis, CAAAELII & other Executive Directors of CAAAELII member agencies	More fundraising handouts: 1) 10 tips for effective board development; 2) approaching corporations for funding; 3) different avenues for fundraising; 4) fundraising through websites; 5) what board members should know about fundraising; 6) volunteer management
Wed October 24, 2012, 6 pm – 9 pm	**7. You're Connected to the Internet:** Technology, Social Media, Communications & Marketing	Dale Asis, CAAAELII Community Media Workshop (to be invited)	Website links, technology links

Groupwork Interventions for Women and Children Experiencing Domestic Abuse: Do They Work & Do They Last?

Stephanie Holt, Gloria Kirwan and Jane Ngo

Abstract

This chapter draws selectively on the findings of a study exploring the impact of a concurrent group work programme for mothers and children (6-7 years of age) who have experienced domestic abuse. This group was delivered by statutory child welfare services in Ireland in conjunction with a voluntary sector child support service. The chapter illustrates how participation in the group work programme impacted positively on the relationship between the participating mothers and their children and also explores what benefits were sustained over time. Employing a mixed methods approach, both quantitative and qualitative data was collected from three distinct populations and at three points in time. The findings of this study confirm the usefulness of the group environment in helping participants share the full extent of their personal experiences in a therapeutic and supportive setting. Participant outcomes included pro-social modelling of positive parenting, awareness raising and information-sharing regarding the impact of the experience of domestic abuse on both child development and parenting capacity. These factors were reported by participants to have impacted on the quality of the mother-child relationship. This chapter concludes by highlighting the key features of the group work programme which were central to facilitating and sustaining these positive outcomes.

Introduction

The complexities and challenges of working with families affected by domestic abuse are considerable and have been extensively documented, particularly within a statutory child protection and welfare context (Hester, 2011; Humphreys, 2010; Humphreys & Absler, 2011). These challenges include a lack of understanding of the dynamics of domestic abuse, which Humphreys (2010) concludes results in an attack on the mother-child relationship, where a gendered approach to social work intervention holds mothers responsible for the protection of their children whilst simultaneously failing to hold abusive men accountable for their actions. Not surprisingly, therefore, much research concludes that families experiencing domestic abuse and as a result receiving services from child protection social workers, are ambivalent if not apprehensive about this type of involvement in their family life, finding it neither helpful nor appropriate (Humphreys & Absler, 2011).

Group work interventions, however, can offer an empowering method of working with some parents as the focus of the work is to engender support networks between the group participants and to reduce the isolation individual members experience as an integral feature of domestic abuse (Peled & Davis, 1995). Peer support groups have proven useful in helping people to cope with many personal, emotional and health challenges (Ussher, Kirsten, Butow, & Sandoval, 2006; Rowan, 1999; Bolibok, 2001). For example, Peled and Davis (1995) report on their work with children of mothers exposed to domestic abuse and highlight consistent benefits such as 'breaking the secret', sharing personal experiences, assertive conflict resolution and protection planning. Research on group work with mothers exposed to abuse also highlights increased insights into the impact of this experience on their mothering and subsequently on their children's behaviour as direct outcomes of this intervention (Cunningham & Baker, 2004).

The usefulness of the group environment in helping participants share the full extent of their personal experiences has been recognised as an essential and distinctive element of groupwork practice (Yalom, 1995). Drawing on the extensive literature on group work with vulnerable populations, this chapter reports on a group work programme with women and children experiencing domestic abuse, reflecting on the extent to which it has provided the opportunity for participants to benefit from the therapeutic factors that a positive group work experience can provide. By following up with the participating mothers one year after the ending of the group work intervention, the evaluation reported here has also captured new knowledge on the potential for benefits, gained through group work intervention with mothers and children with histories of domestic abuse, to endure over time. Contrary to existing research on the nature of statutory social work involvement in families experiencing domestic abuse, the findings concur with Øverlien (2010) who argued that social work has much to offer within this field.

Literature Review

A gendered perspective of domestic abuse which reflects an understanding of this phenomenon as the intimate context within which *women* are abused by *men,* underpins the research from which this paper is drawn and may be legitimised based on empirical data concerning the nature and impact of this crime. Firstly, the numeric extent of woman abuse exceeds that of the intimate abuse of men (Walby & Allen, 2004; Watson & Parsons, 2005). Secondly, the impact of the abuse is likely to be greater for women than men, both emotionally and injuriously (Walby & Allen, 2004; Watson & Parsons, 2005). Thirdly, women are at far greater risk of serious and lethal abuse at the hands of their male partner than men are at risk from their female partner (World Health Organisation, 2002).

Exposure to domestic abuse can potentially infiltrate multiple aspects of victims' lives, which may result in detrimental short- and long-term effects on their physical and psychological health (Coker et al., 2002; Taft, 2002). This next section will focus firstly on the impact of exposure to domestic abuse on children before moving on to consider the empirical evidence on the impact of domestic abuse on mothering. It will conclude with a discussion on the evidence base for group work with women and children who have experienced domestic abuse.

Impact on Children

While there is undoubtedly a certain level of commonality in children's experience of domestic abuse, it would be erroneous to assume that either impact or outcomes are predictably similar for all children (Magen, 1999). As such, exposure to domestic abuse is not a "homogeneous uni-dimensional phenomenon" (Jouriles et al., 1998, p. 178), the impact of which can be neatly examined in isolation from the potential impact of other stressors or traumas in a child's life.

That said, however, due to the intimate nature of domestic abuse, children are very likely to be exposed to the violent incidents involving their caregivers (Carpenter & Stacks, 2009) as well as become victims of abuse (Alessi & Hearn, 2007; Moylan et al., 2010; Tajima, 2004), thus increasing the likelihood of developing posttraumatic symptoms (Courtois, 2004; Graham-Bermann & Levendosky, 1998) as well as negatively affecting their health and development (Evans, Davies & DiLillo, 2008). In addition, exposed children are at risk of developing internalised (i.e. depression or anxiety) or externalised behavioural difficulties (i.e. conduct or oppositional defiant disorder) that may further complicate existing relationships within the home, school or amongst peers (Buckley, Holt & Whelan, 2007; Holt, Buckley & Whelan, 2008; Graham-Bermann, Lynch, Banyard, DeVoe,. & Halabu, 2007; Grych, Jouriles, Swank, McDonald, & Norwood, 2000; Guerra, Huesmann, Tolan, Van Acker, & Eron, 1995; Moylan et al., 2010). Furthermore, developing maladaptive behaviour and/or having negative worldviews may inadvertently have long-term, detrimental effects that could lead to substance abuse, becoming victims or perpetrators of domestic abuse in adulthood, criminal involvement and increased mental health issues (Ehrensaft et al., 2003; Widom, 1998).

Helping children to reduce self-blame and anxiety, to problem-solve, and to cope are some strategies that various interventions have explored to reduce the effects of domestic abuse (Graham-Bermann et al., 2007; Sullivan, Egan & Gooch, 2004). Furthermore, children who have a safe and secure attachment to a non-violent parent or significant carer-giver are more likely to exhibit less behavioural and emotional issues than their counterparts (Cunningham & Baker, 2004). Thus, fostering and strengthening the mother-child relationship is essential within domestic abuse, but sustaining this relationship may prove difficult, as the next section illustrates.

Impact on Mothering

The empirical evidence clearly states that women who have previously experienced or are currently living with domestic abuse tend to exhibit and suffer from mental health issues (i.e. anxiety, fear, posttraumatic stress, low self-esteem, suicidal ideation and/or attempts), economic hardship, substance abuse, physical injuries and social isolation (Briere & Jordan, 2004; Humphreys & Thiara, 2003; Lafta, 2008; Woods, 2005). Even after separation, abused women may be obliged to have some form of contact with their violent ex-partner (Grip, Almqvist & Broberg, 2011; Holt, 2011), because of continuing shared factors such as parenting, finances etc. Such issues not only potentially affect abused women's ability to parent, but the attack on their mothering capabilities by their violent partners[1] also further undermines the mother-child relationship, whether it is through abuse or threat of abuse, manipulation, controlling, blaming, and/or legal or threat of legal action (Bancroft, 2011; Jaffe, Johnston, Crooks & Balla, 2008; Keeling & van Wormer, 2012; Lapierre, 2010). By weakening the mother-child relationship, the perpetrator can potentially gain increased control over the family's well-being (i.e. finances, material resources, access to services) (Lapierre, 2010). Some studies have found a positive correlation between abused women and the use of abusive tactics on their children, suggesting that domestic abuse adversely affects women's parenting (Holden & Ritchie, 1991; Levendosky & Graham-Bermann, 1998; Levendosky & Graham-Bermann, 2000). However, such results are not consistently found across similar research, where abused women are found to be adopting strategies that alleviate the stress and impact of exposure for their children (Casanueva, Martin, Runyan, Barth & Bradley, 2008; Létourneau, Fedick & Willms, 2007; Levendosky, Huth-Bocks, Shapiro, & Semel, 2003; Radford & Hester, 2006).

Peled and Gil (2011) found that abused mothers rarely linked the effects of the violent acts they had experienced to their children's well-being and were often able to completely separate the "children's world" from the real "violent world" by reframing the impact such violent acts had on their parenting and striving to maintain a positive image of their motherhood. Furthermore, these mothers learnt techniques to decrease the severity of fathers' violent outbursts in the presence of their children and would discuss the father in a positive light to their children in order to maintain harmony (Peled & Gil, 2011). Although such techniques are crucial to mediate living in a stressful environment by contributing positively to their self-image (Levendosky, Lynch & Graham-Bermann, 2000), such experiences may have hindered the mothers' capability to emotionally meet their children's needs, or provide nurturance and protection (Grip et al., 2011; Peled & Gil, 2011).

Groupwork with Women and Children Who have Experienced Domestic Violence

Engaging in groupwork can be a valuable form of intervention for victims of domestic abuse as it has the potential to enhance self-efficacy, promote empowerment and encourage the development of interpersonal skills critical to strengthen the mother-child relationship (Graham-Bermann et al., 2007; McWhirter, 2011; Basu, Malone, Levendosky & Dubay, 2009). Furthermore, group intervention has the potential to "decrease feelings of isolation...sharing problem-solving, coping strategies, and resources among group members" (Basu et al., 2009, p. 92). This has particular relevance in the context of domestic abuse, a phenomenon which thrives on isolating the victim from support. Yalom (1995) highlighted eleven therapeutic factors that intricately contribute to therapeutic change in group therapy. These factors are: (1) instillation of hope; (2) universality; (3) imparting information; (4) altruism; (5) the corrective recapitulation of the primary family group; (6) development of socialising techniques; (7) imitative behaviour; (8) interpersonal learning; (9) group cohesiveness; (10) catharsis; and (11) existential factors (Yalom & Leszcz, 2005, pp.1-2). Understanding how these factors impact group dynamics is essential in order to ensure the effectiveness of therapeutic groupwork and to foster an environment that promotes acceptance, healing and positive behaviour change. Although the therapeutic factors are identified individually, they function interdependently and therapeutic outcome depends on the holistic incorporation of these factors (Yalom & Leszcz, 2005). However, the effectiveness of the group programme may be contextually dependent on external group factors such as the existing relationships within families, situational circumstances, readiness of the mother and/or child to engage as well as the motivation of organisations and workers to provide a service that meets the victims' needs (Humphreys, Thiara & Skamballis, 2011).

Very little research has been conducted on groupwork with both women and children simultaneously, and less so within the community compared to shelter-based settings[2] (Basu et al., 2009; Graham-Bermann et al., 2007). Conducting interventions concurrently with women and children exposed to domestic abuse has been found to be effective (Basu et al., 2009; Graham-Bermann, et al., 2007; Sullivan et al., 2004; Thomspon & Trice-Black, 2012), especially since parenting and mothers' psychological well-being affects their interaction and ability to support their children (Jouriles et al., 2001; Levendosky & Graham-Bermann, 2000). Furthermore concurrent group intervention allows the involvement of women and children who may not have participated due to the lack of childcare (Basu et al., 2009; Graham-Bermann et al., 2007). Currently extant group interventions with domestic abuse victims vary in framework, structure, recruitment and analyses. McWhirter (2011) conducted two types of community-based group therapies with abused women and their children. Women who had been exposed to domestic abuse within the year of the onset of the study were recruited from a temporary family homeless shelter (McWhirter, 2011). In addition, their children must have been present for at least one incident of domestic abuse (McWhirter, 2011). Forty-six women and forty-eight children were randomly assigned to either a social supportive, emotion-focused or goal-oriented (reduction of family conflict and/or alcohol use) group therapy. Both therapy groups produced positive results. Children assigned to both groups reported an increased rating of their emotional well-being and self-esteem and a decrease of family and peer conflict (McWhirter, 2011). Concurrently, women found the groups to have increased self-efficacy and bonding within their families and rated themselves as less depressed (McWhirter, 2011). When analysed further women assigned to the emotion-focused group significantly reported a greater increase in social support than the goal-oriented therapy group, while women in the goal-oriented group were significantly found to experience less family conflict compared to the emotion-focused group (McWhirter, 2011).

Grip et al. (2011) also conducted community-based interventions with abused women and children separately in Sweden over a 15 week period. In the first report of this research, Grip et al. (2011) analysed the psychological outcome of participation in a group intervention for abused mothers and found that at an aggregate level, the self-reports indicated a significant improvement in mental health and a reduction of trauma-related symptoms immediately post-intervention and at the one year follow-up. Despite yielding strong results at group-level analyses, results at the individual-level demonstrated a more complicated relationship between participation in groupwork and mental health outcome (Grip et al., 2011). The majority reported feeling less distressed but their current symptom levels were still within the clinical range (Grip et al., 2011).

In a follow-up study of children who had undergone the group intervention, Grip, Almqvist and Broberg (2012) found that children receiving treatment improved their behavioural functioning immediately post-intervention but this was not sustained a year later. Although the group intervention was not attachment-focused, Grip et al. (2012) acknowledged that attachment as an issue indirectly surfaced in their data and concerns were raised in regards to the mother-child relationship in the aftermath of exposure to domestic abuse. They concluded that future interventions perhaps need to focus on parenting to promote and strengthen the mother-child relationship and be flexible with its objectives to better cater for the specific needs of victims (Grip et al., 2011).

Similarly, Sullivan et al. (2004) implemented a 9-week group intervention programme with 46 abused mothers and 79 exposed children. Groups were conducted based on a systemic and cognitive-behavioural approach, and were held conjointly as well as concurrently (Sullivan et al., 2004). Based on feminist principles, the objective of the group did not consist of victim blaming but rather holding offenders accountable while ensuring the safety of women and children (Sullivan et al., 2004). Their research found that the groupwork intervention was effective in reducing self-blame and trauma-related symptoms among children (Sullivan et al., 2004). In addition, children considered to have had clinically challenging behaviours benefited most from the group intervention. Future research may need to investigate intensifying or prolonging the intervention programme, but overall mothers claimed that they believed the intervention helped their children more than themselves even though they reported feeling less isolated, decreased health problems and lower stress levels at the end of the group intervention (Sullivan et al., 2004).

Although the above-mentioned research found improvements based on pre- and post-test results, unfortunately those studies lacked a control group that would enable analyses to compare impact on participants' well-being against those that did not receive any intervention. Graham-Bermann et al. (2007) recruited 221 mothers and children for a 10-week intervention programme through the community and allocated 62 children to the child-only (CO) condition, 61 to the child-plus-mother condition (CM), and 58 children to a wait-list comparison (CG). As hypothesised, the CM group showed the greatest improvement regarding children's attitudes towards abuse and in their externalising and internalising difficulties from post-intervention and at the 8-month follow-up (Graham-Bermann et al., 2007). Not only was the study group's intervention effective, Graham-Bermann et al. (2007) also demonstrated that group work programmes run concurrently with mothers and their children were most effective, perhaps due to the opportunities provided to address the specific needs of both groups, which permitted them to apply learnt skills in their day-to-day interactions.

The Groupwork Programme and Participants

A group work programme for mothers experiencing domestic violence was first established by the statutory social work service and located within a Family Resource Centre (FRC) in Dublin (Ireland) in 1995. That initial groupwork programme, known as SIN (Strength in Numbers) focused on the women's experience of domestic abuse. Since 1995, this programme has been expanded to include a second subsequent groupwork programme with a focus on understanding the impact that living with domestic abuse has on children, parenting and on the mother-child relationship. Completion of the first SIN group was a pre-requisite to the mother's involvement in the second mother and child group work programme.

For the programme under discussion here, five women, ranging in age from 31 to 40 years, participated in the ten week mothers' group. Only four of those women participated in the research and between them they had eleven children aged between 18 months and 17 years at the time of the first interview. The base line data collected in Phase One detailed that these women had experienced a broad range of domestic abuse, reporting also that the children had both indirect and direct exposure to that abuse. All of the participating women had sought protection from domestic abuse under the Domestic Violence Act, 1996. There were four children in the children's group, with the child of the fifth mother not being given permission to attend by his father who had joint custody of him. The influence of the abusive parent on the participation of the mothers and children in their respective groups, and in particular the possibility that participation in the group could become another control event, emerged as an issue requiring for future groups more attention and planning on the part of the facilitators and in particular, the lead group organiser. The four children, three boys and a girl were aged between six and seven years when the group work programme commenced.

The mothers' group followed a ten week programme employing a psycho-educational approach which involved both educational activities and opportunities for the women to support each other by sharing child-related needs and concerns. The children's ten week programme was arts based and focused on facilitating a discussion with the children on feelings and relationships.

Methodology

This study design was informed by the 'Intervention Research Model' developed by Rothman and Thomas (1994). This model accommodates both quantitative and qualitative methods and is appropriate for use with small population samples, and where the research is conducted in on-site practice conditions. It also supports the inclusion of practitioners' insights within the overall research design, and is thus of particular worth in this study where the investigation sought to accommodate the views of both the service users and service providers.

A multi-stage data collection strategy was carried out, with data collected at three distinct points in the delivery of the group work programme. Phase One of this research involved establishing base line data on the group participants. This was achieved with the completion of a structured questionnaire by participating mothers. This questionnaire gathered standardised information on each family including socio-demographic information, experiences of domestic abuse and perceived impact on mothers and children. Phase Two took place following the completion of the intervention for the group participants. Qualitative semi-structured individual interviews were conducted with participating mothers to explore in detail, their experience of the group work programme and its impact on them as participants and as parents and their perceptions of impact on their children from their participation in the children's group. A qualitative semi-structured focus group interview was also conducted with the participating children. Finally Phase Two also included qualitative semi-structured focus group and individual post-group interviews with the professionals delivering the programme to gain insight into the issues surrounding the group work programme implementation and the outcomes they perceive it to have achieved. The qualitative approach employed in Phase Two was deemed the most appropriate given the need to understand the reasoning behind the interviewees' viewpoints and also the sensitive nature of the topic (Rubin & Rubin, 2005).

Phase Three involved a return to the research site, one year later, where the qualitative interviews with the mothers were repeated. The findings of Phase Three were compared with Phases One and Two to explore the sustainability of outcomes arising from the group work programme intervention for both mothers and children.

Findings

The findings presented capture the outcomes and benefits reported by mothers, children and workers at Phase Two and by mothers at Phase Three of the evaluation. A key focus of the evaluation of this group at Phase Three was to establish the extent to which any positive gains by mothers and children, identified at the end of Phase Two, endured for a period of one year or longer. As a preamble to the findings presented below, it is relevant to note that all the mothers completed their group to its natural end and that in general it was a productive group in which the members self-reported and were reported by the facilitators to have fully participated.

Findings at Phase Two Evaluation

Phase Two of the research methodology marked the end point of the group work programme. The findings presented here record how the informants discussed the factors inherent to the group process that benefitted participants and also the general benefits achieved that relate to the participants' overall sense of wellbeing.

The legacy of domestic violence

Like a thread running through the evaluation interviews, it emerged from the data that although all the participating mothers had separated from their abusive partners before the commencement of the mother and children programme, the historical legacy of that experience remained a fresh and constant theme for the mothers. For all of them, there was still some form of ongoing contact with their former partner due to the many connections that still existed between them, including their children. Therefore, not surprisingly, the details of the historical violence and abuse surfaced repeatedly during the evaluation interviews at Phase Two. It also emerged that while the actual violence was now in the past, the threat of violence and the other forms of abusive control exerted by their former partners over them was, for many of the mothers, a continuing reality. The violence they had endured, the related trauma experienced by their children, the impact on their confidence, self-esteem and mental health were intertwined with how they reported on the benefits for themselves and their children arising from the group. One woman, commenting on how she had been while still living with her abusive partner:

> *(I had)* no sense of anything else going on around me. Just had to get on with the day to day violence – survival – accept it as my lot – like I had accepted dying – *(I had)* gave up completely on myself.

All of the women interviewed reflected back on life with their partner and the sense of losing self-agency, of finding day-to-day life unpredictable and dangerous, and of varying levels of emotional availability (or unavailability) to their children. All participants indicated that the abusive context of domestic life had impacted on their children for whom the violence and danger was not invisible. The reality for their children is captured in these following quotes from two mothers:

> *They saw everything especially the 11 year old. She was the oldest left to protect the others – heard a lot too – she had to escape to call the Garda [Irish Police Service]. She saw the effect on her Mum, saw me being punched in the head, arms body, saw broken ribs and that I couldn't work.*

*Between ages 3-5 he saw me being hit, saw Dad smack my head against the
wall and he screamed at his Dad to stop....he has seen Garda involvement,
saw his Dad smash up the whole house and he still sees heated discussion
from the car at access. He witnesses my panic attacks and worries about
me all the time.*

This last quote captures the link between the present and the past,
which permeated the accounts of all the mothers interviewed. In this
instance, the mother connects her son's current concern for her and
the anxiety they share about her continued panic attacks with the
experience in his younger years of seeing his father seriously assault his
mother on more than one occasion. A recurring theme throughout all
of their accounts was the presence of anxiety and emotional damage
suffered by their children arising from witnessing or being aware of
the violence between their parents when they lived together.

Confirming this past-present connectivity, the group facilitators
reported that dealing with the present parenting/family issues
brought by the participants to the group meetings required devoting
considerable attention to the past. For them it was clear that the
current mother-child relationships were resting on the foundations
of the past, and moving forward required addressing the historical
as well as the current contexts. The evaluation identified that the
support offered by the facilitators, and in particular their in-depth
awareness of the dynamics of domestic violence, enabled both the
children's and mother's groups to achieve high levels of performance
in which therapeutic factors supported the participants to recognise
the influences of the past while also realising the potential they held
to change the present.

Therapeutic factors in the group programme

The evaluation uncovered a range of issues related to the planning,
format, timing, content and process of the two concurrent groups.
It is not possible to report in full on all the issues that emerged from
the evaluation so the discussion will focus on how the existence of
certain key therapeutic factors (Yalom & Leszcz, 2005) supported
the positive outcomes that the evaluation identified for both mothers
and children. From a thematic analysis of the evaluation interviews,
it emerged that certain factors permeated the process of both groups
and these appear to have been instrumental in supporting the overall

gains found at Phase Two.

The "Instillation of Hope" (Yalom & Leszcz, 2005) was a pervasive therapeutic factor across all aspects of this group programme. The participating women had already completed the Strength In Numbers (SIN) programme, and had previously found group intervention useful. This was a clear motivating factor for them in deciding to participate in the mother and children programme where they carried with them into this group the sense of hope that group intervention could be of benefit to them. The evaluation confirmed that the participating mothers viewed their involvement in the group programme with positive anticipation and that on completion they continued to believe that the group had offered them much needed support and information.

"Imparting of Information" (Yalom & Leszcz, 2005) was a central therapeutic factor found in both the mother's group and the children's group. The evaluation identified that discussions involved the group in deep level and meaningful exploration of the many challenges facing group members regarding their parenting, past and present. One facilitator's comment captured this element:

> *The women were all at different stages and that's also how the group worked really well I think because where one woman was ten steps forward, another one was ten steps in a different direction and she could say 'Oh I remember that when I was like that and you will get through it and you'll come to this step. They gave each other hope.*

Of interest was the extent that information sharing also acted as a therapeutic factor in the children's group. The evaluation found that bringing the children into discussion of feelings, memories and past experiences required sustained effort by the facilitators, but that when it was achieved in the group, then transformative conversations took place. It was clear from the evaluation interview with the children and from the reports from their facilitators, also supported by information provided in the evaluation interviews with the mothers, that for all of the children, the group had offered them a first time experience of meeting other children who had similar domestic violence histories and discussing with others what that had been like for them. A legacy issue for all of these children was confusion about emotional wellbeing and understanding or being able to identify their feelings. How the group had made a difference in this regard is captured in this account by one of the children:

> *I feel different now because I know all about my feelings...I feel safe*

(because there is) no fighting and people being mean to each other. (this group) is different to other clubs I go to. I go to homework club but you don't talk about feelings there.

A key point to note in this example is how this child identifies that they "feel different now" and "I feel safe". They are also able to differentiate this group experience from other groups in which they participate, again confirming that the content and process of the children's group had a therapeutic component of which the children were aware.

Linked with "Imparting of Information" (Yalom & Leszcz, 2005), the evaluation found that "Universality" (Yalom & Leszcz, 2005) contributed to the positive benefits reported by the participants. Discovering that they were not the only people with similar histories who felt that history impacted on their parenting, liberated the mothers in many ways to articulate and find solutions to the parenting challenges they faced. By hearing each other's stories, the participants could adopt a more objective perspective on their own experience and recognise the shared patterns of parenting-disruption arising from the legacy of domestic abuse. One mother explained this very clearly:

I couldn't put a name on a lot of things, listening to the other girls has made me really aware that it's not me. I always thought it was me and because of my past I was blaming myself, it must be me. Hearing other people's stories made me think that these guys all went to the same school you know, they're all doing the same things, you know they might do it a bit differently but their end goal is the same.

A similar dynamic occurred within the children's group where the children expressed relief to discover that they were not alone in coming from a family where domestic violence occurred. This sense of shared experience fostered "Altruism" (Yalom & Leszcz, 2005) within the groups and the evaluations contain many examples of assistance received and assistance given which participants found useful and rewarding. The information-sharing norm established within the mother's group in particular, fostered a strong sense of group identity and the members worked collectively to explore solutions to each other's problems. This beneficial dynamic was articulated by one of the facilitators of this group and also displays how this promoted the overall functioning of the group itself:

The women can challenge each other and it's not taken in an offensive way where if we were to challenge, it's like, it might come across as like 'oh they're doing something wrong' but if another women challenges, it's like their peers so that worked really well in our own group, that like we could step back quite a lot of the times and let them challenge each other and keep us outside you know, steering but not directing.

External to the group sessions, the evaluation at Phase Two discovered that the issues addressed within the group fed into the mother-child relationships in the home contexts. In the evaluation interviews, the children and mothers identified improvements gained, particularly in the area of communication between them, reduction in tension and arguments, improved behavioural management approaches and generally a greater sense of openness in their relationships with each other. Central to these improvements was the heightened awareness on the part of the mothers that their children had been victims too and also carried a legacy of emotional hurt from the experiences of domestic abuse. The position of the children caught in the middle between two parents of a disrupted relationship was also brought sharply into focus during the programme and this helped the mothers appreciate the thin tightrope their children often traversed in trying to simultaneously manage relationships with separated parents. The key to unlocking this increased awareness appeared to be the level of discussion devoted to feelings in both groups.

The following quote from one of the mothers captures many of the benefits recorded within the evaluation at Phase Two:

I am more positive now, more aware of what I am doing as a parent and where we are going as a family. Before I was an emotional wreck. First I suppose the experience of the group...the learning from the group –the realisation that these men are all branches of the same tree, they are all thinking the same, doing the same stuff. What they might be doing from one woman to the next, the outcome for us all and our kids is the same. Realising that was good for me – it made me see that I am not what he sees. I don't think it is just time, more it has been the support from (children's group facilitator),since the group finished, for all the kids and me as their Mum.

The positive experience of the group for the children is captured by one of the child participants:

I wish I could stay here forever...

Findings at Phase Three Evaluation

The evaluation team returned one year later to elicit the sustained benefits, if any, that participating mothers could identify for themselves and their children. The interviews with the mothers at Phase Three focused on the extent to which the positive reports they had provided regarding the confidence in parenting and their heightened awareness regarding the emotional wellbeing of their children had persisted and endured over the intervening year.

The findings at this stage of the evaluation depict a broadly positive but perhaps more mixed set of outcomes across the participating mothers and children. The mothers all recalled participation in the group as pivotal in helping them acquire a sense of personal agency, of becoming aware of their power to shape the relationship they developed and sustained with their children, albeit in the context of ongoing disharmony with their child's father. The mothers remained committed to working on building and maintaining positive relationships with their children despite and not dependent on the state of the relationship between them and their estranged partner. The mothers also recounted how the group experience had helped restore their sense of the world as a safe place where help can be available and where their histories and experiences could be accepted non-judgementally. The boost to their confidence was reportedly retained by all of the women who expressed a wish that the group could continue in some shape or form as it had been central to the uplifting of their self-esteem and had enhanced their confidence as parents. They expressed a similar wish for the children's groups as they reported the children still talked about the group and how they had enjoyed it. One mother, whose child had not had a good year in school or in the family context, strongly expressed a concern that the group had been too short and that its ending had been yet another loss in her child's life.

A paradoxical finding from the Phase Three evaluation related to the experience of the mothers of receiving statutory child protection social work involvement. Prior to joining the mother and child programme, many of the participants had not been involved in direct receipt of statutory child protection services. They had preconceived misgivings about engaging with child protection social work provision, arising from anecdotal hearsay from neighbours, acquaintances or the media. Some had been nervous and sceptical of taking part in the programme, concerned that what they perceived as their deficient parenting might attract the negative attention of the group facilitators. However, the experience of participation in the group had replaced this concern with a strongly positive view of the gains to be made by working with professional services. Paradoxically, this had impacted negatively on their view of other professional services they had encountered since the group programme ended. The level of understanding, empathy and expertise on the issue of domestic abuse that the participants had received from the programme facilitators was not so automatically replicated among professionals in other services or fields. Some mothers commented on the limited understanding of teachers regarding the impact on their children of domestic violence or the persistent acrimony between the parents. One mother, who had engaged with a child mental health setting, reported feeling very let down and abandoned by the therapists there whom, she believed, failed to acknowledge the impact of the domestic history on her child's current health and wellbeing.

A key message from the findings at Phase Three was that providing a positive group experience is an important step in helping families successfully mediate the transition after separation in domestic abuse contexts but that the programme itself is not sufficient. A message strongly articulated by many of the participating mothers at Phase Three was that follow-up group contact would have cemented the gains achieved by them and their children. While they all felt stronger as a result of the programme, their ability to translate their increased knowledge and skills into daily life varied depending on external factors and waivered when the pressure within the parent to parent or parent to child relationship became intense. It was also challenged by the lack of domestic violence awareness pervasively encountered by families in their dealings with many institutions and contexts in society.

Conclusion

The findings of this research have highlighted a number of issues worth a concluding mention. In response to Keeling and van Wormer's (2012) and Lapierre's (2010) call that social work must create and provide an environment whereby abused mothers and their children feel safe to discuss their experiences, this groupwork programme has demonstrated the clear capacity for social work to provide that environment, build rapport between a vulnerable service user group and build capacity in parenting in order to enhance parent-child relationships. Through building rapport and learning more about women's experiences, this social work agency is better informed and equipped, as Yoshioka and Choi (2005) suggested, in providing a holistic plan of intervention. Going forward, this evaluation has highlighted, not only the importance for this agency to concentrate on how the abuse has affected abused women's mothering capabilities, but also the importance of focusing on the men's abuse as it directly affects the family environment (Lapierre, 2010). Just as the abusive adult relationship does not exist in a vacuum, this research concludes that the group process in itself may not be enough to maintain and sustain positive change and that social work needs to consistently challenge societal perceptions of domestic abuse, motherhood, and social systems and procedures currently in place for handling domestic abuse cases if better outcomes that will ensure the safety and eventual empowerment of abused women and children are to be achieved (Anderson, 2003; Fox & Cook, 2011; Stanley, Miller, Foster & Thomson, 2011; Yoshioka & Choi, 2005). Undoubtedly, collaboration between disciplines directly and indirectly involved with issues related to domestic abuse is needed to better address and provide effective intervention that will yield long-lasting, positive results (Busch-Armendariz, Johnson, Buel & Lungwitz, 2011; Schewe et al., 2011).

Notes

1   Abusive fathers also tend to adopt parenting techniques and strategies that are potentially not conducive to the general well-being and development of children (i.e. being rigid and authoritative, uninvolved in children's lives, self-absorbed, possessive, manipulative and physically punitive) (Bancroft, 2011; Bent-Goodley & Williams, 2007; Holden & Ritchie, 1991; Sternberg, Lamb, Greenbaum, Dawud, Cortes & Lorey, 1994).

2   The majority of group interventions for domestic abuse outside of shelter settings tend to be for male perpetrators (see Augusta, Scott & Dankwort, 2002).

References

Alessi, J. & Hearn, K. (2007). Group treatment of children in shelters for battered women. In A. Hearns (Ed.), *Battered Women and their Families.* (3rd Ed., pp.159-173). New York, NY: Springer.

Anderson, C. (2003). Evolving out of violence: An application of the transtheoretical model of behavioral change. *Research and Theory for Nursing Practice: An International Journal, 17*(3), 225-240.

Bancroft, L. (2011). *The Batterer as Parent: Addressing the Impact of Domestic Violence on Family Dynamics.* London: Sage.

Basu, A., Malone, J., Levendosky, A. & Dubay, S. (2009). Longitudinal treatment effectiveness outcomes of a group intervention for women and children exposed to domestic violence. *Journal of Child & Adolescent Trauma, 2*(2), 90-105.

Bolibok, B. (2001). 'The plural "self": group therapy with Bosnian women survivors of war'. *Smith College Studies in Social Work, 71* (3), 459- 467.

Briere, J. & Jordan, C. (2004). Violence against women: Outcome complexity and implications for assessment and treatment. *Journal of Interpersonal Violence, 19*(11), 1252-1276.

Buckley, H., Holt, S. & Whelan, S. (2007) 'Listen to me! Children's experiences of domestic violence', *Child Abuse Review, 16*(5), pp. 296–310.

Busch-Armendariz, N., Johnson, R., Buel, S. & Lungwitz, J. (2011). Building community partnerships to end interpersonal violence: A collaboration of the schools of social work, law, and nursing. *Violence Against Women, 17*(9), 1194-1206.

Carpenter, G. & Stacks, A. (2009). Developmental effects of exposure to intimate partner violence in early childhood: A review of the literature. *Children and Youth Services Review, 31*(8), 831-839.

Casanueva, C., Martin, S., Runyan, D., Barth, R. & Bradley, R. (2008). Quality of maternal parenting among intimate-partner violence victims involved with the child welfare system. *Journal of Family Violence, 23*(6), 413-427.

Coker, A., Davis, K., Arias, I., Desai, S., Sanderson, M., Brandt, H. & Smith, P. (2002). Physical and mental health effects of intimate partner violence for men and women. *American Journal of Preventive Medicine 23*(4), 260-268.

Courtois. C. (2004). Complex trauma, complex reactions: Assessment and treatment. *Psychotherapy, 41*(4), 412-425.

Cunningham, A. & Baker, L. (2004) *What About Me! Seeking to Understand a Child's View of Violence in the Family.* London, Ontario: Centre for Children & Families in the Justice System.

Domestic Violence Act, 1996. Available at: http://www.irishstatutebook.ie/eli/1996/act/1/enacted/en/html

Ehrensaft, M., Cohen, P., Brown, J., Smailes, E., Chen, H. & Johnson, J. (2003). Intergenerational transmission of partner violence: A 20-year prospective study. *Journal of Consulting and Clinical Psychology, 71*, 741-753.

Evans, S., Davies, C. & DiLillo, D. (2008). Exposure to domestic violence: A meta-analysis of child and adolescent outcomes. *Aggression and Violent Behavior, 13*, 131-140.

Fox, K. & Cook, C. (2011). Is knowledge power? The effects of a victimology course on victim blaming. *Journal of Interpersonal Violence, 26*(17), 3407-3427.

Fugate, M., Landis, L., Riordan, K., Naureckas, S. & Engel, B. (2005). Barriers to domestic violence help seeking: Implications for intervention. *Violence Against Women, 11*(3), 290-310.

Graham-Bermann, S. & Levendosky, A. (1998). Traumatic stress symptoms in children of battered women. *Journal of Interpersonal Violence, 13*(1), 111-128.

Graham-Bermann, S., Lynch, S., Banyard, V., DeVoe, E. & Halabu, H. (2007). Community-based intervention for children exposed to intimate partner violence: An efficacy trial. *Journal of Consulting and Clinical Psychology, 75*(2), 199-209.

Grip, K., Almqvist, K. & Broberg, A. (2011). Effects of a group-based intervention on psychological health and perceived parenting capacity among mothers exposed to intimate partner violence (IPV): A preliminary study. *Smith College Studies in Social Work, 81*(1), 81-100.

Grip, K., Almqvist, K. & Broberg, A. (2012). Maternal report on child outcome after a community-based program following intimate partner violence. *Nordic Journal of Psychiatry, 66*(4), 239-247.

Grych, J., Jouriles, E., Swank, P., McDonald, R. & Norwood, W. (2000). Patterns of adjustment among children of battered women. *Journal of Consulting and Clinical Psychology, 68*(1), 84-94.

Guerra, N., Huesmann, L., Tolan, P., Van Acker, R. & Eron, L. (1995). Stressful events and individual beliefs as correlates of economic disadvantage and aggression among urban children. *Journal of Consulting and Clinical Psychology, 63*(4), 518-5828.

Hester, M. (2011). The three planet model: Towards an understanding of contradictions in approaches to women and children's safety in contexts of domestic violence. *British Journal of Social Work, 41*, 837-853.

Holden, G. & Ritchie, K. (1991). Linking extreme marital discord, child rearing, and child behaviour problems: Evidence from battered women. *Child Development, 62*(2), 311-327.

Holt, S. (2011). Domestic abuse and child contact: Positioning children in the decision-making process. *Child Care in Practice, 17*(4), 327-346.

Holt, S., Buckley, H. & Whelan, S. (2008). The impact of exposure to domestic violence on children and young people: A review of the literature. *Child Abuse & Neglect, 32*(8), 797-810.

Humphreys, C. (2010). Crossing the great divide: Response to Douglas and Walsh. *Violence Against Women, 16*(5), 509-515.

Humphreys, C. & Absler, D. (2011). History repeating: child protection responses to domestic violence. *Child & Family Social Work, 16,* 464-473.

Humphreys, C. & Thiara, R. (2003). Mental health and domestic violence: 'I call it symptoms of abuse'. *British Journal of Social Work, 33*(2), 209-226.

Humphreys, C., Thiara, R. & Skamballis, A. (2011). Readiness to change: Mother-child relationship and domestic violence intervention. *British Journal of Social Work, 41*(1), 166-184.

Jaffe, P., Johnston, J., Crooks, C. & Balla, N. (2008). Custody disputes involving allegations of domestic violence: Toward a differentiated approach to parenting plans. *Family Court Review, 46*(3), 500-522.

Jouriles, E. N., McDonald, R., Norwood, W. D., ShinnWare, H., Collazos Spiller, L. & Swank, P. R. (1998) Knives, guns and interparent violence: Relations with child behaviour problems. *Journal of Family Psychology, 12*(2), 178–194.

Keeling, J. & van Wormer, K. (2012). Social worker interventions in situations of domestic violence: What we can learn from survivors' personal narratives? *British Journal of Social Work, 42*(7), 1354-1370.

Lafta, R. (2008). Intimate-partner violence and women's health. *Lancet, 371,* 1140-1142.

Lapierre, S. (2010). More responsibilities, less control: Understanding the challenges and difficulties involved in mothering in the context of domestic violence. *British Journal of Social Work 40*(5), 1434-1451.

Létourneau, N., Fedick, C. & Willms, J. (2007). Mothering and domestic violence: A longitudinal analysis'. *Journal of Family Violence, 22*(8), 649-659.

Levendosky, A. & Graham-Bermann, S. (1998). The moderating effects of parenting stress on children's adjustment in woman-abusing families. *Journal of Interpersonal Violence, 13*(3), 383-397.

Levendosky, A. & Graham-Bermann, S. (2000). Behavioral observations of parenting in battered women. *Journal of Family Psychology, 14*(1), 80-94.

Levendosky, A., Huth-Bocks, A., Shapiro, D. & Semel, M. (2003). The impact of domestic violence on the maternal-child relationship and pre-school-age children's functioning. *Journal of Family Psychology, 17*(4), 544-552.

McWhirter, P. (2011). Differential therapeutic outcomes of community-based group interventions for women and children exposed to intimate partner violence. *Journal of Interpersonal Violence, 26*(12), 2457-2482.

Magen, R.H. (1999). In the best interests of battered women: Reconstructing allegations of failure to protect. *Child Maltreatment, 4*(2), 127-135.

Moylan, C., Herrenkohl, T., Sousa, C., Tajima, E., Herrenkohl, R. & Russo, M. (2010). The effects of child abuse and exposure to domestic violence on adolescent internalizing and externalizing behavior problems. *Journal of Family Violence, 25*(1), 53-63.

Osofsky, J. (2003). Prevalence of children's exposure to domestic violence and child maltreatment: Implications for prevention and intervention. *Clinical Child and Family Psychology Review, 6*(3), 161-170.

Øverlien, C. (2010). Children exposed to domestic violence: Conclusions from the literature and challenges ahead. *Journal of Social Work, 10*(1), 80-97.

Peled, E. & Davis, D. (1995). *Groupwork with Children of Battered Women: A Practitioner's Manual.* London: Sage.

Peled, E. & Gil, I. (2011). The mothering perceptions of women abused by their partner. *Violence Against Women, 17*(4), 457-479.

Radford, L. & Hester, M. (2006). *Mothering through Domestic Violence.* London: Jessica Kingsley Publishers.

Renner, L. & Slack, K. (2006). Intimate partner violence and child maltreatment: Understand intra- and intergenerational connections. *Child Abuse & Neglect, 30*(6), 599-617.

Rothman, J. & Thomas, E. J. (Eds.). (1994). *Intervention research: Design and development for human services.* New York: Haworth Press.

Rowan, J. (1999) Crossing the great gap: Groupwork for personal growth. *Groupwork, 11*(3), 6-18.

Rubin, H.J. & Rubin, I.S. (2005). *Qualitative Interviewing: The Art of Hearing Data.* 2nd edition. Sage: London.

Schewe, P., Bell, C., Bennett, L., Goldstein, P., Gordon, R., Mattaini, M., O'Brien, P., Riger, S., Risser, H., Rosenbaum, D., Schuck, A., Simmons, B. & Ullman, S. (2011). University of Illinois at Chicago's Interdisciplinary Center for Research on Violence: Changing systems to prevent violence in Chicago and beyond. *Violence Against Women, 17*(9), 1176-1193.

Stanley, N., Miller, P., Foster, H.R. & Thomson, G. (2011). A Stop-start response: Social services' interventions with children and families notified following domestic violence incidents. *British Journal of Social Work, 41*(2), 296-313.

Sullivan, S., Egan, M. & Gooch, M. (2004). Conjoint interventions for adult victims and children of domestic violence: a program evaluation. *Research on Social work Practice, 14*(3), 163-170.

Taft, A. (2002). Violence against women in pregnancy and after childbirth. *Australian Domestic & Family Violence Clearinghouse, 6,* 1-23.

Tajima, E. (2004). Correlates of the co-occurrence of wife abuse and child abuse among a representative sample. *Journal of Family Violence, 19,* 399-410.

Thompson, E. & Trice-Black, S. (2012). School-based group interventions for children exposed to domestic violence. *Journal of Family Violence, 27,* 233-241.

Ussher, J., Kirsten, L., Butow, P. & Sandoval, M. (2006). 'What do cancer support groups provide which other supportive relationships do not? The experience of peer support groups for people with cancer'. *Social Science and Medicine, 62,* 2565-2576.

Walby, S. & Allen, J. (2004). Domestic violence, sexual assault & stalking: Findings from the British crime survey. *Home Office Research Study,* 276.

Watson, D. & Parsons, S. (2005). *Domestic Abuse of Women and Men in Ireland: Report on the National Study of Domestic Abuse.* Dublin: National Crime Council.

Widom, C.S. (1998). Child victims: Searching for opportunities to break the cycle of violence. *Applied & Preventative Psychology, 7*(4), 225-234.

Woods, S. (2005). Intimate partner violence and post-traumatic stress disorder symptoms in women: What we know and need to know. *Journal of Interpersonal Violence, 20,* 394-402.

World Health Organisation (2002). *World Report on Violence and Health.* Geneva: World Health Organisation.

Yalom, I. (1995). *The Theory and Practice of Group Psychotherapy.* (4th Ed). New York: Basic Books.

Yalom, I. & Leszcz, M. (2005). *The Theory and Practice of Group Psychotherapy.* (5th Ed). New York: Basic Books.

Yoshioka, M. & Choi, D. (2005). Culture and interpersonal violence research: Paradigm shift to create a full continuum of domestic violence services. *Journal of Interpersonal Violence, 20*(4), 513-519.

Group Work with Mothers with Multiple Sclerosis: A Second True Self Emerges

Rebecca Halperin

Introduction

Using a narrative approach, this chapter looks at a second "True Self" that is nurtured within each member of a support group I facilitate for mothers with Multiple Sclerosis (MS). Prior to the start of the support group, I was familiar with both the authentic self and inauthentic self of each participating woman. The inauthentic self was the self that masquerades in front of friends, families, strangers and even health care professionals. Masquerading is discussed at length, as it is a common habit formed by individuals with chronic illness (including Multiple Sclerosis). The authentic self I was familiar with was a version of each mom that had sat, at some point prior to the start of the group as well as throughout the duration of participation, in my office and cried. The women in the support group are all also women I see for individual counseling. In individual counseling, each woman shared feelings of hopelessness and desperation. It was anticipated that one of the familiar versions of the self would emerge in group; instead, a second authentic self surfaced – one that was realistic but hopeful. The focus of this paper is to examine the support group's role in creating the second authentic self.

Background, Planning, and Recruitment

Although there are close to sixty social workers employed by New York

University Langone Medical Center, I am the sole social worker at the Multiple Sclerosis Comprehensive Care Center, an outpatient clinic under the neurology department of the medical center. I am accustomed to patients coming to me eager for advice and keen for answers. I know not every social worker shares this experience. There is something about working at a doctors' office that makes people appreciate you for being the expert that you are. The reverence our patients hold for their neurologists spills over to me. I spend my day being presented with problems and finding – sometimes more successfully than others – solutions.

It caught me by surprise when a patient, explaining her recent frustrations one day in my office, stated, "I know what I need!" She proceeded to tell me that what she would find most helpful was a support group for other mothers with Multiple Sclerosis. "Can you start a group for us?" she continued while my excitement immediately matched hers. I am very lucky to work in a setting that values my clinical skills. All welcomed the idea of the group and it only took a matter of weeks before it was up and running.

There was not much difference between the group as it existed in the planning stages and the group after it was born into reality. MOMS, short for Move Over Multiple Sclerosis, is a support group for mothers who have MS. It is an open group that meets weekly for one hour. It is loosely structured. I welcome participants and encourage everyone to "check in" by sharing something – anything – with the group. After my brief introduction I most often become a silent observer, speaking up again only as the hour draws to a close. From time to time, I interject in order to push a participant to think more deeply or to free the air space from being monopolized. It is a support group and simply that; there is no educational piece except for what participants learn from each other. There are no required tasks and the only goal, albeit an important one, is that each participant feels more supported and less isolated than they did prior to joining the group. (This is measured with a questionnaire that is given on the first day of participation and again at intervals throughout participation.)

Eligibility requirements are two-fold: a diagnosis of Multiple Sclerosis or similar neurological condition/symptoms, and motherhood. The age of children or stage of motherhood is not specified although the majority of participants have children under the age of eighteen. Recruitment was approached from several angles. I spoke to women I saw regularly for counseling, and I sent letters and made phone calls to patients who were identified by other staff members. I hung a sign in my office for patients to notice and the patient program assistant at my clinic kept our waiting room stocked with flyers.

Prior to the start of the group, I had seen all of the participating women for individual counseling, some for just one session, several for weekly appointments, and most for something in between. Meeting with me was not a requirement to join the group, it just happened that women who were interested in a support group were women who were already reaching out for support through individual counseling. Each and every one of them had sat in my office and cried, sobbed even. Each and every one had voiced that they felt like they were alone with their struggles, and that even the support of their friends and families would only go so far. They shared joys and triumphs as well; I knew they were capable of recognizing and enjoying positive things in their lives. It was not as if they were all so depressed that they could not function.

In other words, these are normal women. They get out of bed every day, they dress themselves (no matter how long it takes – MS slows you down), they dress their children, they prepare meals, they get around to their appointments. They are not so paralyzed with sadness and fear that they cannot function. Some of them come dangerously close to that point from time to time, but for the most part, these are women that can pull themselves together. But after you peel back that layer of "being fine" and you take away the smiles that reassure their children that "mommy's okay", that genuine part of the self, that True Self that they feel like they can not show anyone, appears.

It happens so easily in my office because they do not need to "have it together" like they do for their children, spouse, parents, etc. They do not need to worry about how I will react. They do not need to feel guilty for "bringing me down". They know I can handle it; they know I am a professional, no matter how familiar and friendly the relationship may start to feel.

The Beginning of the Group

I expected these nuggets of True Self to appear in the group setting as they had in my individual sessions with each woman. I anticipated a room full of crying women, uninhibited and safe to express their dark feelings. I assumed that if this did not occur, then I had not done my job to create an environment fit for a True Self. Perhaps it was possible that I could create that environment for one-on-one sessions but not for a group?

The positive energy buzzing in the room was palpable during our first session. As a facilitator, I felt inspired, almost moved to tears. These women were like stronger, happier, calmer doppelgangers of themselves. *"First session enthusiasm,"* I thought, still convinced my expectation of mass misery would come to fruition. Sessions passed and it became the norm and not the exception that these women were showing and sharing strength. It was not that they avoided the tough subjects or wiped away their tears before being seen; they talked about deep disappointments, fears, dissolving marriages – the list could go on and on. The content of what they discussed was the same as what many of them had shared during individual sessions, but it was the package in which it was delivered that was different.

My expectations for the group were incorrect and although I was enjoying seeing this other side of each participant, I could not help wondering, *"what is going on here? Which setting, individual or group, is soliciting the genuine, authentic woman?"* I knew that group work can elicit different outcomes than individual work – after all, they are two distinct types of intervention – but I wanted to discover if there was anything specific to my population (mothers with MS) that could speak further to this phenomenon.

Living with Multiple Sclerosis

This led me to wonder, *"what is unique about people with MS?"* I could have potentially gotten stuck here, as that is a rich question with many answers. Recognizing a need to be more specific, I rephrased my question to include *"what is unique about people with MS and social relationships?"* My ongoing work with patients helped me answer this question.

There is a great deal of masquerading with MS, and perhaps with all chronic illnesses. After the crisis of diagnosis, patients report that they do not feel that family and friends really want to hear "how they are doing." The truthful answer, which could range from "today is a good day, I feel pretty good" to "I am not sure if I can wake up and take another day" may serve as a reminder to the loved one that there is nothing, no amount of love, support or prayer, that can cure the illness. And that is hard for family and friends to accept; it is hard to feel that we cannot take away a loved one's suffering. It is a crushing, heartbreaking feeling that we as humans take precautions to avoid. So when a patient has the opportunity to list the pains, fears and disappointments that occupy their mind most of the day, often "I'm fine" is a substitute.

A person with a chronic illness may be positive most, if not all of the time, but it is not necessarily always genuine. The masquerade artist is not always born overnight; during and immediately after diagnosis the individual – now "a patient" – is in crisis mode. Their crying, worrying and fragility are accepted. No one questions their shaky voice or the fear in their eyes. After the crisis of diagnosis is over, life goes back to normal. At least that is what we as a society, as a family, and as a social group expect. It has to, after all; the very nature of crisis mode makes it unsustainable over a long period of time.

Family members worry if the newly diagnosed patient is crying too much or "just not themselves." Newly diagnosed individuals begin to notice that family and friends do not really want to hear how they are doing. Casual greetings become opportunities for deception and the masquerade becomes habit. It is important to state that, of course, this is a generalization and that there are always exceptions, especially when we are describing humans.

The True Self, The False Self and the Literature

"The trait of deceptiveness", described by Mary Jacobus (2005) as "the mask which conceals the subtle reservation of all control under intellectual rationalizations, or under feigned compliance and superficial politeness," (p.37) led me to think about Winnicott (1965) and his concept of False Self. The False Self is a consortium of behaviors that in their sum act in accordance with others' expectations, rather than the genuine wishes and instincts of the individual. The False Self can make it difficult to connect with others and is often considered an inauthentic version of the self. The False Self is not entirely without merit and use. Acting without societal norms also can lead to alienation. Protecting vulnerable parts of ourselves is a vital skill in facing the challenges of each day (pp. 140-152). Similar to Freud's Super Ego (Freud, 1923), the False Self gives us guidance as to how we interact with our environment and other people. As with the Super Ego, it can be too harsh and controlling, leaving little to no space for the True Self (Jacobus, 2005).

Both in individual sessions and during group meetings, the participants in the MOMS Group have voiced that they feel they are not able to share how they are really feeling with family and friends. They confirmed my assumption that they protect their loved ones from the heartbreak of their suffering. They have built up a fierce False Self with which to face their post-diagnosis world. Although each woman has a mask she is able to put on to minimize or hide altogether her suffering, each also has a True Self.

According to Winnicott (1965), "only the true self can be creative and only the true self can feel real," (p. 140). The True Self is spontaneous and unforced. It is honest and open. Both versions of each woman fit the description for True Self. The True Self that is revealed when we are alone in my office is a desperate, vulnerable, scared self. It is a self that is not able to share her fears with her loved ones and has difficulty even saying them aloud to herself. The True Self present in group sessions is bold and hopeful. It is a self that acknowledges challenges but trusts in herself and her resources to face them.

Group Structure and Environment, Group Process and Dynamics

Instead of presenting another opportunity for each woman to masquerade, the group produced a chance to expand and strengthen a genuine part of the self. The process itself of engaging in group work provided support to each participant in a way that individual counseling could not. More specifically, I found that the following characteristics of group work contributed to accessing this second self.

A Unique Holding/Containing Environment

The Holding Environment, another concept championed by Winnicott, is usually discussed in the context of individual psychotherapy. It refers to a replication, by a therapist, of an atmosphere created between a mother and baby. For some individuals, the safe space of a Holding Environment is created for the first time during treatment. The Holding Environment consists of a designated time, space and way of interacting. This creation allows for "the opportunity for a constructive and meaningful engagement with the patient's inner world," (Yogev, 2008, p. 379).

The structure of our MOMS group meets the criteria for a Holding Environment: there is a designated time, space and way of relating. While the content of the group is not predetermined or rigid, the construction of the group is solid and unchanging. There are ground rules (respect, commitment and confidentiality) that are non-negotiable for participation. The group is able to act as a holding environment that can contain the struggling individual, providing support and soothing while the individual is able to strengthen her ability to self-heal.

Mirroring Between Members

The group environment serves as a mirror that reflects aspects of an individual. Often an individual is not able to acknowledge or accept a part of oneself until they observe it in a peer. An individual may identify a strength in a fellow participant and only then are they able to call on that strength in themselves. There is a strength that comes from receiving messages of how multiple people – women in the same situation – view you. The women reflect back versions of themselves that they are not easily able to see.

The best mirrors are ones that are truly in tune with the individual, just as a mother is with her baby. Group members prove to be better mirrors than a clinician, as other members are closer to what an individual is experiencing. Group members share experiences, feelings and traits with each other, and those commonalities can be more potent than all of the empathy a clinician may show. Even just one peer with a similar experience can be more in tune with needs than a therapist; a room full of peers provides several mirrors, all reflecting a similar, yet slightly different message, providing many opportunities to gain knowledge about the self. As the different prisms of the self are being reflected back, the self becomes more integrated, whole and healthy.

Members Identify and Label Feelings

Participants in a group are able to identify and label feelings that the individual may not have been able to label themselves. Language allows us to express what we are feeling, and once a feeling is expressed, an individual is able to manage, regulate and change emotions. Language takes the feeling out of the internal experience and shares it with the external world, and the process of this "in to out" communication can lead to insight and growth. Sometimes giving a name to a feeling diffuses it and leaves it with less power; it is no longer an amorphous shadow hiding in the corners of the mind. A name is a classification, a grouping, a signifier; names allowed participants to realize that their feelings had been experienced by others. Without a name, a feeling feels more unique and personal; it is hard to imagine anyone else sharing the experience of having a particular emotion. When a feeling is put into a category, one can understand and be reassured by the fact that others have "felt that, too."

Normally Unacceptable Feelings Expressed and Validated

Participants were able to openly discuss the feelings that are usually hidden behind the mask. Mothers reported that they feel guilty, embarrassed, and ashamed about symptoms, especially as they may impact their caregivers. As a society, we do not always welcome a constant account of symptoms. We call it complaining, a trait that holds a very negative connotation. As a society, we might label an individual who has steady problems a "Debbie Downer;" to avoid this label it becomes easier to withhold the sharing of symptoms and associated feelings.

The MOMS group offers a chance for individuals to not only share their feelings, but for those feelings to be validated by others. In this environment their emotions are not taboo and the sharing of them is not considered complaining. For individuals who are made to feel different and "the other" on a regular basis, joining with others who can truly empathize is a powerful tool. Feeling marginalized can decrease an individual's sense of hope and purpose; likewise, feeling a sense of normalcy can increase hope and positive attitude.

Members Became Involved in a Social Setting and Built a Sense of Community

Multiple Sclerosis is a condition that causes social isolation for physical reasons, for emotional reasons, but most often for both reasons. The progression of the disease brings difficulty with physical functioning. Changes happen to the body which make it difficult to leave the home: impaired balance, difficulty or inability to walk, urinary and bowel urgency and incontinence, vision deficits, debilitating fatigue, chronic pain, muscle stiffness, and the list could go on. Emotional weights also begin to prevent individuals from engaging in previously enjoyed activities. It is exhausting to masquerade. It is embarrassing to have a bladder or bowel accident. It is frightening to fall in public.

As the disease progresses, so does the social isolation. Interactions become limited to immediately family and medical teams. At the heart of the purpose of this group is to connect individuals with others. The group was established on the premise that, "people's lives are enriched when the need for a strong human connection is met – one that is accepting, genuine, and empathic" (Northen & Kurland, 2001). While some groups aim to socialize participants and teach them the importance of relationships, the members of this group already understood this. We simply sought to replace dissolved relationships with strong, present ones.

Practical Help Shared Between Members

Suggestions for abstract and emotional matters, as well as advice on concrete issues, flowed between members from the time of the first meeting. Altruism enhances self-worth and an integrated sense of the self, as participants learn they can offer help to others. Often giving help to others is more healing than receiving helpful information in return. The mutual aid that occurs in the group is especially beneficial to chronically ill individuals who feel they are a constant burden on others. The group establishes a give and take atmosphere, allowing individuals to contribute, reducing the feelings of dependency.

None of the women in the group are still working; they all left their jobs and are currently on Social Security Disability. Although they all care for their children, each of them have expressed a generalized doubt about their "abilities," ranging from social to financial and from physical to emotional. Sharing advice with each other in the setting of the group is more than "just sharing advice;" it is a dynamic problem-solving process that unfolds involving all members. It is an activity in which these women are not often able to participate. This process of reciprocity and mutual aid not only benefits each individual member but it profits the group as a whole, strengthening it and making it an even more cohesive unit.

Conclusion

Although the discovery of this second True Self was a joy to witness and has been even more of an honor to nurture, I do not mean to imply that individual therapy has no place with these women or others with chronic illness. The negativity and hopelessness that is revealed during individual sessions has its place, for fears and disappointments deserve to be examined and given a voice. This may be controversial, but I believe that being completely positive all of the time (masquerading) is not a long-term plan for mental health. Finding a safe space to break down and fall apart is important in order to stay put together in the long run. But just as constant and unrelenting positivity is an inauthentic road to walk down, wallowing in sadness on a prolonged basis has its (maybe more obvious and dangerous) downfalls as well. The space created in our MOMS group allows a third, healthy option. Difficult feelings are explored and joys are shared; the negative and the positive are integrated and balanced.

For individuals with Multiple Sclerosis, maintaining a sense of self and authenticity is paramount. There is so much that is taken away, both physical ability and dreams of the future. The second True Self that has been cultivated and nurtured in our MOMS group breathes life into the authentic self for each participant, a self that, for some, has been lost for some time. Being in touch with the authentic self makes the moments of masquerade less difficult and taxing; being in touch with the authentic self makes the fleeting free falls into sadness feel safer.

As clinicians we do not have all of the right answers. Sometimes we must allow our patients to lead the way and tell us what they need. Most importantly, we must allow ourselves to be surprised – to take chances knowing the results may not match up with our expectations. Sometimes they might just surpass them.

References

Freud, S (1923), "Neurosis and Psychosis". The Standard Edition of the Complete Psychological Works of Sigmund Freud, Volume XIX (1923-1925).

Jacobus, M (2005). *The poetics of psychoanalysis: In the wake of Klein.* Oxford, UK: Oxford.

Northen, H., & Kurland, R. (2001). *Social work with groups* (3rd ed.). New York, NY: Columbia University Press.

Winnicott, D.W. (1960). Ego distortion in terms of true and false self. *The maturational process and the facilitating environment: Studies in the theory of emotional development, 1965* (pp. 140-152). New York: International UP Inc.

Yogev, H. (2008). Holding in relational theory and group analysis. *Group Analysis, 41(4),* 373-39.

An Evaluation of a Psycho-Educational Program for Pregnant Women Living with HIV in Toronto, Canada

Simone Shindler, Stephanie Bell, & Mary Tangelder

Introduction

This chapter presents an evaluation of The Teresa Group's Prenatal Program for women living with HIV in Toronto, Canada. The evaluation was designed to answer the following questions: (1) Which factors promote participation in The Teresa Group's Prenatal Program for pregnant women living with HIV?; (2) Which factors act as barriers for participation in the program?; and (3) How does participation in the program impact a participant's experience of pregnancy? The methodology used in this evaluation included focus groups (FGs), surveys with program participants, and interviews with professionals associated with the program.

The findings reported here indicate that opportunities to interact with other women living with HIV, to ask questions about disclosure and their children's health, and to share personal experiences were key factors facilitating women's participation in the program. Barriers to participation included stigmatizing experiences and feelings of powerlessness within the health care system.

Post participation in the program, participants reported improvements in social support, confidence and hope, capacity to cope with stigma, and adherence to new complex drug regimens. The dearth of published research on similar programs suggests a clear need for additional research and evaluation on the supports that are available to pregnant women living with HIV in different contexts.

Background

Between 1985 and 2011, a total of 74,174 cases of human immunodeficiency virus (HIV) were diagnosed in Canada (Public Health Agency of Canada, 2012). Seventeen percent of these cases were in women of childbearing age (Public Health Agency of Canada, 2012). During the same time period, 3,567 infants were born to HIV-infected women (Public Health Agency of Canada, 2012). Although the number of infants exposed to HIV perinatally has increased over time, the number of infants confirmed to be HIV-positive each year is steadily decreasing (Public Health Agency of Canada, 2012). Pregnant women receive HIV testing according to the opt-in or opt-out system in place in their province; in Ontario's opt-in system 97% of pregnant women are tested (Public Health Agency of Canada, 2011; 2012).

A diagnosis of HIV is a stressful event that can cause substantial psychological distress and intense depression and anxiety (Eller et al., 2010; Kagee & Martin, 2010; Mello, Segurado, & Malbergier, 2010; Olley, 2008; Sanders, 2008). This distress is often amplified during pregnancy. Many women living with HIV experience intense and conflicting emotional responses to pregnancy, regardless of when their diagnosis was received (Sandelowski & Barroso, 2003). Women living with HIV often experience the same elation about having a child as other pregnant women, but these feelings can be mixed with fear, shame, anxiety, doubt and depression (Ross, Sawatphanit, Draucker, & Suwansujarid, 2007; Sanders, 2008; Simpson & Forsyth, 2007). These emotions are often related to concerns about their own physical health and that of their child; disclosure of their serostatus, especially in the context of decisions not to breastfeed; stigmatization and the perceptions of family, community members, health care professionals, and others around them; parenting; and inadequate support systems (Hanh, Rasch, Chi, Gammeltoft, 2009; Kotze, Visser, Makin, Sikkema, & Forsyth, 2013; Lester, Partridge, Chesney, & Cooke, 1995; Mawar, Joshi, Sahay, Bagul, & Paranjape, 2007; Ross et al., 2007; Sanders, 2008). Despite these concerns, and knowledge that emotional well-being during pregnancy is crucial for a successful transition to parenting, there is little published research about the psychosocial wellbeing of pregnant women living with HIV (Lester et al., 1995; McLearn, Minkovitz, Strobino, Marks, & Hou, 2006; Sanders, 2008). In a study by Pereira and Canavarro (2012), pregnant women living with HIV reported increased negative emotional reactivity, fewer social relationships, and worse overall quality of life. Similarly, Blaney et al.

(2004) report increased levels of depression among pregnant women living with HIV who experience social isolation. This psychological stress can have negative health outcomes for both mothers and infants, including decreased adherence to antiretroviral regimens and missed health care appointments (Bhatia, Hartman, Kallen, Graham, & Giordano, 2011; Chronis, 2007; Collins, Dunkel-Schetter, Lobel, & Scrimshaw, 1993; Do et al., 2010; Hobfoll, Ritter, Lavin, Hulsizer, & Cameron, 1995; Lobel, Dunkel-Schetter, & Scrimshaw, 1992; Oswalt & Biasini, 2012; Pearson, Cooper, Penton-Voak, Lightman, & Evans, 2010).

There have been repeated calls for interventions and programming to begin to address the psychosocial and informational needs of pregnant women living with HIV but, to our knowledge, no formal programs have been presented or evaluated in the literature (Blaney et al., 2004; Hanh et al., 2009; Orr et al., 1996). This evaluation was designed to answer the following questions: (1) Which factors promote participation in The Teresa Group's Prenatal Program for pregnant women living with HIV?; (2) Which factors act as barriers for participation in the program?; and (3) How does participation in The Teresa Group's Prenatal Program impact participant's experience of pregnancy?

Program Description

The Prenatal Program for women living with HIV is a psycho-educational program for pregnant women at The Teresa Group in Toronto, Canada. It serves as an entry point to The Teresa Group's spectrum of programs and services that provide practical and emotional support to children and families affected by HIV.

Program Delivery

The Prenatal Program was initiated in 2004 as a series of six one-hour sessions delivered over a six-week period. Based on informal feedback from program participants and attendance data, the delivery format was modified in June 2008 to include two six-hour, intensive sessions. Sessions are presented by program affiliates, comprised of a group of staff from local hospitals who specialize in HIV and include a psychiatrist, obstetrician-gynecologists, nurse practitioners, a midwife, and a nutritionist. All of the presenters interact with program participants in their respective clinical settings. Social workers employed by The Teresa Group are also involved in delivering program content.

Program Participants

Women from the Greater Toronto area, who are pregnant and diagnosed with HIV, are referred to The Teresa Group by their health care providers. Between 2004 and 2010, 71 women attended the program. About half of the participants attended for the first time during their first pregnancy; of those 12.9% returned during a subsequent pregnancy. The majority of program participants were newcomers to Canada; 61.4% were originally from Africa, 20% were from the Caribbean and South America, 11.4% were from Canada and the United States, and 7.1% were from Asia. More detailed demographic information was not collected in order to respect the privacy of participants and to alleviate concerns about confidentiality.

Program Themes

During the program, participants receive information and have opportunities to discuss issues related to antiretroviral therapy, nutrition, labour and delivery, perinatal care and support, and financial support. An introductory session is offered to ensure participants are prepared for the emotional discussions that will take place during the program.

Methods

An independent consultant who had no affiliation with The Teresa Group was hired to undertake the evaluation, which consisted of focus groups (FGs), surveys with program participants, and interviews with professionals associated with the program.

Focus Groups

FG participants were women who had taken part in the Prenatal Program between January 2004 and January 2011. Every woman who participated in the program received a letter in the mail inviting her to participate in the FGs. Each letter was followed by a telephone call. In the letter and/or during the telephone conversation, the women received information about: the purpose of the FGs; their duration; scheduling options; assurances about confidentiality; and information about the provision of child care, local transportation tickets, and a $50 food voucher. Twenty former program participants were interested in taking part in this evaluation. These participants were divided into two FGs of ten participants each, which were held at The Teresa Group office in Toronto in April 2011. Each FG lasted roughly 90-120 minutes.

The FG guide covered several themes: motivating and inhibiting factors for attending the Prenatal Program, the value of the Prenatal Program, the ways in which it differed from other prenatal care and support programs, and how it could be improved. The discussions were moderated by the female evaluation consultant, who was experienced in the facilitation of groups of marginalized women. All participants provided verbal informed consent for their involvement in the evaluation.

Notes and audio recordings were taken during the FGs. Thematic codes were identified manually from the notes and recordings. To test for coding reliability, a second person undertook a process of re-coding. Minor variations were identified and discussed, and a revised set of codes was agreed upon.

Surveys

All 71 Prenatal Program participants during this period were asked to complete an anonymous survey following their session. The survey asked participants to rate the session and the group facilitator on a 4-point Likert scale, and included open-ended questions about the highlights of the program and suggestions for future sessions. The responses from the open-ended questions informed the development of thematic codes from the FG recordings and contributed some of the participant quotations presented in this paper.

Semi-Structured Interviews

Professionals who delivered presentations during the Prenatal sessions were invited by e-mail to participate in semi-structured interviews to share their views of the program. Interviewees participated in one 30-minute telephone interview conducted by the external evaluation consultant in April 2011. Five members of this group, including a psychiatrist, an obstetrician-gynecologist specializing in high-risk pregnancies, two nurse practitioners specializing in HIV, and a midwife who works in partnership with a local hospital and specializes in HIV care, agreed to participate in the interviews. Two Teresa Group staff members who were involved with the design and implementation of the program were also interviewed.

The interview guide included questions about: the importance of a Prenatal Program specifically for women living with HIV, the primary needs and concerns of women attending the Prenatal Program, the ways in which participants benefit from the program, new learning about the needs of mothers with HIV and the ways in which these may be impacting the interviewee's professional practice, and the strengths and limitations of the program. Each interview was recorded and notes were taken during the interview. Thematic codes were identified manually from the notes and recordings. To test for coding reliability, a second person undertook a process of re-coding two of the interviews. Minor variations were identified and discussed, and a revised set of codes was agreed upon.

Results

Psychosocial Context

Many FG participants reported a number of complex and interrelated psychosocial issues in their daily lives. These issues included domestic conflict; immigration and settlement issues, including loss of social status; and poverty, food insecurity, and housing instability. Interviews with program delivery staff revealed that many program participants had also experienced gender-based violence, including domestic abuse and rape; and that some had experienced female genital mutilation.

FG participants described experiences of HIV-related stigma and discrimination in all aspects of their lives. Many of the women had been rejected and shunned by family, friends, and community members; had lost jobs; or faced reduced access to food and housing. Some participants were in discordant relationships and shared experiences of HIV-negative partners using the threat of disclosing the woman's HIV status to others in order to manipulate and control her behaviour.

Factors that Promote Access to the Program

Opportunities to Interact with Other Women Living with HIV

The social isolation that FG participants experienced as a result of stigma in all aspects of their lives limited opportunities to meet and interact with other women living with HIV. FG participants commonly reported, "we had never met anyone like us". While nearly all of the women said they had a strong desire to meet others with similar experiences, many had never interacted with another person with HIV.

The first person I met with HIV was me. I desperately wanted to meet someone else who was going through my experience. (FG participant)

Questions About Disclosure and Their Child's Health

FG participants acknowledged that although they had serious concerns about attending the program, related primarily to experiences of stigma and powerlessness in interactions with health care professionals, their concerns about their baby's wellbeing were greater. They believed that the health of their child was more important than the potentially negative experiences they feared facing at the Prenatal Program, and that they might gain valuable information by attending. Program participants suggested that they had no other place to go to seek answers to questions about their child's health, managing disclosure, and confronting stigma in the health care system

I didn't know what would happen to my baby. You hear "HIV" and you hear a death sentence. (FG participant)

Focus on Personal Experience and Sharing

Several FG participants and health care professionals agreed that the opportunity to share personal experiences and engage in informal dialogue with peers was a profound shift from deep isolation to a strong sense of mutuality and support. FG participants also suggested that exchanging personal practices and experiences also helped to normalize new behaviours, like bottle-feeding and new medication regimes.

> *The greatest benefit I see is that women come together to talk openly. Through talking together in a circle, their experiences are normalized.* (Nurse practitioner, interviewee)

Reflecting upon the experiences of other mothers provided some FG participants with important insights into their own experiences.

> *Hearing [another mom] describe herself as brave made me feel tearful. I've never thought of myself that way. I've been living with HIV for over 10 years and I'm proud of who I am, I'm happy. But hearing her call herself brave [for making the choice to have a baby] was really important to me.* (FG participant)

Barriers to Program Participation

Program staff noted that despite efforts to describe the potential benefits of participation in the Prenatal Program to pregnant women living with HIV, attracting women to the program was challenging.

Stigmatization by Health Care Professionals

Many FG participants recounted traumatic and stigmatizing experiences related to their HIV status within the Canadian health care system. Although all participants accessed specialist HIV care, many reported incidental and ongoing negative interactions with mainstream health care providers, including pharmacists, nurses and physicians in emergency room and walk-in clinics, and office administrators.

Experiences of ignorance, judgement, shaming, and violations of confidentiality were common.

> *I had to go to a walk-in clinic for something minor, unrelated to HIV... I overheard the doctor say to the nurse: "She needs blood work, but you don't have to do it if you don't want to, because she's HIV positive". Even though he didn't say my name, I was standing right there ... it was so awful.* (FG participant).

Participants indicated that they believed this stigma was a result of ignorance and moral judgement. Program staff confirmed the presence of widespread stigma within the health care system.

> *I fight within my own hospital to break down barriers...people look at [people with HIV] differently, they touch you differently.* (Physician, interviewee)

As a result of these experiences within the health care system, FG participants acknowledged that they initially felt anxious and fearful when they were invited to attend the Prenatal Program. Several participants indicated that they felt safer in isolation and that they avoided seeking professional services of any kind.

Feelings of Powerlessness

FG participants described interactions with health care and social service professionals in which they felt powerless and unable to negotiate for their own interests and preferences. Some noted that they did not always know what to say during conversations with professionals or how to refuse particular requests. Specifically, one woman indicated that she was very uncomfortable with the presence of a medical student during her appointments, but she did not feel empowered to refuse when asked whether she agreed to the student's participation.

Participants who had recently claimed refugee status expressed particular concern about the consequences of appearing non-compliant in consultations with health and social service professionals and how this might impact their refugee status. *"If you are new to Canada, you need support from [doctors]; you can't reject them."* (FG participant).

These feelings of powerlessness were reflected in the participants' hesitation to attend the Prenatal Program. They did not want to find themselves in another situation where their privacy would be compromised because they felt unable to advocate for what they wanted.

Impact of the Prenatal Program

Social Support

Both survey respondents and FG participants reported a new sense of belonging and reduced isolation. Many women described the crucial importance of this social and emotional support in the context of fear of disclosure and experiences of stigma. *"Listening to other moms makes me stronger."* (FG participant). Some women described the Prenatal Program as their only source of social support during pregnancy, and the only space where they could openly share their concerns and experiences without judgement or fear.

> *The first time I came, I cried and cried. I had so many different feelings. I couldn't believe there were so many women...I felt such relief.* (FG participant)

Confidence and Hope

Many FG participants indicated that before attending the program, they did not believe that, as women living with HIV, they could be healthy mothers and raise healthy babies. Through participation in the program, they learned that both mother and baby can be healthy and found renewed hope for the future.

> *I realized that I used to have dreams for myself. Big dreams. But when I found out I had HIV, I lost those dreams. I am still scared that I won't be there to see my child grow up, to see him get married. But slowly, I am beginning to have these dreams again.* (FG participant)

When asked to describe their feelings before attending the program, many women painted bleak pictures of darkness. Words that were used to describe these feelings included "living under something, feeling heavy, doomed, and tangled and caught up". One woman drew an image of several circles, coloured with progressively lighter shading. She wrote,

> *These are the different stages for me. This picture shows how, over time, things began to feel lighter.* (FG participant)

Capacity to Cope with Stigma and Self-Advocate

During FG discussions, program participants shared positive experiences of being able to discuss examples of stigmatizing experiences and new strategies they had learned to manage these situations. Some program participants indicated that they understood that the process had become easier with time and practice, and would continue to improve:

I still wish I could stand up for myself better, but...my capacity to deal with [these issues] has [improved]. It helps to know what to expect, and I'm better prepared to deal with them now. (FG participant)

Support for Adhering to New Drug Regimens

FG participants described improvements in adherence to the complex drug regimens that women living with HIV face for themselves and their babies during and after pregnancy. Specifically, they identified the following experiences that contributed to better adherence: opportunities to receive information, ask questions, and seek clarification from peers and professionals; opportunities to make social connections with other mothers who could lend peer support; and participation in a group that normalized routines of taking medications.

Discussion

In this evaluation of The Teresa Group's Prenatal Program for pregnant women living with HIV, we investigated the factors that promote and hinder participation, and the impact of the program on participants' experiences of pregnancy.

Many participants in the evaluation were acutely affected by the social determinants of health. They were often victims of gender-based violence, socioeconomically and ethnoculturally marginalized, and socially isolated. Other authors have found that these factors accentuate the psychosocial challenges experienced by pregnant women living with HIV, particularly when study subjects are immigrants from low-income settings to high-income settings, such as in Canada (Blaney et al., 2004; McMahon & Ward, 2012; Webel et al., 2013).

The evaluation found that the main factors promoting participation in the program were the opportunities to interact with other women living with HIV, seek answers to their questions, and share their personal experiences with others. This is consistent with other studies that found that women living with HIV in general, tend to seek interaction with other HIV-infected women for social support and shared experiences (Heath & Rodway, 1999). In her studies of pregnant women living with HIV, Ross et al. (2007) found that women sought support from other seropositive women and found informal peer support beneficial to their overall health and wellbeing. Others reported that knowing other women living with HIV was associated with improved active coping skills (Kotze et al., 2013). Heath and Rodway (1999) confirm that other women living with HIV also express the need for information and support from healthcare professionals to assist with planning for the care of their children.

Barriers to participation included previous experiences of stigmatization by healthcare professionals and feelings of powerlessness during interactions with healthcare and support professionals. This finding is consistent with a study by Sanders (2008), who found that pregnant women living with HIV in New York had a wide range negative experiences in the health care system related to their serostatus that impacted their access to health care professionals. Studies in other regions also report findings that suggest women living with HIV are frequently discriminated against within the health care system, and that they are less likely to continue to visit healthcare providers with whom they feel stigmatized (Hanh et al., 2009; Hardon, Ngoc, Nguyen, Oosterhoff, & Wright, 2008; Lester et al., 1995; Ross et al., 2007; Varga, 2008).

In terms of the overall impact of the Prenatal Program, women who participated reported enhanced social supports, feelings of confidence and hope, increased capacity to manage stigma and self-advocate, and support for adhering to new drug regimens. These findings are consistent with those Ross et al. (2007) and Goggin et al. (2001) exploring the importance of finding hope for pregnant women living with HIV. Other studies have found positive correlations between improved coping skills and lower levels of internalized stigma and depression, improved self- esteem, social support, knowing other people who have HIV, good physical health, and adherence to drug regimens (Chan, 2006; Chida, 2009; Kotze et al., 2013; Vervoort, 2009; Vyavaharkar, 2012).

Limitations

There are methodological limitations inherent in the design of this study. The evaluation process spanned a period of nearly ten years, and the Prenatal Program underwent several changes based on anecdotal participant feedback during this time frame. These changes and variations may have led to differences in the experiences of women who participated in the FG discussions. Since FG participants had participated in the Prenatal Program at any time since between 2004 and 2011, it is possible that recall bias may have been present during discussions about the program. The relatively small number of FG participants was not randomly selected and therefore may not have been representative of the total population of women who participated in the program or of pregnant women living with HIV in general. The women who participated in this program live in the socio-political context of Toronto, Canada and came from very diverse ethnocultural backgrounds. The findings of this study cannot be generalized to other contexts.

Since the FG discussions were held at The Teresa Group office and the surveys were submitted to Prenatal Program staff, there is a risk of acquiescence bias. Similarly, although interviews with program professionals and FGs were carried out by an external evaluation consultant who was not otherwise affiliated with The Teresa Group or the Prenatal Program, respondents may have been hesitant to offer critical perspectives.

Despite these limitations, this study is the first to evaluate a psycho-educational program for pregnant women living with HIV and is therefore a valuable contribution to the existing literature.

Conclusions and Implications for Future Research

This evaluation of The Teresa Group's Prenatal Program sought to determine: (1) The factors that promote participation in the program; (2) The factors that act as barriers for participation in the program; and (3) How participation impacted participant's experiences of pregnancy. Opportunities to interact with other women living with HIV, ask questions about disclosure and their children's health, and share personal experiences were key factors facilitating participation. Barriers to participation included stigmatizing experiences and feelings of powerlessness within the health care system. Participants reported improvements in social support, confidence and hope, capacity to cope with stigma, and adherence to new complex drug regimens after participating in the program. The paucity of published research on similar programs suggests a clear need for additional research and evaluation on the supports that are available to pregnant women living with HIV in different contexts.

References

Bhatia, R., Hartman, C., Kallen, M. A., Graham, J., & Giordano, T. P. (2011). Persons newly diagnosed with HIV infection are at high risk for depression and poor linkage to care: Results from the Steps Study. *AIDS and Behavior*, *15*(6), 1161–1170. doi:10.1007/s10461-010-9778-9

Blaney, N., Fernandez, M., Ethier, K., Wilson, T., Walter, E., Koenig, L., & Perinatal Guidelines Evaluation Project Group. (2004). Psychosocial and behavioral correlates of depression among HIV-infected pregnant women. *AIDS Patient Care & STDs*, *18*(7), 405–415.

Chan, I. (2006). Illness-related factors, stress and coping strategies in relation to psychological distress in HIV-infected persons in Hong Kong. *AIDS Care*, *18*(8), 977–982.

Chida, Y. (2009). Adverse psychosocial factors predict poorer prognosis in HIV disease: A meta- analytic review of prospective investigations. *Brain Behavior and Immunity*, *23*(4), 434–445. doi:10.1016/j.bbi.2009.01.013.

Chronis, A. M. (2007). Maternal depression and early positive parenting predict future conduct problems in young children with attention-deficit/hyperactivity disorder. *Developmental Psychology*, *43*(1), 70–82.

Collins, N. L., Dunkel-Schetter, C., Lobel, M., & Scrimshaw, S. C. (1993). Social support in pregnancy: psychosocial correlates of birth outcomes and postpartum depression. *Journal of Personality and Social Psychology*, *65*(6), 1243–1258.

Do, N. T., Phiri, K., Bussmann, H., Gaolathe, T., Marlink, R. G., & Wester, C. W. (2010). Psychosocial factors affecting medication adherence among HIV-1 infected adults receiving combination antiretroviral therapy (cART) in Botswana. *AIDS Research and Human Retroviruses, 26*(6), 685–691. doi:10.1089/aid.2009.0222

Eller, L. S., Bunch, E. H., Wantland, D. J., Portillo, C. J., Reynolds, N. R., Nokes, K. M., Tsai, Y.-F. (2010). Prevalence, correlates, and self-management of HIV-related depressive symptoms. *AIDS Care, 22*(9), 1159–1170. doi:10.1080/09540121.2010.498860

Goggin, K., Catley, D., Brisco, S. T., Engelson, E. S., Rabkin, J. G., & Kotler, D. P. (2001). A female perspective on living with HIV disease. *Health & Social Work, 26*(2), 80–89.

Hanh, N., Rasch, V., Chi, B., & Gammeltoft, T. (2009). Posttest counseling and social support from health staff caring for HIV-infected pregnant women in Vietnam. *Journal of the Association of Nurses in AIDS Care, 20*(3), 193–202. doi:http://dx.doi.org/10.1016/j.jana.2009.02.003

Hardon, A., Ngoc, Y. P., Nguyen, T. A., Oosterhoff, P., & Wright, P. (2008). Barriers to access prevention of mother-to-child transmission for HIV positive women in a well-resourced setting in Vietnam. *AIDS Research and Therapy, 5*(7). doi:10.1186/1742-6405-5-7

Heath, J., & Rodway, M. R. (1999). Psychosocial needs of women infected with HIV. *Social Work in Health Care, 29*(3), 43–57. doi:10.1300/J010v29n03_03

Hobfoll, S. E., Ritter, C., Lavin, J., Hulsizer, M. R., & Cameron, R. P. (1995). Depression prevalence and incidence among inner-city pregnant and postpartum women. *Journal of Consulting and Clinical Psychology, 63*(3), 445–453.

Kagee, A., & Martin, L. (2010). Symptoms of depression and anxiety among a sample of South African patients living with HIV. *AIDS Care, 22*(2), 159–165. doi:10.1080/09540120903111445

Kotze, M., Visser, M., Makin, J., Sikkema, K., & Forsyth, B. (2013). Psychosocial variables associated with coping of HIV-positive women diagnosed during pregnancy. *AIDS & Behavior, 17*(2), 498–507. doi:http://dx.doi.org/10.1007/s10461-012-0379-7

Lester, P., Partridge, J. C., Chesney, M. A., & Cooke, M. (1995). The consequences of a positive prenatal HIV antibody test for women. *Journal of Acquired Immune Deficiency Syndromes and Human Retrovirology: Official Publication of the International Retrovirology Association, 10*(3), 341–349.

Lobel, M., Dunkel-Schetter, C., & Scrimshaw, S. C. (1992). Prenatal maternal stress and prematurity: A prospective study of socioeconomically disadvantaged women. *Health Psychology: Official journal of the Division of Health Psychology, American Psychological Association, 11*(1), 32–40.

Mawar, N., Joshi, P., Sahay, S., Bagul, R., & Paranjape, R. (2007). Concerns and experiences of women participating in a short-term AZT intervention feasibility study for prevention of HIV transmission from mother-to-child. *Culture, Health & Sexuality, 9*(2), 199–207.

McLearn, K. T., Minkovitz, C. S., Strobino, D. M., Marks, E., & Hou, W. (2006). The timing of maternal depressive symptoms and mothers⊠ parenting practices with young children: implications for pediatric practice. *Pediatrics, 118*(1), e174–182. doi:10.1542/peds.2005-1551

McMahon, T., & Ward, P. (2012). HIV among immigrants living in high-income countries: a realist review of evidence to guide targeted approaches to behavioural HIV prevention. *Systems Review, 1*(56). doi:http://dx.doi.org/10.1186/2046-4053-1-56

Mello, V. A., Segurado, A. A., & Malbergier, A. (2010). Depression in women living with HIV: Clinical and psychosocial correlates. *Archives of Women's Mental Health, 13*(3), 193–199. doi:10.1007/s00737-009-0094-1

Olley, B. O. (2008). Psychological distress in the first year after diagnosis of HIV infection among women in South Africa. *African Journal of AIDS Research, 5*(3), 207–215.

Orr, S. T., James, S. A., Miller, C. A., Barakat, B., Daikoku, N., Pupkin, M., ... Huggins, G. (1996). Psychosocial stressors and low birthweight in an urban population. *American Journal of Preventive Medicine, 12*(6), 459–466.

Oswalt, K. L., & Biasini, F. J. (2012). Characteristics of HIV-infected mothers associated with increased risk of poor mother-infant interactions and infant outcomes. *Journal of Pediatric Health Care: Official Publication of National Association of Pediatric Nurse Associates & Practitioners, 26*(2), 83–91. doi:10.1016/j.pedhc.2010.06.014

Pearson, R. M., Cooper, R. M., Penton-Voak, I. S., Lightman, S. L., & Evans, J. (2010). Depressive symptoms in early pregnancy disrupt attentional processing of infant emotion. *Psychological Medicine, 40*(4), 621–631. doi:10.1017/S0033291709990961

Pereira, M., & Canavarro, M. (2012). Quality of life and emotional distress among HIV-positive women during transition to motherhood. *Journal of Psychology, 15*(3), 1303–1314.

Public Health Agency of Canada. (2011). HIV/AIDS epi updates - July 2010. Retrieved August 29, 2013, from http://www.phac-aspc.gc.ca/aids-sida/publication/epi/2010/8-eng.php

Public Health Agency of Canada. (2012). At a glance - HIV and AIDS in Canada: Surveillance report to December 31st, 2011. Retrieved August 29, 2013, from http://www.phac- aspc.gc.ca/aids-sida/publication/survreport/2011/dec/index-eng.php

Ross, R., Sawatphanit, W., Draucker, C., & Suwansujarid, T. (2007). The lived experiences of HIV-positive, pregnant women in Thailand. *Health Care for Women International, 28*(8), 731–744.

Sandelowski, M., & Barroso, J. (2003). Motherhood in the context of maternal HIV infection. *Research in Nursing & Health, 26*(6), 470–482. doi:10.1002/nur.10109

Sanders, L. (2008). Womens voices: the lived experience of pregnancy and motherhood after diagnosis with HIV. *Journal of the Association of Nurses in AIDS Care, 19*(1), 47–57. doi:http://dx.doi.org/10.1016/j.jana.2007.10.002

Simpson, B. J., & Forsyth, B. W. C. (2007). State-mandated HIV testing in Connecticut: Personal perspectives of women found to be infected during pregnancy. *The Journal of the Association of Nurses in AIDS Care: JANAC, 18*(5), 34–46. doi:10.1016/j.jana.2007.07.008

Varga, C. (2008). Factors influencing teen mothers enrollment and participation in prevention of mother-to-child HIV transmission services in Limpopo Province, South Africa. *Qualitative Health Research, 18*(6), 786–802. doi:10.1177/1049732308318449

Vervoort, S. C. J. M. (2009). Adherence to HAART: Processes explaining adherence behavior in acceptors and non-acceptors. *AIDS Care, 21*(4), 431–438. doi:10.1080/09540120802290381

Vyavaharkar, M. (2012). Factors associated with quality of life among rural women with HIV disease. *AIDS and Behavior, 16*(2), 295–303. doi:10.1007/s10461-011-9917-y

Webel, A., Cuca, Y., Okonsky, J., Asher, A., Kaihura, A., & Salata, R. (2013). The impact of social context on self-management in women living with HIV. *Social Science & Medicine, 87*, 147–154. doi:http://dx.doi.org/10.1016/j.socscimed.2013.03.037

"Why do WE Have to Come in Here?": Using Group Work to Reduce Conflict and Stigma Among Boys in a Youth Development Setting

Dara Kammerman

Introduction

One of the potential dangers of doing social group work with a targeted population of youth is further stigmatization of an already stigmatized group. This is particularly relevant in school and youth development settings in which there are large, heterogeneous populations and youth are being "pulled out" to participate in groups. At an after-school youth development agency with boys, I worked with a group of seven boys aged 7-10 who attended a special education school for children who had been labeled "emotionally disturbed" on their Individualized Education Plans (IEPs). Some members of the group also had diagnoses of Attention Deficit and Hyperactivity Disorder (ADHD), Oppositional Defiant Disorder (ODD), Autism Spectrum Disorder and various learning disabilities. At the beginning of the group, most of the members resented the further stigma of having to come into the social work office twice a week upon arrival at the program rather than joining the rest of the population for homework or activities. By using several interventions, I was able to facilitate a group experience for the members that allowed them to feel less of a negative stigma and more of a positive sense of membership within the group.

Group Formation and Structure

When I began to work at the program, my supervisor told me about the group. He said that the group members attended the same school and then rode the same bus to the program. Conflicts that arose at school or on the bus often continued at the program and the boys were often fighting as they literally entered the doors of our building. My supervisor asked me to help reduce the amount of verbal and physical fighting occurring in the group. Some of my colleagues thought that the boys needed to be separated upon arriving at the program because they were just spending too much time together and needed a break from each other. While I thought there was some validity to that idea, the fact was that they *had* to interact as a group in their classes, on the bus and even sometimes at the after-school program. Therefore, I made a seemingly counterintuitive decision to facilitate a group with them, which would require them to spend a little extra time together once they arrived at the program. The structure of the group was that we met twice a week for about a half an hour per session from late October until early June of one school year. For the first 3-4 weeks of the group, most members passionately protested having to come to the group rather than going to homework help, gym, swimming or the other activities in which their peers were participating. In the beginning sessions, one boy, a 10 year old named Milo, repeatedly asked me, "Why do *WE* have to come in here?" thus expressing the group's frustrations. I explained that the purpose of the group was for us to all relax and get to know each other better and most importantly to reduce the amount of fighting happening among everyone. After the first few weeks of the group, the members were coming to me each day and asking to have more than two sessions per week. By June, they were expressing genuine sadness that the group had to end and the amount of conflict among members had been greatly reduced to a point where they could engage in activities without being consumed by interpersonal conflict.

Honing the Purpose of the Group and Purposeful Use of Activities

Through observation of the members' most challenging behavior, I was able to hone the purpose of the group and choose activities that best moved us toward that purpose. Verbal and physical fights were the biggest concern about this group; the members just did not seem to be able to get along. From the agency's perspective, the physical fighting was of the utmost concern because it posed a physical danger for these boys and any other boys who may be in the vicinity of their fighting. I decided to be as transparent as possible with the members about the purpose of the group. Kurland and Salmon (1999) support this stance and state that this transparency of purpose is integral to the formation of a group. During the first session, I told the members that we would be meeting in order to get to know each other better and relax a little before moving into the rest of the afternoon and evening programming. I also was clear that the purpose of this was to reduce the amount of fighting that happened among them. This purpose was very much informed by the needs of the agency. Letendre and Wayne (2008) acknowledge that in some settings, adults who are frustrated with children's unruly behavior will expect social workers to, "teach" the offending youngsters how to behave more appropriately" (p. 290). I felt some of this pressure as the social worker who was charged with the duty of reducing conflict among the members of the group. In retrospect I may have taken some more time to make the formation of purpose more of a collaborative effort because the members definitely had some pushback at the beginning. They said things like, "I don't want to spend MORE time with these guys!" I also heard, "We don't need to stop fighting, we are only playing. We just want to go to the game room." My response was, "Well, I think it could be great to have a little time to relax together, have a snack, and play some games together when you first come into the club. Let's try it for a little while and see what you think." After explaining the purpose of the group at the beginning of the first several sessions, I asked the group to come up with a name for themselves. They decided on "Team No Fight." Clearly this was an aspirational name and I also had the sense that the group was pandering to my wish for the group rather than genuinely "buying into" the purpose, but I checked in with them many times about the name and they never wanted to change it. Kurland and Salmon (1999) note that group workers commonly make the mistake of not involving the members of the group enough in the articulation of group purpose. They write that, "Even if a group's Purpose can be stated clearly, if that Purpose is not connected integrally to members' perceptions of what they want and need, if need is not identified, understood and acknowledged by members, the group is doomed to failure" (p. 109). This group was not a failure, despite a lack of member involvement in defining the purpose at the start of the group. Perhaps on some level, members did believe in the purpose I had determined for them even though they voiced resistance, but the group purpose also evolved slightly during the life of the group and perhaps members were able to buy into group purpose more as it evolved.

The first two months of the group were extremely challenging because the members constantly wanted to engage in physical fighting despite my redirections, my reminders of the group guidelines we had collaboratively established (including, "Keep your hands to yourself"), and my attempts to process the conflicts in a constructive way. During one particular session early in the group when members were physically fighting with each other, I felt my frustration level rising. I decided to hang back instead of intervening immediately and to observe the group in action, while at the same time making sure the members were safe. I noticed that as the members "fought" they were smiling and sometimes appeared to enjoy the physical interaction. Wayne and Gitterman (2003) discuss the importance of paying attention to "offensive" behaviors in groups because it can be a form of hidden communication. The physical fighting was happening consistently during every session and it seemed that it was a form of communication about the needs of the group. During the next session, I asked the group why they were fighting so much. Eight year-old Adam said, "We aren't 'fighting'! We're having fun." Several other members echoed Adam's sentiment that even though it looked like they were fighting, they were playing. Although there was definitely a great deal of genuine interpersonal conflict occurring among group members, their physical fighting was sometimes mistaken by me, the facilitator, as motivated by anger rather than as an enjoyable experience. I developed a hypothesis that the group members were seeking to have physical contact with each other and the only socially acceptable way to achieve this was through fighting. The play fighting, however, sometimes led to real issues of people's feelings being hurt. Undoubtedly, this is a common phenomenon among boys in particular because they still need physical proximity to others, but they are socialized to think that they, as boys, should not want to be physically close to others, especially with other boys. Wayne and Gitterman (2003) note that paying attention to the underlying meanings of offensive behavior can often allow the facilitator to have "unconditional acceptance of group members" as the behavior often leads to an understanding of group needs (p. 24).

This new understanding of the group's need for physical interaction helped me hone the purpose of the group. The purpose of the group became more about fostering positive ways of interacting with each other rather than just not fighting. Although I became aware of this new purpose as the facilitator, the process of revising the group purpose was probably not as collaborative as it could have been. Kurland and Salmon (1999) are strong proponents of the concept that a truly effective group purpose must be dynamic and constantly changing as the needs of the group change or as the facilitators and members get a deeper sense of need. However, they believe that this process always needs to be transparent with group members, as stated earlier.

In order to work towards this slightly nuanced purpose, I chose activities that allowed members to interact physically with each other in safe, constructive ways and then I would be sure to have members reflect on their positive interactions after activities. Wright (2000) acknowledges the importance and power of choosing the most effective activities for a group when she writes that, "The stimulation of verbal communication of feelings, the facilitation of problem solving, the development of relationships and the enhancing of self-esteem through skill mastery emerge as values pervasive in much of the literature on activity-oriented group experiences" (p. 34). Several activities were central to the group's desire for "closeness" in both a physical and emotional context. For example, I created one activity in which I wrote several objects down on a piece of paper. A member chose an object out of a hat and then they had one minute to create the object with their bodies. Each member was responsible for being one part of the object. Some of the objects that they became included Beyblades (a popular toy among the members), a shower and a tree. The activity gave the members an opportunity to interact physically with one another in a safe and constructive way and then to reflect on what it was like to be part of a bigger whole. In another activity, created by the members, they would hide quietly together somewhere in the room and I would play a "monster" who was searching for them. The activity was so popular with the members that it was often used as a sort of reward at the end of a session. I believe that this activity was effective for two reasons. First, when members hid they always hid in close proximity to each other. For example, they might all crowd into a corner of the room and hide behind big beanbag chairs. This may have satisfied a need for physical contact with each other and they bonded over pretending to be scared and then laughing when they were discovered. Also, because they always wanted me to be the monster, it may have given them an opportunity to feel like they were all on a team together, united against a fictional common enemy. Other activities that required group members to hold each other's hands or wrists were also successful and seemed to decrease violent interactions among them and may have fulfilled a similar purpose in giving them an opportunity to have physical closeness with each other in a safe, but socially acceptable way.

Creating Mutual Aid

The purposeful use of activity was also integral to the success of the group in that I scaled their experience of positive interactions with each other by having them move from low-risk to high-risk activities. For the first two months, many of the activities we engaged in allowed members to simply get to know each other better. The goal was to help the members create empathy for each other as they found common ground and to begin to develop a cohesive group identity. In her article about facilitating a conflict resolution group with boys, Abrams (2000) explored the importance of helping group members find common ground with each other before being able to explore the differences and the conflicts among them. She also acknowledges the need for a balance between honoring individuality of members and fostering feelings of unity and commonality. These approaches proved to be important for Team No Fight as well. As a group, we found that even though the members had spent a lot of time together in school, on the bus and at the after school program, they did not know a lot about each other. Through activities, they discovered that they loved the same video games, watched the same TV shows and five out of the seven of them had parents who were divorced or separated. The most important commonality they had was that they all disliked being in special education classes. During the middle and end stages of the group, the members were able to acknowledge their frustrations with the other kids who had behavior issues in their classes and many members expressed a desire to "get out of special education class." Some of the activities that were used to find common ground and also acknowledge individuality were "The Big Wind Blows..." (Jones, 1998, p. 208) in which members sit in a circle in chairs. One member is in the middle of the circle and says, "The Big Wind Blows If you have an older brother," or some other identifying characteristic. All members who have that same identifying characteristic run to find a new seat and a new member ends up in the middle. During a round of this game, one member named Jason said the following:

> Jason: *The Wind Blows If... you hate being in special education (all members of the group run and find a new seat indicating that they all hate being in special education classes.)*
> Milo: *Yeah, I can't wait to get out of my class because the kids are so crazy and dumb there.*
> Andre: *The kids in my class never listen.*

The conversation proceeded like this with members talking about how much they disliked their classes. Their common frustrations helped build mutual aid in the group as they realized that they were all in the same boat. Other activities that helped them get to know each other and also build some mutual aid included Agree/ Disagree in which members moved to different sides of the room depending on whether they agreed or disagreed with a series of statements that are read aloud. Another getting-to-know-you activity was to ask members to draw images on a shield to represent different aspects of themselves and share them with the group.

In the middle and late stages of the group, as a higher level of cohesion was achieved, the group was able to engage in higher- risk activities. Wright (2000) notes that in the middle stages of a group, "risks of self-exposure, which once seemed inconceivable in the beginning of the group, now come more freely" (p. 214). Wright goes on to acknowledge that this willingness to take risks leads to mutual aid. The activities I chose at this stage required the group to cooperate in order to achieve goals. I was careful to choose activities that could challenge the group, but still give them a sense of competency and a sense that they have the ability to collaborate successfully. One game was called Bop, a game I learned from my clinical supervisor, in which members stand in a circle and hold each other's hands (or wrists) and attempt to keep a balloon up in the air as long as possible. I sometimes timed the group during this activity to see how long they could keep the balloon in the air and they tried to beat their previous times. They were very motivated to continue trying to beat their time as a group and several members would say, "Can we try one more time to beat that time? Please?" After games like these, we would take time to debrief and reflect on the most effective ways to collaborate and how to deal with the conflict that sometimes emerged. For example, sometimes members would express that one member in particular was "the weakest link" who held the group back from making progress overall. While playing Bop one day, one particular member repeatedly allowed the balloon to drop to the ground. When members began to express their frustration and disappointment, I asked them, "What could you do to help Alexander out in a situation like this?" A member said that they could make sure he had back up when the balloon came his way.

Developing an Effective Incentive System

At the formation of the group, I decided I wanted to use an incentive system in order to encourage group cohesion and positive interactions among members. This was a suggestion from my clinical supervisor based on her knowledge of the members and the fact that because of their challenging behaviors, many of them were used to attention being focused on their negative rather than positive behaviors. During our first session, we generated five group guidelines including: Participate in activities and conversations, keep your hands to yourself, try to use words instead of hitting, no cursing, one mic (one person speaking at a time). I explained to the group that during each session, they could earn a sticker on a chart if they made a good effort to follow the group guidelines. In writing about doing group work with school age children, Abrams (2000) notes that it is important to give members an experience that feels very different from a school experience because members need to interact with the facilitator in a less hierarchical way than they would with a teacher. A group experience should give members a sense of agency that, unfortunately, is not commonly fostered in typical public school classrooms. Similarly, Gitterman and Wayne (2003) note that for groups that occur in schools there is a tendency to structure them with a "behavior management" approach that does not allow for the normal testing behaviors of school age children (p. 26). Bearing these concepts in mind, I wanted to find a way to both honor personal agency in the group and reward positive behavior in a structured way. The fact is that some of the members of the group did have very challenging behavior. Many of them struggled to self-regulate when they felt angry or upset.

Low self-esteem was endemic in the group, perhaps due partially to their experience of being labeled as "special ed" or "emotionally disturbed" throughout their school careers and this low self-esteem sometimes led to bullying behaviors. I had a hunch that they could benefit from a formal reward system that reinforced positive behaviors. I spoke with the two guidance counselors at their school and found out that the boys' school used a very structured token economy to reward good behavior. The school used a point system in which students earned points during every period of the day and there was a corresponding system of rewards.

The reward system that I originally developed resembled their school's system in that it was based on individual behavior. If a member put in good effort to meet the group guidelines, he would receive a sticker. At the end of a certain period of time, individuals who had earned a certain amount of stickers would be invited to a pizza party. However, as the weeks went by, I realized that the reward system was not group-oriented enough and I wanted there to be more of a collective effort to earn the rewards. I decided to change the system so that whenever the group *collectively* earned 50 stickers, the whole group would earn a pizza party and movie session in my office. This had a positive effect on the group. It became a ritual at the start of every session for one member to count how many stickers the group had and to remind everyone that they could earn the pizza and movie by following the group guidelines. The members who were more self-regulated often reminded others in the group to treat each other with respect so that they could all benefit from the reward. At the end of one group, one of the internal leaders said, "Guys, we've earned 40 stickers already. That means if everyone earns a sticker the next time we meet, we can probably get pizza and a movie in the next week or so." The group ended up earning four pizza and movie sessions throughout the year and because the system was collective, all members could feel like they had contributed to the success of the group. Steinberg (2010) defines mutual aid as "various forms of help that people can offer one another (process) or experience together (result)" (p. 55). The incentive system in our group embraced both aspects of mutual aid since group members earned points by showing kindness, respect and empathy for one another and then were able to collectively celebrate their achievements in this regard. Because of these qualities, Steinberg also defines mutual aid as being inherently a strengths- driven process. Likewise, the incentive system that helped to develop mutual aid among members focused on rewarding positive behavior rather than punishing negative behavior.

Unconditional Positive Regard

Every group experience presents its unique challenges. In many respects, this group was a very challenging one to facilitate. The group had a great deal of interpersonal conflict and as previously stated, some members had not developed the ability to self-regulate when experiencing negative emotions. During one session, two members began to have an argument with each other while were all having a snack of yogurt. Before I knew it, containers of yogurt were flying around the room and the members were not only angry at each other, but also covered in yogurt. There were times when it was difficult for me as the facilitator to provide an experience that would be empowering for members, but at the same time to maintain safety and structure for the benefit of everyone in the group. Being able to maintain unconditional positive regard for this group, despite the fights, conflicts, disagreements and, occasionally, the flying containers of yogurt, proved to be essential to the success of the group. Letendre and Wayne (2008) discuss the merits of process-oriented groups in which children with behavior issues organically explore behaviors and conflicts as they arise rather than through a curriculum geared at reducing troublesome behaviors. With this approach, members are able to gain self-awareness that could ultimately improve relationships with others. The authors write that, "In this approach, unruly, deviant and rebellious behavior that does not directly hurt others is tolerated and accepted as the worker expresses unconditional acceptance of the members" (p. 292). Using this strategy with Team No Fight may have been effective because some of the "unruly" behavior may have been a way of testing me as the facilitator to see if I would be pushed away, like many of the adults in their lives. After several challenging sessions, I believe that they began to see that I could not be pushed away and that we would have to work through these behaviors and conflicts together.

From the beginning of my work with this group, I had a sense that they felt stigmatized because of how often they asked why they had to participate in the group and also from their conversations about being labeled as "special ed" students and hating this designation. Because of this, I made efforts to help them feel like participation in the group was a positive and special thing. At our program, boys usually do homework and then get to have snack before participating in activities. On the days we had sessions, I would have snacks ready for them and we would all have a snack together while doing some sort of check-in.

This way, they got snack earlier than usual and we had the common experience of sharing some food to start the group. The sessions were almost entirely activity-based rather than discussion-based because I learned very quickly that that format fit the needs of the group and it kept the group fun. I sometimes gave the group special privileges that made them feel positively about the group. For example, on days when the weather was nice, we would go outside on our play roof and do activities there instead of in the office. These experiences helped the group build trust with me and helped them feel like I had their best interests in mind. There was at least one session during which physical fighting among the members got to a point where I was concerned for everyone's safety and I chose to end the group early and direct some of the members to other staff members for discipline responses. When this and other issues arose in the group, I was sure to acknowledge and discuss them with the group, but not to dwell on them. When there were conflicts in the group, the group as a whole was invited to discuss the situation and as a group we would figure out how to move on together in a way that felt safe for everyone.

More About Dealing with Conflicts

Many group work practitioners have acknowledged the benefits of working through conflicts in a group work setting. Conflict is inevitable in groups as it is inevitable in life and effective groups provide a helpful forum for working through difficult disagreements and issues. Salmon and Steinberg (2007) write extensively about the importance of group workers "staying in the mess" with groups. They explore the idea that effective groups will almost inevitably have to wade through the swamp of some of life's most challenging problems and practitioners have to be willing to stay in this mess rather than immediately trying to find a way out. There is an important balance that must be struck of exploring the conflict to its fullest extent and then moving to possible solutions. In staying with the swamp metaphor, Salmon and Steinberg refer to this process of problem solving as "helping others to also negotiate that swamp in a meaningful way" (p. 83). Northen (2002) also writes about the challenges of addressing conflict in groups. She acknowledges her own discomfort with conflict and the conscious efforts she has made not to avoid conflict in groups as a practitioner because she knows that, "Learning how to resolve conflicts through the group experience is expected to carry over to more effective coping with the conflicts that occur outside the group" (p. 43). The group of boys that I worked with, Team No Fight, was conceived because the agency wanted the conflict among members to decrease. For safety and liability reasons, this is understandable. However, sometimes a great deal of conflict had to emerge in the group in order for the members to learn how to "negotiate that swamp."

When conflicts occurred in the group, I usually asked members, in a structured way, to express their individual points of view. All group members, not just the ones involved in the conflict were invited to contribute. There was space for members to get angry or sometimes to cry because their feelings had been hurt. Members often expressed their frustration about certain peers whom they felt stalled the group and prevented them from doing activities that they wanted to do or reaping rewards that they wanted for themselves. One strategy that I employed to address conflict was to try to empower certain members of the group to be role models for other members. I had private conversations with two members in the group who were older and tended to be more self-regulated than the others. They often got frustrated with the group and did not want to be associated with it. I reminded them that they could function as important role models for the group and acknowledged the social cache they had with the group. This was effective and I saw both members stepping into positive leadership roles within the group after the conversations. When conflicts occurred in the group, I was sometimes able to step out of the role of mediator as these members became more willing to step into that role of being an internal leader. This increased the group's sense of agency as a whole as it was able to resolve some conflicts on its own.

In retrospect, I would have devoted more time in the group to explicitly navigating conflicts. Perhaps one reason I did not do this was because of agency context. The group, like most groups with school age children, was chaotic at times and I was sometimes self-conscious about that chaos. What would a staff member think if he or she walked by my door and saw members yelling at each other? In this sense, more education about social work with groups is needed in youth development and school settings in order for groups to function at their utmost potential. In some youth development settings or schools, there may be a widely held belief that a group that is effective is one that is quiet, calm and polite. In reality, groups often get "messy," as mentioned above, and the process does not always look neat. Non-social work professionals may not be aware of this potential or the benefits of a group going through a genuine conflict resolution process and it may be up to a social worker in a setting like this to explain the concepts either through formal training or informal conversation.

Conclusions

Although group progress is never linear, it was clear that certain changes had occurred in Team No Fight by the ending stage. Members were more willing to openly process conflict, they had gotten to know each other better, they needed me less and less as a facilitator for the successful functioning of a session and they were proud of being associated with this group rather than resentful of it. For our last session, I made a collage with some photographs I had taken during a few sessions. I asked each member to write a brief reflection on one positive thing they had gained from the group and to glue it to the collage. Members also acknowledged things about the group that they did not like and things that they wished had happened. The collage is still in the social work office and members of the group often visit and look at the collage. They speak about the group fondly and say that they wish the group had continued. With these members, I am able to talk about what they gained from the group and how they use it in their lives this year. Salmon and Steinberg (2007) discuss the "muck" and the "swamp" of group work by writing that:

> It demands courage- courage to open Pandora's box; tenacity- tenacity to lift the lid no matter how heavy; and faith- faith that some vision will take shape for what to do when the mess contained therein flies out (p. 91).

Of all the interventions I made with Team No Fight, perhaps the most important one was having a sense of faith that things could be different among the group members. Despite very challenging behaviors, a lot of conflict and feelings of stigma, I tried consciously to stay in the mess of the group and have faith that together we would emerge in a different place. In my experience, young people are particularly intuitive and they sense when adults believe in them and believe in their capacity for change. As youth workers, and as group workers, it is imperative that we stay with our youth through "the muck" and always give them the sense that we know things can change and can be better.

A group like Team No Fight would not have been possible without the presence of a social worker on staff. Some, but not all, after school youth development settings have social workers on staff. These settings are ideal in many ways for social work, particularly in the form of group work, to occur. As in schools, youth are interacting in naturally-formed groups and conflict inevitably arises in these groups. Participation in a group experience can allow youth to feel a sense of community and to learn conflict resolution skills that they can use in social interactions outside of the group. At a time when there is increasingly less funding for social workers in schools, it is especially important to increase funding for social workers in after school settings.

References

Abrams, B. (2000). Finding common ground in a conflict resolution group for boys. *Social Work with Groups, 23*(1), 55-69.

Jones, A. (1998). 104 Activities That Build: Self-Esteem, Teamwork, Communication, Anger *Management, Self-Discovery And Coping Skills.* Rec Room Publishing.

Kurland, R. & Salmon, R. (1999). Purpose: A misunderstood and misused keystone of group work practice. *Social Work with Groups* 29(2-3), 105-120.

Letendre, J. & Wayne, J. (2008). Integrating process interventions into a school based curriculum group. *Social Work with Groups, 31*(3-4), 289-305.

Northen, H. (2002). I hate conflict, but .... *Social Work with Groups, 25*(1/2), 39-44.

Salmon, R. & Steinberg, D. (2007). Staying in the mess: Teaching students and practitioners to work effectively in the swamp of important problems. *Social Work with Groups, 30*(4), 79-94.

Steinberg, D. (2010). Mutual aid: A contribution to best-practice social work. *Social Work with Groups.* 33(1), 53-68.

Wayne, J., & Gitterman, A. (2003). Offensive behavior in groups: Challenges and opportunities. *Social Work with Groups, 26*(2), 23-34.

Wright, W. (2000). The use of purpose in on-going activity groups: A framework for maximizing the therapeutic impact. *Social Work with Groups* 22(2-3) 31-54.

Things I didn't learn in graduate school: A survival guide for leading involuntary groups

Francis S. Bartolomeo

Introduction

This chapter is based on an invitational lecture and provides advice, in the form of a survival guide, for working with involuntary groups. The guide represents the distillation of 25 years of group work practice with involuntary groups with diverse populations in an array of settings combined with the findings of my doctoral research, a qualitative study that explored the process of negotiating group purpose with non-voluntary adolescent groups in therapeutic day schools (Bartolomeo, 2007). Eight essential guidelines for social group work with involuntary groups are illustrated by personal experiences, anecdotes from practice and research findings.

Background

In June 1989, the night before I was to lead my first group at a residential treatment center for adjudicated adolescent males with my freshly minted Master's Degree in Social Work, I had a nightmare: after entering the group room, the group members physically attack me. Awake, I attributed my nightmare to the natural anxiety of starting a new job and working with violent youth. I did not know at that time that my dream presaged a more protracted emotional pounding that I was to endure: I was totally unprepared for the hostility, aggression, silences, avoidance, and emotional (and physical) intimidation I experienced as a social group worker during my first two years following graduation.

The setting, a residential treatment center, operated within the juvenile justice system, emphasized group treatment, and thus, it seemed to be a good fit given my enthusiasm for group work. With little preparation, I was soon leading and co-leading racially diverse groups with teens who had committed crimes such as manslaughter, violent assault, drug trafficking, theft, and sexual offenses. Though I had majored in group work and was privileged to have been taught by notable professors and skilled practitioners, few of the practice skills that I learned in graduate school were effective in this real life group setting. Furthermore, my agency supervisor and more seasoned colleagues appeared equally frustrated in their group work; they frequently resorted to conducting individual treatment with the group-as- audience (Shulman, 1992), or structured the group to such a degree that it more resembled a classroom. Unfortunately, when social workers resort to these approaches, by default or intentionally, the potentially therapeutic or helpful factors of group treatment are minimized or lost (Corder, Whiteside, & Hazlip, 1981; Shulman, 1992; Yalom, 1995).

In retrospect, there was a host of organizational, systemic, and clinical factors that interfered with good social group work practice within that residential treatment center. Client needs, group purpose and group composition, for example, presented formidable practice challenges because the residents, though sharing a common diagnosis of Conduct Disorder, presented with a complex mix of educational, social, familial, substance abuse and psychiatric needs. Therefore, groups were comprised of residents with varied and erratic levels of cognitive and social-emotional functioning. This chapter explores the formidable practice challenges and opportunities associated with providing compulsory social group work services.

Review of Literature

Influential models of social group work assume group members are voluntary (Levin, 2006; Rooney, 1992). It is surprising, given social work's rich tradition of working with clients in criminal justice, child protection, and substance abuse treatment programs, that social work research and pedagogy paid little attention to the varied demands of working with involuntary clients. This state of knowledge fortunately began to change in the early 1990s. This section will provide a cursory review of the literature related to group work with involuntary clients that began to surface at that time.

Rooney (1992) is one of a small number of social work scholars who focuses on social work practice with mandated and pressured clients. In an important social work text, dedicated entirely to practice with involuntary clients, Rooney devotes a chapter to group work with this challenging population. He introduces the theory of psychological reactance, which plays a vital role in understanding and working effectively with involuntary clients.

Rooney (1992) asserts that there are two types of involuntary groups. A mandated group includes members with legal requirements (or legal ramifications for noncompliance) to participate in group treatment. A non-voluntary group is composed of members who have non-legal pressures (family, agencies, and referring parties) to participate in group treatment. Rooney also notes that some groups may be comprised of both legally mandated and pressured clients such that there are varying degrees of voluntarism within a group.

Rooney accentuates the pre-group planning and beginning phases of group work with involuntary clients. As a component of client preparation, group workers should distribute a written description of the purpose and goals of the group, basic rules, expectations of the clients, qualifications of the leaders, and methods to be employed to prospective group members. The goal of the beginning session of an involuntary group, according to Rooney, is to develop a semi-voluntary contract, which "is the convergence of agency-mandated purposes and rules and goals expressed by participants" (1992, p. 291).

In mandated treatment groups for adults with substance abuse disorders, Milgram and Rubin (1992) suggest a number of intervention strategies. The authors take the position that resistance is a normal and adaptive response to painful self-exploration. Incorporating psychodynamic perspectives, Milgram and Rubin argue that resistance is both an unconscious and conscious phenomenon that can occur in individual group members or the group-as- a- whole. They, too, stress the significance of the beginning phase of groups. If group leaders fail to assist the group in temporarily resolving their resistance at the start of treatment, then "resistance can retard the group development to the point where members will engage in stereotyped conversations about the unfairness of probation officers, urinalysis, and the need to be in treatment" (p. 96).

Behroozi (1993) distinguishes different types of involuntary applicants and considers the term, 'involuntary client' an oxymoron, and suggests that 'client' refers to, and should be limited to, persons who volitionally enter into mutual agreements or contracts for professional services. Behroozi contends that the principal aim of social workers is to assist involuntary applicants to transform into clients through mutual agreement. Moreover, social workers should not pronounce involuntary applicants as unmotivated, but rather explore the sources of reluctance that involuntary applicants characteristically present. Like Rooney (1992), Behroozi contends that special attention should be conferred to the pre-group and beginning phase of groups with involuntary applicants because it is during this period that the process of socializing the applicant into the role of client begins.

In mandated groups for men who batter their intimate partners, Trimble (1994) reports that in his earliest group work with these men, he attempted to apply a *personal growth* group model with the assumption that empathy, rapport building, and an acceptance would result in client insight and greater control of their abusive behaviors. Based on high client attrition rates and professional exchanges with workers at battered women shelters, Trimble determined this model to be ineffective. He concluded that men with histories of violence generally need external pressure to remain in the group, "past their usual tolerance level for self-confrontation" (p. 261). Thomas and Caplan (1999), also working with involuntary groups of men who batter, provide 56 valuable techniques for facilitating involuntary clients, which they cast into three categories: process, inclusion, and linking. By attending to group process, the group worker can surface the emotional content expressed by an individual member, which can then be potentially linked to a group-as-a-whole theme. Inclusion techniques are employed to engage uninvolved or disconnected group members.

Goodman, Getzel, and Ford (1996) describe a group work approach with high-risk urban adolescents of color who are on probation for a range of criminal activity. The authors suggest that the probation officers facilitate the groups' transformed relationship with authority by decreasing the social distance between them and the group, while simultaneously clarifying the boundaries of authority and responsibility.

More recently, Rooney and Chovanec (2004) and Chovanec (2009) have made substantial contributions to the development of a theoretical framework for group work with involuntary groups. Incorporating the stages of change model (Prochaska, Norcross & DiClemente, 1994) and relatedly, motivational interviewing (Miller & Rollnick, 2002), Rooney and Chovanec have produced an integrative and valuable approach to involuntary groups.

Researching the engagement process with involuntary groups, Levin (2006) recognized the vital role that anger plays, when harnessed effectively, in the creation of a productive group culture. Levin recommends that group leaders of involuntary groups should expect group members to test authority and boundaries and that the group members are carefully observing the leader's reactions to these tests. Group norms are established by the manner in which the group leader responds to individual and collective anger related to the compulsory nature of the group. Levin therefore advises that group leaders demonstrate patience and acceptance: "The group member must feel accepted 'anger and all,' to be accepted as real, in order for the group member to engage (p. 78)."

Practice strategies with involuntary groups

Despite differences in population and presenting problems, there appear to be some recurrent themes in the social work literature regarding involuntary groups. Many of the writings emphasize the critical importance of the pre-group and beginning phase of groups for involuntary clients. Nearly unanimously, the literature notes the importance of acknowledging the sources of coercion as well as normalizing client reactions to infringement on their autonomy. Similarly, whether client reactions are framed as reactance or resistance, the authors perceive these responses as expectable and adaptive. Another recurring idea in the literature is the value of providing involuntary clients with as many choices as possible and/or to acknowledge the remaining areas of choice. This can be facilitated through the development of honest, clear, and explicit contracts that identify non-negotiable items and areas for compromise, as well as client rights. Finally, the social work literature on group work with involuntary clients highlights the need to identify client strengths and capacities as a means, in part, to counteract feelings of incompetence and powerlessness.

These practice strategies from the social work literature summarized above are consistent with several of the techniques and approaches that evolved organically from my social group work practice with involuntary clients, which are now described in the form of a survival guide.

The Survival Guide

Though it seems obvious now, involuntary clients are different from voluntary clients (Levin, 2006), in that the dynamics of a coercive therapeutic context differ from a voluntary one, and pressure to participate in clinical services triggers client reactions and strategies to restore their sense of self-agency (Rooney, 1992). Though recognizing that I was employed by an agency with social control purposes (Garvin, 1981), and that the residents were committed to the treatment center through judicial means, I was employing techniques, theories, and models that were primarily developed and applied to clients who voluntarily sought or desired help. Lacking an appropriate framework, the adolescents' negative responses and lack of progress in group treatment could be simply attributed to their lack of motivation, resistance, and psychological defenses.

In the late 1980s and early 1990s, my graduate training, the social work literature and even the Association for the Advancement of Social Work with Groups (now IASWG), the professional organization for social group workers, provided minimal guidance for leading groups for involuntary clients. Similarly, though I was acutely aware of the ethical tension between the social control purposes of my agency and the social work value of client self-determination, I could find little direction or resolution. As previously mentioned, there was no theoretical or research-informed paradigms for group work with involuntary populations at that time.

The survival guidelines defined below represent an integration of my 25 years of group work experience with a range of involuntary populations, findings from my doctoral research, which focused on negotiating group purpose with involuntary groups of adolescents, and the theories and practice models that have emerged over the last 25 years. These general guidelines inform my practice with involuntary groups with respect to technique, interventions, and leadership stance; these are applied differentially to correspond with varying population needs and presenting problems, and with fluctuating degrees of involuntariness –from court-involved clients to those who face non-legal pressures from family and/or parents to participate in social work services. The survival guide is comprised of the following recommendations:

1. Use the right map
2. Take off the rose-colored glasses
3. Beware of deviancy training

4. Know your stages of group development—with a twist
5. Be an authoritative leader
6. The truth shall set you free, so tell it
7. Do not feed the victim narrative
8. Do not cheat the group of its suffering: The existential choice

Survival Tip # 1: Use the Right Map(s)

Applying treatment models predicated on voluntary participation are ineffective because the dynamics of a coerced therapeutic context differ from that of a voluntary context; voluntary clients are characteristically ready to change and generally have hope or positive expectations for good outcomes. The relationship between the social worker and the voluntary client is usually collaborative as goals and objectives are developed through mutual agreement. Involuntary clients, in contrast, may not acknowledge problems and, therefore, have no need for changes, and bring their negative reactions to compulsory services. Other involuntary clients may acknowledge problems, but do not believe change is possible, but also have negative responses to coercion. The relationship between the social worker and the involuntary client at the outset may be marked with mistrust, suspicion, disagreement and antagonism.

Therefore, my first survival tip for practitioners is to locate and employ the appropriate theory and practice maps for working with involuntary clients in groups. Group work is a complex activity, especially treatment groups, which require knowledge of the clients' specific problem (e.g., addiction, emotional and behavioral dysregulation), population characteristics (e.g., normative developmental needs, gender, and race), and organizational context (e.g., agency purposes and culture). It is the responsibility of the social group worker to be informed in all these domains.

In addition to familiarity with the literature on the strategies and models for group work with involuntary participants that now exist and best practices related to specific problems and populations, it is essential that social workers also be knowledgeable about the theory of psychological reactance and the transtheoretical model of the stages of change (Prochaska, DiClemente, & Norcross, 1994).

Next, I will discuss these two important components of the "right map" in work with involuntary groups.

Reactance theory

Reactance theory, as developed by Brehm (1966), a social psychologist, describes the attitudes, feelings, and behaviors typical of individuals in reaction to real or perceived threats to autonomy. Reactance is a motivational state in which the intent is to oppose those forces that threaten to interfere with individual liberties. In contrast to psychological resistance, originally a psychoanalytic construct that described an unconscious opposition to consciously agreed upon goals and treatment methods, and which in contemporary usage is often used pejoratively, reactance is a normal reaction to a forced situation. Mental health professionals frequently misperceive reactance-based behaviors and attitudes as indicators of pathology, and label clients as resistant, oppositional, or unmotivated (Rooney, 1992).

Reactance theory describes five direct and indirect response patterns intended to reclaim those freedoms and/or reduce the degree of reactance (Rooney, 1992). These attitudinal and/or behavioral response patterns are: 1) actively attempting to restore lost or threatened freedoms (e.g., directly refusing to attend group sessions); 2) indirectly reclaiming freedom through partial compliance (e.g., attending group meetings, but refusing to participate; arriving late), finding loopholes, or exhibiting behaviors similar to the banned ones (e.g., after being told that headphones are not allowed during group, a group member begins reading a book); 3) observing others trying to restore their freedoms, or by inciting others to do so (e.g., encouraging another group member to walk out); 4) the attraction to the forbidden behavior increases (e.g., a group leader asks group members to cease side conversations and more side conversations erupt) ; and 5) hostility and aggression, which adolescents are more likely to directly exhibit.

According to Rooney, reactance theory provides a means to understand circumstantial responses to "involuntary situations under the pressure of coerced and constrained choices" (p. 129). Reactance theory assumes that people have valued behaviors that they are free to exercise. Reactance will arise when these valued freedoms are threatened, diminished, or eliminated. Reactance theory describes thoughts, emotions, and behaviors that typically ensue from restricted freedoms. It is a transactional theory that assumes that these responses are normal reactions to threat of loss of valued freedoms.

Reactance-based responses are highly likely to occur when problems or the need to change are imposed on individuals, which threaten the client's freedom to engage in behaviors of their choice—even if self-destructive or harmful to others. Reactance theory helps to explain why techniques and approaches that were developed with voluntary clients often evoke negative responses from clients who do not see the need for change, or those who are not yet ready for change. A theory of change is also indispensable for practice especially with involuntary clients.

Transtheoretical model of change (a.k.a. stages of change)

The model of stages of change (Prochaska et al., 1994) is a well-researched model of the process of how people, with professional assistance and without, consider, enact, and maintain long-term behavioral and lifestyle changes. Though there are, as Chovanec (2009) notes, challenges and limitations to the application of an individual change model to groups, it is crucial to match interventions to a group member's respective stage of change, and assuming that members are in a similar stage, to the group-as-a-whole. It was based, initially, on research on smoking cessation, and is now extensively utilized in the substance abuse field and public health campaigns.

Though referred to as stages, the research-based model asserts that the change process is non-linear, represented as a spiral rather than ascending stairs, with five stages: beginning with the *precontemplation* stage, not thinking or being aware of a problem to *contemplation*, awareness of a problem, but undecided about change. Once an individual has sufficiently resolved his/her ambivalence about changing, and is committed to changing, s/he enters the *preparation* stages, literally developing a plan, which could include seeking professional assistance, to *action*, which entails implementing the plan. When the objective, for example, curtailing nicotine use is reached, individuals enter into *maintenance*, to reinforce and sustain their achieved changes. Prochaska et al. (1994) found that making long-term changes frequently involves relapse and recycling through the stages of change. Their research on smoking cessation, for example, indicated that individuals generally required three to four attempts before successfully quitting. Relapses are approached as learning experiences.

The stages of change model has profound significance for those working with involuntary clients because it provides practitioners and healthcare workers a paradigm for matching specific interventions and processes to respective stages. The model of stages of change posits that prior to desiring change, or being internally motivated, there is generally an external pressure or instigator that impinges on a person's belief that there is no problem. A person who smokes cigarettes, or has an unhealthy diet, or abuses substances may become aware of a problem when his/her physician provides education about risks. If education about risk, however, is an insufficient motivator a person may, in turn, develop health problems, which may then serve to prompt the individual into considering, or contemplating that there is a need to stop smoking or eating more healthily.

With individuals with substance use disorders, it may not be their physician but a legal consequence, such as an arrest for driving under the influence (D.U.I.), which initiates the movement from a state of precontemplation to contemplation. Contrary to the cliché that people "have to want to change," research in the field of addiction and the use of "drug courts" or diversion programs has repeatedly found that treatment does not have to be voluntary to be effective. The longstanding popular notion that a person with a substance use disorder (SUD) needs to "hit rock bottom" before help can be useful is not only dangerous, but inaccurate.

When working with precontemplators, corresponding interventions include consciousness-raising and an examination of the role of psychological defenses. Unlike strategies for voluntary clients, practitioners involved with involuntary clients often attempt to increase client anxiety through information about the effects of unhealthy or risky behaviors rather than trying to soothe or reassure. Defenses such as denial, externalization (i.e., blaming) and minimization are commonly associated with those in precontemplation. A technique for treating individuals with substance use disorders (SUDs) in the precontemplation stage involves a detailed examination of the impact of substance use across multiple domains of functioning: work performance, relationships, and family and leisure activities. Also, agency context influences the type and intensity of techniques that can be employed. Clients in outpatient treatment, with non-legal pressure to receive services, are likely to terminate services if defenses are overly challenged whereas clients in residential and correctional facilities may require more intensive strategies such as family or victim impact statements.

According to Prochaska et al. (1994), relationships that help precontemplators, include those which caringly confront harmful or self-destructive behaviors and the facilitating defenses; that insist on responsibility and accountability for choices and actions; that give and permit consequences for negative behavior; and that directly and regularly recommend behavior change. This approach is in sharp contrast to the accepting, client-directed style that is commonly employed with voluntary clients who are likely in the *preparation* or *action* stage of change.

Reactance theory and the stages of change model are essential elements to navigate individual and group practice with involuntary clients. Since reactance is a predictable response to coercion and encroachment on personal autonomy, difficult behavior as exhibited by clients can be attributed, in large part, to the *situation* rather than the *person*. Ascribing objectionable client behaviors and attitudes to the nature of their involvement allows social workers to be more empathic to their circumstances and accepting of their responses, which is critical in the formation of an alliance and the creation of a therapeutic group culture. The Transtheoretical Model of Change offers guidance to reduce reactance because certain principles and processes of change work best at each stage.

Survival Tip # 2: Remove the Rose- Colored Glasses

Individuals who behave in antisocial, aggressive and self-destructive ways may become involuntary clients. It is important to remember that the group is a social microcosm and therefore it is likely that involuntary clients will exhibit or reenact in the 'here and now' of the group the very attitudes, values and behaviors that got them in trouble in the first place. Challenging behaviors in the group include verbal aggression, intimidation or threats, physical aggression or posturing, noncompliance or silence and telling "war stories" i.e., bragging about their drug use and misdeeds. These behaviors are generally antithetical to therapeutic group norms and the creation of a group climate of safety.

My experience as a forensic social worker taught me that involuntary clients are capable of deception, manipulation, and often employ intentional self-presentation strategies to avoid legal consequences and/or to further their self-interests. In my groups with adjudicated adolescents, I repeatedly discovered that group members would misuse my empathy and good intentions to violate residential or milieu policies and procedures (of course with my so called permission), which undermined my credibility and working relationships with residential care staff who worked so hard to maintain consistent boundaries necessary for a safe, predictable environment.

The challenges of developing respectful therapeutic relationships with individuals who have impulse control problems, low distress tolerance, relational detachment, lack of empathy, and/or have a need for interpersonal dominance are magnified many times when the treatment method is group. Utilizing techniques and group models designed for voluntary clients with the capacity for self-regulation of emotions and behavior is not only ineffective, but potentially harmful. Not only did I allow myself to be regularly verbally assaulted by the juvenile offenders in my groups, I recall an incident in which a group member pulled the chair out from a residential staff person causing him to fall hard to the floor as the other group members laughed, adding to his humiliation. I did nothing in response, neither setting a limit, nor giving a consequence to the group member or assisting the victim of the prank. Later, I explained my inaction to the humiliated staff person by framing the incident as "normal adolescent fooling around." I did not appreciate that the resident had reenacted to a lesser degree the same attitude and behavior, including a lack of concern for others, which led to his involvement with the juvenile justice system; nor did I use the incident to reinforce acceptable and unacceptable behavior in the group.

Social group work with involuntary client populations who have histories of interpersonal and relational violence (as victims and victimizers) necessitates a values-driven leadership approach that communicates "good people can do hurtful things" and that people and feelings are acceptable; however, all behaviors are not. Separating behavior from the person helps involuntary clients assume responsibility for their choices and actions. Individuals recovering from addiction and men who batter their partners, for example, frequently experience shame, guilt, and humiliation when they expose their behavior to a group of others. Similarly, belligerent client presentations often belie underlying feelings of profound inadequacy. Avoidance of these painful emotions interferes with the acceptance of responsibility for past or present actions that caused harm to others or oneself.

In relationships, involuntary clients due to shame, secrecy, and self-protection frequently engage in fight, flight, and "fool" (Brendtro, Mitchell & McCall, 2009, p. 50). Involuntary clients with adequate moral development and social awareness will hide those parts of themselves that they find unacceptable or fear that others will find unacceptable. A person in recovery from addiction may not disclose that he traded sex for drugs or that he is experiencing urges to relapse. Involuntary clients will not respect mental health professionals who are easily manipulated or shocked; these clients cannot feel known by naïve practitioners and consequently their destructive impulses have less chance for containment. Involuntary clients frequently want to be known, warts and all, and feel relieved when shameful secrets, disavowed impulses, and parts of self (e.g., the violent offender who can acknowledge that a part of him *enjoyed* the power he felt when he physically dominated another person) can be identified and contained. However, as will be discussed later, groups for involuntary clients require clear boundaries and structure necessary for the containment of anti-relational behaviors and the creation of interpersonal safety.

Survival Tip # 3: Beware of Deviancy Training

When working with involuntary groups, there is a significant risk that the well-known dictum of Marsh (1931), "by the crowd they have been broken, by the crowd they shall be healed" could devolve to: "by the crowd they have been broken, by the crowd they shall be made worse." The research by Dishion and his colleagues (1999) provided evidence that group intervention for high-risk youth in early adolescence can have negative iatrogenic effects. That is, the problem behavior that the intervention was to ameliorate was actually reinforced by peers and, thus, increased. This research, though limited to a specific age group and developmental period, has major implications for group work with involuntary client populations. The potential for group interventions to reinforce and exacerbate negative behaviors should not be surprising given that modeling, imitation, social learning, and mutual aid are factors that are frequently associated with the unique power of groups. To minimize the risk that group interventions with certain population may harm, social group work with involuntary populations necessitates thoughtful evaluation of several interrelated issues: group composition, organizational policies and practices, and simplified or one-dimensional views of mental and behavioral health problems.

When composing groups that appear to be homogenous with respect to problem area, it is critical to consider the degree of severity evidenced by each group member. Substance abuse disorders, for example, fall along a continuum of severity from use, abuse, to addiction. It is common practice to mix individuals with wide variations in severity yet in similar early stage of change, such as precontemplation, which creates the risk that the group members will reinforce each other's denial and minimization of the problem and expose those with milder presentations to those with more advanced conditions. Similarly, including individuals in the contemplation stage with group members predominately in the precontemplation stage frequently results, through the process of emotional contagion, in backsliding.

As an example, an agency that provides outpatient substance abuse services to teens consulted me due to concerns about the lack of efficacy of their groups and a decrease in community referrals. A discussion of group composition revealed that, due to administrative pressure to get groups started, teens who were abusing marijuana were placed in groups with adolescents with more severe poly-substance use disorders, including heroin abuse. The net result was that the less experienced substance abusers were essentially being inducted into a pro-drug culture and the groups developed a reputation, not unwarranted, in the community for "making kids worse."

It is critical that social group workers assume an organizational perspective when working in agencies that provide services to involuntary clients and to intervene at the system level when indicated. Though it may be an organizational philosophy, cherished historical practice, or fiscal pressure, agencies that serve involuntary clients often overlook the possibility that there are disadvantages to creating groups with coerced clients, especially if done improperly. Some clients, for example, do not do well in groups, or are insufficiently prepared, and can thereby ruin the experience for other group members. Further drawbacks of group work for involuntary clients, as Dishion et al. (1999) have demonstrated, include negative peer modeling in which antisocial behaviors are reinforced. For the social work administrator or program manager, I recommend the development of exclusionary criteria for participation in certain types of groups and to consider creative alternatives such a dyadic treatment with the gradual and incremental introduction of additional members.

Survival Tip # 4: Know your Stages of Group Development with a Twist

It is widely accepted that small groups evolve over time through discernable developmental stages (Bennis & Shepard, 1956; Berman-Rossi, 1993; Garland, Jones & Kolodny, 1965; Lacoursiere, 1980; Rutan

& Stone, 1984; Tuckman, 1965: Yalom, 1995). Group development is conceived as an underlying dynamic process that is manifested in changes in such areas as task performance, group cohesion, role behavior, and capacity for mutual aid (Bartolomeo, 2009; Berman-Rossi, 1993; Garland et al., 1965; Lacoursiere, 1980). Theories of group development provide group leaders with a structure in which to understand complex group processes, and that progression can be facilitated through interventions attuned to the group's stage of development (Berman-Rossi, 1993).

During graduate school, I was deeply immersed in the study of *A Model for Stages of Group Development for Social Work Groups* by Garland, Jones, and Kolodny (1965) also known as "The Boston Model" (Bartolomeo, 2009), and it served as my primary frame of reference for group work with the adjudicated youth in the residential treatment center. Garland et al. proposed a five stage model: preaffiliation, power and control, intimacy, differentiation, and termination.

Following is a brief review of the Boston Model which will be limited to the first two stages of group development, *preaffiliation and power and control* because it is during the first stage that establishing purpose and safety are critical, and the second stage involves themes of power and revolt, which have particular significance for non-voluntary groups. At the outset of the first stage, *pre-affiliation*, a collection of individuals with a shared task or identity does not yet exist (Berman-Rossi, 1993; Lacoursiere, 1980). Because trust in others or the situation has not yet developed, anxiety is present and new group members engage in superficial, stereotyped interactions. Group members are, to varying degrees, ambivalent about committing to and making an emotional investment in the group. Even when there are positive expectations for the group experience, new members normally need to be self-protective, as manifested in cautious, approach-avoidance behavior and attitudes toward the group and its activities (Garland et al., 1965). In this stage, the social worker attempts to help an aggregate of individuals to become a functioning group. The social worker facilitates this effort by attending to the task needs of the group especially the group's purpose, and by providing sufficient structure, direction, and boundaries to promote safety, thereby reducing the level of interpersonal anxiety.

Once members have adequately resolved to be part of the group and have established basic trust in the group situation and the other members, the group-as-a-whole theme shifts to concerns about dominance, authority relations, rebellion and autonomy (Bennis & Shepard, 1956; Garland et al., 1965; Yalom, 1995). If the primary relational dynamic in the first stage of group development was ambivalence, the preoccupation of the second stage is "power and control" (Garland et al., p. 272). In stage two problems of influence and status also appear. In the attempt to establish a social hierarchy, scapegoating of more vulnerable members may occur, and internal cliques or dyadic alliances form (Garland et al.).

The relationship between the worker (and the authority he/she represents) and the group is central to the power and control stage. Garland et al. (1965) regard the second stage as crucial because it is through the groups' grappling with the authority of the worker that power is redistributed to the group itself. The group-as-a-whole may struggle with the group leader through testing limits, non-participation, and rebelliousness. The group reacts to the structure or format they previously found necessary to feel safe, but which now feels oppressive, or as an arbitrary expression of the leader's power. It is imperative that the group worker not respond punitively to the group's challenge to his/ her authority, which is "a necessary prerequisite to helping members feel more secure in expressing themselves freely and in permitting autonomy in their relations with one another" (Garland et al., p. 273). The power and control stage, therefore, is profoundly relevant to the value of empowerment in social work practice. A social work group cannot become a system of mutual aid (Shulman, 2006) unless the power and expertise of the group leader, which was vital in the preaffiliation stage, is dispersed and embraced by the group members.

Garland et al.'s description of the power and control stage decisively captured what I was perceiving and experiencing in the groups with adjudicated youth, however, the groups, or more accurately the sequence of stages were out-of-order because the primary tasks of the pre-affiliation stage, establishing purpose, safety, and sufficient trust which are *preconditions* for movement into the power and control stage had not been adequately achieved. In Garland et al.'s model, as well as in other prominent group development paradigms (see Bennis & Shepard, 1956; Dies, 19996; Lacoursiere, 1980; Rutan & Stone, 1984; Tuckman, 1965: Yalom, 1995), the stages develop and progress in a sequential fashion, with the preceding stage serving as the foundation for the next. According the Boston Model, the group begins the transition to the power and control stage only *after* members have adequately resolved their ambivalence about being part of the group and have established basic trust and safety in the group situation and the other members (Garland et al., 1965).

The limitation of the Boston Model and other eminent concepts of stages of group development were based on groups of voluntary clients who could chose, even if ambivalently, to be part of a group or exercise their choice not to; and challenges to the leader's authority occurred after the group members felt sufficiently secure to do so. The Boston Model and other mainstream theories of group development do reflect the impact of client coercion and concomitantly, reactance-based attitudes and behaviors, on the processes and maturation of the group. Recognizing the differences in group development with involuntary clients, I discuss an applicable model below.

A model for group development with involuntary clients

In his comprehensive review of theories of group development, Lacoursiere (1980) discerns a pattern of group development related to groups with involuntary clients. A group developmental sequence was uncovered that began not with the typical positive, albeit apprehensive, orientation stage, but an initial stage characterized by "negativity, resistance, and sometimes open hostility" (p. 128). Lacoursiere calls this type of group beginning *the negative orientation stage*. Lacoursiere notes that this negative sequence appears "particularly when participation is not completely voluntary, such as in therapy groups with delinquents or alcohol or drug abuse patients, or in training and learning groups with required participation" (p. 37).

The author explains that because the group members are engaging in orienting behaviors, albeit antagonistically, this negative stage does not generally transform into the more typical positive one. Rather, the negative orientation stage blends into a less discernable dissatisfaction stage, which results in a prolonged negative stage. The negative stage can merge with the resolution stage in which sensible goals are established and the group begins to work toward them.

Lacoursiere's negative orientation sequence of group development is consistent with my practice experience and findings in my doctoral research. In groups with involuntary clients, and to a lesser extent, with the non-voluntary, there is a merging of the emotional themes of forming and storming (in Tuckman's parlance) into a single stage or a convergence of the preaffiliation stage and power and control stage in Garland et al.,'s "Boston Model." Thus, at the beginning of a non-voluntary group, when the group's dependence on the leader to provide structure, purpose and focus is high, the group is reacting to the mandate in the embodiment of the group worker and wrestling with the worker's authority. The group is requiring direction from the group work while paradoxically needing to divest him or her of the power to provide such leadership. Stated another way, at the same time the group worker is attempting to engage the group, create a safe environment, and establish the group contract, which includes the group purpose, the group-as-a-whole may be expressing anger (Levin, 2006) or hostility (overtly or silently) related to the impingement on their autonomy directed toward the person and authority of the social worker who (unfairly or not) represents the source of the mandate, but which potentially undermine the capacity to establish safety and trust. All of these dynamics are pithily captured in an actual exchange I had during an involuntary group for adolescent offenders: After asking the participants for their understanding of the purpose of the group, a dominant teen replied, "to f#*k you over."

The leadership style and skills necessary to meet the paradoxical tasks of managing expressions of anger and reactance while establishing trust and safety are addressed next.

Survival Tip # 5: Be an Authoritative Leader

The clinical challenges produced by the compression of the preaffilation and power and control stages can be mitigated by thorough pre-group planning and individual preparation, which is emphasized in the extant literature. Rooney (1990), in particular, accentuates the pre-group planning and beginning phases of group work with involuntary clients. As a component of client preparation, group workers should distribute a written description of the purpose and goals of the group, basic rules, expectations of the clients, qualifications of the leaders, and methods to be employed to prospective group members. The goal of the beginning session of an involuntary group, according to Rooney, is to develop a semi-voluntary contract, which "is the convergence of agency-mandated purposes and rules and goals expressed by participants" (1992, p. 291).

The research on parenting styles is highly applicable in understanding the leadership stance necessary for involuntary groups. The parenting literature describes three broad styles of parenting: a) authoritarian, b) permissive, and c) authoritative (Baumrind, 1991). Within these parenting styles are differing approaches to balancing connection and discipline, or control, of children. The authoritative style represents the middle ground between the extremes of permissiveness and authoritarianism.

Analogous to an authoritative style of parenting, the social workers with involuntary groups need to adopt an authoritative style of group leadership. This stance blends warmth, acceptance, and interest in clients' perspective while creating clear boundaries for their authority and responsibility. In turn, this establishes and maintains limits for the creation of an emotionally safe group climate. Thus, social group workers need to be comfortable in their role of authority figure and in the judicious exertion of their authority.

Anger plays an important role in the beginning stage of involuntary groups (Levin, 2006), which requires social group workers to be comfortable and accepting of appropriate expressions of anger. There is an important distinction between expressing anger about the circumstances and requirement of the group and denigrating the group leader. With involuntary adolescent groups, group workers may need to educate the group members about the difference between feelings and behaviors and teach them how to appropriately and effectively communicate anger. I will consistently emphasize with the group that all feelings are permissible, but not all behaviors are acceptable.

With involuntary groups, I strongly recommend that social workers, especially in the beginning stage, prioritize the conditions necessary to create a safe climate and vigorously counteract and limit anti-relational behavior, including verbal assaults toward the group worker. Creating safety refers to a group condition in which group members and the social worker can feel sufficiently free from anxiety that they will be harmed emotionally or physically in the group. Social group workers need to be cognizant that many involuntary clients have histories of interpersonal trauma and social maltreatment such as peer rejection and ridicule. The consequences of these negative social experiences include relational mistrust, social anxiety, difficulty with self-disclosure, and concerns about emotional safety, all of which present significant obstacles to developing a working group with the capacity for mutual aid. Therefore, one of the first tasks that I implement with involuntary groups is the co-creation of a set of agreements (rather than rules), or a covenant, which includes values, attitudes and behaviors that will guide how we treat each other. I explain that agreements are necessary so that collectively we can feel comfortable in the group. The primacy of creating safety is captured by a social worker in my doctoral study:

My goal is to make sure everybody is to feel safe in this room. ... How do people feel safe? ... That is the first problem they [the members] solve together" (Bartolomeo, 2007, p. 108).

Group members are more likely to adhere to agreements they have created and, when a group member is violating an agreement, the leader and the group members can ask the group member, with curiosity rather than judgment, why s/he is struggling to observe the agreements. It is important to note that the agreements are a vital element of the structure and boundaries, which are critical for clients lacking adequate inner-controls. That is, the structured group environment provides the controls, or *containment*, from the outside in and thereby helps clients to express rather than act out their feelings.

Survival Tip # 6: The Truth Shall Set You Free, So Tell It

Nearly unanimously, the literature on involuntary groups emphasizes the importance of acknowledging the sources of coercion as well as validating and normalizing client reactions to the infringement on their autonomy, and whether client reactions are framed as reactance or resistance, their responses are perceived as expectable and adaptive. In addition to acknowledging the reality that the group members are being pressured or required to participate in the group, it is important to be clear about the agency's purposes for the group.

Group purpose can be difficult to achieve under general clinical circumstances. Group workers can sometimes fail to state the group purpose in simple, clear language that helps the group members to understand the focus of the group. In addition, concerns about exerting too much control over the group can lead social workers to be reluctant about sharing their perceptions or the host agency's view of the group purpose. If the agency-perceived purpose(s) of the group is not transparent, group members will sense a hidden agenda, which will increase mistrust and undermine the development of an authentic relationship between the group worker and the group participants.

Achieving group purpose with non-voluntary clients is even more complicated because group members have reactions to coercion that interfere with their willingness to embrace the role of client. A straightforward discussion of group purpose, i.e., an examination of "what this group is for," is the vehicle through which group members can first grapple with their responses to compulsory treatment and is the means by which members can become a group with a shared task. In my study of social group workers in therapeutic day schools for adolescents, most of the social workers dealt directly with the compulsory nature of the group during the first few group meetings. The social workers often assumed a clear, no-nonsense approach, as this statement reflects:

> This is the drill. This is what is expected of me. This is what is expected of you. At the end of it, you're not going to receive a grade but you will receive a certificate and that's important. To some of you it will be important because it's on your IEPs. Some of you, it will be important because it is a condition of your probation, who knows. This is your job, participating in the group. My job is to be leading the group (Bartolomeo, 2007, p. 128).

This social worker makes clear the programmatic expectation that these students participate in a group, which in this case is a psychoeduational-type group whose formal purpose is "fire safety" for group members with histories of low-level firesetting. She indicates that she too must cope with the expectations of her employer, and she mentions, without singling out any student, that there are other stakeholders and forces (IEPs and/or probation) adding to the requirement.

Another means of speaking the truth with involuntary clients is to acknowledge the limits of the group worker's power and the client's remaining areas of choice (e.g., the amount of self-disclosure). This can be facilitated through the development of honest, clear, and explicit contracts that identify non-negotiable items and areas for compromise, as well as client rights and responsibilities. Adolescents in mandated groups, for example, will attempt to draw the group worker into fruitless power struggles by directly and indirectly challenging the group worker to try and force them to change. I have found it helpful to recognize that, while they can be compelled to attend a group, I, nor anyone else, have the power to make them change from the inside out. The group member's remaining area of choice is his willingness or unwillingness to change. This intervention is comparable to Trimble's (1994) statement to his groups for men who batter, in which he underscores their freedom to choose: "...no one can reach into your mind and heart and order a change ... that's where you have complete control" (p. 262). This intervention also reflects the reconciliation of the ethical tension between compulsory services and the client's right to self-determination.

Survival Tip # 7: Don't Feed the Victim Narrative

While it is important to validate, normalize and empathize with the group members' normative reactions to a mandatory situation, it is important to not get stuck in, or over-identify with their indignation or potential sense of victimization. Although geared to preserving a sense of self-agency, psychological reactance can become maladaptive by interfering with members' ability to use and receive benefit from services that are intended to help and eliminate future involvement with social control agencies and/or compulsory services. When reactance behaviors become protracted, groups for involuntary clients can, as Rooney (1992) observes, "...start, end, or persist indefinitely in power struggles between leaders and participants" (p. 290).

Reactance in involuntary groups for adolescents is magnified by their developmental need for greater autonomy, and power struggles can become a norm, thus deeply entrenched, and their need to demonstrate 'who's in charge' can become the group's raison d'être. I have led or co-led numerous adolescent groups that spent enormous time railing against the unfairness of having to participate in groups and all of the reasons they should not have to participate, which can become a way of avoiding the work of the group.

Members of involuntary groups are notorious for their efforts to shift responsibility or blame others for their predicament, which is reflective of defenses associated with the precontemplative stage. Men who batter their intimate partners frequently blame their victims for provoking them; persons who are addicted hold family members or situations responsible for their substance use. The group worker with the involuntary group must repeatedly emphasize the importance of personal responsibility, honesty, and our capacity to make choices even under severe circumstances. In my experience, involuntary group members have had numerous opportunities to correct negative behaviors and I will remind them that they are currently "living the consequences of their choices and actions."

Survival Tip # 8: Don't cheat the group of its suffering: The existential choice

As noted previously, involuntary groups appear to start with a dissatisfaction stage or negative orientation stage (Lacoursiere, 1980) conjoined with the preaffiliation or forming stage. This dissatisfaction can continue, and will often increase after the task of creating safety through shared agreements is done. This dissatisfaction is expressed with varying degrees of directness from "this group is a waste of time" to "this group really sucks." Earlier in my career, I would work hard at trying to make things better or encouraging the group to consider ways to improve the situation, which frequently led to a complete avoidance of the agency's or other stakeholder's purpose for the group. Even in those cases, the group would frequently end up disgruntled and resentful. I no longer rush in to rescue the group from the discomfort, boredom or irritation. Nor do I engage in futile discussions about ways to be rid of the requirement of the group; in fact, I support the members to accept the group as a reality, which will not disappear no matter how much they complain, push against it, or struggle.

Transforming the group

Viktor Frankl's (1959) axiom, "when we are no longer able to change a situation - we are challenged to change ourselves (p. 135)" captures what I refer to as the involuntary group's *existential crisis*. There is usually a moment when the group collectively confronts the reality that the group is here to stay, that it cannot be avoided and that the group worker does not have the power (which the group has repeatedly emphasized) to make it better. It is at this juncture that the frustration reaches a crescendo, or a crisis point, in which the group is faced with an *existential choice*. In other words, the group members make choices as to how they will ultimately use the group and the members realize they have the power to influence the quality of their group experience.

Here, a seasoned group worker in a therapeutic day school for youth with emotional and behavioral disturbances (Bartolomeo, 2007) presents this choice to her mandated group:

> I understand that you guys don't want to be in group, but this is what we have to do. It can go either two ways. Either we can make it an enjoyable experience that we all hopefully look forward to at some point, or it is going to be miserable. I really don't want to have that happen. I really need your thoughts on what we should do (p. 161).

In the above example, the group worker is validating the reality that the group is mandatory, but she is also establishing that the group members they are not passive recipients and thus are able to make moment-to-moment decisions as to how they will respond to the requirement. For many involuntary clients this is a new perspective and provides a means by which they can reposition themselves in tense or conflicting situations.

In another example, also with adolescents in a therapeutic day school, the group worker responds:

> They were just so, 'This is stupid.' I said, It is stupid. It is stupid to get together for once a week for an hour and do some stupid crap. That is stupid. It is your group. Do you want to have a stupid group (p. 129)?

This group worker is not engaging in a debate, rather she is resonating with the group's frustration and communicating that they have the power to create a different group experience. She is asking the group to share responsibility for its functioning. The group worker is sharing leadership through acknowledging the power already held by the group to create a more satisfying group experience.

Group workers with involuntary groups need to be firm and clear that the group is necessary and that members have a choice to work together to create a group that is productive, useful, and enriching—or not. Emphasizing clients' roles as co-creators of experience is an indispensable intervention and leadership posture. A point that I repeatedly highlight with involuntary groups is the distinction between willfulness and willingness. Group members do not need to want or feel like transforming group into something useful, all that is required is the willingness to do so. For many involuntary clients, this is a new and empowering perspective and provides a means by which they can reposition themselves in conflicting situations or unwanted events: that clients, though involuntary, can choose how they respond to undesirable circumstances is an empowering and optimistic stance in relation to undesirable realities.

Conclusion

Group work with involuntary clients is challenging and complex. It can also be extraordinarily rewarding both professionally and personally to observe group members evolve from their roles as involuntary applicants, or resisters, to those of clients and collaborators, and to witness a required group transform into a desired group or at least into a collectively created, productive experience. This transformation is accomplished when involuntary group members can sufficiently resolve their feelings and reactions about the required service, with the help of skillful interventions by the group worker, then assuming or sharing some of the group worker's leadership functions necessary to establish emotional and physical safety within the group.

The mandated group is an exquisite venue to explore how members respond, individually and collectively, to an unwanted circumstance. The existential choice involves the social group worker standing firm and clear that the group is both necessary and unavoidable. And, by allowing the group to experience the ensuing frustration, the group-as-a-whole will confront an existential crisis: the group members individually and collectively must choose how they will respond and what they will make of the group experience. In response to the existential crisis, the social group worker presents the group with a choice to work together to create a group that is productive, helpful, and enriching—or not. When the group-as-a-whole chooses to create a climate that is safe and purposeful, members can serve as therapeutic agents for one another. Being able to help others can be an antidote to the negative self-perceptions prevalent among involuntary clients. Instead of viewing themselves as damaged or inadequate, involuntary clients who offer assistance, comfort, or understanding toward their peers can move toward a new self-perception as resilient, capable, and compassionate.

References

Bartolomeo, F. S. (2007). *Social group work with adolescents in therapeutic day schools: Discovering group purpose with involuntary clients* (Doctoral dissertation). Retrieved from http://library.simmons.edu/search/o503561972

Bartolomeo, F. (2009). Group stages of development: Boston Model. In A. Gitterman & R. Salmon (Eds.), *The encyclopedia of social work with groups.* (pp. 103-105). New York: Routledge Press.

Baumrind, D. (1991). The influence of parenting style on adolescent competence and substance use. *Journal of Early Adolescence, 11*(1), 56-95.

Behroozi, C. S. (1993). A model for social work with involuntary applicants in groups. In J. Garland (Ed.), *Group work reaching out: People places and power.* (pp. 13-26).

Bennis, W. G., & Shepard, H. A. (1956). A theory of group dynamics. *Human Relations, 9*(4), 415-457.

Berman-Rossi, T. (1993). The tasks and skills of the social worker across stages of group development. *Social Work with Groups, 16*(1/2).

Brehm, J. (1966). *A theory of psychological reactance.* New York: Academic Press.

Brendtro, L.K., Mitchell, M. L., & McCall, H. J. (2009). *Deep brain learning: Pathways to potential with challenging youth.* Starr Commonwealth, Albion, MI.

Chovanec, M. (2009). You can't make us change: Use of stages of change in involuntary group development. *Encyclopedia of Social Work with Groups,* Gitterman A. and Salmon, R., (Eds.) New York: Routledge

Corder, B. F., Whiteside, L., & Hazlip, T. (1981). A study of the curative factors in group psychotherapy with adolescents. *International Journal of Group Psychotherapy, 31,* 345-354.

Dies, K. R. (1996). The unfolding of adolescent groups: A five-phase model of development. In P. Kymissis & D. A. Halperin (Eds.), *Group therapy with children and adolescents.* Washington, D.C.: American Psychiatric Press, Inc.

Dishion, T.J., McCord, J., & Poulin, F. (1999). When interventions harm: Peer groups and problem behavior. *American Psychologist 54*(9), 755-764.

Garland, J. A., Jones, H. E., & Kolodny, R. L. (1965). A model for stages of development in social work groups. In S. Bernstein (Ed.), *Explorations in group work: Essays in theory and practice* (pp. 17-71). Hebron, CT: Reprinted by: Practitioner's Press.

Frankl, V. (1959). *Man's search for meaning.* Boston: Beacon Press.

Garvin, C. D. (1981). *Contemporary group work.* Englewood Cliffs, N. J.: Prentice-Hall, Inc.

Goodman, H., Getzel, G. S., & Ford, W. (1996). Group work with high-risk urban youths on probation. *Social Work, 41*(4), 375-381.

Lacoursiere, R. (1980). *The life cycle of groups: Group developmental stage theory.* New York: Human Sciences Press.

Levin, K. G. (2006). Involuntary clients are different: Strategies for group engagement using individual relational theories in synergy with group development theories. *Groupwork, 16(2),* 61-84.

Malekoff, A. (1997). *Group work with adolescents: Principles and practice.* New York: The Guildford Press.

Marsh, L. C. (1931). Group treatment of the psychoses by the psychological equivalent of the revival. *Mental Hygiene in New York*, 15, 328-349.

Milgram, D., & Rubin, J. S. (1992). Resisting resistance: Involuntary substance abuse group therapy. *Social Work with Groups, 15*(1), 95-110.

Miller, W. R., & Rollnick, S. (2002). *Motivational interviewing: Preparing people for change.* (2nd ed.). New York: The Guilford Press.

Prochaska, J., Norcross, J., & DiClemente, C. (1994). *Changing for good.* New York: Avon Books.

Rooney, R. H. (1992). *Strategies for work with involuntary clients.* New York: Columbia University Press.

Rooney, R. & Chovanec, M. (2004). Involuntary groups. In A. Gitterman, L. Gutiérrez & M. Galinsky (Eds.), *Handbook of social work with groups.* (pp. 257-271). New York: The Guilford Press.

Rutan, J. S., & Stone, W. N. (1984). Psychodynamic group psychotherapy. New York: Macmillan Publishing Company.

Shulman, L. (1992). *The skills of helping individuals, families, and groups.* (3rd ed.). Itasca, IL: F.E. Peacock Publishers, Inc.

Thomas, H. & Caplan, T. & (1998). Spinning the group process wheel: Effective facilitation techniques for motivating involuntary client groups. *Social Work with Groups, 21*(4), 3-21.

Trimble, D. (1994). Confronting responsibility: Men who batter their wives. In A. Gitterman & L. Shulman (Eds.), *Mutual aid groups, vulnerable populations, and the life cycle.* (2nd ed., pp. 257-271). New York: Columbia University Press.

Tuckman, B. W. (1965). Developmental sequence in small groups. *Psychological Bulletin, 63*, 384-399.

Yalom, I. D. (1995). *The theory and practice of group psychotherapy.* (4th ed.). New York: Basic Books.

Proceedings of the XXVI International Symposium
of the International Association for Social Work with Groups,
Detroit, MI, USA, October 21th-24th, 2004
'Revitalizing Our Social Group Work Heritage:
A Bridge to the Future'

Selected Papers

Edited by Alice Lamont and Dale Swaisgood

Introduction

The theme of the Symposium was "Group Work reaching across boundaries: disciplines, seasons of life, practice settings, cultures and nations." The five papers published here present a fascinating diversity of subjects.

Beginning with a rich review of the literature, *David Bargal and Charles Garvin* report "on a project to reduce inter-group conflicts." A manual was produced for the bi-weekly sessions of two groups of high school students: one in a college town and one from an industrial city school. The interactions in sessions are described and as well as the evaluation at the end of the school year.

Steven Hartsock and Karen Harper-Dorton identify groups as the most effective treatment for sex offenders. Cognitive Behavioral Therapy (CBT) is their theoretical framework. They illustrate its application through case illustrations and excepts from progress notes.

Jessica Rosenberg found that the 4.5 million grandchildren living with grandparents were more likely "to live in poverty" and "more likely to to be without health insurance." than other children. She examined physical and emotional challenges experienced by these grandparents and illustrates the advantages of group support for the grandparents and for the group of group leaders providing support.

John Mansfield, Debra Cuda, Pamela Oliver and Amy Sill describe one of their approaches in teaching a beginning course in group work. Students formed groups of four to six . The culminating assignment was for each group to produce a video illustrating a theory from the class content and for each group member to lead part of the class session.

The instructor evluates the experience and identifies further work.

McIntyre and Mitchell describe "Girl Talk", a Healthy Sexuality Program they have developed for girls in grade five. The program is based "on the assumption that girls' sense of self and agency regarding sexual identity and relationships will be stronger if we assist them to understand and exercise choice early."

The People

The Conference Committee was led by Ann Alvarez, Althea Grant and Robert (Bob) Sisler shared the work. Their guidance, patience and focus made the Symposium "go". Members of the Committee were: Tony Alvarez, Cassandra Bowers, Peggy Brunhofer, Lila Cabbil, Mygene L. Carr, Lois Garriott, Charles Garvin, Ted Goldberg, Polly Hardy, Loren Hofman, Alice Lamont, Sally Jo Large, Charlene McGunn, Kathy Ransome, Mary Robinson, Henrietta Reaves, Mavis Spencer, Jean Teschner, Kay Tulupman, Phyllis Vroom .

The Abstracts Committee - Each member was asked to review at least three abstracts. Several members reviewed even more. Members were Paul Abels, Ann Alvarez, Tony Berman-Rossi, Peggy Brunhofer, Cassandra Bowers, Susan Ciardiello, Paulene Everette, Louise Kerlin, Sherry Fairchild, Laura Farley, James Garland, Lois Garriott, Charles Garvin, Jean Gill, Ted Goldberg, Althea Grant, Alison Johnson, Carolyn Knight, Alice Lamont, Elen Sue Mesbur, Kenneth Reid, Robert Sisler, Nancy Sullivan, Dale Swaisgood, Kay Tulupman, William Vanderwill, Michael Wagner, Betty Welsh, Mary Wilson.

A special note of thanks to Phyllis Vroom, Dean of the School of Social Work at Wayne State Universitry who supported the Symposium in many ways including assigning Susan Titus to staff the Symposium.

We wish to express our great appreciation to all those who served on the Committees and to everyone who contributed to the behind the scenes work and success of the Symposium.

Alice Lamont and Dale Swaisgood
Editors

Reducing inter-group conflict through the use of group work

Charles Garvin and David Bargal

Introduction

This paper reports on a project to reduce inter-group conflicts. It provides a theoretical base for understanding such conflicts as well as describes intervention principles which were applied. Such conflicts are prevalent in many societies and are frequently related to people's ethnic, religious, national and social class affiliations. These conflicts may be found among people in the same country as well as between countries that compete for rare resources such as in the Middle East, or in central Europe or Northern Ireland. In the U.S. inter-group conflicts exist for example, between African-Americans and those of European origins, Latinos and Anglos, Native Americans and those whose ancestors immigrated to this continent comparatively recently.

This project focused on group work with adolescents because in contemporary Western societies youth are at a stage of life that emphasizes development of social and personal identities (Erickson, 1968). Peer culture also plays a central role in adolescent development (Brown, 1990). During this stage people are open to educational influences that may change their perceptions and attitudes towards other social groups. The small group context also provides a setting for considering participants' views regarding their own group as well as other groups with whom they may be in conflict.

Inter-group relations and inter-group conflicts: Theoretical explanations

The study of inter-group conflict is viewed as a derivative of inter-group relations, which are an inseparable facet of the structure and composition of almost every modern pluralistic society. Tajfel (1982), a prominent contributor to this area of study, has described inter-group relations as 'one of the most difficult and complex knots of problems which we confront in our times' (p. 1). Another renowned scholar in the field of inter-group conflict, Sherif (1966), defined inter-group relations as follows:

> Whenever individuals belonging to one group interact, collectively or individually, with another group or its members in terms of their group identification, we have an instance of inter-group behavior. (p. 12)

On the basis of their 'ingroup', individuals develop stereotypes, prejudice, and discrimination toward other group members. Moreover, conflictual inter-group relations may escalate toward hostility, animosity, and even violence. These negative emotions and their concomitant behaviors in the forms of delegitimacy, aggression, and in some cases even deprivation of human rights, emanate from several sources (for detailed surveys of the topic, see Brewer & Brown, 1998; Stephan & Stephan, 2001). Numerous attempts to understand inter-group conflict and discrimination have focused on the following main factors:

- social cognitive processes;
- personality development;
- social-cultural influences;
- social identity, and conditions of inter-group conflict; and
- competition for realistic resources.

Social cognitive processes

Regarding social cognitive processes, Fiske and Taylor (1991) define social cognition as a theoretical perspective that explains how information is processed and stored. The assumption underlying the social cognition approach is that humans have limited cognitive capacity to manage the overload of daily social and interactive stimuli. Therefore, the mind categorizes information about situation, object and people 'before engaging memory or inferential processes' (Howard, 2000, p. 368). The cognitive products of these processes are schemata, or representations, regarding one's self or one's social world. Regarding the role of schemata in social interaction, Howard (2000) points out that they lead us to reduce and summarize information by its basic elements. Such categorization is a cognitive device for storing information, but important facts may be lost in the process. Moreover, categorization frequently implies the evaluation of some categories as better or worse than others. Thus social cognitive processes are not only related to perception but actually define social relationships. In addition, they have an impact on the development of biased stereotypes (prejudice) and discriminatory behavior.

Attribution processes also manifest themselves in the service of social cognitive processes (Stephan, 1985). Attribution processes provide the 'rules' used by humans to perceive and explain other people's behavior. Because very little information is available to the perceiver, who is also biased by in-group affiliation, he or she tends to attribute bad characteristics to the other group members and to blame those characteristics on their personalities rather than on circumstances or on social, political, and historical contexts. For example, whites may perceive blacks as lazy, uncivilized and underachievers. Much of the blame in this instance is put on the individual black person rather than on economic, political, and cultural circumstances.

Personality development

The second theoretical approach regarding the development of inter-group discrimination is rooted in the dynamics of personality development. According to the psychodynamic approach (Adorno, Frenkel-Brunswick, Levinson, & Sanford, 1950), manifestations of prejudice and discrimination reflect a deep personality conflict that stems mainly from an authoritarian personality makeup. The expression of prejudice serves as an outlet for hostility that is harbored as a result of harsh methods of upbringing during childhood. Although the authoritarian personality construct has been a topic of numerous studies, a direct link could not be established between socialization practices and the prejudice of one group against another (Ashmore & Delboca, 1976). More recent research (Altmeyer, 1998) established the empirical existence of a new type of authoritarian personality.

Socio-cultural influences

The sociocultural explanation for the development of prejudice and discriminatory behavior is based on the assumption that these patterns are learned in the same way as other preferences, beliefs, and values – through interaction with one's sociocultural environment (Ashmore & Delboca, 1976). Socialization, which embodies the various mechanisms through which culture is transmitted from one generation to the next, operates through various channels. Four major channels of socialization have been distinguished: parents, peers, schools, and mass media. However, most of the research evidence on this issue is correlational, and

> it is not clear exactly how cultural patterns are transformed into the prejudice of individuals and the relative importance of the various agents of socialization is not known. (p. 97)

Social identity theory

According to social identity theory (Tajfel & Turner, 1986), prejudice and inter-group tension originate in the individual's affiliation with a group. The group serves as the individual's main source of social identity: the in-group is perceived in positive terms, and its members are viewed in a differentiated and personal way, whereas the outgroup is perceived in a negative light, as a depersonalized collective. Inter-group discrimination is motivated by a desire for a positive social identity that can enhance self-esteem,

Competition for realistic resources

'Realistic group conflict theory' is the fifth approach toward explaining the development of inter-group discrimination (Campbell, 1965; Sherif, 1966). According to this theory, prejudice is the product of a negative interdependence between different social groups. Such interdependence is manifested in relations between a conqueror and the conquered population – or between a dominant majority and suppressed minority. In this context, the dominant group uses its power and status to keep the subordinate groups in an inferior position. Members of the dominant group tend to view their subordinates in terms of negative stereotypes and act accordingly. Ultimately this approach is used to rationalize the attempt to maintain the inferior status of less powerful groups and even justify their exploitation. Prejudice may also be part of a psychological reaction to competition between two groups for valued, scarce, or limited resources (Sherif, 1966). The next section will deal with the principles guiding attempts to reduce inter-group tension.

Theoretical approaches and principles for reducing inter-group conflicts

Two major approaches have been employed to reduce inter-group tension and improve inter-group relations: Facilitative conditions and conflict management workshops or encounters.

Facilitative conditions

Facilitative conditions are based on Allport's (1954) contact hypothesis. This hypothesis, which was elaborated by Amir (1969) has recently been upheld and reconfirmed empirically (Pettigrew, 1998; Pettigrew & Tropp, 2000). According to this approach, the following conditions may strongly contribute toward the improvement of inter-group relations between adversarial groups (Fisher, 1997).

- Contact in an intimate, pleasant, and rewarding organizational climate.
- Equal status between the two groups

- The existence of cooperative superordinate goals (Sherif, 1958), which participants in the groups work together to accomplish.
- Strong institutional support for the program.

Conflict management workshops

The conflict management approach derives its principles of intervention from several sources:

- *The notion of reeducation* (Lewin, 1945/1948b) (resocialization), which suggests that individuals may undergo changes in knowledge, values, and standards, emotional attachments and conduct mainly through *interaction in small groups* (Lieberman, 1980, 1983).
- *The course of change* that occurs among participants in the group is characterized by three phases: 'Unfreezing', 'movement', and 'refreezing'. 'Unfreezing' is the phase where the motivation and readiness for the change are emphasized. 'Movement' refers to the phase in which the participants gradually change their attitudes and reframe their cognitive beliefs toward their own group and towards out-group members. 'Refreezing' refers to the institutionalization of the change in the form of new habitual attitudes or behavior to be applied within as well as beyond the group's meetings (Lewin, 1947/1958).
- *The facilitators of the group* are the most important agents of change that help participants modify their attitudes, emotions, and behavior. The facilitators employ basic counseling skills such as positive regard, empathy, and support for the participants (Carkhuff, 1969; Egan, 1986) who may engage in a prejudiced discourse in the group sessions. In this context, the facilitators convey the message that the encounter is a safe setting where participants can renounce biased beliefs about members of other ethnic and social groups. The facilitators also give mini-lectures concerning issues related to prejudice, stereotypes, group processes, and inter-group conflicts. The lectures are intended to help the participants understand and incorporate the changes, which they undergo more fully (a detailed example of the facilitator's activities is provided later in this paper).

According to Bargal and Bar (1994), the optimal encounter focuses on three main targets: the individual, the small group and its dynamics, and inter-group relations. The following is a general description of each of the three target units.

1   *The individual participant's personality* which is at the center of the intervention. The components of the participant's personality include cognitive mechanisms for organizing his or her impression of the social world, such as stereotypes regarding members of the other group and feelings toward them. Specifically, the intervention focuses on prejudiced and discriminatory behavior manifested by participants toward each other. The principal psychological processes by which stereotypes and prejudice can be modified are: creation of a supportive climate by the facilitators; catharsis of feelings when needed; and planned confrontations regarding participants' biased perceptions of others or themselves. The facilitators are in charge of developing intimate and meaningful contacts among members of the group, in addition to encouraging discussions about beliefs and feelings, and enhancing participants' insight into biased attitudes and feelings they hold towards themselves and others.

2   *The individual group member and group affiliations.* The second target of intervention is at the group level. At the center are the participants' multiple group affiliations, which generate multiple identities. As mentioned, the participants' ingroups are perceived in positive, differentiated terms, while outgroups are perceived in a negative, generalized way. The group achieves its goal of molding participants to its standards and norms by exerting pressure (Tajfel & Turner, 1986). The participants are sensitized to these mechanisms as a first step toward alleviating these pressures and developing a more individualistic, independent perspective toward their group affiliations and identities.

3   *Inter-group relations in a diverse, pluralistic society.* The third target of intervention focuses on the inter-group level and on relations among ethnic, gender, and social groups in a pluralistic society. Topics dealt with in mini-lectures, discussions, and experiential activities focus on issues of inequality and injustice in the relations between the majority group and the minority group. Common behavioral manifestations of minority-majority relations such as respect, patronage, and exploitation are examined. Participants become aware of the need to play an active role as agents of change and point to ways in which they can mitigate social injustice. In this spirit, cooperative projects continue even beyond the duration

of the workshop. The projects generally focus on educational and social activities, which are conducted in schools and surrounding communities.

Action research

In a paper written by Lewin a year before his untimely death at the age of 57 (in 1947) he characterized action research as a methodology and a means of intervention. Using his own words, 'The research needed for social practice can best be characterized as research for social management or social engineering. It is a type of action-research, a comparative research on the conditions and effects of various forms of social action and research leading to social action (Lewin, 1946/1948:202-203). In the same paper he defined action research as follows: 'Action, research, and training as a triangle that should be kept together for the sake of any of its corners' (p. 211)

Based upon his writings (Lewin, 1947, 1946/48a, 1947/1958) the following are the seven main principles that characterize action research:

1. *A recursive process of data collection to determine goals, action to implement goals, and assessment of the action.* In action research the researchers take into account the dynamic nature of the object of inquiry and its interaction with the intervenors. Therefore, the research is being planned where this cycle takes place. This cycle of planning-action and evaluation reflects the paradigm of the problem-solving process.
2. *Action research demands feedback regarding the results of the intervention to all parties involved in the research.* Feedback is a term drawn from the open system terminology and is originally aimed toward two objectives. As a correction mechanism and as a means for choosing action directions. When a system is in action, like the intervention in an action research, it may deviate from the original course planned at the beginning. The feedback to the parties may discover deviations, alterations, misfits, which can be corrected in real time.
3. *Action research implies a continuous cooperation between*

researchers and practitioners. In the scientific model of research, the researcher is the director of the operation. She or he sometimes is the only one to know the hypotheses to be examined, the way subjects are chosen, etc. But in action research, the practitioners are equal partners in many decisions arrived at in the research. The underlying principle to guide cooperation is that the subjects should be responsible for decisions which pertain to their fate, knowing the rationale that guides the intervention. This keeps the subjects' motivation to be high during the intervention.

4. *Action research relies heavily on the rules of group dynamics and is anchored in the principles of change.* The change process is comprised of three phases: unfreezing, moving, and refreezing and it is based on participatory decision making in the small group.

5. *Action research takes into account issues of values, objectives, and power needs of the parties involved.* Because each party to the action research has its own system of preferences and values, the only way to get along with the enterprise is to deal openly with conflicts which arise regarding their realization by the parties. Continuous ongoing process of managing and solving these conflicts guarantees that the research will go on as planned. This is in contrast to an ordinary research project where the principal investigator usually has the sole power even to coerce decisions.

6. *Action research serves to create knowledge and to formulate principles of intervention* and also to develop instruments for intervention and evaluation. Action research is expected to generate knowledge: the ordinary data gathered in every research project as well as 'actionable knowledge'. This knowledge is important for the intervention itself, but it is also expected that the intervention will improve the functioning of the particular group or organization. The intervention instruments or packages and the measurement devices may serve the organization even beyond the period of the action research intervention.

7. Within the framework of action research there is much emphasis on recruitment, training, development, and support of the change agents (the trainers)

Because action research strives to achieve a social change, there is a major importance to invest in the change agents. They are the main means for effecting change in human systems. *Training* is the first component in the triangle mentioned in Lewin's definition of action research. Two more sides of this triangle are *intervention* and *research*.

In contrast to ordinary research, the trainers do not serve only in the capacity of collectors of data or evaluation. In action research they need to understand deeply the subjects of the intervention and to be equipped with the appropriate means to achieve the goals of the research. Hence, the crucial need to select the right trainers as well as to train and support them during the intervention.

The seven principles elaborated above are the interpretations of action research as developed by Bargal (2008) based on theoretical writings by Lewin and others (1946/1948). The reader can easily identify almost all of the principles in the research reported in this paper.

The current project

The project was conducted in two schools that were selected in view of the fact that they had culturally diverse student bodies but differed in the economic circumstances of their students. We shall call one high school 'College Town High School (CT)' and the other Industrial City High School (IC). CT has a student body of about 2000 with 55% of the students white, 20% black, 10% Arab-American, 10% Asian American, and the rest either Latino or Native-American. IC has a student body that is almost equally divided between white and African-American students although Arab-American families are beginning to move into the area. CT students tend to come from professional families, many of whom are employed by the major university located in the community. IC students largely come from families who are employed in local factories or in the service sector.

We initiated the project by meeting with the principals of the two schools. This was facilitated by the fact that one of the project staff members, as a member of the Education faculty of the University, had served in a consultative capacity to these individuals. The principals were receptive to the project although neither thought that major ethnic conflicts existed in their school at this time. In the spirit of action research, we indicated that the intervention will be developed and overseen by a task group composed of representatives of the University and of their schools. We added three students from each school to this task group after we had spoken to a group of students referred to the project although this was after the manual had been drafted. This was undoubtedly a mistake as some problems with the manual might have been avoided if students had been consulted earlier. Nevertheless, it was always intended that the student participants will select the inter-group problems to be addressed by the project and will work on resolving these problems. There were some difficulties with this approach that we shall describe later.

The principals each assigned a staff member to be part of this task group; At CT, an assistant principal was the representative of the school from the beginning. At IC, the initial representative was a teacher but she was soon supplemented by an assistant principal from that school as she was too new to the school to be sufficiently aware of school history and context. The project task group consisted of Charles Garvin and Tony Alvarez from the School of Social Work, Henry Meares from the School of Education, doctoral student research assistants (Alexandra Crampton, Linda Cunningham), the assistant principals, the school social worker of CT, the group facilitators (when they were chosen), and the six student representatives (chosen when the participants were selected).

A first task was to acquire information about the history and current situation of the Schools with respect to inter-group relations. The assistant principals identified a series of key informants including school counselors, social workers, teachers, and personnel assigned to maintain discipline (such as adult hall monitors). These persons were selected because of their knowledge of inter-group issues in the school.

The informants agreed that no major conflict currently existed in the Schools although both have had their history of such conflicts. By this we mean that there was no situation likely to become violent. Nevertheless, there are significant tensions in the schools between ethnic groups. Both schools have a significant degree of informal segregation as manifested in the proverbial separation of ethnic groups in the lunchroom. In addition, extra curricular activities such as sport teams, orchestra, and choir tend to be largely composed of one ethnic group. At CT, some informants noted that certain corridors in the school were the 'turf' of particular ethnic groups.

The task group met bi-weekly throughout the 2003-2004 school year. Initial meetings were devoted to sharing the material secured from informants and obtaining the group's perceptions of inter-group relations in the schools. Following this, the director of the project presented an overall plan for the weekly sessions to be held with the students. He indicated that he would bring in detailed plans for sessions at each meeting, the group will critique it, and he will incorporate the group's ideas into a revised plan.

It was stated that the eventual 'manual' should not be followed rigidly by the facilitators and they will be free to alter it as required by circumstances unfolding in the groups. They will be expected, however, to take notes of how and why they altered the manual. Observers also will write narratives of each session and these will be available to facilitators so they may consider the responses of students to sessions as they make changes in the manual. This is in the spirit of action research in which an intervention is seen as an evolving entity, the product of continuous feedback from all of the participants.

The group concluded its work on the manual by the spring of 2003. A conference was then held, attended by several authorities from the U.S. and abroad who reviewed the manual and the plans for its implementation and evaluation. This meeting was tape recorded and minutes were taken so that ideas emanating from it could be retrieved. Following this, the manual was further revised and a final evaluation plan was adopted. A meeting was also held with principals of the schools to provide them with an update on the progress of the project and to obtain their ideas.

In the fall of 2003, the task group met again to make decisions on how participants will be selected, who the facilitators will be, and what kinds of physical facilities will be required. The students will be nominated by teachers and staff based on two criteria: they have an interest in improving inter-group relations and they are influential with their fellow students. The school's representatives made the final selection of students so that the students will represent the diversity of the school in terms of ethnicity and gender. We sought about 30 students in each school for the actual workshop so we planned to invite about 40 students to an orientation meeting. This number of students was agreed upon in terms of having the group represent the diversity of the school while having each ethnic group 'represented' by several students to avoid any student being the sole person from his or her group.

A meeting was planned to inform teachers as they were asked to nominate students. A meeting was held with nominated students to ask them to join the project and to answer their questions about it. Assent forms, to be signed by the students, and consent forms, by parents, were distributed at the student meetings attended by about 40 students at each school. Students who wished to participate were to signify this by returning these forms.[2]

The group determined that there will be two facilitators for each workshop. One facilitator would be a staff member of the school; the other a social work student doing field work with the project. The staff members chosen were program administrators within the schools who had an interest in the project and experience in facilitating groups.[3] The facilitators met with the directors of the project (Garvin and Meares) on a weekly basis to clarify the manual, consider changes required by emerging events, receive training to enhance their group work skills, and solve problems arising as the program unfolds. The facilitators also received three sessions of training in January as the student groups began in February at the beginning of the second term. The project staff did not assume that this amount of training was sufficient but was bound by the time available to the facilitators, especially the school personnel.[4] This training dealt with the following issues:

- How to work as co-facilitators by resolving conflicts between facilitators, determining a division of labor, and developing the ability to work as a team.
- The overall logic of the program as embodied in the manual
- The legitimacy of altering the manual as required by the development of the group and the nature of interactions among students
- How do deal with expected group interactions and issues such as intragroup conflicts, the emergence of subgroups, challenges to the facilitators, and the emergence of indigenous leadership

The teachers' and students' meetings were held in December, 2003. The former occurred as an agenda item on regularly scheduled teacher's meetings. The teachers were told of the nature of the project and the kinds of students that were sought. They were encouraged to nominate students if they had contact with 3rd year students (juniors) who met the criteria and they were given forms on which to record their names; they were asked to tell the students that they had been nominated but that all could not be accepted in view of size limitations.

The faculty and staff nominated about 45 students. After this, the school representatives to the planning committee met to make the final selection. Primarily this involved identifying groups that were not sufficiently represented, leading to recruiting additional names of members of those groups.

Student meetings were held in both schools. Most of the students who were nominated attended, numbering about 40 students in each school. They were told the purposes of the group and introduced to the facilitators who each talked briefly about themselves. They asked many questions about the content and format. They were also told the main reward for participating in the program will be their increased skill in negotiating group conflicts. They were promised, in addition, a certificate of completion that might be listed on college applications.

The intervention in action

We shall now describe the sequence of topics along with some examples of how the session actually occurred as recorded by observers hired for this purpose. Space does not permit us to give more than a few brief examples and to avoid confusing the reader, we shall only give examples from the IC school.[5]

Session 1. Discussion of purpose of this 'workshop' and initial activity for getting acquainted -icebreaker type.

Example

J (the white male facilitator) introduced the 'All my neighbors' exercise. This involved each students standing in the center of the circle and saying their name and something about themselves that the other students could not see (e.g. My name is X and I have two brothers; My name is Y and I like music). There is one less chair in the circle than the number of students. After the person in the center makes a statement, all the other students in the group who have that in common get up and move about the circle to find another chair to sit in. The student who is left standing in the circle after everyone else sits down is the next to share.

Students began by sharing 'safe' kinds of responses that were not very personally revealing (e.g. I love ice-cream, I love cookie dough). After about four or five minutes of this activity, a student shared something more personal: 'My name is C. and I'm part Hispanic.' The students really seemed to enjoy this exercise as evidenced by their attentiveness, and frequent laughter and smiling throughout the exercise. Students who knew something about each other prior to the session occasionally commented to another student after hearing something about them they did not know prior to the exercise, 'I didn't know you'd been to Europe – aren't you just the world traveler?'

The next activity was a 'get acquainted' exercise. N. (the other facilitator, an African-American woman) said 'My name is N. and I am a teacher and an African American.' An African American female student responded with an enthusiastic 'Oh yeah'. J. shared 'My name is J. and I am half Irish and half Italian and I'm married.' A female student asked him where his wedding ring was and he said he didn't have one.

The following are some of the responses from students:

I am ...

Somalian
light skinned and I am loud
oldest of 11 siblings and crazy
very sociable
Mexican Puerto-Rican and wild
Part Black, part white, part Native-American
a baseball player
a certified childcare provider
Indian and a little Black and quiet; a runner; an athlete; bow legged.

Session 2. More getting acquainted activities in which students learn more about each other. (e.g. take turns interviewing each other)

Example

During the session an activity called 'Cross the Line' was introduced in which, as categories are read, students 'cross the line' if the category applies to them. When 'tall' was read, tall people crossed and others didn't. When 'middle class' was read, most people crossed the line but a handful didn't. A student asks 'is that poor?' before he decides to cross the line. Another student mocks a student who stayed behind saying 'He thinks he's rich!' The next categories were 'parents born in the US' and 'visited Europe' and nothing noteworthy happened. When 'hang out at the mall' was read, students giggled and mocked the phrase 'hang out'. Only 2 cross the line and many are giggling. When 'hang out at the

University of Michigan campus' was read, 3 crossed the line and there is no giggling. J. reminded the students to notice who crosses the line and who does not and for them to think what it brings up for them. There is a group of 3-4 boys who seem to be laughing a lot and don't seem to be taking the activity too seriously. When 'religious' was read, about half the group crosses the line, One girl straddles the line and another girl says she can't do that. She stays straddling the line and explains that is how she feels about it. When 'person of color' is read. All people who appear to be of color cross the line. The room is very silent and students take this category very seriously. When 'if you plan on going to college' was read, all students but one cross the line. Students mock the girl (white) who did not cross the line and one boy says, 'What are you going to do with your life?' The student left standing looked a little uncomfortable, but holds her head high. There is quiet chatter among those who crossed the line. The next category was 'If you plan to go to college and are worried about how you will pay for it'. The group was silent and serious and about one-third of the students do not cross the line. They looked at those who crossed and vice-versa.

Session 3 -4. Discussion of inter-group situation and history in U.S. and local area.

Example

Students watched portions of a film entitled 'Skin Deep' which portrayed students discussing their reactions to their own ethnicity and the ethnicity of others. There are no side conversations during the playing of the video but a few students do exchange glances with each other silently at different times indicating some sort of disbelief or shock that something is being said on the video. Their eyes appeared wide as if to express that what one of the students said in the video was rather bold. At one point, a student exclaims 'damm' in response to an African-American in the video saying to another student that because you are a white male, people are going to hate you. There is a lot of laughter and giggling when an African-American male in the video shared a story about shoplifting and how he believed that whites are likely to think that all Blacks do that. There is small chatter among the students in response to the girl in the video sharing how she believes whites still benefit from historical oppression.

J. asked what the students thought about the video. Students' responses include some whites who were offended; an African-American female said she was offended at how Blacks in the video were 'coming at' whites; another African-American male said he was surprised at how angry people were for 'something that went on 1000 years ago'. A white female said 'it was mean'. N. asked was anyone <u>not</u> surprised. One female student reiterated surprise at Blacks mad at white people for something that happened long ago. A white male student said that she obviously had not been to a trailer park. A white female commented on scholarships to college Blacks have that whites do not have. Another Black student said that whites do benefit because 80% of students in college are white and that's why scholarships are there for Blacks.

Later in the discussion, a white female student comments on how groups tend to be segregated in their school; even in this group, students tended to sit among students of their same race. Two Black students defended that these seating arrangements were not deliberate, but 'just happened' to be the way that people sat down since they were near their friends. Most students expressed the idea that since they were not intentionally segregating themselves, that this doesn't count as 'real' segregation.

Session 5-6. Discussion of inter-group relations at your high school and beginning identification of problems and issues. Participants perceptions of 'causes' of these conditions. Discussion of multiple identities. Discussion of stereotypes.

Example

J. introduced the first discussion activity which was what kinds of groups exist in their school? Student responses include: jocks/athletes, gothic, punks, homosexual, thug 'wannabe', drama students, druggie. Students were very excited in their eagerness to share responses. There is a lot of joking and friendly teasing. Students seem to clearly know which groups they identify themselves as belonging to and they also seem to know where the other students in the group belong. More student responses were added to the list: preps, ethnic groups, smart/geeks, outcasts, grade levels, band. J. prompts for other groups besides social groups. Students respond with gender and physically challenged. An

African-American female suggests 'Black' and receives a loud 'thank you, I'm glad someone said it' from another African-American male student. Another male student shares 'light skinned'. Many students are talking at once and it is difficult to hear. N. tries several times to settle the group down but this doesn't seem to be working too well. N. asks how the existence of these groups can lead to conflict. The students mention diversity, discomfort, misunderstanding, stereotyping, ignorance, closed-minded, low self-esteem, loss of trust, social status. When discussing stereotyping, one African-American female student comments 'like Black folks eat chicken, that's not true, I eat exotic foods'. Another student asks her, 'Does that mean you don't eat chicken?' She answered, 'No, but that makes it sound like that's all I eat'.

Session 7. Discussion of situations that lead to tensions between groups

Example

J. leads a discussion on what students perceive to be some of the sources of conflict in the world. Students offer the following and J. records them on a poster board: religion, race, money, hate, knowledge, power, gender, family background, values, age, ignorance, stereotypes and prejudices. He then asks students to decide which of these sources of conflict lead to conflicts in their own school. Students reach consensus that all are sources of conflict in their own school but some are greater than others. Students take some time to discuss stereotypes. J. asks them 'who is stereotyped?' One answer is 'everybody', another says 'Kids are stereotyped by adults , they think they'll do something dumb'. A student brings up the recent news article about a college official who publicly states that the school is considering lowering its academic standards so it can recruit more talented Black athletes. He points out how this is a stereotype that Black athletes are not as smart as other students and that White students are not the best athletes. N. asks if athletes are stereotyped at this school. One student says 'No, a lot of them are really smart'. Another said 'Coaches here will talk to teachers about getting grades up for someone if their grades are getting so low that they might not be able to play'.

Session 8. What role can participants play in change?

Example

Students were asked to indicate things they could do if there was a conflict in their school. Student responses include 'set a good example', 'speak your mind', 'try to see both sides and the root of the conflict,' 'set up a neighborhood watch', 'be willing to put forth effort necessary and don't give up', 'bring together groups in the community', and 'raise awareness through personal conversation, community meetings, write to a newspaper'. N. comments that all of their suggestions are good but they are only good when people know a conflict exists. How would they go about educating others about a conflict that exists when people are unaware of it? Students reply that they could inform others about a conflict by making flyers or other posters to educate the public.

N. then brings up the example of the conflict in this school about graduation and whether or not seniors should be allowed to walk across the stage at commencement. (Note: the significance of this issue is that the principal ordered that students stand in their place when their name is read and diplomas should be distributed after the ceremony; this was to change the pattern in which a lot of families blow horns and cheer when the student 'walks' and this interferes with the decorum of the occasion. It is significant that the Black students see this kind of celebration as the way they would like the ceremony to be while some white students see this as undignified and, consequently, this clearly represents a conflict between the two sets of students.

There was a lengthy discussion of this issue. One student, a Black student, remarked that for some students, they may be the first person in their family to graduate high school and the school had no right to tell their families that they couldn't scream and holler if that's how they behave when they express their pride in their kids. Suffice it to say (the observer) I didn't notice any diverging views along racial or gender lines and all students seemed to have very strong and passionate feelings one way or another about this issue.

Session 9-10 Techniques of peaceful negotiation of conflicts

Session 11-13 - These techniques are used in the workshop as

participants work on issues identified in previous sessions.

Space does not permit details of these sessions; the students did pick on the graduation conflict as the one they wished to work on in terms of conflict resolution.

Session 14. Where do we go from here?

In the final session, the students selected a subgroup to meet with the facilitators to finalize plans to resolve the graduation issue. They also indicated their interest in returning in the fall to be trained as junior facilitators for next year's cohort and to continue their discussions of inter-group conflict and its resolution.

The logic behind this sequence of topics was that first we would clarify the purpose of the workshop and help the students begin to develop trusting relationships with one another. This included learning about each other's cultural and social backgrounds. This process was intended to continue throughout the workshop as students would be asked to talk about their own feelings, attitudes, and views of the world and to reflect on these and to trust each other to listen in supportive ways. The students would subsequently discuss how their personal backgrounds and experiences related to the history of inter-group relations in the United States as well as their local communities. This would lead into a discussion of inter-group relations in their school. We hoped that this discussion would help them to identify issues that might be the foci of actions they would take in the final sessions of the workshop to resolve conflicts that exist among participants of this workshop and were likely to exist in the larger school environment.

Up to this point in the workshop, the work would be similar to that done in groups to promote inter-group dialogues which are increasingly being conducted in educational settings. This is the point that our workshop began to diverge from these programs so as to focus on conflict and conflict resolution. This was to be done through a discussion of sources of conflict between groups. The idea would be introduced that conflicts can be resolved and that these students have a role to play in this. A major approach to conflict resolution is the process of negotiation between groups and the participants will be taught techniques for the peaceful negotiation of conflicts. The final stage of the group will be when the participants identify actual conflict situations, hopefully represented in microcosm within their group, and will use what they have learned throughout the workshop to deal with such conflicts.

In many ways the objectives of the workshop were achieved and in many ways they were not. It would take more space that we have to explore all of these in detail. Instead we shall select some that we believe will be most important in designing the next set of workshops in these schools and we shall discuss these. A later section will report on specific responses of students on written questionnaires and verbal interviews. *We note that the following were not true for everyone or at all times but were true for some students at specific times. It should also be noted that there were more negative comments from CT than from IT.* Our preliminary analysis suggests this was due to two factors:

• The facilitation at CT was viewed more negatively than the facilitation at IT
• The students at CT are of a higher social economic class and are more likely to come from professional families and tend to deny the existence of inter-group conflicts even though informants are certain these exist in the school and there is also considerable informal segregation in the school. Our hypothesis is that these factors lead them to have more anxiety about discussions of tension among ethnic groups in the school, especially since we believe there is a belief prevalent in the community that this is an 'ideal' town in which everyone 'gets along'.

Examples of ways the workshop achieved its purposes for some students and at some times

• Students explored each other's cultures and backgrounds
• Students talked about their identities in ways that have not done before
• Students learned about the cultures of other students
• Students learned about the ways other students have felt oppressed
• Students explored the concept of privilege
• Students discussed conflict situations in their school

Examples of workshop 'failures' for some students and at some times.

• Lack of clarity on purpose of workshop and how topics relate to purpose

- Disappointments regarding failures of workshop to meet some student's expectations
- Lack of frank discussion of views of inter-group relations
- 'Acting out' of students when dealing with anxiety provoking topics
- Lack of confidence in facilitators
- Difficulty in selecting conflict situations to be resolved through the workshop

Evaluation

We had two major sources of data for assessing the impact of the program on students. One was an individual interview held with the students. The other was a questionnaire that was administered at the first and last sessions. We shall first present data from the individual interview.

The interview was conducted by a person employed by the project who also attended all of the sessions and prepared a process record of each session. The interviews were conducted shortly after the workshop ended. We were able to obtain more interviews (20) from CT because the researcher was also the school social worker and she was able to invite students into her office when she saw them in the halls. We obtained fewer (13) at IC because the interviewer was employed by the project and was not customarily at the school; she phoned students and arranged to meet them at the school or, more typically, interview them over the phone. Many students were not home when she called (repeatedly) and/or failed to return her calls.

The questions asked of the students, together with the responses, were the following:

1. *How would you describe your experience in the program so far?*
   At IC, 7 students (out of 13) said they liked the program and none said that they disliked it. At CT, 15 students (out of 20) said they liked the program and 2 said that they disliked it. One student at CT commented that it was repetitive.

2. *What are some memorable activities that you have participated in during the programs?*

Star Power: 5 students at IC (out of 13) and 10 students at CT (out of 20)

Crossing the Line: 2 students (out of 13) at IC and 5 students at CT (out of 20)

3. *What was interesting about these activities?*
    Experienced different classes (5 at CT)

    Learned about each other (3 at IC and 5 at CT)

    Learned about people's backgrounds and ancestors (1 at IC and 2 at CT)

    Learned about power (2 at IC and 6 at CT)
    People 'stuck in their positions' like in real life (1 at CT)

4. *Can you tell me about some of the experiences that you have had as a participant in this group that you might not have had otherwise?*
    Contacts with new people (3 at IC and 8 at CT)

    Changed perceptions (1 at CT)

    Others interested in what I had to say (1 at CT)

    Criticisms were kept 'in the group' (3 at CT)

    Discussion of issues (1 at IC)

    Found I was not alone on issues (2 at IC)

5. *What was the best part of being a participant in this program?*
    Meeting new people (4 at CT)
    Learned awareness and understanding (1 at IC and 7 at CT)
    Learning conflict resolution (1 at IC)
    Could speak freely (1 at IC and 2 at CT)

6. *In what ways has the program influenced the way you think about inter-group relations and conflict?*
    No influence (1 at IC and 3 at CT)

    Changed my thinking (1 at IC and 2 at CT)

    Helped me listen (1 at IC and 1 at CT)

    Learned this was more complex than I had thought (1 at CT)

    Saw this as more important than previously (1 at CT)
    I look more for solutions now (2 at CT and 2 at IC)

7. *Has the program influenced how you think about yourself and others from different social groups than your own?*

   No influence (4 at IC and 7 at CT)

   Neutral effect (1 at CT)

   I better understand where I fit in (1 at CT)

   Learned to be less judgmental (2 at IC and 1 at CT)

   Learned others have similar feelings (2 at CT)

   I became more aware of differences (1 at IC and 4 at CT)

8. *What did you hope to get out of the program?*
   More education (1 at IC and 2 at CT)

   Learn about the culture of others (1 at IC and 7 at CT)

   Don't know (2 at IC and 2 at CT)

   Be more vocal (1 at IC)

9. *Were expectations met?*
   4 said yes at IC, 11 said yes at CT

   No one said 'no' at IC; 6 said 'no) at CT.

   At IC, 2 students commented that they spent time 'talking' but not 'solving'.

10. *How do you think you will be able to use what you learned in the program?*
    Make better decisions (1 at IC and 2 at CT)

    Know what to say in conflicts (2 at IC and 7 at CT)

11. *What would you change about this program? Why?*
    3 at CT said 'interact with the community

    1 at IC and 3 at CT said 'like it the way it was'

    Change the order of sessions (1 at CT)

    Add current event conflicts (1 at CT)

    Add controversial topics (1 at CT)

    More discussion on race (1 at IC)

12. *How would you make the program better?*
    More participation (None at IC, 7 at CT)

More interesting (1 at CT)

More relevant (3 at CT)

Journals would be completed (1 at IC)

We also noted whether students in these open-ended individual interviews made comments about the facilitators. At IC, 2 students volunteered positive comments and none were negative. At CT, one student made positive comments and 5 made negative ones.

It should be noted that the number of responses may be fewer than the number of students as some students did not produce responses that could be coded to the question. In some cases the number is greater than the number of students because some students gave several answers to the question.

While the number of students completing the questionnaire at the final meeting was about 2/3 of the students at each school, there was indication that students' assessment of the program differed depending on the gender of the students. We report here on the significant findings in this respect although, because of the small numbers, we see this primarily as an opportunity to generate hypotheses for future study than as a definitive finding. We first indicate the ethnicity and gender of the students completing this survey in each school.[6]

CT
Male　11 (2 African American, 4 white, 1 Latino, 1 Arab-American, 3 Asian American)

Female 15 (6 African-American, 3 white, 2 multi-racial, 1 Arab-American, 3 Asian American)

IC[7]
Male 9 (7 African-American, 1 white, 1 'other')

Female 11 (5 African-American, 3 white, 1 Latino, 2 multi-racial)

Gender Differences in Responses

- At IC, 66% of the male students thought that people from groups that do not get along with each other should avoid contact; Only 18% of the female students thought this. (p = .04). Is this some indication that male students are more concerned about the outcome of conflicts than women students?

- At IC, women students were more likely to say they were aware of their biases (100%) than male students (33%) (p.= .015). Is this some indication that women students are more sensitive to discrimination issues than male students?
- At CT, male students favored expulsion of those who participate in inter-group conflicts (54%) to a greater degree than female students (13%) (p. = .02). Are male students more likely to be punitive in their responses than women; this implies that women students might be more likely to favor interactional and educational approaches?
- At CT, male students are more likely (54%) to think students are taught prejudice by their teachers than female students (13%) (p. = .02).
- At CT, male students are more likely (73%) to think that people from certain groups bring disapproval on themselves by their socially unacceptable behavior than female students (6%) (p. = 0). Again, this might suggest that male students tend to be more judgmental than female students.
- At CT, male students were more confident of their ability to be open to beliefs, attitudes and behaviors that are different than their own (90%) than female students (67%) (p. = .03). We wonder if this is the 'truth' or whether male students have less insight than female students into their biases.
- At CT, male students are more likely to think about the amount of power different groups in society have (72%) than female students (27%) (p. = .05). This suggests that male students may be more likely than female students to think in terms of power issues.
- At IC, Women are more likely (45%) to think about gender than male students (0%) (p. = .03). This fits with the notion that 'oppressed' groups think more about the circumstances of oppression than those who are not in that category.

Summary and conclusions

This paper presented details of a program that utilized group work principles and practices to enable high school students to become leaders in the peaceful resolution of inter-group conflicts. The paper described the theoretical grounding of the project in knowledge about the source of inter-group conflicts as well as the reduction of such conflicts. Another important contribution to the project was that its methodology was derived from principles of participatory action research. The paper described the way the group was composed, the content of the group's discussions, and the nature of the partnership with school systems. The paper concluded with preliminary data that were collected to evaluate the program.

Notes

1   This project has continued in the ensuing years after this paper was written and continues till this day. A more recent report of the project is presented as a special issue of the journal *Small Group Research* (Garvin & Bargal, 2008).

2   The content of this form is prescribed by the University's Institutional Review Board which also must, and did, approve all details of the project as consistent with the ethical principles governing such research

3   The facilitator at CT was a white woman and the one at IC was a black woman. The student was a white man who had considerable experience before entering the MSW program leading adolescent adventure groups. We would have preferred the facilitators to be from different genders and ethnic groups but this was not possible in terms of who actually was available. The facilitators were paid a modest honorarium of $1250 for the entire 15 week term.

4   It was clear to the project staff that the optimal circumstance would have been the availability of facilitators who were trained group workers but the limited resources available to the project did not make this possible.

5   The full narratives will be presented in a book we are preparing on the project although we shall disguise names in order to protect the identities of facilitators, students, and other individuals who were identified.

6   We began the program with about 35 students in each school. The impression of the facilitators is that the number of students at the last session, all of whom completed the questionnaire, is not necessarily a reflection of drop-outs but of the variation in attendance due to conflicts with classes and activities as well as school absences.

7   We note that the African-American students at IC were more likely to

attend regularly than the white students. This appears to be a pattern at IC inasmuch as, according to school informants, most activities at the school tend to become primarily either white or African-American in this roughly evenly divided school.

References

Adorno, T., Frenkel-Brunswick, E., Levinson, D, & Sanford, R. (1950) *The authoritarian personality*, New York: Harper.

Allport, G. (1954) *The nature of prejudice*. Cambridge, MA: Addison-Wesley

Altmeyer, B. (1998) The other authoritarian personality. In M. Zana (Ed.) *Advances in Experimental Social Psychology* (Vol. 30, pp. 47-92). New York: Academic Press.

Amir, Y. (1969). Contact hypothesis in ethnic relations. *Psychological Bulletin*, 71, 310-342.

Ashmore, R. and Delboca, F. (1976). Psychological approaches to understanding intergroup conflict. In P. Katz (Ed.) *Toward the elimination of racism* (pp. 73-123). New York: Pergamon.

Bargal, D. and Bar, H. (1994). The encounter of social selves approach in conducting intergroup workshops for Arab and Jewish Youth in Israel. *Social Work with Groups*, 17(3), 39-59.

Bargal, D. (2008), Action research: A paradigm for achieving social change. *Small Group Research*, 39(1), 17-27.

Brewer, M., and Brown, R. (1998). Intergroup relations. In D. Gilbert, S. Fiske, & G. Lindzey (Eds.). *The Handbook of social psychology* (Vol. 2, pp. 554-593). Boston: McGraw-Hill.

Brown, B. (1990). Peer group and peer cultures. In S. Feldman and G. Elliot (Eds.), *At the threshold: The developing adolescent* (pp. 171-190). Cambridge, MA: Harvard University Press.

Campbell, D (1965). Ethnocentric and other altruistic motives. In D. Levine (Ed.), *Nebraska symposium on motivation* (pp. 283-311). Lincoln: University of Nebraska Press.

Carkhuff, R. (1969). *Helping and human relations*. New Yok: Holt, Rinehart & Winston.

Egan, G. (1986). *The Skilled helper: A systematic approach to effective helping*. Monterey, CA: Brooks-Cole.

Erickson, E (1968). *Identity, youth, and crisis*. New York: Norton.

Fisher (1997). *Interactive conflict resolution*. Syracuse, NY: Syracuse University Press.

Garvin, C., and Bargal, D.(Eds.) (2008). *Enabling high school students to cope with intergroup conflict: An action research study*. Published as a special issue of *Small Group Research*, Vol. 39 (1).

Fiske, S., & Taylor, S. (1991). *Social cognition* (2nd ed.). New York: McGraw-Hill.

Howard, J. (2000). Social psychology of identities. *Annual Review of Sociology*, 26, 367-393.

Lewin, K. (1945/1948a). Conduct, knowledge and acceptance of new values. In G.W. Lewin (Ed.) *Resolving Social conflicts* (pp. 56-70). New York: Harper & Row.

Lewin, K. (1945/1948b). Group decision and social change. In E. Maccoby, T. Newcomb, & E. Hartley ((Eds.), *Readings in social psychology* (pp. 197-211). New York: Holt.

Lewin, K. (1946/1948). Action research and minority problems. In G.W. Lewin (Ed.) *Resolving social conflicts*. (pp. 201-216). New York: Harper & Row.

Lewin, K. (1947). Frontiers in group dynamics. Part II. *Human Relations*, 1, 143-153.

Lieberman, M. (1980). Group methods. In F. Kanfer & A. Goldstein (Eds.), *Helping people change* (pp. 470-536). New York: Pergamon.

Lieberman, M. (1983). Comparative analyses of change mechanisms in groups. In H. Blumberg. P. Hare, V. Kent, & M. Davies (Eds.), *Small groups and social interaction* (Vol. 2. pp 239-252), New York: John Wiley.

Pettigrew, T., and Tropp, L. (2006). A meta-analytic test on intergroup contact theory. *Journal of Personality and Social Psychology, 90(5), 751-783.*

Pettigrew, T. (1998). Intergroup contact theory. *Annual Review of Psychology*, 49, 65-85.

Sherif, M. (1958). Superordinate goals in the reduction of intergroup conflicts. *Journal of Sociology*, 63, 349-356.

Sherif, M (1966). *In Common predicament: Social psychology of intergroup conflict and cooperation*. Boston: Houghton & Mifflin.

Stephan, W.G., and Stephan, C.W. (2001), *Improving intergroup relations*. Thousand Oaks, CA: Sage.

Tajfel, H., & Turner, J. (1986). The social identity theory of intergroup behavior. In O. Worchel and W. Austin (Eds.), *Psychology of intergroup relations* (pp. 7-24). Chicago: Nelson-Hall.

Tajfel, H. (1982). The social psychology of intergroup relations. *Annual Review of Psychology*, 33, 1-39.

Groups as a medium for reducing sex offender recidivism

Steven Hartsock and Karen V. Harper-Dorton

Introduction

Explosion of awareness of victimization and containment of sexual offenders who are reentering communities and neighborhoods have increased understanding of this difficult to treat population (Allam & Browne, 1998; Kimberley & Osmond, 2003; Stalans, 2004). As identified sexual offenders return to community living, public safety and reduction of future sexual offending acts are critical concerns. In response to public and community concerns, programs are increasing for treatment, supervision, community containment and reduction of reoffending (Stalans, 2004). Recent literature identifies group therapy as the preferred medium for treatment of sexual offenders, particularly as increasing numbers of sexual offenders are identified for services upon their return to living in communities and neighborhoods throughout the nation (Bates, Falshaw, Corbett, Patel, & Friendship, 2004; Ephross, 1997; Kimberley & Osmond, 2003). This account of an ongoing community-based treatment group for sexual offenders in Maryland presents a model for group treatment of sexual offenders intended to bridge transitioning from institutional confinement to community reentry.

Upon their return to community living, offenders are required to attend group treatment as a condition of discharge. New group members are court-ordered to present without escort or supervision and to have their attendance reported to appropriate legal jurisdictions. It is intended that this community-based group experience be valued positively for daily living and even for life-long support. In addition to attendance reporting, group members must personally pay for their weekly treatment sessions. While payment is on a sliding-fee scale according to ability to pay, requiring offenders to pay for their own treatment is one effort to help establish a greater sense of responsibility, often a weak character quality among the perpetrator population.

Having completed various sentences for their crimes of sexual offending and perpetrating, nearly all participants have recently participated in sexual offender treatment while incarcerated. Some have had years of sexual offending therapy including both individual and group treatment. Some with extended prison sentences have had much less treatment and a few present with minimal experiences of any psychotherapeutic intervention. Others come from closed settings where pre-therapy groups and interventions often use confrontation as a major means for getting members to divulge the nature of their offenses and personal responses. Offenders react differently to sharing accounts of deviant sexual behaviors and victimization in great detail in the group environment. Nevertheless, listening to details of other group members' offenses does serve to establish some commonalities among offenders as well as their offenses. The group medium provides each participant the experience of verbalizing perhaps some of the most stigmatized acts that humans can exercise upon each other (Griffin, Williams, Hawkes, & Vizard,1997; Newbauer & Blanks, 2001). Likely there is no other social network outside the treatment group environment where sexual offenders can talk about sexually offending, molestation of children, and their feelings about being labeled the 'lowest of the low.'

Concerns of public safety and awareness

The number of sexual offenders who are incarcerated continues to grow, with many returning to society, frequently under community supervision and with mandates for probation and treatment. The public is very concerned about assurances for public safety and prevention of reoffending. Public registries, notification of residents that a sexual offender has moved into their neighborhood, letters to school principals, and other efforts to build awareness of potential risk are viewed as protective measures but increase stigma and raise privacy questions for the offenders. Nevertheless, community awareness is believed to be helpful in reducing reoffending and protecting potential victims.

In addition to fear of personal victimization, many people are confused about incidence rates and recidivism. Criminal justice and social work literature are replete with studies of recidivism. Reports of rates of repeat offenses vary widely. For example, (Stalans, Seng, & Yarnold, 2002) report a recidivism rate as high as 65% for child molesters who are noncompliant with treatment and a rate of 36% for those with strong aggressive or psychopathic tendencies. In another review of the literature, Wakefield and Underwager (1998) place the sexual offending recidivism rate at or below 40%, even as long as 15-20 years after conviction. A five-year study of 23,393 subjects released after incarceration and exposure to a range of treatment therapies found that only 13.4% committed new offenses (Hanson & Bussière, 1998). It is noted that there is variation among studies as well as classification of offenders being charged versus those who have one or more convictions.

Group treatment with sexual offenders

Group therapy is recognized as the primary treatment modality for sexual offenders (Freeman-Long & Knopp, 1992; McLean, 2001; Newbauer & Blanks, 2001; Tharp, 1997). The milieu of the group brings together those who have committed similar or the same offenses and creates an opportunity to realize commonalities and gain some sense of belonging or comfort. Group therapy is a powerful medium that can bring together offenders at different levels of treatment and in various states of awareness of self, responsibility, anger, denial, cognitive distortion, and relapse. Secrets are less important than open discussion and feedback about inappropriate sexual behavior, convictions, and once hidden secrets. The commonality of membership in a sexual offenders group for those caught in some inappropriate sexual activity provides a peer network where confrontation, feedback and support occur.

Sexual offenders bring the commonality of being found guilty of inappropriate sexual behavior to the treatment group. Being known for having committed sexual offenses has the capacity to place offenders at the lowest rung of those adjudicated, regardless of diversity in age, race, religion, education, and psychosocial functioning. For most, the openness, trust, feedback, and confrontation that are part of group treatment are new experiences in sharing, supporting, and being supported. Denial, depersonalization, and minimization are mechanisms that sexual offenders use to alleviate responsibility for offending behaviors (Schneider & Wright, 2004). Having operated in a web of denial, negativism, and distorted reality, group members are court ordered to attend upon discharge from prison and/or as a condition of probation, generally a period of from three to five years. Not expecting to get caught and not having been open about their sexual feelings, sharing experiences in this group milieu is foreign and strange. Frequently denying the destructive nature of their actions, trust in the group environment comes slowly for members. Having offended, being caught, being classified as lowest of the low even in prison, entering this 'peer' environment of other 'lows' can be quite a bruising experience.

Cognitive behavioral therapy

Cognitive behavioral therapy (CBT) is empirically supported as being useful in treating a wide variety of problems such as mood disorders, substance abuse, sexual abuse, eating disorders, and personality disorders including psychotic disorders. Cognitive-Behavioral Therapy with groups of sex offenders is the preferred method for reducing recidivism of sex offenders in communities.

Having its roots in psychoanalysis, client-centered therapy, and behavioral therapy, CBT is used in treating many emotional and behavioral problems. This empirically supported therapy focuses on identifying and treating maladaptive patterns of thinking and underlying beliefs. With the therapist's help, patients are encouraged to identify cognitive errors and to focus on correcting them. In others words, people identify erroneous thought processes and messages and work to change them.

CBT helps people learn how thinking patterns and interpretation of their environment produce a distortion of reality in daily life and events. Feelings of denial, anxiety, frustration, and anger are often evident. Continuing with and responding to this cognitive distortion of reality can provoke actions that are dysfunctional and harmful to self or others. Learning to restructure negative thought patterns is essential for both perception and behavior to become more acceptable and appropriate. Changing thoughts, beliefs, mental imagery and attitudes represents cognition while changing actions and responses is behavioral. Conceptually, CBT teaches offenders to recognize faulty thinking. Proficiency enables the offender to avoid potential situations where re-offending is most likely. Developing skills in these areas enables the offender to be contained in the community.

Treatment tasks: Sexual offenders group

This program for adult sexual offenders consists of nine tasks. These tasks are clearly presented to the group as tasks to be accomplished. Some offenders take issue with the fact that they simply cannot complete them in order, pass some test, and be on their way. Instead, group members are there for the duration of their court-ordered probation time.

Figure 1: Group treatment tasks

Building social competence
Reducing cognitive distortion
Providing sex education
Increasing anger management
Providing support and nonsepecific counseling
Involving family systems
Preventing relapse
Increasing commitment to accountability and responsibility
Preparing for positive community reentry

This group is a semi-structured, open-ended group where some members may be leaving and new members joining. Size of the group will remain under twelve members with the average time of treatment in the group being about four years. As offenders enter the group, ongoing members and leaders explain group boundaries. The first important boundary is to establish an understanding that each offender's history of offending, sentencing, conviction, and prior treatment is known to the group leaders and probation officers who are working together. Second, group treatment is the best 'game' in town and a condition of their probation. Third, offenders are required to arrive on time and to pay for treatment. Fourth, benefits from treatment are greatest for those who take responsibility for their recovery as sexual offenders.

Co-leadership

In this treatment program, co-leaders are an integral part of group therapy. The role of the group leaders is critical to treatment in this semi-structured, open-ended group treatment model. These groups need to run regularly to be effective. The use of co-leaders is an effective means of running these groups. Sex offender groups are needy from both the perspective of setting limits and boundaries and in terms of individual dependency. Co-leaders help to provide sufficient emotional support for the group. Co-leaders also offer one another support when trapped by seductive group members and can give each other breaks and time for redirection.

Sex offender treatment groups are overwhelmingly male. Female co-leadership works to help the sex offender learn appropriate interaction with females. The presence of the female leader helps in keeping offender interaction more appropriate. When the female leader is not present the group can quickly move into more 'locker room,' anti-female conversation. In some cases the group member begins to act out some of the inappropriate and seductive interaction with the female. The co-leaders are then able to address this inappropriate interaction by using in vivo exposure to the communication and thought errors that exist in the group. Male and female co-leaders serve as role models for interaction among males and females.

In CBT group treatment, therapists are active in engaging patients in group process. They will focus on problems in a present-centered context and use past histories and recall as necessary to help explain cognitive distortions or apperceptions. Encouraging change in thoughts and actions requires the therapist to be goal-directed and action oriented so that more patients can achieve more adaptive alternatives in response to thoughts and misguided patterns of thinking and perceiving. In this group example, co-leaders discuss issues pertinent to the group, confront expressions of thought errors, provide education and encourage the group to take on leadership in treating each member of the group. For example, co-leaders identify negative interaction and provide confrontation in instances when a member is singled out for unfair judgment or harassment by other group members.

Group composition and selected treatment examples

Sexual offenders group members have areas of commonalities as well as very different experiences and boundaries in their own lives. Some may be dealing with struggles in managing their fears of not being able to get through their first year of probation without reoffending while others may be entrenched in taking steps to deal with situations such as substance addictions. Vast differences in age, gender preference, and commitment to treatment in a particular stage of recovery create boundaries to be recognized and managed within the group. For others, convictions for pedophilia often create serious blocks to group membership that have to be processed by other involuntary members.

Figure 2: Group participants

F	Predator type, schizophrenic, bi-sexual alcoholic, urban background, high school graduate
E	Sexual relations with step-daughter (age 12), works in power plant of a nuclear submarine
A	Child pornography, road rage, 18 years old, fills soda machines
M	Paid grand-daughter to have sexual relations and wants to continue to pay as she dates boys and why not him? Retired from military, and now aged 53
D	Sexual relations with 12 year old who seduced him, wife leaving him, 34 years old manager of an airport, waiting sentencing
J	Angry, wanted to commit suicide, but felt that 19 year old girlfriend was too young to die with him, turned in another sex offender for fondling a teenage girl. 50 years old, going to South Carolina with girlfriend, pulled over by police alleges harassment because he was a sex offender
R	Alcoholic, caught a second time, 54 years old, going to prison for rape for 20 years, Florida sending him to West Virginia
T	Substance abuser, molested 12 year-old stepdaughter, served two prison sentence, one for substance, and one for sex offense. On the first sentence, beat up jailmate for being a sex offender.

Commonalities among group members include: alcohol addiction, mental and emotional distress, heterosexual relationships, and noticeable age difference between them and their focus of interest/ victims. Of course the criterion for membership is the greatest commonality of all--sexual offending. While offender commonalities are generally targets for treatment, individual characteristics such as personality and problem solving approaches add rich detail to the group.

Selected group treatment notes

In this on-going group, new members were introduced and their offense shared. As part of introductions, group members typically share their offense and then return to whatever is in process of being discussed. Usually this happens without leader intervention. This group's most senior member is approaching his 4th year. This group has learned to work with the co-leaders and has cohesion among its members. Self-disclosure seems to come easily within the group. There is some evidence of cognitive restructuring and commitment to change. However, therapeutic factors of trust, empathy and intimacy that are necessary for really productive personal growth are weak for all members (Corey, 2004). The absence or weakness of trust, empathy and problems with intimate relations is not atypical of sexual offenders treatment groups. In fact, gaining awareness and mastery in these areas is critical to the success of nonoffending and community reentry. The following excerpts come from notes dictated immediately following the session and provide a view of ongoing treatment and group process.

Admitting New Member

The co-leader opened the session by greeting everyone and introducing a new member who has been in prison for internet child pornography on the internet. The new member shares that he is finding employment to be very difficult and is searching for just about any kind of a job. The group spent time introducing themselves to the new members and each shared their offenses. E. is on probation. T. continues to work but is looking for another job. At times his memory seems impaired. F. was accused of raping a woman but it was determined that the women was delusional. The group expressed appropriate emotions about E. and concern for his well being as he just returned from 60 days of imprisonment for violating probation by getting picked up for fighting. R.

discussed his grandmother passing away. J. discusses his problems with the law, implying that he has re-offended twice and then was set up by an ex wife who was angered.

Denial and distortion

The group focused attention on T. who continues to minimize and distort his offense. This seemed to be good practice for all members to remind themselves of having been in the same place of distortion. At times they quite gleefully grill T. He responds with his own arguments and denial but seems to make some headway. The group seems to be both supportive and confrontive at the same time. Also at one point the group was clearly fantasizing what T's victim looked like. Intervention was made to have them see that perpetration begins at an early stage. The group all were thinking about T's victim and seeing her as a pretty woman. T. said that he was thinking about marrying this woman. He was confronted on this by the group leaders and two group members as it was known that he knew her only as a student. This was another one of his defensive maneuvers.

Group treatment task demonstrated

J. arrives early for group and asks the group leaders if he can have group time to discuss some issues. This is an unusual request for any group member. The understood group format is that members can discuss issues without special permission. However, this request alerted the group leaders to the excitement felt by this group member. The group member had missed a number of sessions and the group leaders wondered if this were not a way to deflect from his absenteeism (Group members are mandated by their parole agents and if they miss, the parole agent is notified.). Nonetheless, J. excitedly presents a summary of what has been happening to him, 'since he is a convicted sex offender.' J. reports to the group that he has been having health issues and has at last found a doctor who identified these issues. He took appropriate action to resolve the medical problems, and he now feels much better. He took a trip to South Carolina where he was roughed up by state police after they did a background check and found that he has sex offenses. J. was with two younger persons ages 18 and 19 (J is 53) which increased the police suspiciousness according to J. He has been having suicidal thoughts but he was prevented from action by his girlfriend who said that she would die with him. He said, 'I told her that she was too young to die. So, we are both still here.' He has been having battles with his ex-wife who has been giving him problems in visitation with his daughters. Because he is a known sex offender, he was chased off the school grounds where he had gone to get his daughter after school. Though J. talks about anger and fighting ('I was going to punch the cop if he said one more word.'), he presents more of a passive attitude in the group. J. is a twice convicted sex offender. The group leaders do not confront J. about absences, nor does this seem to be essential at this time. Group members immediately volunteer responses, and tend to reflect anger and then offer calming comments..

Treatment tasks reflected in group member responses

F. responds by giving a historical view of the group, and how he and J. are the oldest members, All agree that they have been in the group for seven years. This seemed to help provide an anchor for the group and sense of security in that the group has been and will be there for them. They can express hard feelings in the group without the fear of reprisal. This seemed to create a sense of bonding and support, as if to say we have been here for you in group and that this is a safe place. *(Support and Nonspecific Counseling)*

M. supports the view of the unfair police, he then reviews his own interaction with the police when arrested. He becomes agitated and seeks support from other group members. They nod in agreement at first. E. discusses the fairness he received with the police and judicial system. F. who has spent the most time in prison recalls his jail time. This seems to be a valuable exercise for the group, connecting jail time to their actions. At this point the group has conflicting views of punishment. Nonetheless, a behavioral connection is made to the consequence of sexually offending behaviors. The other aspect brought to the group's attention is society's view of their behavior,. The group allows this conflict to abate. *(Community reentry, preventing relapse, cognitive distortion, increasing commitment to accountability and responsibility, anger management)*

E. then becomes more constructive, listens intently to J. and looks at the job loss as a main problem for him since his arrest, a loss more significant than the actions of the police. E. functioned in a high position and now has been forced to take manual labor positions. Others join him in remembering their own losses. The theme of the societal impact in response to their offenses is strong. *(Increasing commitment to accountability and responsibility, building social competence)*

A., who has recently been employed as a truck driver, begins to talk about his job and how people get in front of him, which makes him feel like hitting them. 'They don't know how hard it is for me to stop that big truck.' A. is employed beneath his training and skill. His account. taps into the anger of the group. (Group co-leaders then direct on ways of managing anger, to which all group members listen intently.) *(Anger Management)*

R. is very quiet and thoughtful (unusual for him) and provides very supportive comments for J. R is from the South and readily attests to police issues. *(Support)*

The above expression of the events provided the opportunity for supportive, educational and directive intervention. It also allowed group leaders to assess the progress each member is making in handling pressures of the world outside of the group. The group response is the most valuable aspect of treatment and provides therapeutic value for J. and other group members. In this example, group co-leaders worked to help keep the group focused on the task of developing skills to prevent relapse, manage anger, reduce cognitive distortion, and prepare for positive community reentry. Typically, all treatment tasks identified by this group of sex offenders are addressed in each session.

One issue J. has been working on is that he knows about an active sex offender in the community and is torn about reporting. Interestingly, the group supported him in going to the police. J. did in fact go to the police after the above group session. This person was arrested and currently is in jail awaiting trial. This event brings forth a number of issues, especially that of looking at sex offenders as persons doing harm to others and the need for them to be stopped. New members of the group usually have such high levels of denial that they are unaware of the harm their actions perpetrate.

Discussion

This project for group treatment of sexual offenders using a CBT approach reports our approach to offender reentry initiatives that are going on around the nation. This
community-based initiative serves as a bridge from institution-based treatment that protects society to community-based programs where controlling behavior, restructuring faulty thinking and changing behavioral responses are program goals. This project is consistent with understanding that the importance of behavioral and cognitive orientation to treating sex offenders is an important part of criminal control and is helpful in targeting risk factors that contribute to reoffending. Sexual offenders are a difficult to treat population and threaten feelings of safety and security for many families and children.

Treating sexual offenders in groups is key to successful community reentry and provides rich opportunities for future research. It is in the group where perpetrators share histories, hear how others' perceive them, and hopefully experiences feedback that contributes to personal growth and behavior change. Community reentry programs are helping to reduce sexual offender recidivism by beginning the reentry process from the prison to community-based treatment and on to lifelong support services after probation/parole sentences have ended (Lehman et al., 2002; Wakefield & Underwager, 1991). It is important that sexual offender treatment programs continue to evaluate treatment outcomes, particularly where there are opportunities and funding for longitudinal studies with this population. Groups are a laboratory where concerns such as boundaries, ethics, worker burnout, and management versus treatment arise in working with sex offenders (Shelby et al., 2001)

References

Allam, J. M., and Browne, K D. (1998). Evaluating community-based treatment programmes for men who sexually abuse children. *Child Abuse Review,* 7, 13-29.

Bates, A., Falshaw, L., Corbett, C., Patel, V., and Friendship, C. (2004). A follow-up study of sex offenders treated by Thames Valley Sex Offender Groupwork Programme, 1995-1999. *Journal of Sexual Aggression, 10, 1,* 29-39.

Corey, G. (2004). *Theory and practice of group counseling* (6th ed.,) CA: Bellmont: Brooks/Cole-thomson Learning.

Ephross, P. H. (1997). Group work with sex offenders. In G. L. G. P. H. Ephross (Ed.), *Group work with populations at risk* (pp. 175-187), NY: Oxford University Press.

Freeman-Long, R., and Knopp, F. (1992). State-of-the-art sex offender treatment: Outcome and issues. *Annals of Sex Research, 5(3),* 141-160.

Griffin, S., Williams, M., Hawkes, C., and Vizard, E. (1997). The professional carers' group: Supporting group work for young sexual abusers. *Child abuse and Neglect, 21(7),* 681-690.

Hanson, R.K., and Bussière, M.T. (1998). Predicting relapse: A meta-analysis of sexual offender recidivism studies. *Journal of Consulting and Clinical Psychology, 66,* 348-362.

Kimberley, D., and Osmond, L. (2003). Night of the tortured souls: Integration of group therapy and mutual aid for treated male sex ofenders. In J. Lindsay, Turcotte, D., and Hopmeyer, E. (Ed.), *Crossing boundaries and developing alliances through group work.* Binghampton, NY: The Haworth Press.

Lehman, J., Beatty, T.G., Maloney, D., Russell, S., Seymour, A., and Shapiro, C. (2002, December 6, 2002). *The three 'R's' of reentry.* Retrieved September 15, 2004, 2004, from http://www.ojp.usdoj.gov/reentry/learn.html;

McLean, C. (2001). People like us. *Report/Newsmagazine, 28(16).*

Newbauer, J.F., and Blanks, W.J. (2001). Group work with adolescent sexual ofenders. *The Journal of Individual Psychology, 57(1),* 37-50.

Schneider, S.L., and Wright, R.C. (2004). Understanding denial in sexual offenders. *Trauma, Violence, and Abuse, 5(1),* 3-20.

Shelby, R.A., Stoddart, R.M., and Taylor, K. L. (2001). Factors contributing to levels of burnout among sex offender treatment providers. *Journal of Interpersonal Violence, 16(11),* 1205-1218.

Stalans, L.J. (2004). Adult sex offenders on community supervision. *Criminal Justice and Behavior, 31(5),* 564-608.

Stalans, L.J., Seng, M., and Yarnold, P.R. (2002). *Long-term impace evaluation of specialized sex offender probation programs in Lake, DuPage, and Winnebago Counties.* Chicago, Illinois: Criminal Justice Information Authority.

Tharp, M., 34-36. (1997). *US. News & World Report, 123(1),* 34-36.

Wakefield, H., and Underwager, R. (1991). Sex offender treatment. *IPT-Journal, 3.*

Grandparent caregivers:
Implications for groupwork

Jessica Rosenberg

Introduction

Grandparent caregiver families are rapidly growing in number. According to the Census Bureau (2000), the number of children under the age of 18 living in grandparent maintained households increased from 2.2 million in 1970 to 3.3 million in 1992. By 1997, there were 3.9 million children residing in homes where the grandparent was primary caretaker. In the year 2000, the Census Bureau identified 4.5 million grandchildren living in grandparent headed households, and currently 6.3% of all children reside in homes that are maintained by their grandparent. This dramatic change in family configuration brings with it a host of social concerns. Grandchildren in grandparent maintained families are more likely to live in poverty than other children and are more likely to be without health insurance than other children while the grandparents are at high risk for depression and a myriad of health problems.

Social workers are challenged to understand these family systems and to develop appropriate responses, at the policy and practice level, if these families are to be helped to achieve optimal functioning. This paper provides a discussion of the key characteristics of grandparent caregiver families and examines their issues within the context of role theory and developmental theory perspectives. The impact of culture on family functioning also will be addressed. The paper discusses the use of support groups, an important therapeutic modality that has be shown to be effective with grandparents caregivers, using case examples from ongoing groups to illustrate key points. How group leaders can be supported in their work will be addressed.

Grandparent caregivers: A profile

Grandparents typically assume full time care for grandchildren when parents are unable to assume care of their children. Some of the reasons for this are drug use among the parents, teen pregnancy, AIDS, incarceration of the parents, homicide, and mental illness (Cox, 2003). Grandparent caregivers are keeping families together, often serving as a safety net to keep children out of the formal foster care system.

Five types of grandparent-maintained households have been identified: (1) both grandparents, (2) some parents present; (3) both grandparents, no parents present; (4) grandmother only; and (5) grandfather only. Family structure is strongly associated with the economic well being of the family. The two types of families most likely to be poor are single: grandmother maintained with no parent present (14%) and one parent maintained household with only the grandmother present (29%) What these two families have in common is the absence of a father and/or grandfather. Since men are more likely to be in the labor force and tend to earn more than women, their absence is reflected in higher poverty rates. Thus, 43% of grandparent families do not have a grandfather or father in the home and are likely to be poor (Census 2000). They are more likely be African-American, are often younger compared with grandmothers who live in homes where the parents are present, and are most likely to live in the South.

Psychosocial issues/challenges

Given the prevalence of poverty, particularly among grandmother maintained households, it is not surprising that stressors related to economic insecurity are paramount in this population. Studies suggest that poor economic health compound other psychosocial difficulties

(Minkler et. al. 1997). Furthermore, the involvement of these families with a myriad of government assistance programs, such as public assistance, SSI, and child only cash grants, can take a toll on the well-being of grandparent caregivers, who often experience a measure of shame and anger about having to rely on government assistance as well as confusion about how to negotiate such complex and bureaucratic systems.

Chronic and multiple health problems among this population have been well documented in numerous studies (Minkler & Roe, 1993; Minkler, et. al. 1997; Roe, et al. 1996). Mental health problems have been noted as well with studies finding twice the rate of depression among grandparent caregivers compared with their non caregiving peers (Minkler, et al. 1997).

Decreased socialization with friends and/or relatives is identified as a consequence of grandparent caregiving, with grandparent caregivers reporting that they have less time and energy to spend with friends and families (Cox, 2000). An additional factor exacerbating isolation may stem from a sense of shame about their situation, particularly if their adult child is unable to assume the role of parent because of socially unacceptable causes, such as drug abuse, AIDS, or incarceration. As such, grandparent caregivers may suffer from sense of stigma which further aggravates a tendency toward self-isolation.

Role theory

The special demands placed on grandparent caregivers can be understood within a role theory framework. The challenges facing grandparent caregivers in their new role are formidable. Most grandparent caregivers do not elect, at this stage in their life, to become responsible for raising yet another child. Grandparent caregivers do not generally anticipate nor plan for this new role; rather it is thrust upon them, most often because of unhappy circumstances, such as the death of their adult child or their incapacitation due to illness, incarceration, or drug abuse. How well grandparent caregivers are likely to adapt to their new role is related to a number of issues.

Preparation

Social role theory defines a social role as a set of patterned, functionally interdependent relations between an individual and his/her social circle. Roles typically involve responsibilities and personal rights. In social role theory, people are understood to occupy social positions which assigned norms, behaviors and expectations associated with it. It is hypothesized that an important way that we ease the shock of role transition is through anticipatory socialization in which new roles are prepared for (Kart & Kinney, 2001). For example, expectant parents generally read about childbirth, attend classes, or talk to new parents to prepare for becoming parents themselves. Similarly, training programs and internships are utilized as a means of assisting students in learning a new professional role. Being engaged is a method of providing a couple time to psychologically prepare for their role as married person. Anticipating a new role before one assumes it can significantly ease role transition. However, grandparent caregivers rarely have the opportunity to prepare for the demands of being parents again because their new role is often the result of a sudden family crisis and loss (Cox, 2000).

Physical well being

Parenting is a role that requires physical exertion: cooking, feeding babies at night, chasing a toddler or trying to navigate the public school system is hard work. Grandparents may lack the energy or physical well being commensurate with the demand of child care. Exhaustion and depression can easily set in, especially for grandparents with chronic health conditions.

Timing and role transitions

Most societies and cultures appear to have expectations for when major life events *ought* to *take place.* For example, cultural deadlines is a concept that refers to the age at which most members of society agree that certain family transitions, such as leaving home, marriage, parenthood, grandparenthood, should occur in lives of a man or woman (Kart & Kiney, 2001). Some studies suggest that being 'off time' or 'late' in taking on a social role creates stress stemming from internal factors; namely self judgments regarding what one ought to have accomplished or be engaged in at a certain point in life. External factors such is the reactions of one's peers and the larger community about what role a person is engaged in can cause some distress as well (Sales, 1978). For example, women who do not get married by a certain age may be self critical as well feel some degree of negative judgments by their friends and family. Grandparents who find themselves parents once again are likely to be sensitive to negative social perceptions that there is some implicit failing associated with child rearing at their age. In cases where adult children have engaged in socially deviant behaviors such as substance abuse and/or are incarcerated, feelings of embarrassment or social shame regarding their situation are likely to be exacerbated. Feelings of shame can be problematic particularly when they lead to social isolation.

Role confusion and family structure

Family structures in which a grandparent begins rearing the grandchild are characterized by shifting roles: Grandparents become parents while children may begin to identify their grandmother as mother. However, even when a grandparent has assumed the child rearing role, the parent often will periodically re-emerge and assert, albeit temporarily, a more dominant parenting role. In these families, roles are often in a state of flux which can be confusing and distressful. Grandparents become parents and then may become grandparents again, in the event that the adult child resumes the role of caretaker.

When the adult child is a substance abuser, there is a strong likelihood that the grandparent -adult child relationship is conflictual. In many cases, family court is involved with these families and grandparents may seek legal action to gain custody of grandchildren who they perceive as at risk for neglect and/or abuse at the hands of their parents (Musil, Schrader, & Mutikani, 2000). These grandparents are likely to struggle with strong feelings of anger toward their adult child as well feelings of loss.

Role change as positive

Social gerontologists suggest that a major problem associated with the aging process is the loss of constructive social roles. As people age and retire from the workforce, their sense of being productive members of society can be weakened, leading to loss of self esteem. Rosow (1987) notes that as people age, they are removed from important social roles and consequently suffer status loss. Grandparent caregivers, in contrast, may find renewed purpose associated with the new important role. Some grandparents who become parents again find that it to be full of reward and gratification. Grandchildren can bring life and vitality into the home and provide relief from the loneliness often associated with aging. Grandparents may find joy in caring for someone else. For these grandparent caregivers, the transition is very positive (Cox, 2000).

The extent to which grandparent caregivers embrace their new role as a positive change or resent the demands placed upon them is determined by many factors and most often, grand parenting, like parenting, involves a range of emotions, some positive and others less so. One area that can strongly affect grandparents is the degree of social support that they experience.

Developmental perspectives

In a classic study of personality traits associated with the aging process, Neugarten (1973) conducted one of the first longitudinal research studies about adult personality development. Conducted over a 10 year period with a large sample of adults age 40 80, the study identified a number of specific age related coping styles: 40 year olds exhibited a high degree of perceived control over their environment and a willingness to take risks whereas 60 year olds were more likely to perceive their environment as threatening and less likely to take risks. Neugarten also noted a move away from activity toward greater introspection and self reflection as people grow older.

This finding is consistent with earlier epigenic stage theorists such as Erikson (1950, 1982) who provided a model of psychosocial development. Erikson's theory rests on a number of key assumptions: There are 8 stages of development that occur over the life spam. Each stage is characterized by a different psychological 'crisis', which must be resolved by the individual before he or she can move on to the next stage. The last stage, occurring during old age, is viewed as a time for reflecting upon one's own life and one's accomplishments, particularly within the larger society. The crisis associated with this stage is termed Integrity vs. Despair. Erikson suggested when an adult has achieved a sense of fulfillment about life and a sense of unity; he or she will accept death with a sense of integrity. Conversely, individuals who have not come to terms with life are at higher risk despair and fearing death. Characteristic of the later years in life is that activity decreases while introspection increases.

Another developmental perspective is offered by Levision and his colleagues (1978) who proposed that the life cycle can be separated into a sequence of stages, each lasting 20-25 years. Similar to Erikson, Levinson believed that each stage is marked by a personal crisis with specific developmental tasks that are associated with each stage, although Levinson, unlike Erikson, did not contend that successful completion of developmental tasks at one stage is a necessary precondition for successful completion of developmental tasks at a later stage. According to Levinson's model, a primary task of late adulthood (which begins at around age 60) is to adjust to increasing physical limitations and to find a new balance between active involvement with society and self reflection.

These perspectives differ in many ways but a common theme is that older adulthood is understood as a move away from activity toward introspection. Physical decline in the later years requires a scaling back of activity while the focus shifts to self reflection. The experiences gathered over a lifetime are integrated and given meaning through introspection.

These developmental perspectives do not provide a framework that explains the psychosocial demands associated with the news roles confronting grandparent caregivers. Grandparents who become parents again in their later years are likely to be more engaged in the demands of child rearing than absorbed in reflection about the meaning of their own personal journey. Cox (2000) notes that grandparents raising grandchildren can be viewed as psychologically and socially vulnerable because they are not complying with the expected tasks of later life. However, they may also be seen as posing a challenge to the theoretical developmental frameworks to the extent that they are successfully taking on new risks, expanding their roles and activity level during a stage most commonly conceived a time for restricting activities.

In that these developmental theorists link psychosocial stage developments to chronological progression, some fluidity is to be expected. As people live longer and lead more active lives in their adult years, some of the assumptions about tasks associated with late adulthood are being challenged.

The role of social support

The daily stress associated with grandparent caregiving is very high: financial burdens, physical demands of parenting, family crisis and loss, physical health problems are some of the multiple stressors likely to impact a grandparent caregiver. It is not surprising that they would be a high risk for a host of psychosocial problems such as chronic depression.

Social support, defined as a network that provides caring, compassion, and resources to the grandparent are identified as helping grandparent caregiver families function (Cox, 2003).

Social supports can be informal, such as the support offered by family, friends, neighbors, and church organizations. Formal support is offered through support groups, social services, government social programs and the legal system. Social support has consistently been shown to be key to reducing stress (Musil, Schrader, & Mutikani, 2000).

Unfortunately, grandparent caregivers may have difficulty benefiting from supportive relationships because of a tendency among grandparent caregivers to self isolate from peers for a myriad of reasons: feelings of shame about their new role as parents, limited time and/or energy to participate in social events, lack of finances and fear that they will be criticized for the behaviors of their adult children (Musil, Schrader, & Mutikani, 2000).

Cultural considerations

The social support provided by family members may be considerably influenced by cultural norms. For example, numerous authors suggest that African- American families view child rearing as a shared responsibility among an extended family network (Burton & DilWorth-Anderson, 1991; Goodman & Silverstein, 2002). Intergenerational care giving has historically occurred in African American families with older family members stepping forward to care for children whose parents are unable to do so (Brown & Mars, 2000).

Similarly, Latino family emphasis the role of the family in caring for its members with older persons often stepping in to help care for the younger generation. A strong cultural belief in familism stresses the importance of family over the individual (Cox, Brooks, &V alcarcel, 2000). Nonetheless, while some cultures may provide greater acceptance for grandparent caregivers, the resiliency of such networks cannot be assumed. Despite a traditional emphasis on intergenerational caregiving, qualitative studies of African American grandmothers in urban settings describe financial problems, neighborhood dangers, and stress resulting from raising grandchildren (Burton, 1992),

Formal support on two levels: Grandparents and group leaders

One of the major modalities currently utilized to help grandparent caregivers is support groups. Grandparent support groups are an effective way to help grandparents with the difficult task of caring for their grandchildren. Group members teach and help one another and are themselves, through group process, empowered to reach across intergenerational and cultural lines as they learn to more effectively communicate with their grandchildren. Issues of mourning and loss are addressed as many grandparents are raising their grandchildren due to the death, severe illness, or incarceration of their own adult children.

Support groups provide grandparents with an opportunity to voice feelings, decrease isolation, and importantly, serve as a valuable resource on a range of issues; such as legal problems, parenting concerns, entitlement questions, and health concerns. While support groups differ considerably in regard to structure and leadership, membership composition and activities, a common unifying theme is that they seek to support members through mutual aid, in which members help one another (Cohen, 2000). Issues related to helping grandparents successfully adapt to the demand of their new role as caregiver can be effectively addressed as members learn form one another.

Case examples

Two large grandparent caregiver programs, located in N.Y.C., illustrate the range of services for grandparent caregivers. Grandmothers As Mothers Again (G.A.M.A.) is a Brooklyn based program for grandmother caregivers that serves over 150 members. Support groups are offered at a variety of times to enhance their accessibility. The groups utilize problem solving and members help one another. A strong part of the programming is advocacy based with members lobbying together at the city, state, and federal level. When asked what they valued most about the support groups, members stated that the groups provide them with valuable information that they could not obtain elsewhere. Members additionally expressed feeling a strong degree of trust that they could seek answers to sensitive topics like legal questions in the support groups without any fear of reprisals.

The Family Center, an agency with offices in downtown Manhattan and Bedford Stuyvesant, Brooklyn, provides a range of programming for grandparent families. Originally established in 1993 to meet the needs of families affected by HIV/AIDS, the Family Center has evolved so that a main focus is on serving the needs of grandparent caregivers. Support groups focus on issues such as grief, loss, family conflict, and parenting groups. The groups also participate in recreational outings. Socialization opportunities for the families are provided. Members express that the groups enable them to feel that they are not alone, that they find support from other, and that going to groups is a way to decrease stress. One grandmother who was having considerable difficulty setting limits with her pre-teen granddaughter, reporting learning effective new parenting strategies from other grandmothers in the group.

The Brooklyn Grandparent Coalition: Sustenance for support group leaders

Although it is widely recognized that support groups are an effective yet low cost intervention for grandparents raising grandchildren, support group leaders often find that have little agency support for their groups. The funding for support groups is often tenuous with little consistent attention paid to supervision and training for group leaders. Support group leaders, many of whom are peer consumers, may find themselves overwhelmed by the task of running these groups. Even seasoned group leaders can feel under-prepared because of the complexity of issues (legal, health, parenting, and policy) surrounding grandparent caregivers. Good group work is difficult to engage in when leaders feel that they have to 'go it alone'.

The Brooklyn Grandparents' Coalition serves as a model for providing support for support group leaders. Founded in 1993, the Coalition provides recognition and information for Brooklyn's kinship care families. Currently the Coalition's members represent 10 agencies that provide services and support groups to kinship care providers, including nonprofit, private and government agencies.

The Coalition's objectives are to: increase relative caregivers' knowledge about legal, health care, education, financial, and parenting issues; and outreach to Brooklyn kincare providers who are not connected with supportive services (www.brooklyngrandparents'coalition.org). A central function of the Coalition is that it is a group for group leaders, and as such, is a powerful vehicle for providing a range of support functions including education and training, resources for group leaders, and most importantly, renewing a sense of mission and purpose.

One Coalition member who leads support groups for grandparent caregivers related that because of funding cutbacks, she was uncertain from week to week if her groups would be cancelled or not. The group leader did not know if she would have a job and her group members did not know if they would have a group. This uncertain and difficult state of affairs persisted for a number of months. During this time, the support group leader drew considerable strength from Coalition meetings which enabled her to remain optimistic about the future, thereby helping her to continue to provide a leadership role in her groups. The Coalition also advocated for funding on behalf of the agency. Ultimately her agency found funding and her contract was renewed.

Support group leaders attend Coalition meetings to learn from one another and help one another strategize about how to respond to the many sensitive and complex issues that arise in their groups. Issues such as helping grandparents navigate the legal system or public school systems are 'problem solved'. Support group leaders are then able to utilize such information within their groups.

Joining together in the Coalition nurtures commitment and renews mission and purpose. Support leaders express feeling a stronger sense of commitment to their work when they have an opportunity to share experiences with other support group leaders. As one group leader stated 'Coalition meetings are a way for me to keep on top of issues, to learn and be a better advocate for change in my group'.

Coalition members join their groups together throughout the year for recreational activities such as holiday parties, baseball games and outings, and educational forums. Working together to plan these events helps support group leaders feel energized and encouraged about providing services. This is especially important because some social service organizations fail to adequately recognize the contribution of their staff, who run the risk of feeling underappreciated and supported, which can contribute to burn-The Coalition effectively promotes good group work through bring group leaders together, strengthening their understanding of the issues, helping them have more fun with their groups, and celebrating their mission.

Conclusion

Grandparents who are the primary caretakers for their grandchildren are rapidly growing in number. The challenges they face in their caregiving roles are formidable, ranging from economic difficulty, health problems, and depression to isolation. They also often lack necessary information about parenting issues, entitlements, and legal questions. Support groups are an important modality that can be quite effective in addressing their concerns. Grandparent caregivers voiced feeling better prepared in their caregiver roles as a result of participating in support groups. Decreased anxiety and depression has similarly been reported among grandmothers who attend such groups.

Support group leaders, in order to be effective in their role, also need formal support. While many agencies do not provide training or supervision for support group leaders, one advocacy group, the Brooklyn Grandparents' Coalition, has taken on the task of providing support for support group leaders.

References

Brooklyn Grandparents' Coalition Homepage. Retrieved online from www. brooklyngrandparents.org on 10/2/04.

Burton, L. M. (1992). Black grandparents rearing children of drug addicted parents: Stressors, outcomes, and social service needs. *The Gerontologist*, 32, 744-751.

Burton, L.M. and Dilworth-Anderson, P. (1991). The intergenerational roles of aged Black Americans. *Marriage and Family review*, 16, 311-330.

The Census Bureau (2000). Retrieved online at http://permanent. access.gpo.gov/grandparents.html on 10/2/04.

Cohen, C, (2000). Support groups in the lives of grandmothers raising grandchildren In C. Cox (Ed.), *Perspectives on custodial grandparents*. New York: Springer.

Cox, C. (2000).Why children are going to and staying at grandmother's house and what happens when they get there. In C. Cox (Ed.), *Perspectives on custodial grandparents*. New York: Springer.

Cox, C. (2003). Designing interventions for grandparent caregivers: the need for an ecological perspective for practice. *Families in Societies, 84,* 127-135.

Cox, C. Brooks, L.R., and Valcarcel, C. (2000). Culture and caregiving: A study of Latino grandparents. In C. Cox (Ed.), *Perspectives on custodial grandparents.* New York: Springer.

Erikson (1950). *Childhood and society.* NY: Horton.

Erikson (1982). *The life cycle completed.* NY: Horton.

Goodman, C. and Silverstein, M. (2002). Grandmothers raising grandchildren: Family structure and well-being in culturally diverse families. *The Gerontologist, 42,* 676- 689.

Kart, C. and Kinney, J. (2001). *The realities of aging: An introduction to gerontology.* MA: Pearson.

Levinson, D.J., Darrow, C.N., Klein, E.B. Levinson, M.H. and McKee, B. (1978). *The season's of a man's life.* New York: Knopf.

Minkler, M. and Roe, K.E. (1993). Grandmothers as caregivers: Raising children of the crack cocaine epidemic. Newbury park, CA: Sage.

Minkler, M., Fuller-Thomson, E., Miller, D. and Driver, D. (1997). Depression in grandparents raising grandchildren: Results of a national longitudinal study. *Archives of Family Medicine, 6,* 445-452.

Musil, C., Schrader, S., and Mutikani, J. (2000). Social support, stress, and special coping tasks of grandmother caregivers. In C. Cox (Ed.), *Perspectives on custodial grandparents.* New York: Springer.

Neugarten, B. (1973). Personality change in late life: A developmental perspective. In C. Eisdorfer and M. P. Lawton, (Eds). *The psychology of adult development and aging.* Washington, DC: American Psychological Association.

Roe, K.M., Minkler, M., Thompson, G., and Saunders, F. F. (1996). Health of grandmothers raising children of the crack cocaine epidemic. *Medical Care, 34,* 1072-1089.

Rosow, I. (1987). Status and role change through the life cycle. In R.H. Binstock and E. Shanas (Eds.). *Handbook of aging and the social sciences.* New York: Van Nostrand Reinhold.

Sales, E. (1978). Women's adult development. In I.H. Frieze, J.E. Parsons, P.B. Johnson, D.N. Ruble, and G.L. Zellman (Eds.). *Women and sex roles: A social psychological perspective.* NY: Horton.

Exploring group work concepts presented on video in an undergraduate social work practice with small groups course

**John Mansfield, Debrah Cuda,
Pamela Oliver and Amy Sill**

Introduction

Many academic institutions offer courses that teach group work theory and skills. Social work educators are familiar with offering group work courses and have been doing so for approximately one-hundred years, as suggested by Wilson (1976) some thirty-years ago. The Council on Social Work Education (CSWE) Educational Policies And Standards (EPAS) requires that social work educators incorporate teaching theory and skills relevant to group work. The EPAS is not specific to groups but rather generic to all types of practice including individuals, families, groups, organizations and communities. According to Kurland and Salmon (1999) group work is a key component of social work practice. Furthermore, the proportion of social workers facilitating small groups that have experience is limited and does not seem to be increasing. Berger (1996) posits that many social workers will be asked to facilitate a group some time during their career; therefore, group work knowledge and skills are essential for new social workers.

The CSWE allows the institution through the specific program, department or school of social work to determine the manner in which the practice courses are designed, taught and sequenced as long as the criteria are met. This paper will explore group work concepts that were presented on video during a Social Work Practice with Small Groups class in a CSWE accredited Social Work Program at Mansfield University. Mansfield University is a small liberal arts university located in North-Central Pennsylvania and is part of the state university system.

Literature review

The social work profession, especially social work educators, has been teaching group work knowledge and skills relevant to working with small groups for quite some time. Many social work educators have been interested in studying the impact that teaching different theories and methods has on the student both immediately, in field placements, and after the student graduates (Berger, 1996; Manor, 1988; Parry, 1988; Wayne & Garland, 1990). Undergraduate Social work educators are challenged with preparing students to enter the profession after graduation with the knowledge and skills necessary to function within an agency where group work is often the increasing type of treatment modality.

Manor (1988) suggests that videotape assignments are used extensively for learning skills. The use of video taping for class projects has become widely accepted.

According to Toseland & Rivas (2001), videotaping can be an excellent teaching tool. It allows the student to use the skills learned in class to actively develop his or her own personal style of conducting groups. By viewing the videotaped group sessions, the student was able to critique his or her work and gain insight into the behaviors that required improvement. In cases where there were multiple video sessions, the videotapes were excellent measurement tools for the student to determine how his or her skills have improved, over time.

Finally, the focus of this paper is to ascertain if the concepts that were taught in class were exemplified in the video assignment. There were two research questions. The first question was: What concepts were portrayed in the video assignment? The second question was: Were the concepts portrayed in the video assignment consistent with the concepts taught in class throughout the semester?

Methodology

This was a qualitative research study using a grounded theory approach. Rubin and Babbie (2001) posit that all qualitative research uses grounded theory because inductive reasoning is often generated to complete the project. Although grounded theory does allow for deductive reasoning this project will use inductive reasoning and constant comparisons. The intent was to analyze the videotaped assignments to discover the concepts portrayed for each group. Once the concepts were listed from each of the videotapes, then the five videos were compared to ascertain whether any themes had emerged.

The sample was derived from two sections of a required course entitled, Social Work Practice with Small Groups. Section one had an enrollment of 15 students and section two had 25 students. The students were asked to form groups. Each group consisted of four to six members. There were nine groups combining both sections. This paper will investigate five of the nine videos. The reason four of the videos were not used was, three of the videos had such poor quality after multiple viewings that the information was either hard to hear, difficult to see, or both. The fourth video did not use a theory or model discussed in class.

As mentioned the video assignment was the culminating event in this class; however, there were two assignments which preceded the video assignment. The first assignment was a paper. The intention of the first assignment was to familiarize the group member to a particular theory or model from the journal *Social Work with Groups*. The students were asked to only use this journal. The class emphasized the literature that supported the profession of Social Work and therefore this journal was used exclusively for the paper assignments. Assignment number one as stated in the syllabus was as follows:

Assignment #1

Each student will write a content paper focusing on one group work theory or model. The paper will be 10-12 typewritten pages. A minimum of five references is necessary. The American Psychological Association (APA) format will be adhered to strictly. Check the Mansfield University Library's website for additional information.

The paper will address the following:

What is the most appropriate context for the application of the group theory/model?

Explain the rationale for choosing this theory/model. Please include any empirical evidence that supports this theory/model and ethical standards and principles that should inform the rationale.

Explain the group process. Please include how the process is related to generalist social work practice.

How does the theory/model view the members? Please include any forms of oppression and discrimination, if applicable.

How does the theory/model treat the individual and the group? Please include any forms of oppression and discrimination, if applicable.

What is important in the pre-group phase?

Describe and explain the various stages or phases. How is supervision for the social worker addressed?

Who would benefit the most from this approach?

What population (if any) should this theory not be used? Please include any forms of oppression and discrimination, if applicable.

The intention of this assignment was to firmly ground the student with one specific model or theory that would give him or her an understanding of social work with groups. Furthermore, he or she could base the video assignment on this theory or model. Prior to the student doing his or her research the instructor taught several models and theories during the first several weeks. The models or theories taught in class were most often used in the video assignment, but not always.

The second assignment required the student to discuss the group process over the course of the semester in order to complete the video assignment. The second assignment was as follows:

Assignment #2

Each student will write a process paper describing the small group process over the course of the semester. The focus will be on the meetings that occurred in order to produce the videotapes (assignment #3). The paper will be 10-12 pages and will include a minimum of 5 references. The American Psychological Association (APA) format will be adhered to strictly. Check the Mansfield University Library's website for additional information.

The paper will address the following:

Describe the rationale for joining this group. Please include any ethical standards and principles that should inform the rationale

Explain the small group process

Were the group stages clearly identifiable? Explain.

Did the group have a leader? Explain.

How were meetings conducted?

How was conflict handled?

Did each member have the opportunity to participate? Explain.

When the project was complete how did the group end?

3. Compare this group experience with other types of groups found in the literature.

The student should have gained a thorough understanding of group content and process as a result of assignments one and two. This understanding will promote the student's ability to complete assignment number three, which is the video assignment. The third assignment as stated in the syllabus was as follows:

Assignment #3

Each group will produce a videotape to be viewed in class. The video will portray a group based on one particular model/theory. The group may be either a task focused group or a treatment group. Each member will facilitate the group for approximately 15 minutes. The group will simulate a specific type of group that is indicated by the theory or model. The class will view each of the videotapes. After the tapes have been viewed there will be a discussion based on a critical analysis. A handout will be provided prior to viewing the tapes. The handout will help organize the discussion and provide key ideas upon which to focus.

The data was presented on the videotapes. For the purposes of this paper the instructor viewed each videotape with the form discussed in assignment number three. The form was used to organize the concepts presented. Additionally, three students from the classes volunteered to participate with the instructor on this research project. One of the students that agreed to participate in this project suffers from a severe hearing loss and expressed her concern over her ability to effectively critique the videos. After a short discussion, it was decided that she would view the videos with an emphasis on the non- verbal skills that were or were not demonstrated throughout the videos. The three students viewed the videotapes independently and organized the concepts they witnessed on the same form. A content analysis was performed in conjunction with the instructor to indicate any themes that may have emerged from the videotapes.

Results

There were numerous concepts that were taught in the classroom and emerged as themes as a result of the content analysis. First of all, each group demonstrated the stages of group development. For the purpose of discussion in this paper the stages that were most often represented were the beginning, the middle and the ending. Although the group members portrayed different theories each group did exhibit some stage that can be called the beginning, middle, or ending. Those stages of group development will be discussed further in greater detail.

The beginning stage had several themes emerge that were taught as classroom concepts and expected to be portrayed as practice skills on the videotapes. The second theme to be discussed was 'introductions'. This theme was portrayed on every videotape in some form. The most commonly used method to handle introductions was the round robin. The facilitator would introduce himself or herself and then the round robin would occur. Included in the introduction was the person's name and often the facilitator would request more information, such as the reason the person was coming to the group. Although group purpose was not a specific common theme that emerged, by asking the members to divulge why he or she was attending, the facilitator might have been loosely attempting to establish the group purpose.

The third theme that was identified from the content analysis was confidentiality. The instructor was very pleased to see this portrayed in an overwhelming manner. The students often reviewed confidentiality prior to starting each group. This demonstrated that each student understood the importance of this critical social work value.

The fourth theme that emerged was the 'ice-breaker'. Again, every group had some form of an ice-breaker. By portraying this necessary group concept, the students demonstrated their firm grasp of the necessity to include an ice-breaker. The ice-breaker seemed to work very well, as was evidenced on the videos. The group was often more relaxed during the ice-breaker. The non-verbal cues of sitting in an open manner, smiling, and laughing were observed often during the ice-breaker.

Theme five was group participation. Each group, for the most part, had equal member participation. As mentioned previously, the round robin method was used for introductions. All five of the groups used a round robin approach at multiple times throughout the group video presentation. This helped to establish fair and equal participation. As the group progressed, the use of round robin diminished when free flowing interaction took over as expected.

The final theme that was portrayed overwhelmingly in each video was a strength's perspective focus. The strength's focus was evidenced on the video-tape in a variety of manners. The most often and obvious approach to the strength's perspective was the use of affirmations. The facilitator would often reinforce a positive behavior with affirmations. By doing this, the facilitator would point out the member's strength and make a statement that would reinforce that strength. Each group did some variation of this idea. One group clearly had a strength approach and emphasized only strengths that the member brought to the group and would ask questions from a strength perspective. For example, if a member wanted to work on a goal the facilitator would say, 'You have numerous ways to achieve that goal, which one will you choose'? The students were clearly cognizant of the necessity to apply a strength approach. Additionally, the student demonstrated an understanding of the concept, equifinality.

It is important to discuss one theme separately. As mentioned earlier, one student was assigned to study all of the non-verbal behaviors. She expressed that her extensive training with lip reading and body language, as a result of her genetic hearing disability, had made her sensitive to the way people communicate non-verbally. The student made three general observations that were common in all of the critiqued videos.

First, it was noted when the facilitator presented as attentive, open and engaging with the group members that each member in turn responded in a more positive manner. The more engaging the facilitator became the more the student leader was able to rally individual group members toward a more effective and meaningful group experience. When this occurred, everyone generally paid attention to what was being discussed and acted more relaxed. Facilitators who were not seen as outgoing or attentive and therefore displayed minimal interest in the group member's discussions did not promote good group cohesion. The primary nonverbal behaviors displayed by the facilitator and group members on the videotapes were generally those of acting fidgety and paying less attention to the activities of the group. Conversely, the facilitator who was encouraging interaction elicited a better group experience overall, evidenced by group cohesion.

Second, it was observed that when the group members were in a more natural group setting discussing things that were relevant to them, they participated in the discussions more and displayed fewer signs of being anxious or disinterested (i.e. wringing of hands, not paying attention, appearing disinterested). The group members were able to get over initial nervousness sooner and became engaged in meaningful discussions a lot quicker. In cases where the group portrayed more unfamiliar scenarios, it was clear these groups struggled more with being nervous and fidgety. Often, people in these pseudo-scenarios displayed more distracting nonverbal communication. Members were constantly seen shifting in their seats and exhibiting numerous nervous actions with their hands. The more natural the scenario for group members, ultimately, the more realistic the group process was for those involved.

The third nonverbal theme concerns the issue of the facilitators not picking up on the nonverbal cues of the individual group members. On most occasions, the facilitator failed to pick up on group a member's resistance to the group discussion. It appeared that the facilitator was trying so hard to include all the particulars of his or her stage that the nonverbal signs were not even considered. Even when the nonverbal cues conflicted with what the group member said there was no response made to challenge the discrepancy. By not addressing the nonverbal cues, the facilitator continued to miss vital information that could have helped group members achieve their goals.

When analyzing between those concepts taught in class and those chosen as important to students, it is informative to carefully examine the concepts which were seldom used or not portrayed at all within the student videos.

The first under used concept was the use of a pre-group. Whereas every other group began with introductions, only two of the five groups chose to demonstrate a pre-group phase. The use of a pre-group stage in these particular videos was mostly done to assure confidentiality and the necessity for the group. The absence of a pre-group phase left the instructor and the class guessing as to how the members were referred into their respective groups.

Second, group rules were discussed either minimally or not all. For the purpose of this paper, confidentiality was not considered a group rule. This was taught as an important concept, a value to the profession, and an ethical obligation to the members. The types of rules for this category would be concepts such as using improper language (cursing), showing up on time, coming to each meeting, and consuming food and/or drink during group. Since this was a simulation, the members most likely had a pre videotape discussion on these concepts but they were not portrayed.

The third concept not commonly demonstrated was homework. The instructor spent class time discussing this concept as a strategy to keep members engaged in the group outside of the group session. Furthermore, it was suggested that homework often contributes to achieving goals. However, it was not a concept the majority of students decided was necessary to cover.

A fourth concept 'under addressed' centered around role plays. Again, this was a very important concept that was strongly utilized in class. Although one group did have home work assignments, this was not emphasized to a large extent. The group that did use this strategy did not make a good connection to the members regarding the importance of the homework assignments and how the assignment was tied to achieving goals. Therefore, even though the concept was demonstrated in one video, it was not helpful to the group members in a substantial manner. Each of the other groups choose not to portray role-play (Implication - may not be practical, had to choose what they believe important, and it is time consuming)

As mentioned earlier, group purpose was an important stressed concept but it was not demonstrated in a formal manner. Quite simply, the facilitator did not use the term group purpose, nor was it implied to the extent that every group member was acutely aware of the purpose. Additionally, the concept for group purpose was not portrayed in the videos, which was very disappointing to the instructor. The concept of group purpose was the most commonly discussed idea in the classroom.

The fifth concept, discussed often in class, was conflict/resistance. One group did have an incident where conflict was portrayed. It was a misunderstanding between the facilitator and a member and the member left the group. All of the remaining groups did not address conflict/resistance. For the most part the members were agreeable and motivated throughout the video simulations

The last point regarding seldom demonstrated concepts addressed group endings. The facilitator often ended the group abruptly. The instructor taught in the classroom the importance of summarizing, yet student facilitators often just stated, 'It looks like we are out of time'. Again, the motivated and agreeable members quickly accepted this fact and responded by saying goodbye.

Overall, many important concepts emerged as themes. There were also some concepts that should have emerged as important themes but the students chose not portray them. Each have been mentioned, it is now important to further discuss the ramification of the results.

Implications

The results discussed have multiple implications for group work. Special attention will be given to those concepts not adequately demonstrated by previous students in order to better develop the group work experience and enhance skills for the next class of social work students. In order to become an effective group worker, the emphasis should not only be placed upon the knowledge base of a particular stage, but rather should also incorporate and develop each stage. Additionally, the overall presentation of the facilitator should be the focus of each student. When a student facilitator becomes too consumed with only having a clear understanding of the group stage he or she has chosen to lead, then there tends to be a lack of understanding of each of the other stages. This may stifle the student's ability to comprehend the entire group process.

The five videos demonstrated that each student placed a greater emphasis upon the knowledge and skill base of the stage he or she was leading. As a result of this focus on one stage there appeared to be a lack of interest by the members to fully participate in each group stage. This had a negative impact on group process. The students who were not facilitating often tuned in and out of the group. Since each member varied in his or her ability to remain attentive the group process at times was disjointed. Also, this lack of interest in part, was most likely due to a deficit in understanding of subsequent group stages in which the student held no real responsibility or commitment. Because of this implication, the real question lingers, can these students facilitate a group from beginning to end successfully, if given the opportunity.

Nonverbal communication, although stressed by the instructor was held secondary by nearly all of the groups in priority. Student facilitators held little regard for those nonverbal cues portrayed in group by other members, and if any attention was given it was done minimally instead of with emphasis.

Most facilitators tried to be engaging, warm, and at least superficially interested. Unfortunately, not being more in tune with the nonverbal cues by group members greatly sacrificed the extent to which a member could truly identify and utilize group purpose. The social work student must learn how to incorporate techniques that demonstrate the facilitators ability to fully understand what is happening with each member based on nonverbal communication.

Promoting self awareness is an essential social work skill. The ability to become self aware requires that the student be cognizant of relationships outside of the classroom and how those relationships impact group process. Since each student was encouraged to choose the members for the group simulations, the relationship outside of class will have a greater influence on group cohesion in class because in most instances the members choose friends for the simulation.

Group cohesion was a content area taught in class; however, because prior relationships were already established, some groups appeared to be very cohesive and trusting right from the beginning. Interactions were immediately free flowing among members and did not always simulate a cautious and often distrustful phase that many new members experience. For a minority of students group cohesion was a process demonstrated by increasing trust and self disclosure, which simulates a better example of natural group process.

The importance of establishing clear goals is the next concept for discussion. Goals are tied to the group purpose and when the purpose is not verbally stated, it is left up to each member to loosely interpret why they are attending. If the group purpose was not clear, then the group lacks the ability to work toward the same goals. Often the group loses its focus and the work within the group has no real importance to the members. If this occurs goals will most likely not be achieved.

Another concept that was important to understand, yet was hardly used was conflict/resistance. Because this concept was demonstrated by only one group, it is not clear if other groups did not incorporate it into their simulations because they were unsure how to respond when it arose, or because the term was somewhat unclear to them from the very beginning. Although the concept was taught by the instructor in class, the student tended to not demonstrate it. A reason for the lack of portrayal of conflict/resistance could be because it was easier on the facilitator if members were compliant. Conflict and resistance is often part of the natural group process. It will be a concept that arises frequently once the student begins working as a social worker.

If a social worker has not had much practice in handling conflict/ resistance successfully, it poses two problems. First, when a facilitator is unsure how to proceed in the face of conflict, he or she may lose confidence in leading that group. Secondly, the ability to focus and regain control of the group during a conflict may not occur. Many group workers consider conflict/resistance an important part of the group process because it often facilitates change within the group. It is necessary to understand the importance of conflict/resistance but this may be skill that gets developed more fully in the Field Placement or once the student begins working.

The next concept for discussion was the ending. Each stage had an ending and also the entire group will end, both will be discussed. The ending on most videos was rather abrupt and without summary. Summarizing would have cemented the concepts and ideas portrayed in each. The absence of the use of summarizing could leave the members with many questions about group purpose, group participation, identifying and achieving the goals. Additionally, by not summarizing the videos often appeared choppy and disjointed not allowing the member to reflect on work accomplished. As an ending session with no clear assessment and summary, members leave with an unclear perspective as to what has occurred and how it directs future goals.

Summary

In order to be an effective and confident group facilitator, it is imperative that the student have a very clear understanding of the knowledge and skills necessary to do group work. The implications of having only a partial understanding may indicate only a mediocre understanding of group work. It is simply not enough to have the knowledge or skill. Social workers who want to facilitate groups must incorporate a variety of skills and theories in order to be successful. This is accomplished in several ways: First, by understanding the purpose of the group, as a whole and how it relates to the member; Second, the necessity to have clear, measurable and achievable goals. Next, the ability to recognize and address conflict, and finally, the importance of summarizing each group session in order to have smooth transition and endings that are meaningful to each member.

Social work students who learn how to correctly use group work theory and skills at the college level will be better social work practitioners. The mastering of such practice skills, especially through the use of video tapes assignments, will in turn give social work students opportunities to become better prepared to enter the workforce.

References

Berger, R. (1996). A comparative analysis of different methods of teaching group work. *Social Work with Groups, 19,* 79-89.

Kurland, R., and Salmon, R. (1999). *Teaching a methods course in social work with groups.* Alexandria, VA: Council on Social Work Education.

Manor, 0. (1998). The monitoring of a co-active learning in social groupwork: A pilot study. *Social Work with Groups, 11,* 53-75.

Parry, J. (1988). Organizing principles for developing a foundation group work practice course. *Social Work with Groups, 11,* 77-85.

Rubin, A. & Babbie, E. (2001). *Research methods for social work* (4th ed.. Belmont: Wadsworth.

Toseland, R., & Rivas, R. (2001). The ending stage. In *an introduction to group work practice.* (pp. 401-429). Needham Heights, MA: Pearson Education Company.

Wayne, J., and Garland, J. (1990). Group work education in the Field: The state of the art. *Social Work with Groups, 13,* 95-109.

Wilson, G. (1976). From practice to theory: A personalized history. In *Theories of social work with groups.* (pp. 1-44). New York: Columbia University Press.

Blueprints for awakening desire
The 'Girl Talk' healthy sexuality group program

Maura McIntyre and Naomi Mitchell

Introduction

We have a long history of working together with adolescent (13-17 year old) girls in school groups as clinical therapists at a social service agency in a multi racial, ethnically diverse, predominantly low-income suburb of Toronto, Canada. These eight-week hour-long groups are process oriented with group members identifying topics and issues for discussion. Healthy sexuality education is a critical component in all groups because of the age and developmental needs of the participants. Risk reduction around sexual activity and promoting safe and healthy choices by making real life situations real (like discussing the details of putting on a condom) is central to our work. We model and encourage strategic *and critical* thinking based on issues the girls identify.

Yet a picture has emerged that disturbs us – by grade eight or nine many young women appear to have internalized a negative sexual identity. This is expressed when they describe feeling like passive recipients of the male gaze; when they talk about themselves using sex role stereotypes (such as the virgin / whore dichotomy), when they talk about their vaginas as dirty, and when they bandy about canned and stereotyped versions of attractiveness. We have also observed the censure and ostracizing of adolescent girls by adolescent girls if they express sexual desire, or are alleged to be sexually active. Female society and its stressful socialization can carry with it gossip, labelling, exclusion and sexualizing behaviours – ones that we encourage girls to critique. As Philips notes, girls who name their desire are often

> portrayed as passive recipients of male sexual behaviour, victims of boys or men, who are presumed to be the only sexual initiators; or vilified in media, popular discussion, and sex education classrooms as 'wild', 'loose', or 'lacking self-respect. (Philips, 1998, p. 34)

In our experience doing groupwork with adolescent girls, sexual health as school curriculum has not adequately addressed their developmental needs (balancing peer and familial relationships; developing autonomous relationships and integrating their emerging sexuality). We are concerned that the internal picture of sexual being that emerges for girls is often fragmented and disengaged from the actual wants of the individual (Gilligan, Rogers, & Tolman 1991; Slater et al 2001; Philips, 1998). While many adolescent girls do not feel ready for relationships that include sexual intercourse, desire does not appear to be a partner with abstinence. We encourage girls to assess their emotional readiness for sexual relationships, acknowledging that sexual desire can reside in girls who aren't sexually active in the traditional sense (vaginal intercourse to the exclusion of masturbation and self-exploration). Sexualizing the body through appearance and then coping with the attention sexualized clothing seems to invite leaves no room for the expression of girls' feelings. When sexual desire is alienated from the body, where is sexual desire in relation to the self? How are relationships that incorporate sexual behaviour constructed by pubertal and adolescent girls?

Our experience doing groupwork with adolescents provided the inspiration to work with much younger girls in group to foster at an earlier age a positive internalized vision of emerging female sexuality. The 'Girl Talk' program is premised on the assumption that girls' sense of self and agency regarding sexual identity and relationships will be stronger if we assist them to understand and exercise choice early. This means acknowledging adolescent 'girls' desire and entitlement to sexual pleasure' (Fine, 1988 in Philips, 1998 p. 34).

In this chapter we review the literature in the area of girls healthy sexuality education and present and detail the 'Girl Talk' program we developed for grade five girls, highlighting how we create spaces for girls to name desire. In viewing our group work as a counterculture to traditional sexuality education and popular culture constructions of female sexuality we are particularly aware of our role as gatekeepers and transmitters of values. Through a close up look at our 'Girl Talk' program we encourage sexuality educators and group work practitioners to consider and assess their own values about sex and sexuality and how these translate and manifest in educational and group contexts.

Literature

Developmental theorists

The notion of sexual desire and emerging sexuality in girls has been a small footnote in both the literature on healthy sexuality programs and a faint whisper by feminist developmental theorists. Slater et al (2001), along with Tolman (1991), Fine (1988) and Hedgepath & Hemlich (1996) are notable as developmental theorists because they identify the omission in the literature of pubescent and adolescent girls' emerging sexual desire:

> Most discourses of girls' sexuality have been framed in the context of victimization, disease or morality. Girls may become conflicted by their feelings of sexual desire and the cultural description of their sexuality. The result is a disconnection of true sexual feelings. (Slater et al, 2001, p. 448)

Slater et al also maintain that having to contend with a prescribed feminine ideal can lead to conflict and psychological stress resulting in a false self:

> Girls' concern about their appearance and outside validation is all part of the socially constructed feminine virtue that is at the surface of a girl's denial of self (p. 447)

Tolman (1991) notes the absence of research in psychology on female adolescent sexual desire:

> The glossing over of adolescent girls' sexual desire that Fine encountered

in schools and that I discovered in the literature of developmental psychology reflects the missing discourse of adolescent girls sexual desire in society at large. (p.58)

She identifies Fine's work as key to unlocking a discourse on girls' sexual desire. 'She suggests that

this missing discourse may result in girls failure to know themselves as the subjects of their own sexuality. If girls could conceive of themselves as sexual subjects, they could then potentially make decisions about their sexual behavior and experience that would be healthy for them. (p.59)

According to Tolman:

If girls know about their sexual desire from their experience of their own bodies but encounter a disembodied way of speaking, hearing, and knowing about their sexuality, then a central dilemma is posed for adolescent girls: In what relationship can an adolescent girl be with her sexual desire with her own body, with her own experience? (p. 59)

This is similar to the conflict characterized by Gilligan (1991) and Slater et al (2001).

History of healthy sexuality education

Hedgepath and Hemlich (1996) refer to healthy sexuality education of the 1960s as a time when it was believed that if accurate information was dispensed students would simply abstain. Second generation educators emphasized values and decision making as a way of avoiding risk taking behaviours. Third generation curricula preached 'Just say no!' as a deterrent to premarital sex. Fourth generation focused on postponement and risk reduction albeit with the underlying message that abstinence is best (but, if not practice safe sex). 'Historically, sexuality education has been *reactive* to identified social problems, that is, narrowly focused on prevention of negative sexual consequences such as unintended pregnancy, HIV, and STDs, substance abuse, and sexual abuse or exploitation.' (Hedgepath & Hemlich, 1996, p. 83). Today, fifth generation sexuality education is *ideally proactive* sexuality education ... [it] addresses all needs of the developing sexual person: learning about love, *desire* (our emphasis), intimacy, friendship and commitment; enhancing self-esteem, improving relationship skills and achieving personal success and happiness, within or without a sexual relationship' (p.83).

Healthy sexuality: Theory and methodology

In Britain, Went (1985) addresses the methodology of sex education in her book *Sex Education: Some guidelines for teachers.* Recognizing that 'using fear as a disincentive does not have a very good track record', and that the 'fact giving topic-based approach does not enable people to change their knowledge or behaviour', she advocates 'affective teaching' with its goals of 'self empowerment' and 'autonomy' (p. 36-37). Since group discussion is central to affective teaching, Went acknowledges the challenges inherent in teachers making the transition from teacher to group work facilitator by addressing aspects of group work such as dynamics and process.

Jeffrey Moran's (2000) comprehensive history of adolescence and sex education, *Teaching Sex. The shaping of adolescence in the 20th century* is an accessible, well-researched scholarly text that explores how competing societal agendas that underpin sex education surface in practice according to time and context. Drawing out the social reform (reduce teenage pregnancy and encourage abstinence) and public health (reduce STDs) agendas, Moran suggests that schools should examine sex education within a 'dialogue about which community values the schools should pass on to the next generation' (p. 234). Making reformist agendas explicit requires sex educators to consciously examine his or her own assumptions and articulate 'their reasons for supporting certain kinds of teaching' (p.233). Even more radically, choosing to set these agendas aside would mean teaching sexuality simply by 'fostering a deeper understanding of an important facet of human existence' (p. 234). Sexuality education then might be part of relationship education, and

become a component of the humanities, with history, social studies, and literature courses all consciously exploring the diversity of desire in different ages and places. (p.234

Moran suggests that 'a revised sexuality education might struggle against the educational system's deadening of eros and imagination' (p.234). Pointing toward a more holistic approach toward sexuality education he cites Allan Bloom:

> In a better world sexual education would be concerned with the development of taste. The progress of civilization is intimately connected with the elaboration of erotic sensibility and a real examination of the delicate interplay of human attractions. (Bloom, 1993, pp. 24-25; in Moran, 2000).

Teaching curricula (guides and manuals)

Most healthy sexuality teaching curricula are organized around biology and risk prevention. For example in The Fredericton Planned Parenthood Guide (1984) while there is a brief section on masturbation, it is not integrated into a continuum of information about healthy sexual expression. Great lengths are taken to dispel the myths of masturbation, and while there is a definitional statement about what it is physiologically, notions of pleasure are absent from this mechanical description:

> Masturbation is a sexual behaviour about which many people have misconceptions. Masturbation means the rubbing and consequent stimulation of ones' own sexually sensitive organs such as the penis in males and the clitoris in females' (p.114)

In its size, format and density of biological information and diagrams Campbell and Gollick's (1988) sexuality resource book is typical of a manual style resource book for delivering sex education. The sheer volume of facts around female and male anatomy, pregnancy and disease prevention delivered in a linear, overly descriptive manner obscures important issues around self-concept and sexual feelings such as arousal. Here the danger of prevention information negating normal sexual experience seems high. Campbell and Gollick's discussion of masturbation is situated within a section entitled 'Sexual expression' that includes paragraphs on relationships, sexual expression in relationships, sexual partners, responsible sexual expression, handling sexual involvement and teen pregnancy.

The Durham Board of Education (1992) Teacher Resource Guide is premised on an abstinence model. While the rationale on the first page of the guide purports to present 'accurate information necessary to make wise and safe choices and the living skills required to achieve their personal goals', the very title of the guide, *Delaying teenage sexual involvement: A teacher resource guide on abstinence,* declares its values and intent. Surprisingly it claims to provide

> a safe forum in which to examine and discuss [student's] personal values regarding sexual involvement and the *opportunity to assert and rehearse their views.* [our italics].

From women to girls

The healthy sexuality group work program 'Girl Talk' is based on the premise that mutual support and independent viewpoints can co-exist in a safe atmosphere hospitable to girls' real concerns. Underpinning our delivery of healthy sexuality group work is a definition of wellness that focuses on building strengths rather than identifying problems and pathology.

The voices of the girls emerge as we as mature women model questioning, express independent ideas, and most importantly stop to listen as girls' voices emerge. We echo the optimism expressed by Slater et al

> If girls are allowed to openly express their feelings and desires, their sexual decisions will be grounded within themselves rather than disconnected from their desire' (2001, p. 448).

Also critical to this process is the opportunity to personalize information about pubertal change. Hedgepath and Hemlich (1996) support the use of personalization:

> In sexuality and HIV education more so than in other subjects, personal relevance is a requirement .... students expect sexuality education to be personally meaningful; when it is not relevant or realistic, students may reject it wholesale. (p.72)

'Girl Talk' began in 2000 in response to a need Maura, one of the authors, perceived in her then 10 year old daughter's primary school. As a parent and professional in the school community she recognized how few opportunities girls have to discuss their feelings about entering puberty. Also, in Ontario, while health instruction about puberty is offered in the classroom, it often tends to be fact-based without providing the opportunity for information to be integrated with personal experience. In our experience working with adolescents the separation of content and process (emerging experiences) is insidious and serves to reinforce and assist in alienating sexual desire from bodily function. Working together as parent volunteer and private practitioner we proposed running an eight week girls group at the Island Public School.

Building on the success of the girls group program, when the Vice-Principal moved on to assume a principalship, she invited us to offer the 'Girl Talk' group program at her new school. In particular she was concerned about the pressure the girls at McKee have around performance (music, ballet, academics and sports). She wondered if there were ways that we could support the girls' development of self-esteem without linking self worth to accomplishment. Could we emphasize the value of their being itself, independent of doing? How might this grounding connect with puberty education? (We address the issue of positive self-concept directly particularly through exercises in our program see discussion.)

In shifting our work from middle and high schools to elementary settings, the principles underpinning our group practice remain the same. The groups attempt to help map the current reality of the girls' lives amidst the shifting sands of puberty. They also provide a counterculture to the pressures of popular culture and relief from the isolation girls' often experience in learning about their changing bodies as part of school curriculum. Public education classically assigns function to the body focusing on a functional sexuality with emphasis on reproduction, contraception and disease prevention. Our groups provide the girls with an opportunity to talk about their bodies and to think about them in ways they might not already have had a chance to. We encourage girls to grasp the notion that there is a range of choices to be made about expressing one's sexual identity that is, they need not be drafted into a culture that negatively sexualizes women.

Delivering 'Girl Talk'

When we offer 'Girl Talk' to the grade 5 girls at McKee Public School our delivery is autonomous and distinct from school curriculum. We run three, eight week, fifty minute groups. The groups take place in a corner of the staff room, a spacious, well kept room with good light. The girls sit on couches and big easy chairs in a circle. In providing this special space the school further endorses the importance of the 'Girl Talk' program.

When we introduce ourselves we emphasize the fact that we are not teachers, and that there will be no test or other evaluation of performance associated with participation in the group. We also encourage the girls to adjust the norms of behaviour usually associated with adults and school in order to promote familiarity and comfort. For example, we suggest that they address us by our first names and find a way to speak without interrupting each other that doesn't involve putting up hands. We define and underline confidentiality and establish group guidelines as a way of making the group a safe place to talk.

While 'Girl Talk' is offered to all grade five girls at the school, and while the majority attend all sessions, not all girls are permitted, or choose to participate. The demographics of McKee is predominantly Korean, Chinese, Japanese, Eastern European, and South Asian. The majority of girls come from solidly middle, to high-income homes. Many parents (particularly fathers) work abroad and are away for long periods of time. Since there is no selection criterion, the groups are open to newcomers (grade five girls who have been absent or have transferred to the school) at any time. The size of the groups and the open format impact the groups in a number of important ways. From our point of view as facilitators, in the very large groups we struggle to match names with faces from the beginning to the end. The smaller groups feel by contrast like a bastion of intimacy and cohesion.

Discussion

At bottom is the inevitability of girls entering puberty and beginning menstruation, and our commitment to help them feel prepared for that. For example our exercise 'Pads and tampons – What they look like / How they work', means leaning forward with an actual tampon and pad in hand, and unwrapping it in order to make things real. The inevitable: 'Can we see them?' leads to passing the tampons around and touching them, then relating them back to how they can fit the girls' own bodies. This process often leads to a discussion about the three openings in girls' bodies; that the tampon can only fit in the vagina, not the urethra or anus. Still at this age, the notion that they can touch and feel their own three holes is quite foreign. We invite girls to consider that touching their bodies can be positive and lead to a better understanding of themselves. When the girls ask to put tampons in water to see them expand, they get even closer to the notion that tampons absorb menstrual blood. We speak matter-of-factly about using different brands of tampons – Naomi prefers 'OB' and Maura is used to 'Tampax' – and our own very different cycles, thereby dispelling myths that television commercials engender through their covert language.

Repeatedly we discover that when we attempt to delineate in fine detail the numeric aspect of the menstrual cycle, the group loses interest because the material becomes informational, distant and more abstract. Indeed the very nature of girls' and women's genitalia and reproductive system readily signify the struggle to move from concrete to abstract thinking; an ongoing and developmentally incomplete task for pubertal and adolescent girls (Hedgepath, 1996). The simple gesture of the facilitator placing her hands on her body to indicate where the ovaries sit appears to go much further than a diagram. Simultaneously at work is the paradox that girls 'know' their bodies – but don't. Taking on the role of introducing them to their changing body is a delicate, nuanced process. Part of our struggle is to divine what they need to know and when. In our groups we find it quite easy to make fluid judgements about what is comfortable and appropriate to talk about. It's important to work with what arises; if you don't you reinforce silence. For example we discuss our own and each other's menstrual cycles but do not discuss our own sexual activity.

The girls themselves seem consistently quite capable of intuiting the nuances of self disclosure and boundaries; while they are riveted by our inviting details about which tampon Maura and Naomi prefer and why, they rarely ask personal questions about our sexual conduct. Yet we encourage them to entertain the notion of pleasure – sex is not just for procreation. We'd rather inundate girls with comfort with their own bodies, instill notions of physical pleasure and promote them as experts about their bodies than have them recite by rote the names and workings of reproductive organs. In session seven and eight we use an anonymous Q & A format to get at girls unspoken concerns, questions and notions about their bodies and sexuality. We encourage girls to write out their questions and put them in the hat. We remind them continually that no question is silly and every question is important. We take turns facilitating the answering of the question in concert with the group, clarifying information, flagging concerns, strengthening peer support and ensuring personalization and affective engagement with issues.

A significant number of questions are about periods. On the surface they reveal fear: about getting your period for the first time in class; about when they will start menstruating; about pain and dealing with blood; about swimming and periods; and about how much time and care menstruation requires. In group after group we have found that attending to the immediacy of concerns around the period is essential. We field these questions first, and open up the discussion in order to encourage queries to emerge that aren't primarily technical and fear based. It is only after these issues are thoroughly addressed through group process that girls begin to move into areas of relationships and sexuality. Examples of these questions include:

'What is a good age for dating?'
'Can someone be gay and straight at the same time?'
'If you join a team with boys and they tell you to go away, what do you do?'
'Does one breast get larger than another?'
'What is a wet dream?' Which hole does it come out of?
'What age would be best for sex?' 'Does it hurt the first time you do it?' 'Do you really have to have sexual intercourse?'
'Why are boy's balls wrinkly? Why do nipples go hard? '
'Hows the way we show our sexual feeling like boys get boners?' 'Do we have anything like come? Why do we have a vagina? '
'Have you ever known anyone in person who has been raped? ' 'Why do you get tingly when you make love? '
'Does it hurt to have a boys 'hoo-hoo in your woo-woo'?'

In interpreting questions we always find meaning and the group helps contextualize and deepen discussion. We continue to develop ways of talking about sexual pleasure with the girls. This includes introducing the topic of masturbation as part of the spectrum of pleasure that is normal. We make links to feelings of sensuality girls can easily connect to such as patting a silky puppy, the tingling sensation of scoring a goal in soccer, and the waves of anticipation in unwrapping a chocolate bar. The antecedents to getting girls to investigate their own experience involve simple games like, 'Get the Giggles Out', where girls say the correct words for body parts and begin to feel comfortable saying them. This process moves towards normalizing the experience of puberty and being female, and develops comfort with language that can respectfully depict positive images of self. We have often observed group members who will use slang terms for genitals to differentiate themselves from the group as worldly. We are always on the lookout for age inappropriate language and behaviour (girls who appear to know 'too much' in their use of borrowed language), like the girl for whom 'tits and cock' rolls off the tongue. More similar than she appears (with respect to age appropriate development) is the girl who can name and list reproductive parts by rote as if performing well on a science test. Both communicate disengagement from the concrete reality of their own bodies.

Given the immigrant population specific to the school we reinforce the idea that difference is regarded as a given and requires empathy and respect in group communication. At the same time we look for common ground to foster group cohesion. We encourage narratives about resettlement; often stories about pets left behind in the country of origin along with family members provide a bridge. Girls are given alternatives to engaging in stressful and negative peer communication. Diversity is also acknowledged and explored though girls' physical selves; familial and cultural backgrounds, and home realities. The process of physical maturation varies widely; the process of inclusion and exclusion in peer, familial, and wider society is examined in group. We encourage girls to talk about mothers' and sisters' stories about menstruation emphasizing the fact that not everyone will start their periods at the same age and that you can still be a girl even if you have started menstruating.

As a concluding exercise for our last session we use an activity to promote and reinforce a positive sense of self for the girls. We place oversized homemade word cutouts on a coffee table in the centre of our circle. Each girl is invited to take a turn by choosing as many as she likes. These words such as: Articulate, Warm, Funny, Adventurous and Passionate assist the girls to identify and put in words positive feelings about themselves. Sometimes girls ask each other to help them choose the words. More frequently, however, we find that even the more reserved individuals are able to select words and develop their own stories; often with aplomb. From this flows camaraderie between the girls who further incite each other to select words that define them positively. This exercise and our facilitation of it model a wide range of positive descriptors for self-concept. For example, when a group member appeared withdrawn Maura modeled this by saying that she felt unable to locate a word that captured her feelings. Not only did the group come to her aid with empathy (and several words); the withdrawn member was later able to participate in the activity. We continue to develop ways to enhance girls' positive views of self by reinforcing the idea that puberty is not something one can excel at. All girls were previously tested by their teachers on curricula about puberty. We tell them that not doing well on the test doesn't mean that they've failed at puberty. The measure of success is their ability to relate information to themselves and feel comfortable with the emerging face of puberty.

Reflections and recommendations

Girls' concerns and ideas about puberty are paramount (even if they have misinformation). As adults we need to acknowledge the diverse ways that girls construct their experience. This also means debunking misconceptions about the female body directly. Identifying and developing images that are real and aesthetic in their representation of physical, emotional and social aspects of developing female and male sexuality is an important part of our work.

As facilitators we can convey a spectrum of sexual choice regarding orientation and diversity of desire. This includes reflecting on our values about sex and sexuality education by modeling comfort and tackling taboos. An awareness of one's power as a role model and transmitter of values, information and perspectives is essential. This process includes encouraging critical thinking about sex role stereotypes and how the sexualization of girls and boys occurs, through discussion, and by building on exercises.

If girls are active in expressing and constructing their own blueprints of desire rather than being recipients of a socially determined one that is limiting and embodies passivity, they will likely make choices in their relationships that reflect congruence between thought, feeling and action. This included assisting girls to explore and project their sexuality (through dress and language) in a way that is congruent with their internal experience. We actively promote group work that paves the way for girls to name desire.

Facilitators must listen carefully for girls' desire, instill entitlement to sexual pleasure, validate expressions of it whilst countering messages of victimization and negativity. Facilitators can help girls identify and explore different cultural and familial approaches to sexuality and the ways they validate and invalidate their self-concept. Healthy sexuality group work needs to start early (ages 10-11). By creating process-oriented, small, confidential groups where privacy is possible, girls can begin to name desire.

References

Bloom, A. (1993). *Love and friendship.* New York: Simon & Schuster.

Bourgeois, P. and Wolfish, M. (1994). *Changes in you and me. A book about puberty mostly for boys.* Kansas City, Missouri: Andrews and McMeel.

Cadell, S., Karababow, J., and Sanchez, M. (2001). Community, empowerment, and resilience: Paths to wellness. *Canadian Journal of Community Mental Health,* 20(1), 21-35.

Campbell, J. and Gollick, J. (1988). *Sexuality. An education resource book* Canada: Globe / Modern Curriculum Press.

The Durham Board of Education. (1992). *Delaying sexual involvement. A teacher resource guide on abstinence.* Durham, Ontario: Durham Board of Education.

Fine, M. (1988). Sexuality, schooling and adolescent females: The missing discourse of desire. *Harvard Educational Review,* 58(1), 29-53.

Gilligan, C., Rogers, A. and Tolman, D. (Eds.) (1991). *Women, girls and psychotherapy. Reframing resistance.* Binghamton, NY: Harrington Park Press.

Gulliver, R. and Smith, J. (2002). *Nocturnal admissions.* Sue Johanson and the Sunday night sex show. Toronto, Ontario: ECW Press.

Harris, R. and Emberely, M. (1998). *It's perfectly normal. Changing bodies, growing up, sex, and sexual health.* Cambridge, Mass: Candlewick Press.

Hedgepeth, Y. and Hemlich, J. (1996). *Teaching about sexuality and HIV. Principles and methods for effective education.* New York: NY: New York University Press.

Moran, J. (2000). Teaching sex. *The shaping of adolescence in the 20th century.* Cambridge, Mass.: Harvard University Press.

Orenstein, P. (1994). *SchoolGirls. Young women, self-esteem, and the confidence gap.* Toronto: Doubleday.

Parenthood Federicton (1984). *Sexuality and the teenager: A teaching guide for sex education.* Fredericton, New Brunswick: Planned Parenthood.

Philips, L. (1998). *The girls report. What we know and need to know about growing up female.* New York, NY: The National Council for Research on Women.

Proctor & Gamble Inc. (1990). *The Changing program. Video and resource kit.* Endorsed by the Canadian Association for Health, Physical Education and Recreation.Toronto, Ontario: Proctor & Gamble.

Slater, J., Guthrie, B., and Boyd, C. (2001). A feminist theoretical approach to understanding health of adolescent females. *Journal of Adolescent Health*, 28(6), 443-449.

Tolman, D. (1991). Adolescent girls, women and sexuality: Discerning dilemmas of desire. In Gilligan, C., Rogers, A. and Tolman, D. (Eds.), *Women, girls and psychotherapy. Reframing resistance.* (pp. 55-69). Binghamton, NY: Harrington Park Press.

Went, D. (1985). *Sex Education. Some guidelines for teachers.* London, UK: Bell & Hyman.

Index